AEGIS

Vol. 4

Jinha Yoo

AEGIS

Vol. 4

Jinha Yoo

NETCOMICS

AEGIS Vol. 4

Story and Art by Jinha Yoo

English translation rights in USA, Canada, UK, NZ, Australia arranged by
Ecomix Media Company
395-21 Seogyo-dong, Mapo-gu, Seoul, Korea 121-840
info@ecomixmedia.com

- Produced by **Ecomix Media Company**
- Translator Ernest Woo
- Editor Jeffrey Tompkins
- Managing Editor Soyoung Jung
- Cover Design purj
- Graphic Designers Hyekyoung Choi, Minchul Shin
- President & Publisher Heewoon Chung

P.O. Box 3036, Jersey City, NJ 07303-3036
info@netcomics.com
www.NETCOMICS.com

ISBN: 978-1-60009-103-2

First printing: March 2007
10 9 8 7 6 5 4 3 2 1
Printed in Korea

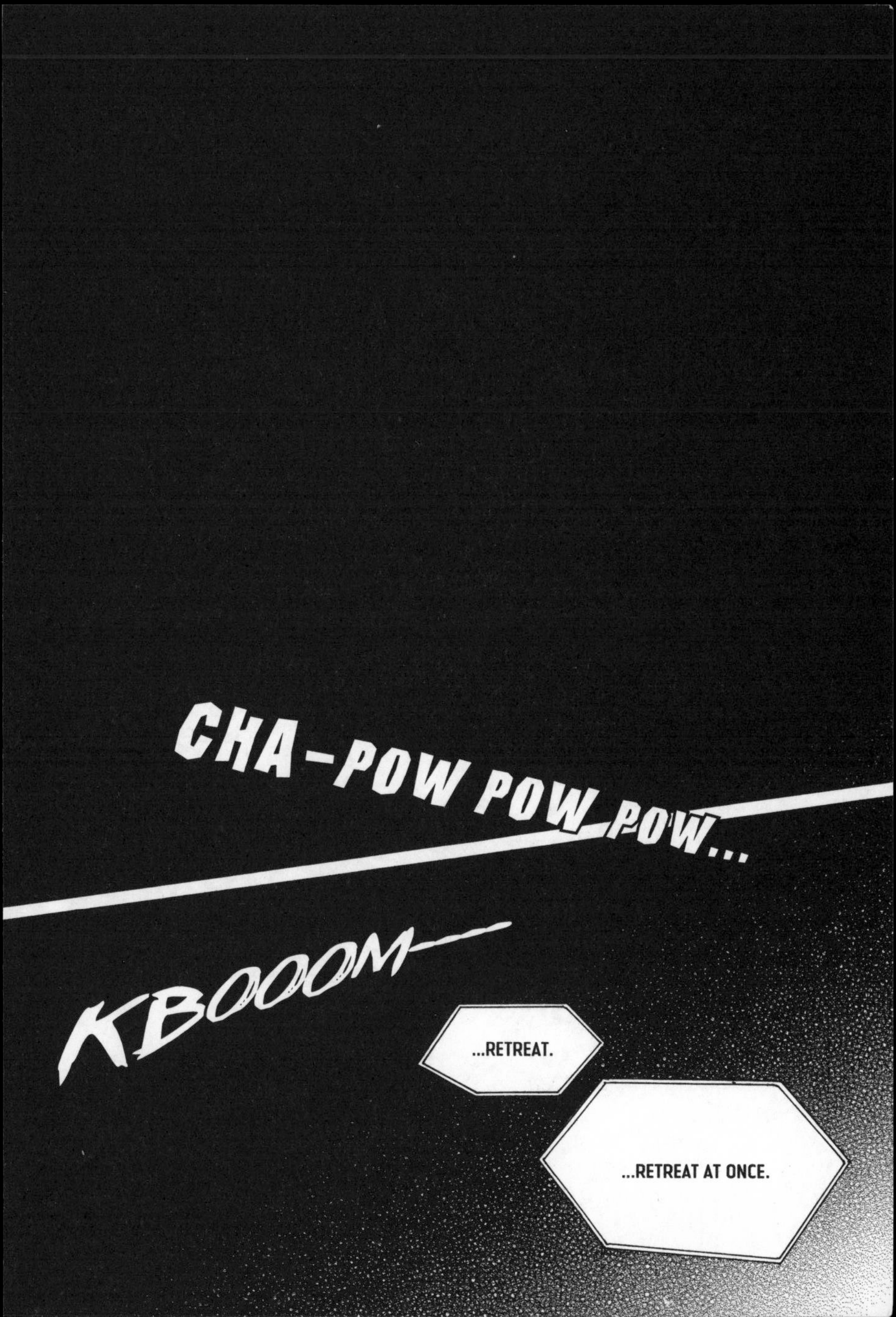
CHA-POW POW POW...
KBOOOM—
...RETREAT.
...RETREAT AT ONCE.

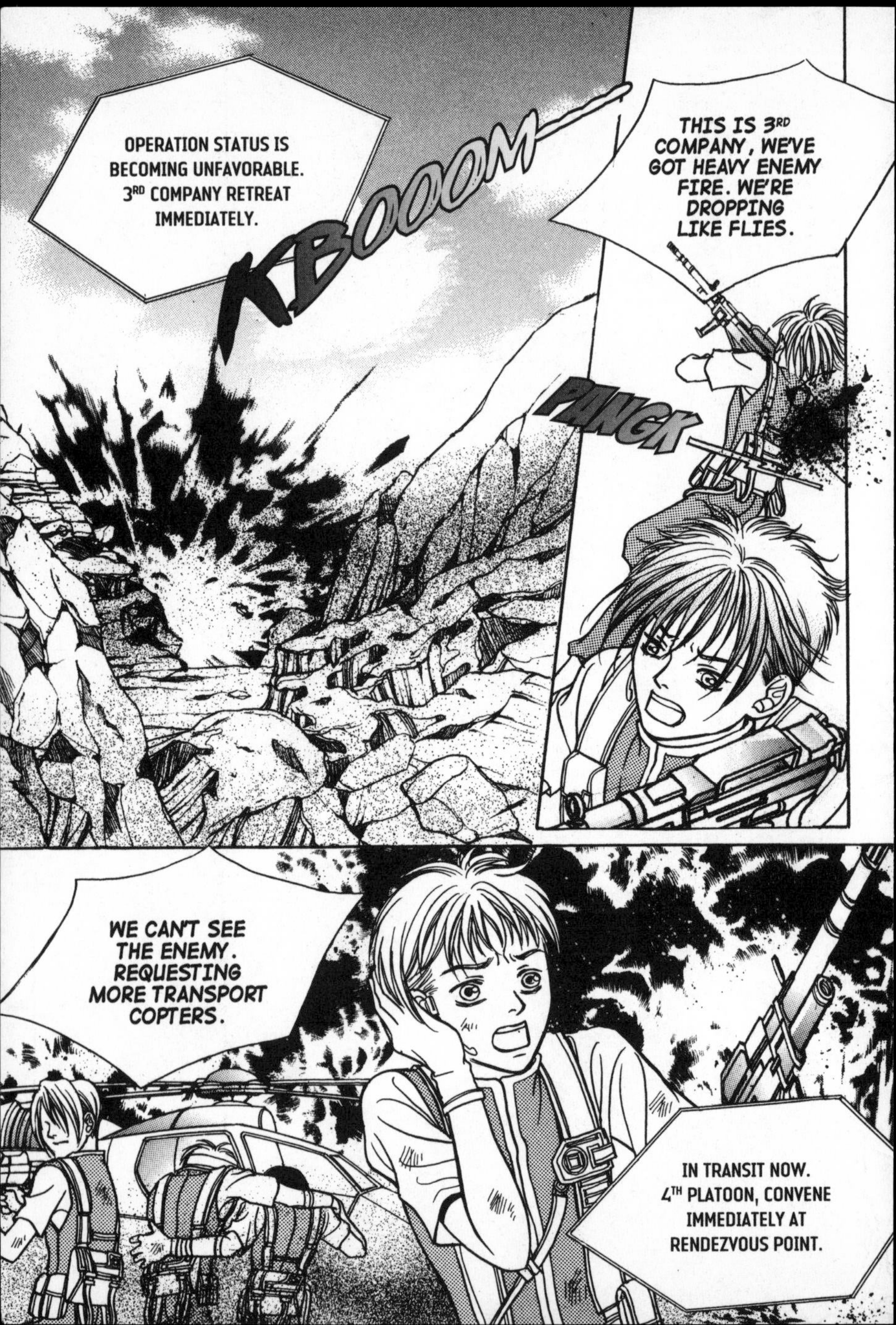
OPERATION STATUS IS BECOMING UNFAVORABLE. 3RD COMPANY RETREAT IMMEDIATELY.
KBOOOM
THIS IS 3RD COMPANY, WE'VE GOT HEAVY ENEMY FIRE. WE'RE DROPPING LIKE FLIES.
PANGK
WE CAN'T SEE THE ENEMY. REQUESTING MORE TRANSPORT COPTERS.
IN TRANSIT NOW. 4TH PLATOON, CONVENE IMMEDIATELY AT RENDEZVOUS POINT.

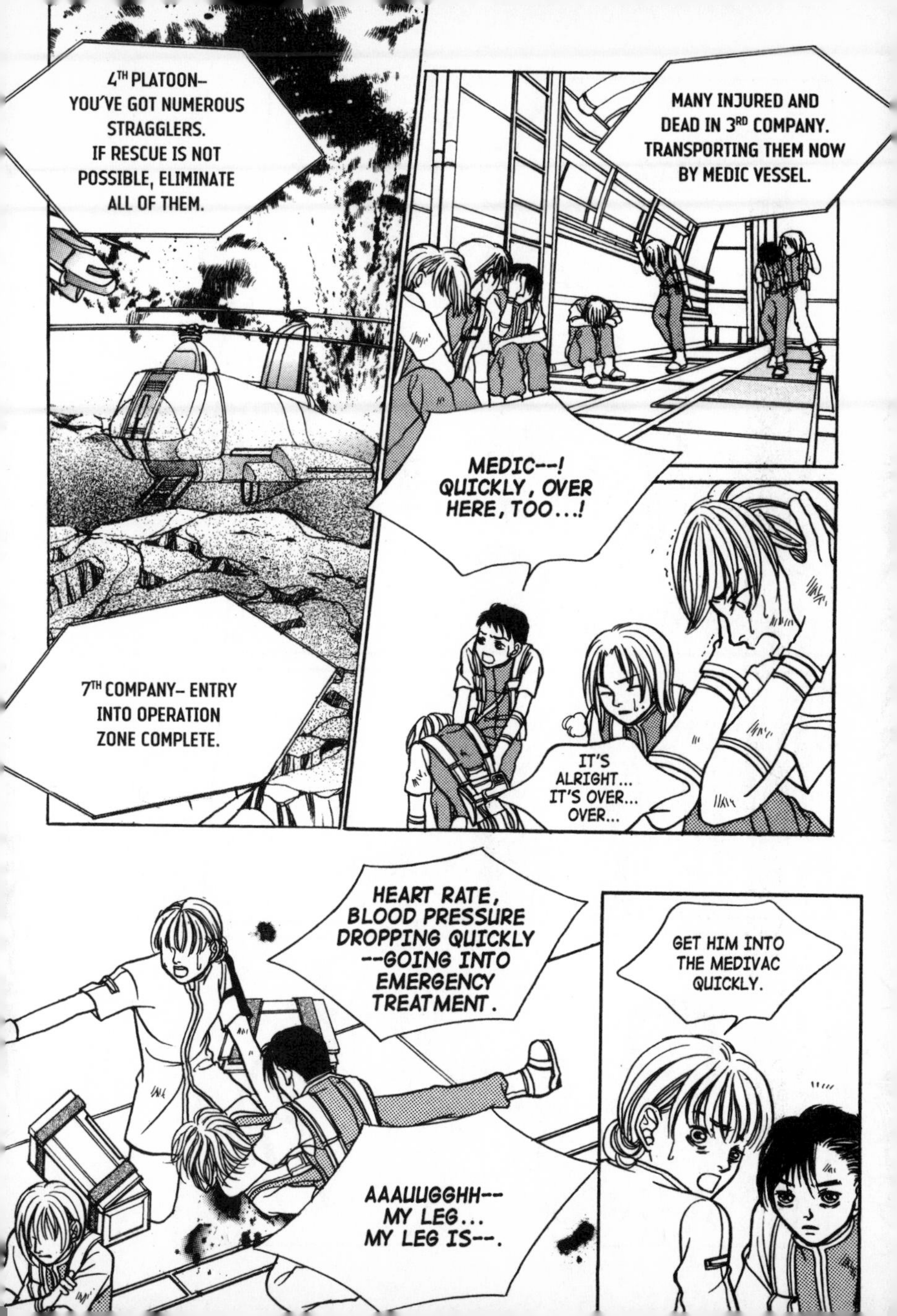
4TH PLATOON— YOU'VE GOT NUMEROUS STRAGGLERS. IF RESCUE IS NOT POSSIBLE, ELIMINATE ALL OF THEM.
7TH COMPANY— ENTRY INTO OPERATION ZONE COMPLETE.
MANY INJURED AND DEAD IN 3RD COMPANY. TRANSPORTING THEM NOW BY MEDIC VESSEL.
MEDIC--! QUICKLY, OVER HERE, TOO...!
IT'S ALRIGHT... IT'S OVER... OVER...
HEART RATE, BLOOD PRESSURE DROPPING QUICKLY --GOING INTO EMERGENCY TREATMENT.
AAAUUGGHH-- MY LEG... MY LEG IS--.
GET HIM INTO THE MEDIVAC QUICKLY.

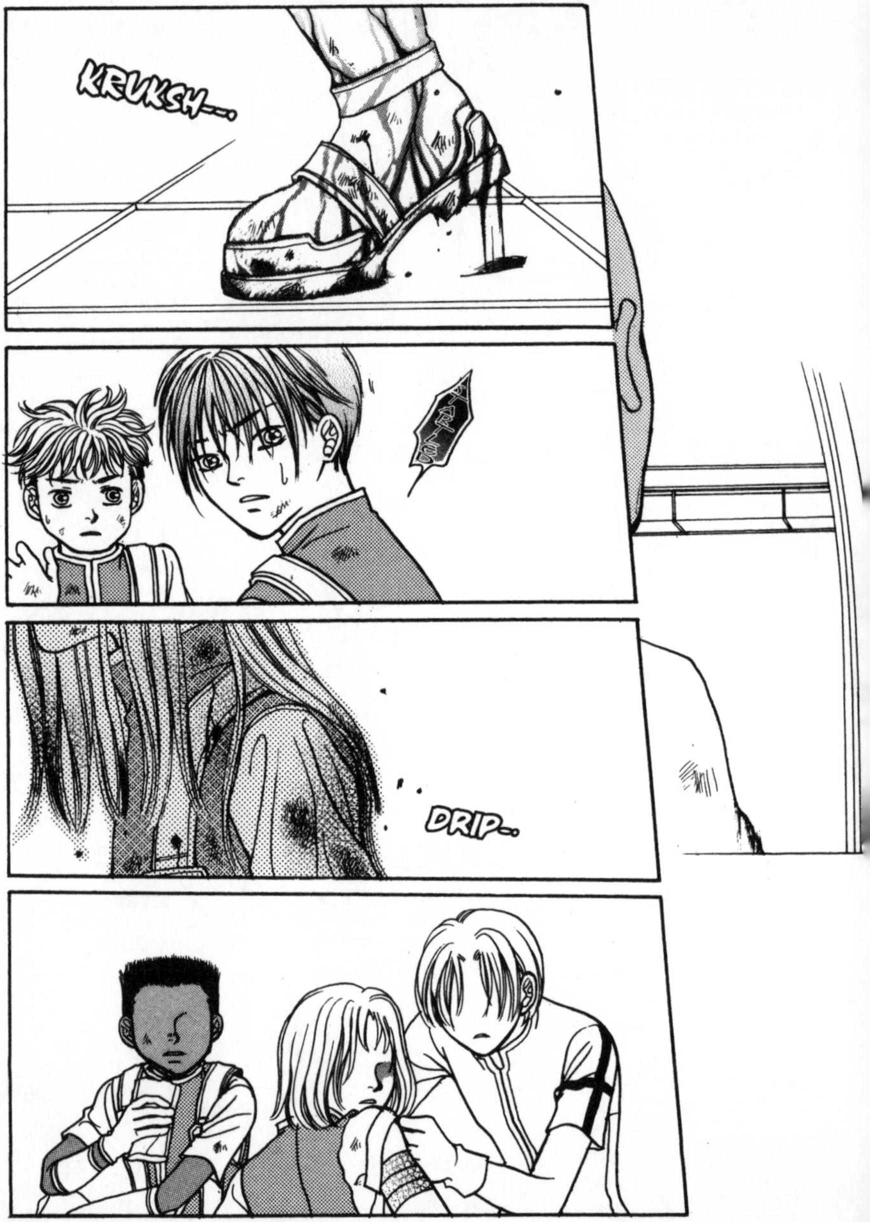
KRUKSH--.
STARTLED
DRIP-.

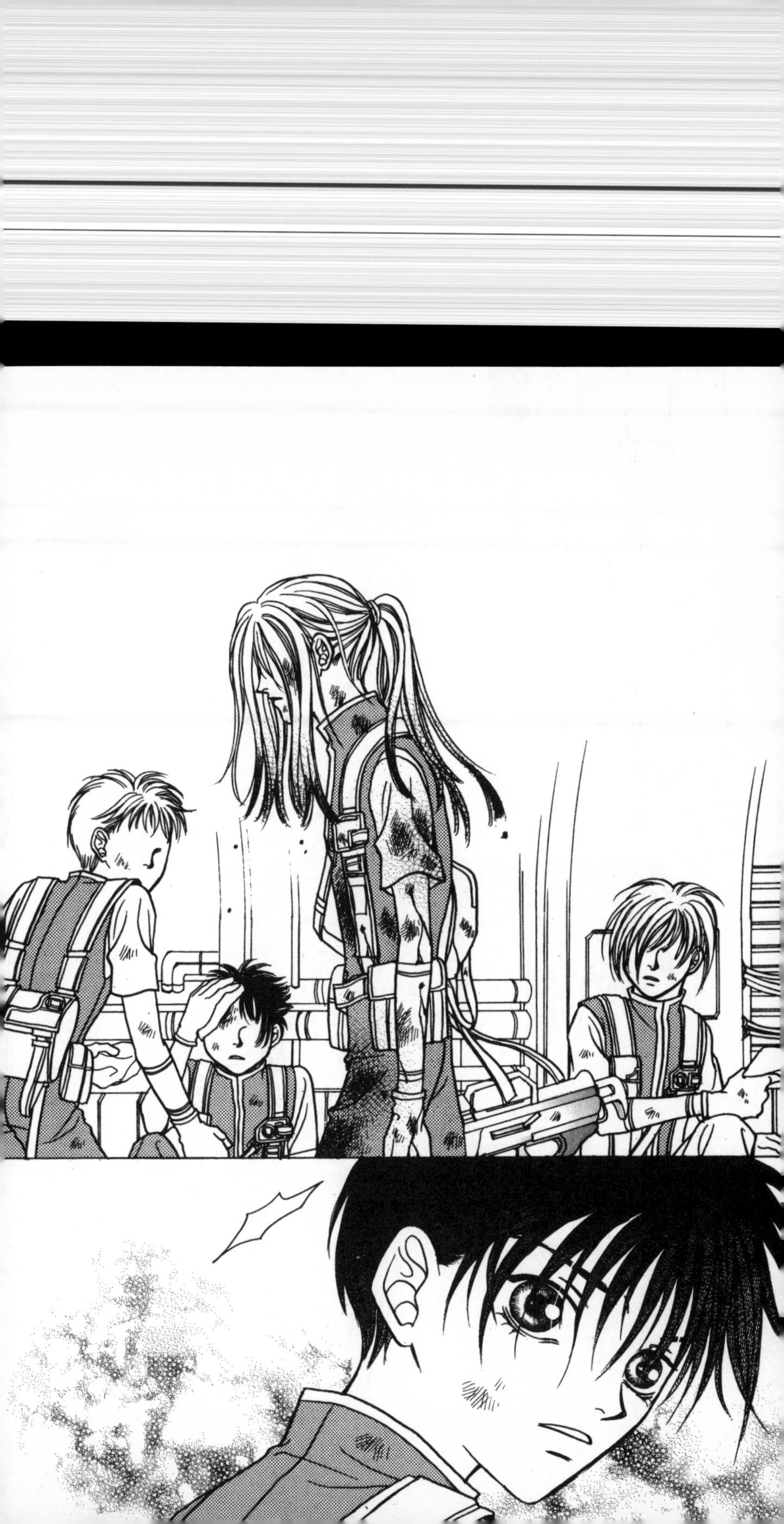

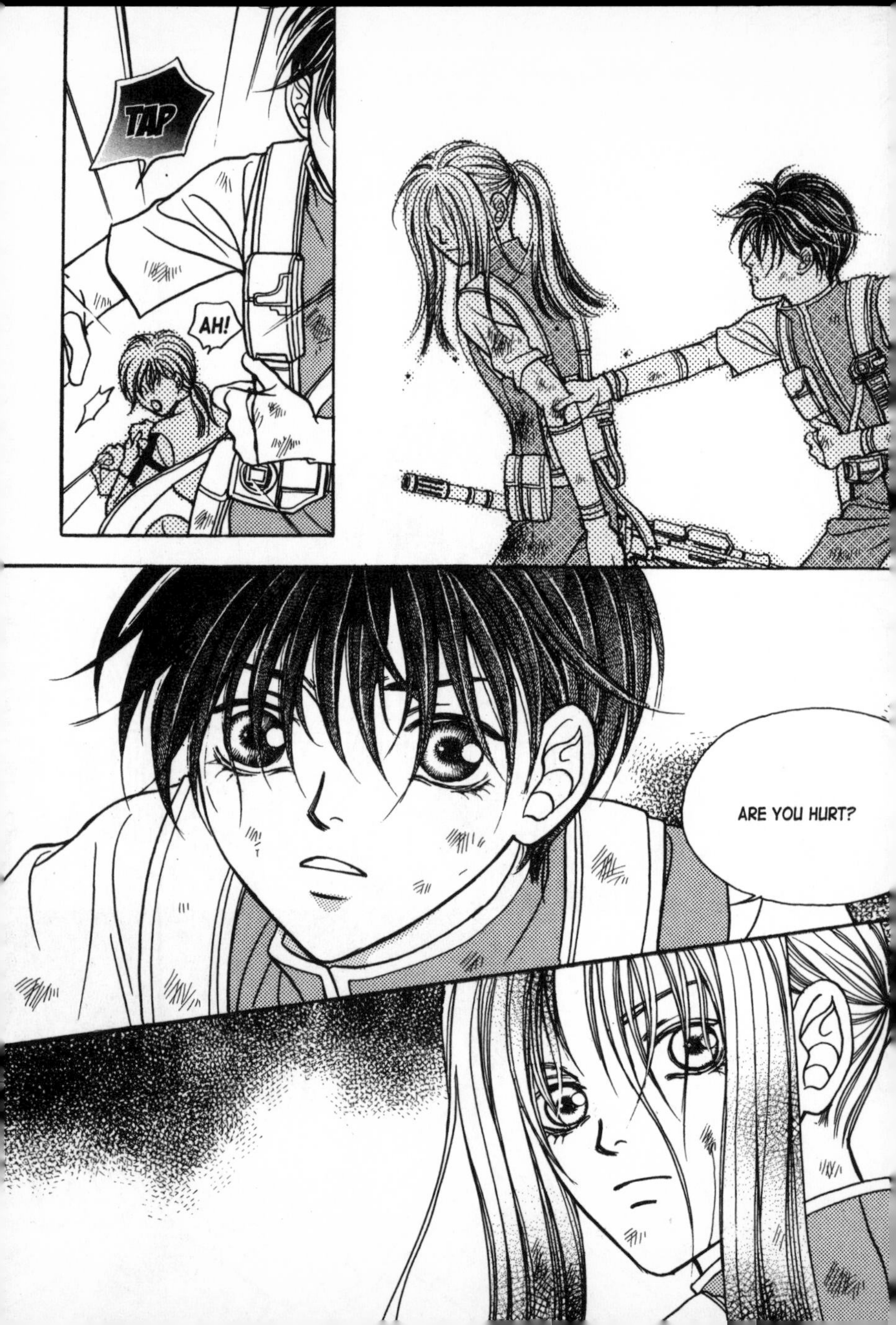
TAP
AH!
ARE YOU HURT?

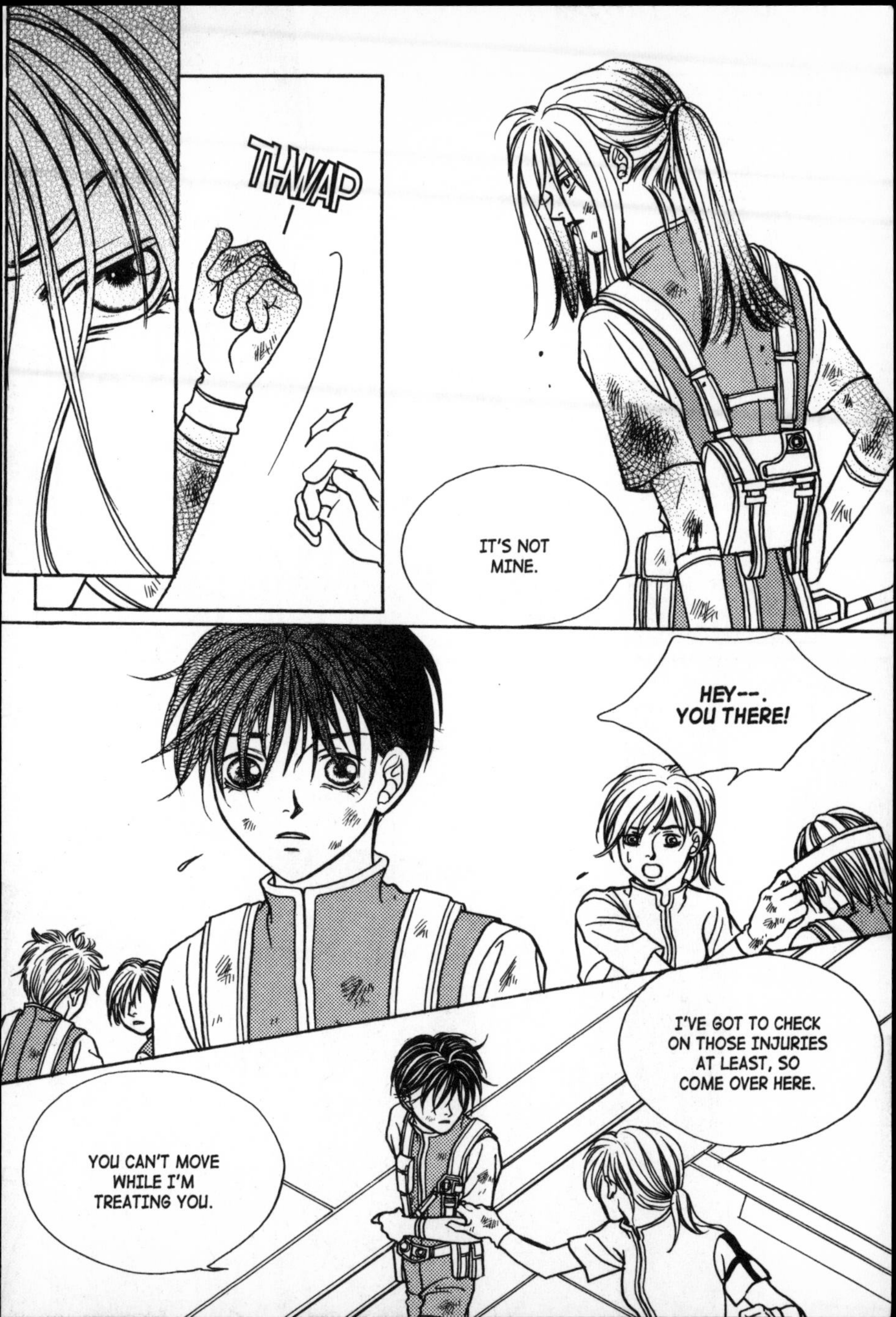
THWAP
IT'S NOT MINE.
HEY--. YOU THERE!
I'VE GOT TO CHECK ON THOSE INJURIES AT LEAST, SO COME OVER HERE.
YOU CAN'T MOVE WHILE I'M TREATING YOU.

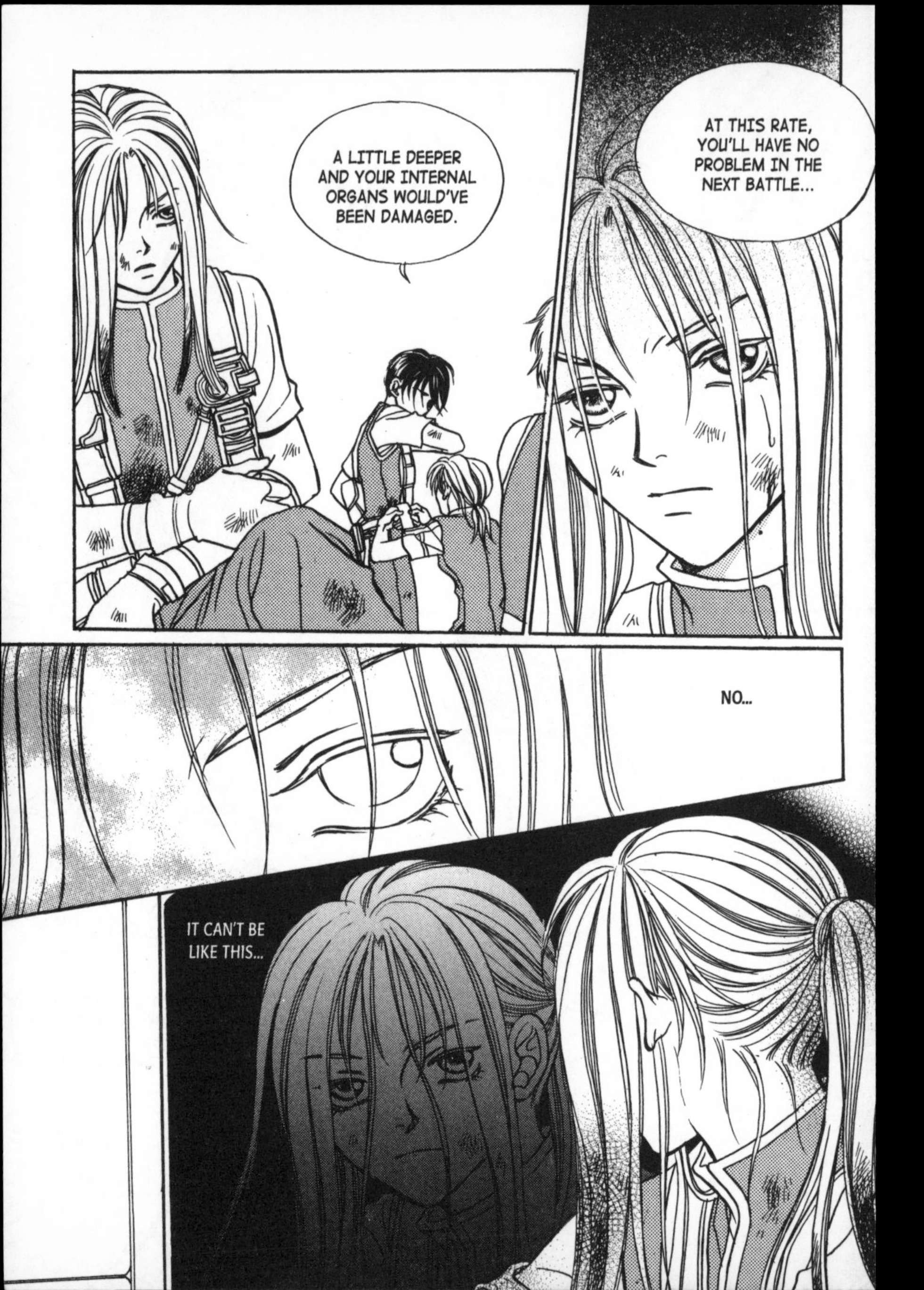
A LITTLE DEEPER AND YOUR INTERNAL ORGANS WOULD'VE BEEN DAMAGED.
AT THIS RATE, YOU'LL HAVE NO PROBLEM IN THE NEXT BATTLE...
NO...
IT CAN'T BE LIKE THIS...

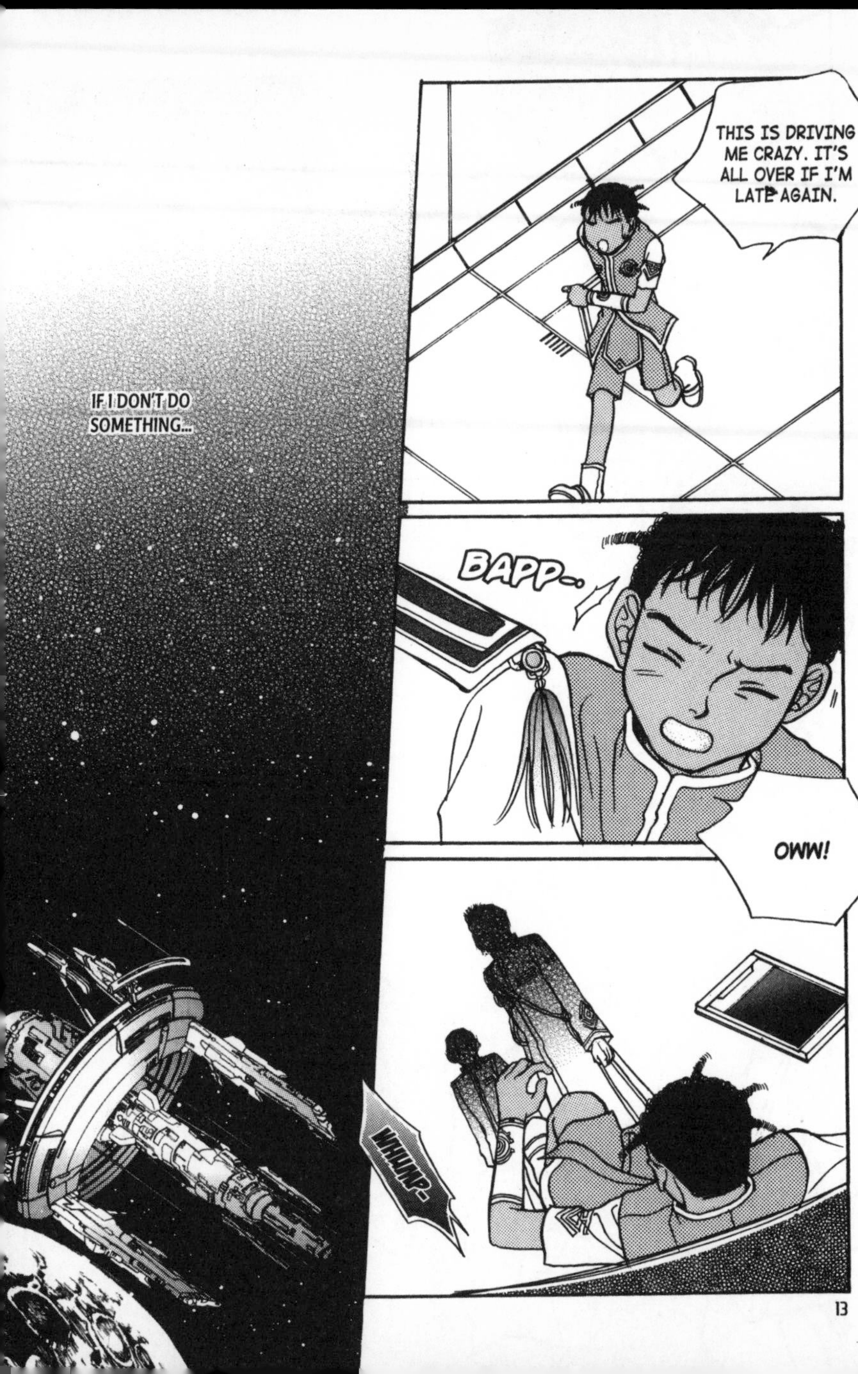
IF I DON'T DO SOMETHING...
THIS IS DRIVING ME CRAZY. IT'S ALL OVER IF I'M LATE AGAIN.
BAPP-
OWW!
WHUMP-

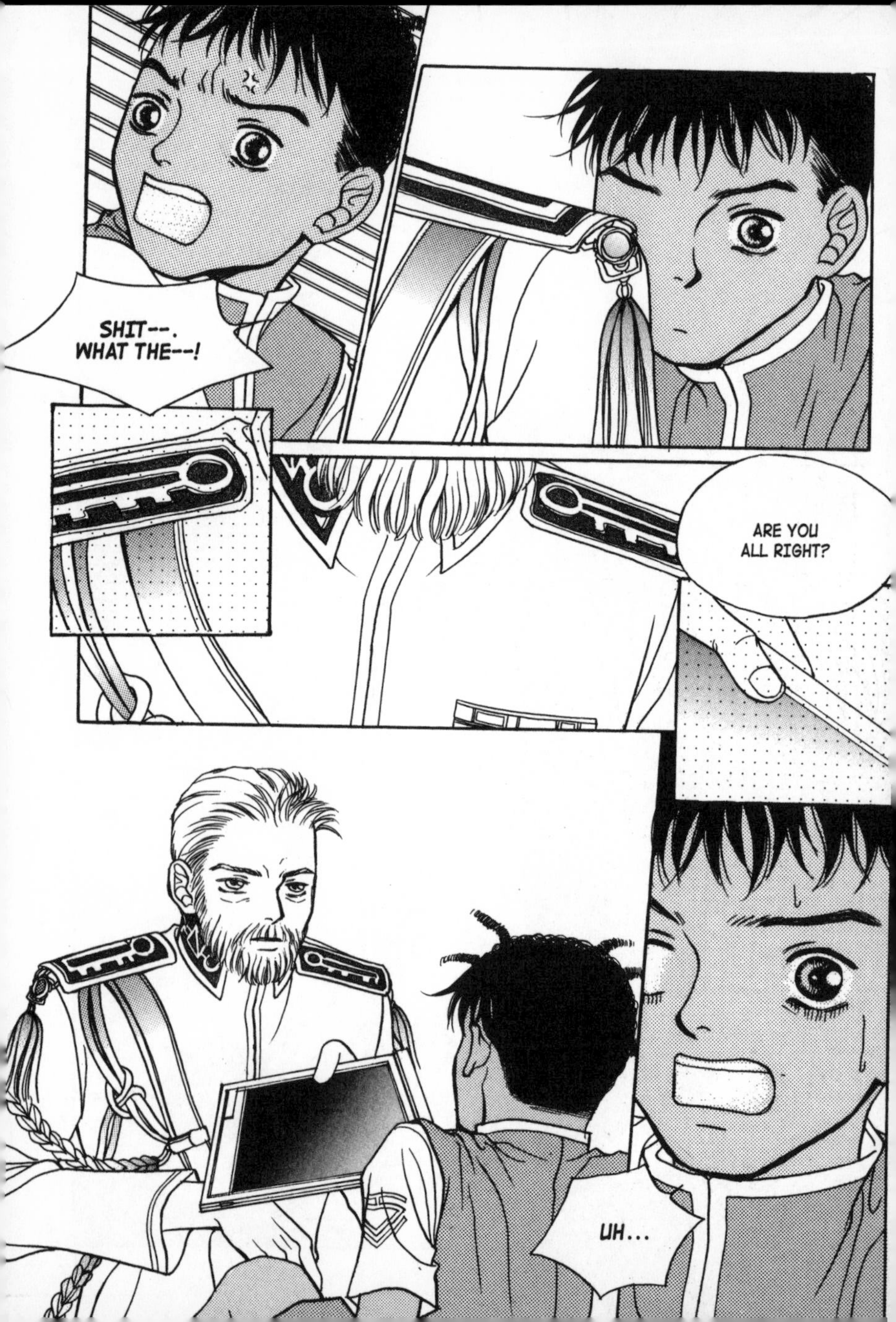
SHIT--.
WHAT THE--!
ARE YOU ALL RIGHT?
UH...

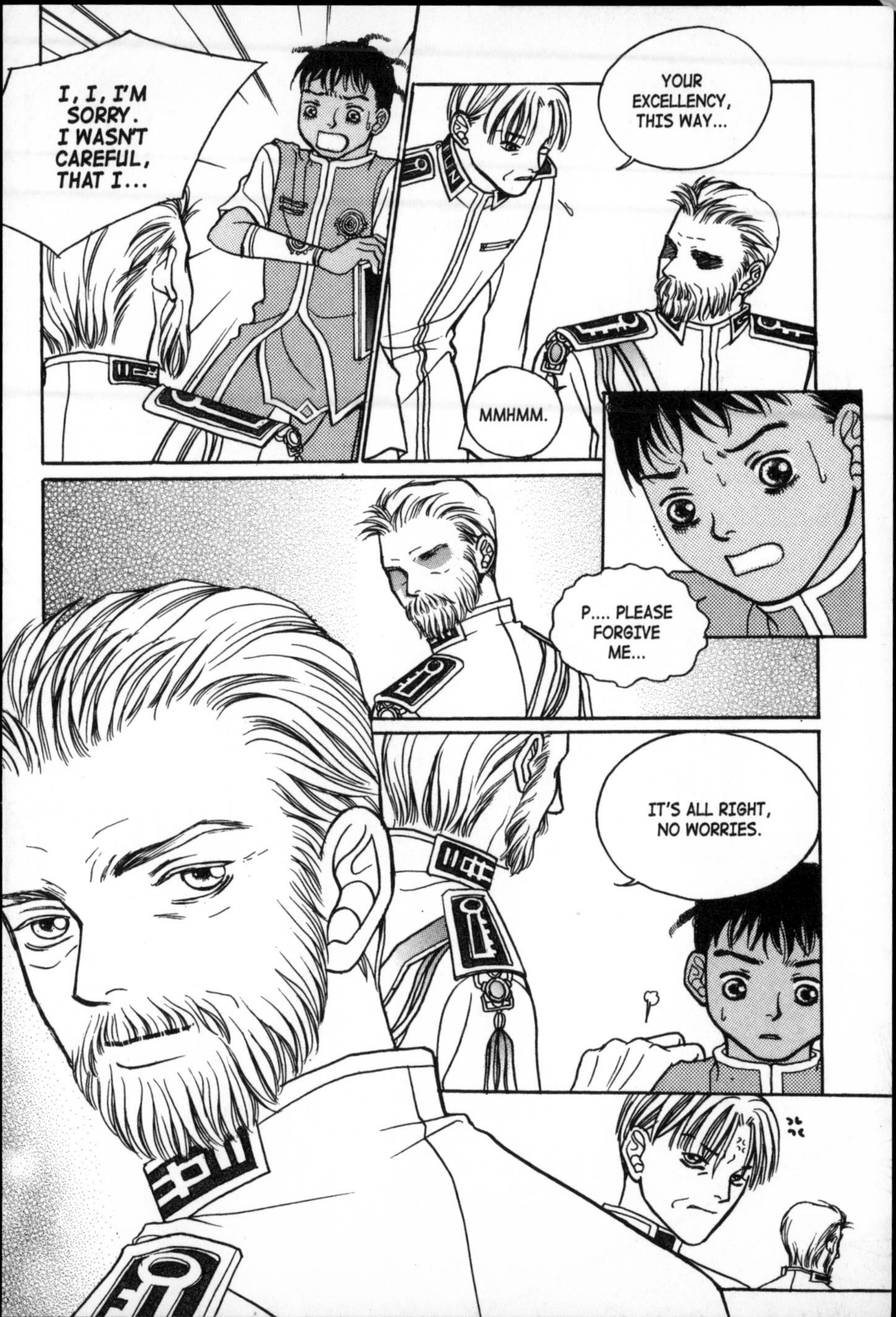
I, I, I'M SORRY. I WASN'T CAREFUL, THAT I...
YOUR EXCELLENCY, THIS WAY...
MMHMM.
P.... PLEASE FORGIVE ME...
IT'S ALL RIGHT, NO WORRIES.

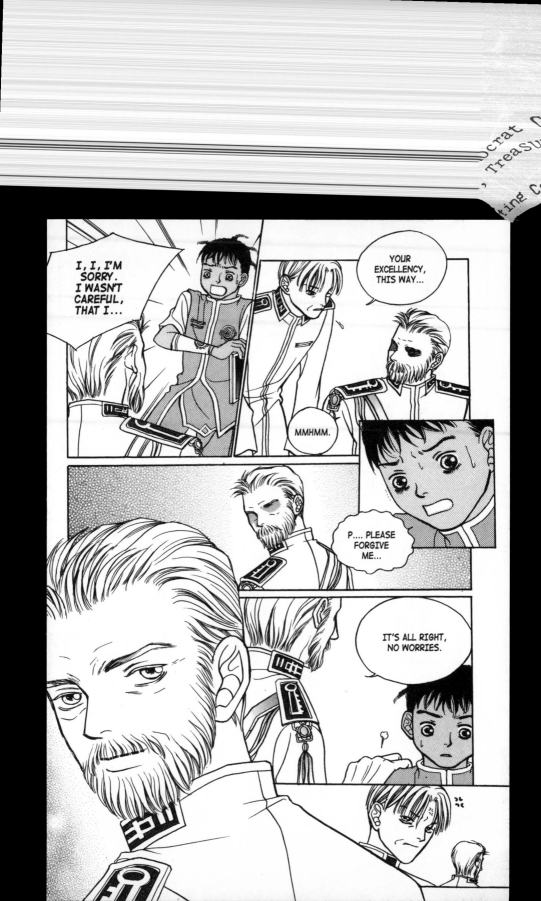

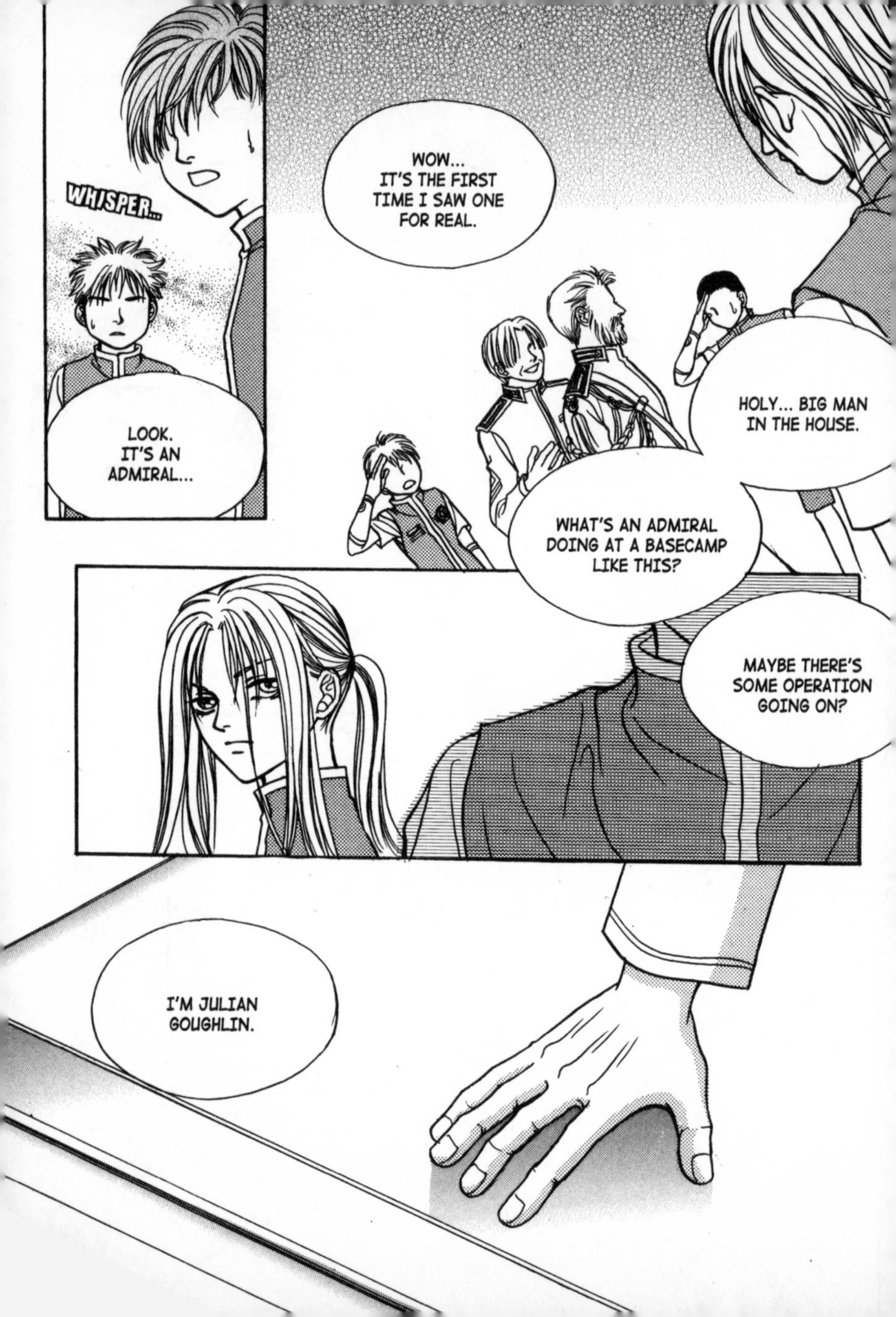
WHISPER...
LOOK. IT'S AN ADMIRAL...
WOW... IT'S THE FIRST TIME I SAW ONE FOR REAL.
HOLY... BIG MAN IN THE HOUSE.
WHAT'S AN ADMIRAL DOING AT A BASECAMP LIKE THIS?
MAYBE THERE'S SOME OPERATION GOING ON?
I'M JULIAN GOUGHLIN.

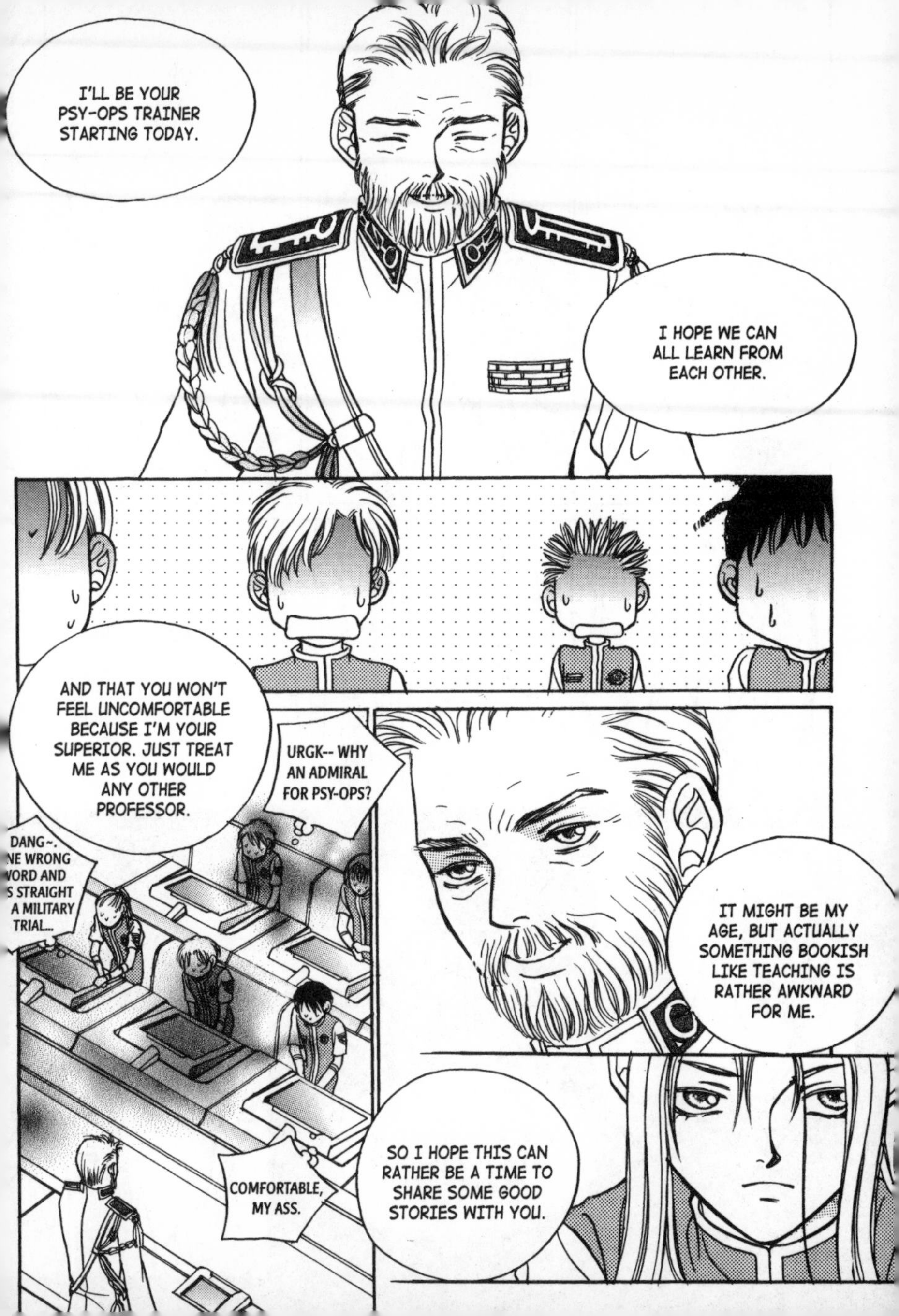
I'LL BE YOUR PSY-OPS TRAINER STARTING TODAY.
I HOPE WE CAN ALL LEARN FROM EACH OTHER.
AND THAT YOU WON'T FEEL UNCOMFORTABLE BECAUSE I'M YOUR SUPERIOR. JUST TREAT ME AS YOU WOULD ANY OTHER PROFESSOR.
URGK-- WHY AN ADMIRAL FOR PSY-OPS?
DANG~. NE WRONG WORD AND S STRAIGHT A MILITARY TRIAL...
COMFORTABLE, MY ASS.
IT MIGHT BE MY AGE, BUT ACTUALLY SOMETHING BOOKISH LIKE TEACHING IS RATHER AWKWARD FOR ME.
SO I HOPE THIS CAN RATHER BE A TIME TO SHARE SOME GOOD STORIES WITH YOU.

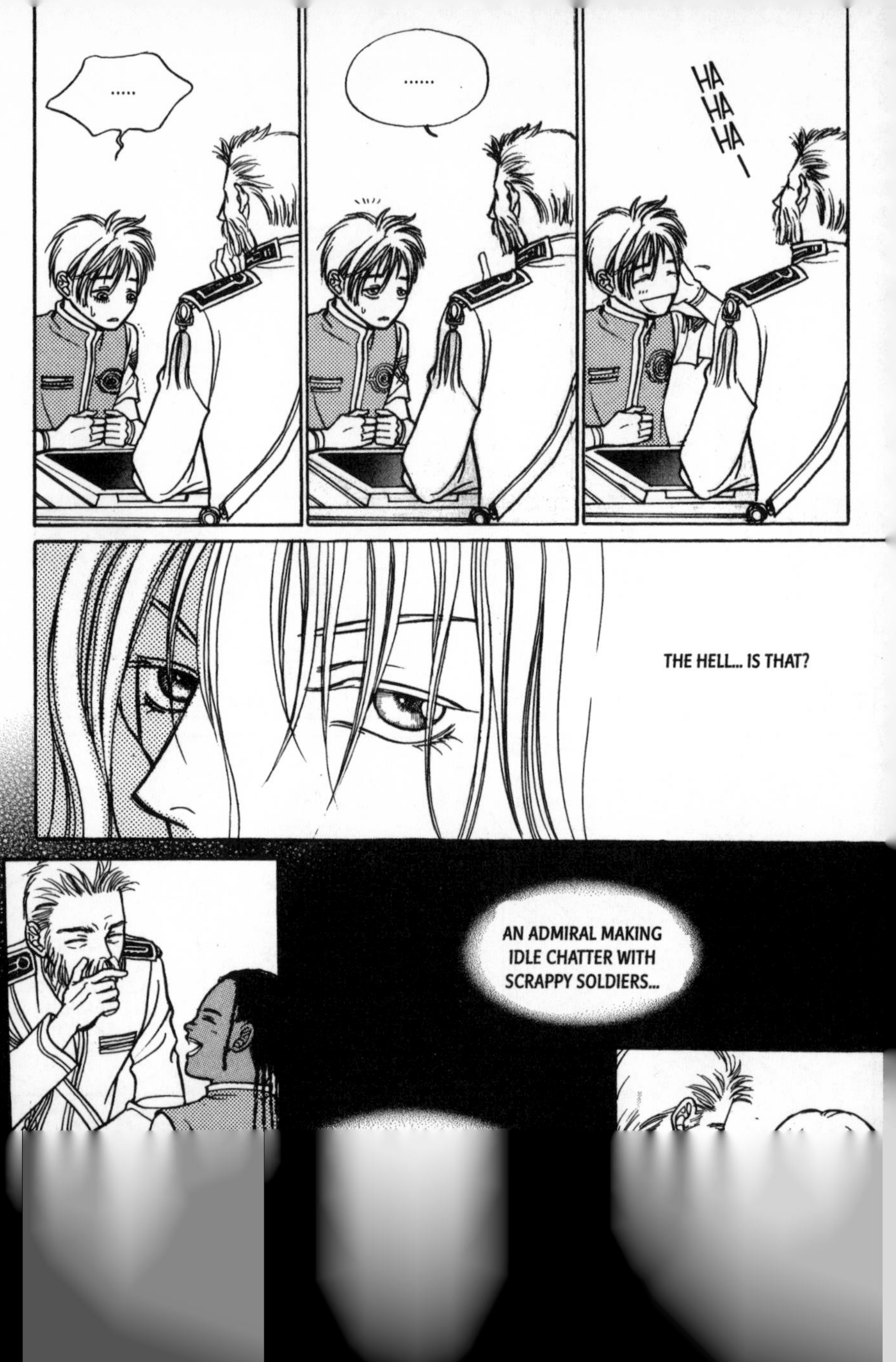
......
....
HA HA HA I
THE HELL... IS THAT?
AN ADMIRAL MAKING IDLE CHATTER WITH SCRAPPY SOLDIERS...

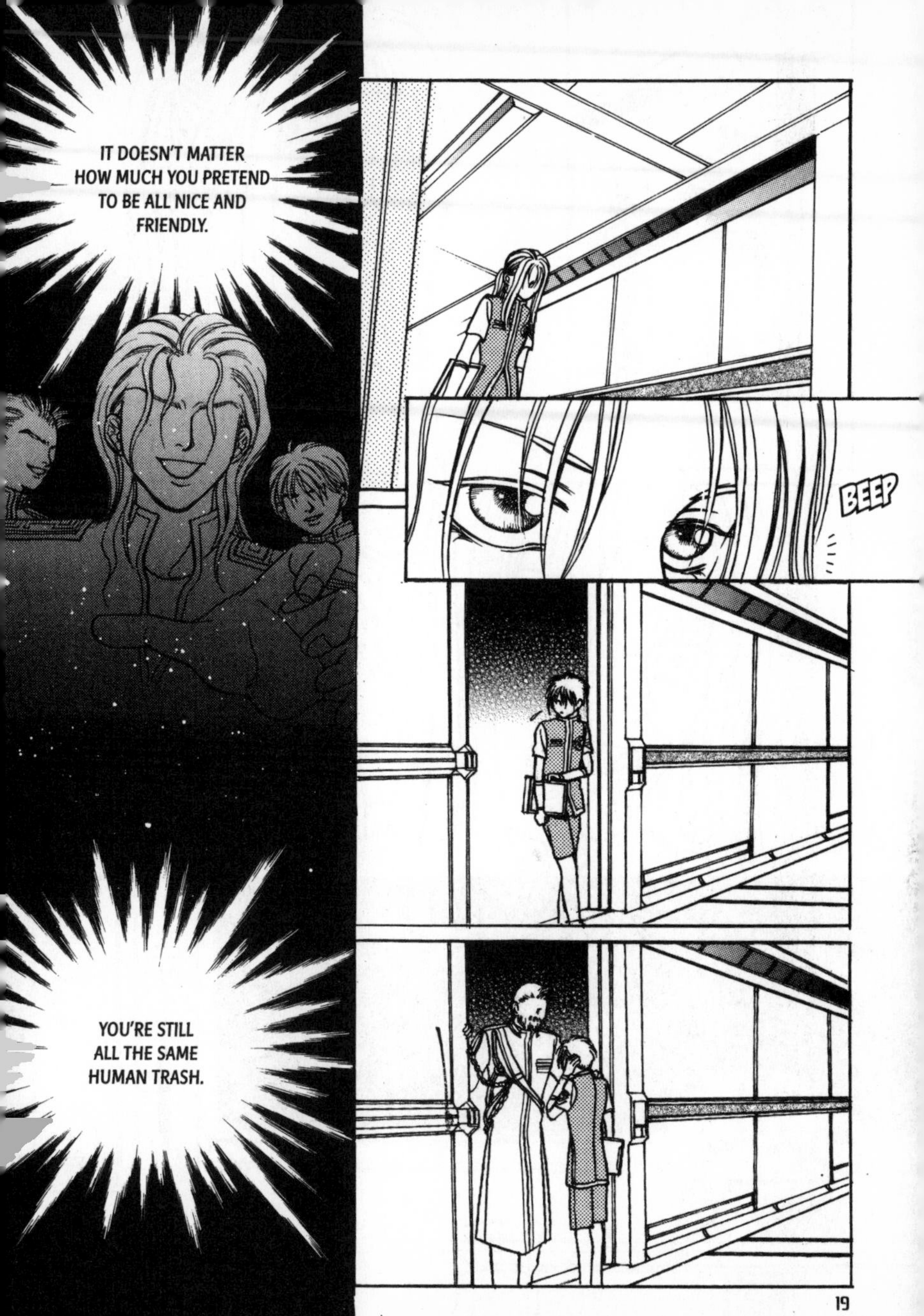
IT DOESN'T MATTER HOW MUCH YOU PRETEND TO BE ALL NICE AND FRIENDLY.
YOU'RE STILL ALL THE SAME HUMAN TRASH.
BEEP

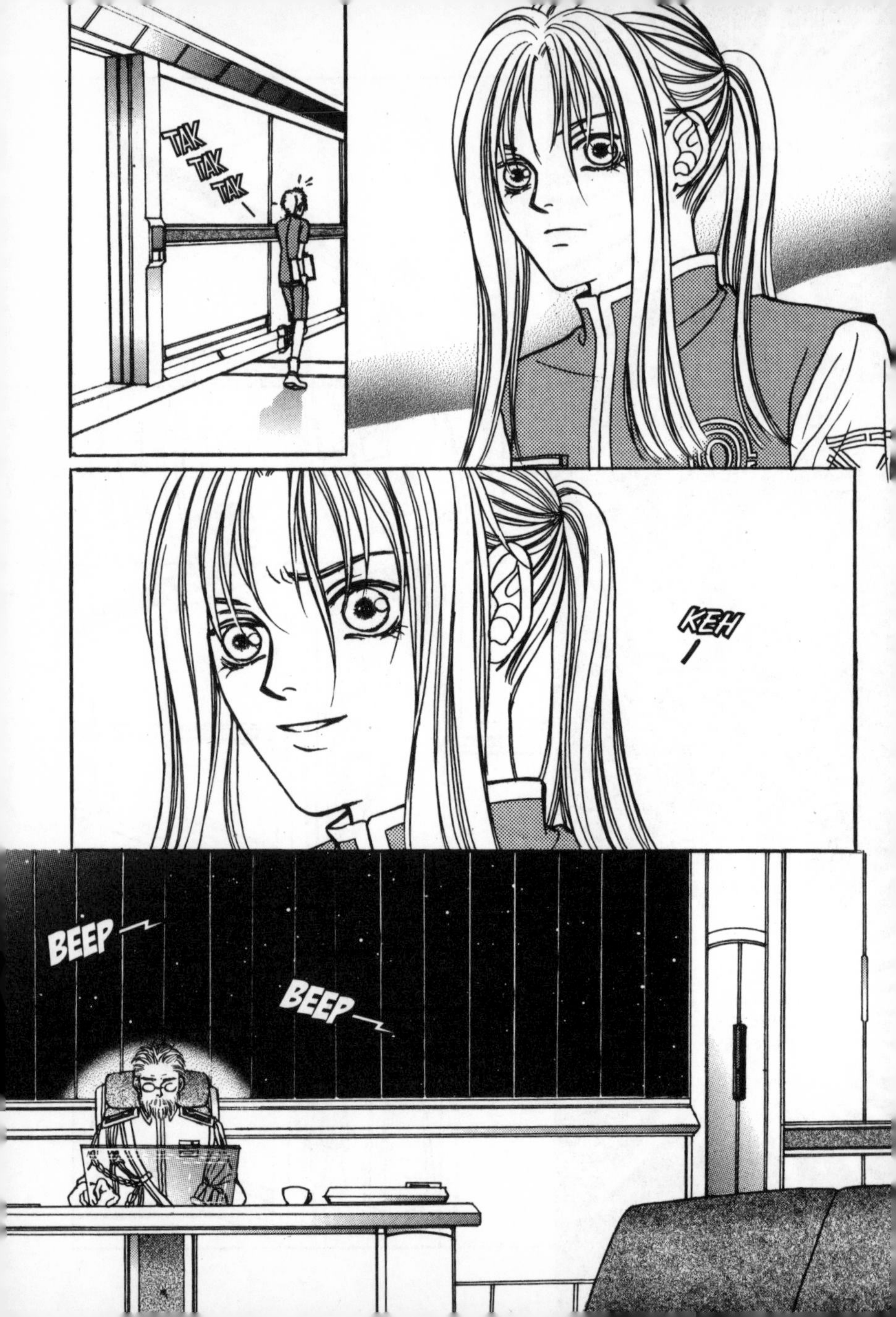
TAK TAK TAK
KEH
BEEP
BEEP

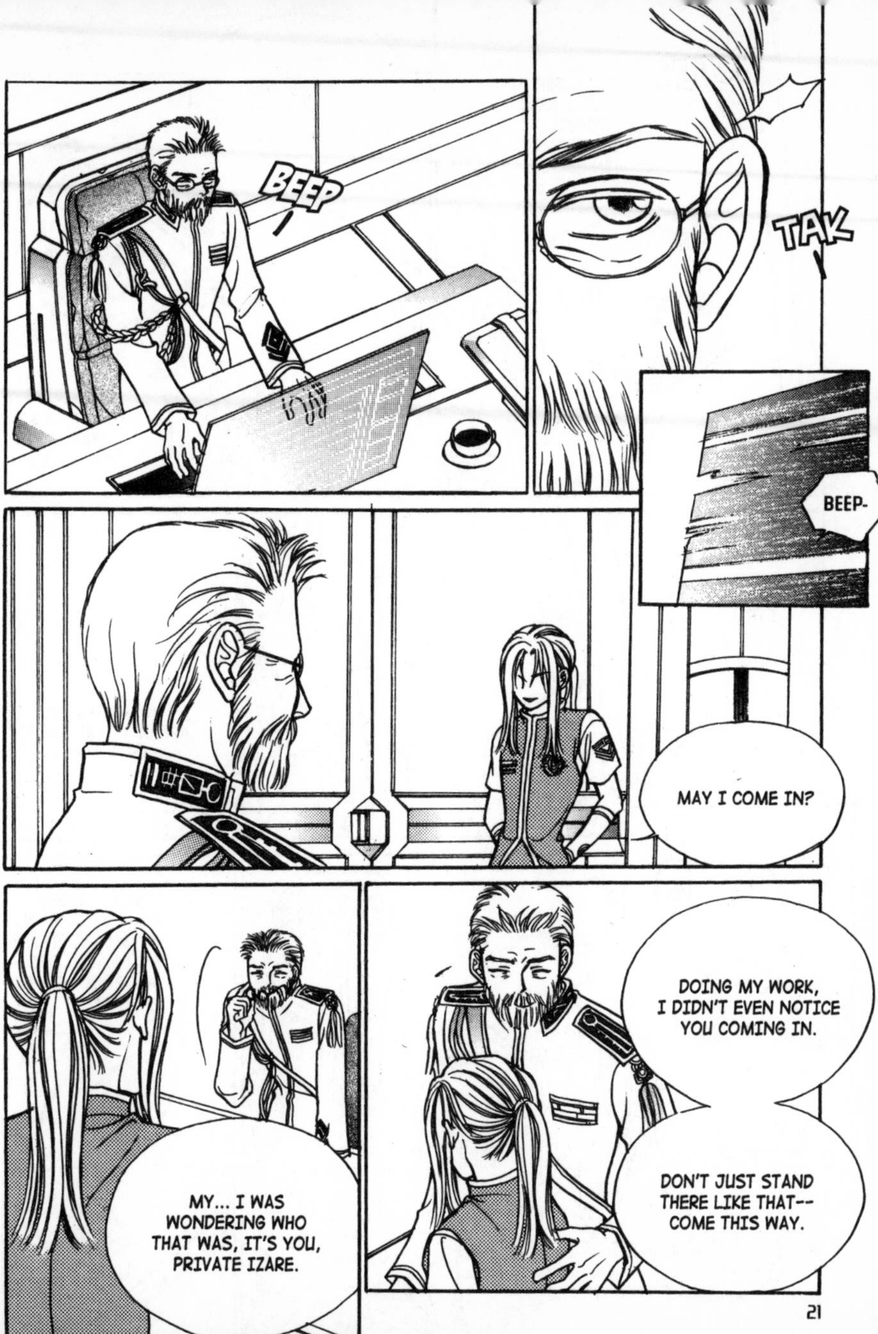
BEEP
TAK
BEEP-
MAY I COME IN?
MY... I WAS WONDERING WHO THAT WAS, IT'S YOU, PRIVATE IZARE.
DOING MY WORK, I DIDN'T EVEN NOTICE YOU COMING IN.
DON'T JUST STAND THERE LIKE THAT-- COME THIS WAY.

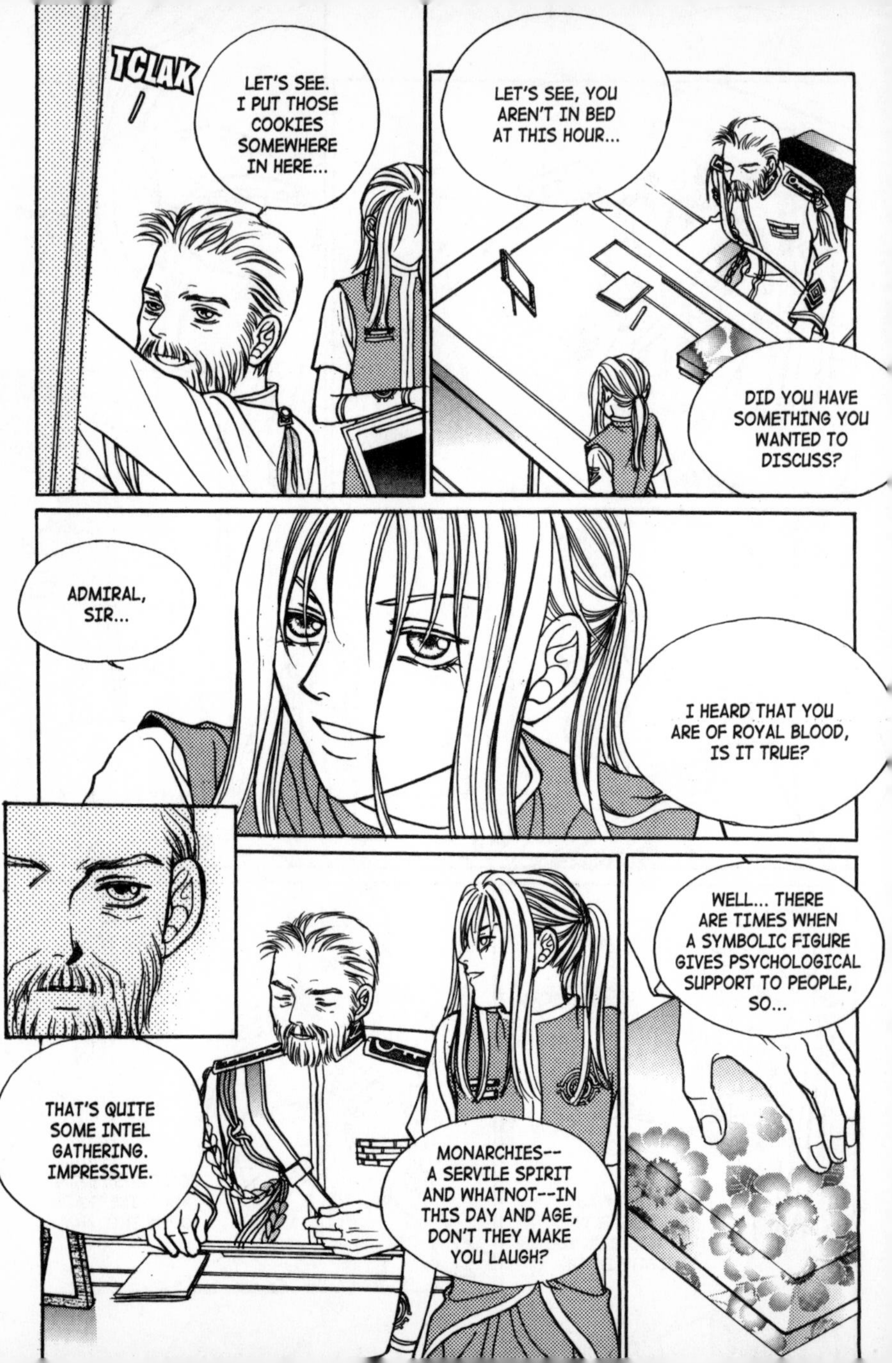
TCLAK
LET'S SEE. I PUT THOSE COOKIES SOMEWHERE IN HERE...
LET'S SEE, YOU AREN'T IN BED AT THIS HOUR...
DID YOU HAVE SOMETHING YOU WANTED TO DISCUSS?
ADMIRAL, SIR...
I HEARD THAT YOU ARE OF ROYAL BLOOD, IS IT TRUE?
THAT'S QUITE SOME INTEL GATHERING. IMPRESSIVE.
MONARCHIES-- A SERVILE SPIRIT AND WHATNOT--IN THIS DAY AND AGE, DON'T THEY MAKE YOU LAUGH?
WELL... THERE ARE TIMES WHEN A SYMBOLIC FIGURE GIVES PSYCHOLOGICAL SUPPORT TO PEOPLE, SO...

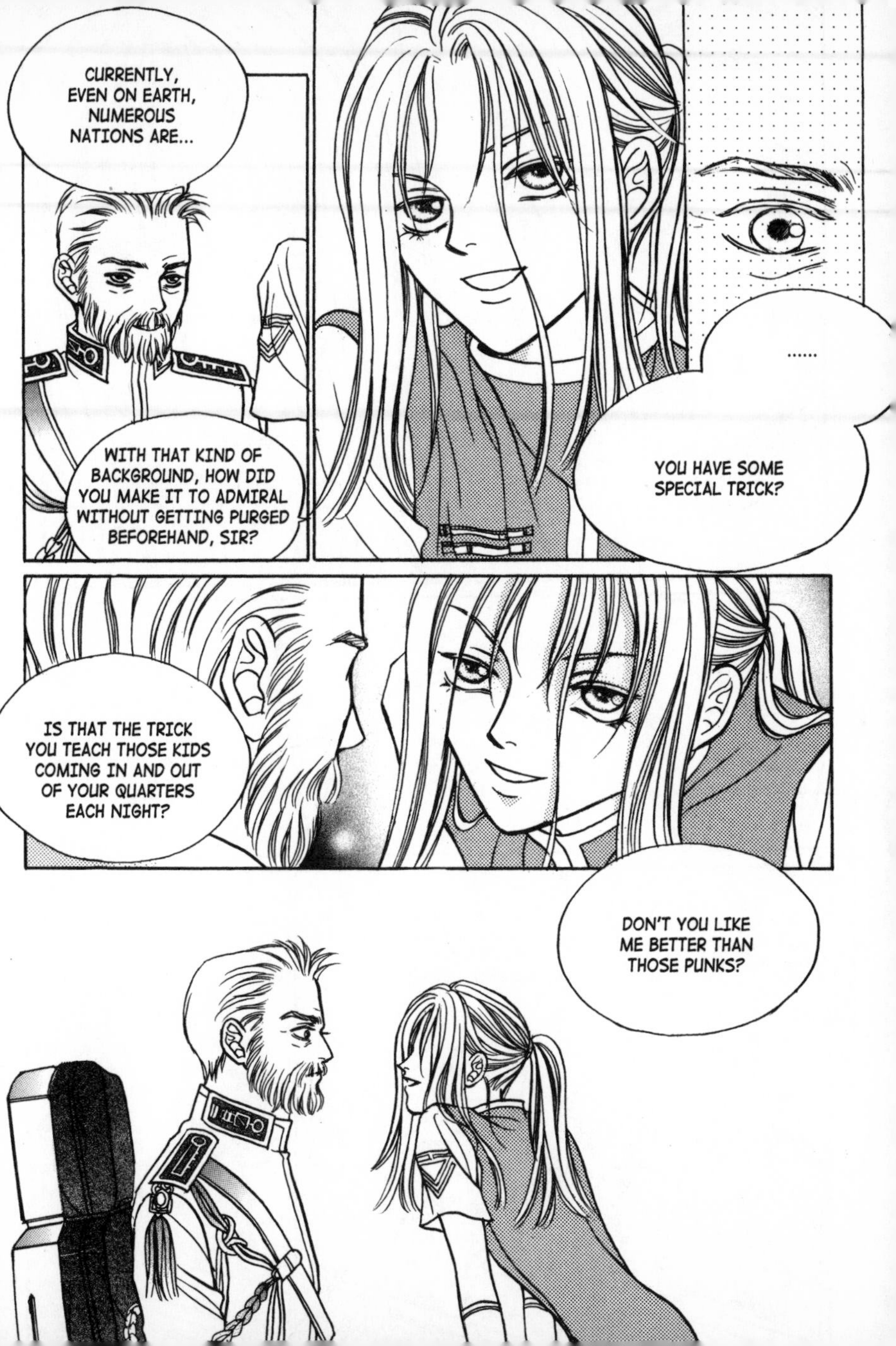
CURRENTLY, EVEN ON EARTH, NUMEROUS NATIONS ARE...
WITH THAT KIND OF BACKGROUND, HOW DID YOU MAKE IT TO ADMIRAL WITHOUT GETTING PURGED BEFOREHAND, SIR?
......
YOU HAVE SOME SPECIAL TRICK?
IS THAT THE TRICK YOU TEACH THOSE KIDS COMING IN AND OUT OF YOUR QUARTERS EACH NIGHT?
DON'T YOU LIKE ME BETTER THAN THOSE PUNKS?

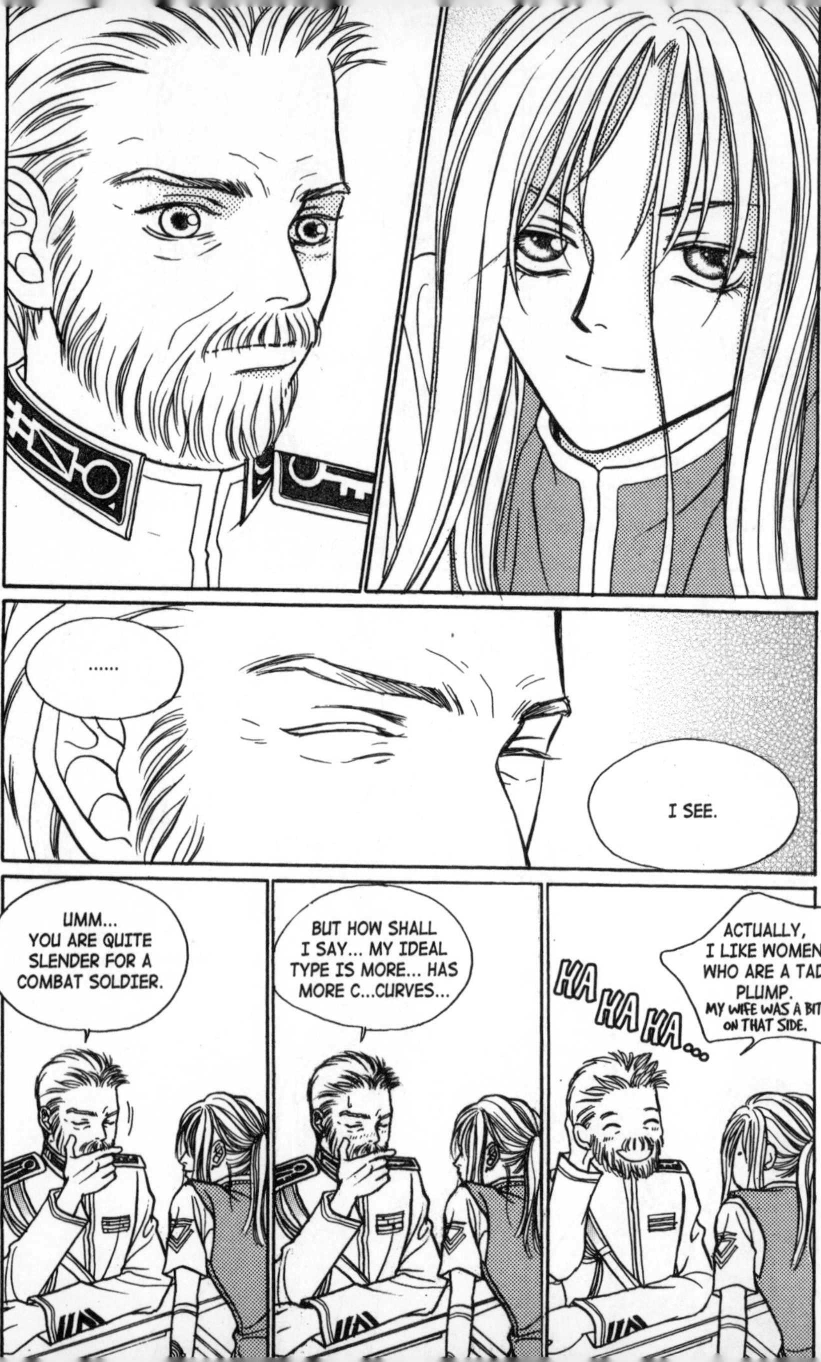
......
I SEE.
UMM... YOU ARE QUITE SLENDER FOR A COMBAT SOLDIER.
BUT HOW SHALL I SAY... MY IDEAL TYPE IS MORE... HAS MORE C...CURVES...
HA HA HA...
ACTUALLY, I LIKE WOMEN WHO ARE A TAD PLUMP. MY WIFE WAS A BIT ON THAT SIDE.

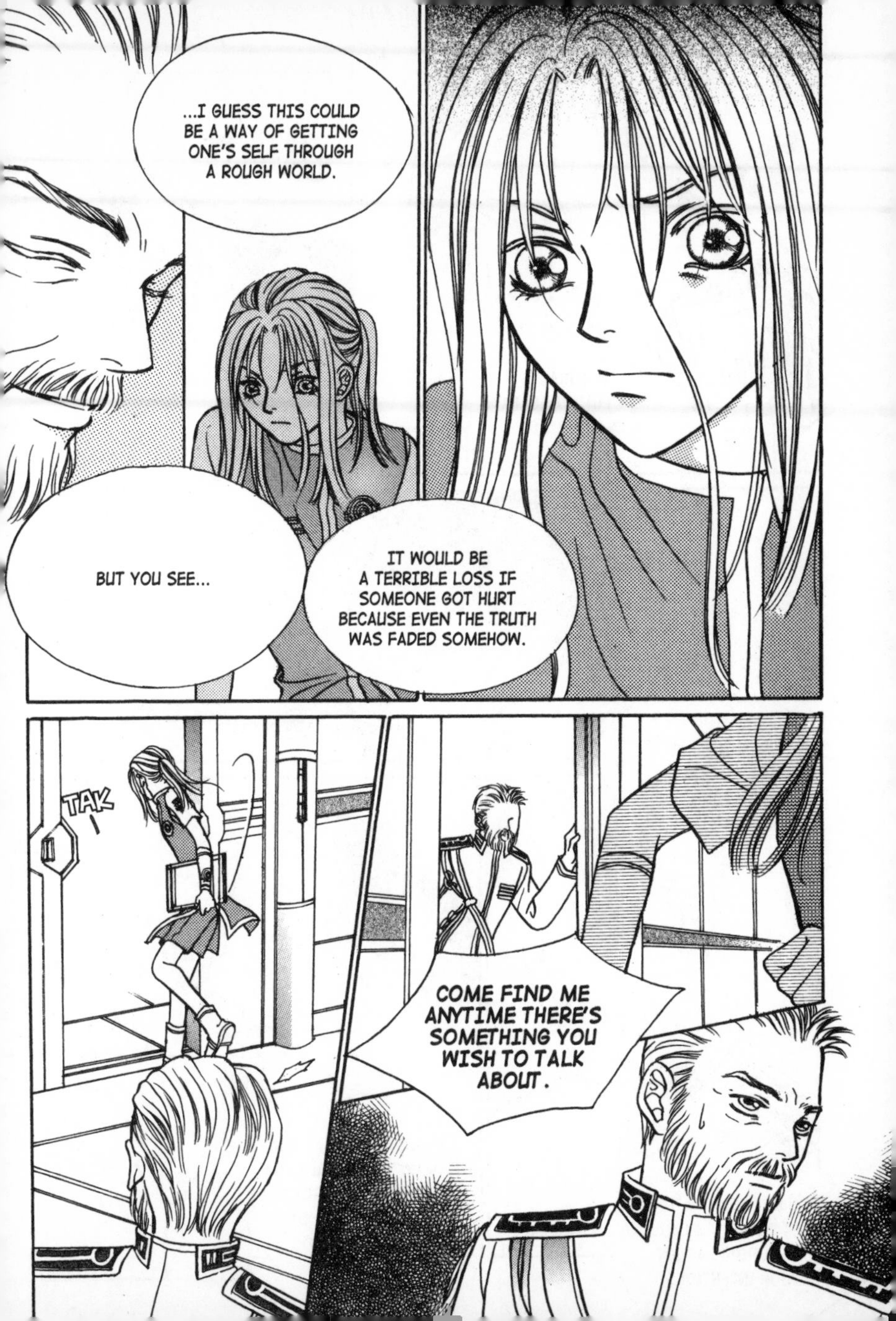
...I GUESS THIS COULD BE A WAY OF GETTING ONE'S SELF THROUGH A ROUGH WORLD.
BUT YOU SEE...
IT WOULD BE A TERRIBLE LOSS IF SOMEONE GOT HURT BECAUSE EVEN THE TRUTH WAS FADED SOMEHOW.
TAK
COME FIND ME ANYTIME THERE'S SOMETHING YOU WISH TO TALK ABOUT.

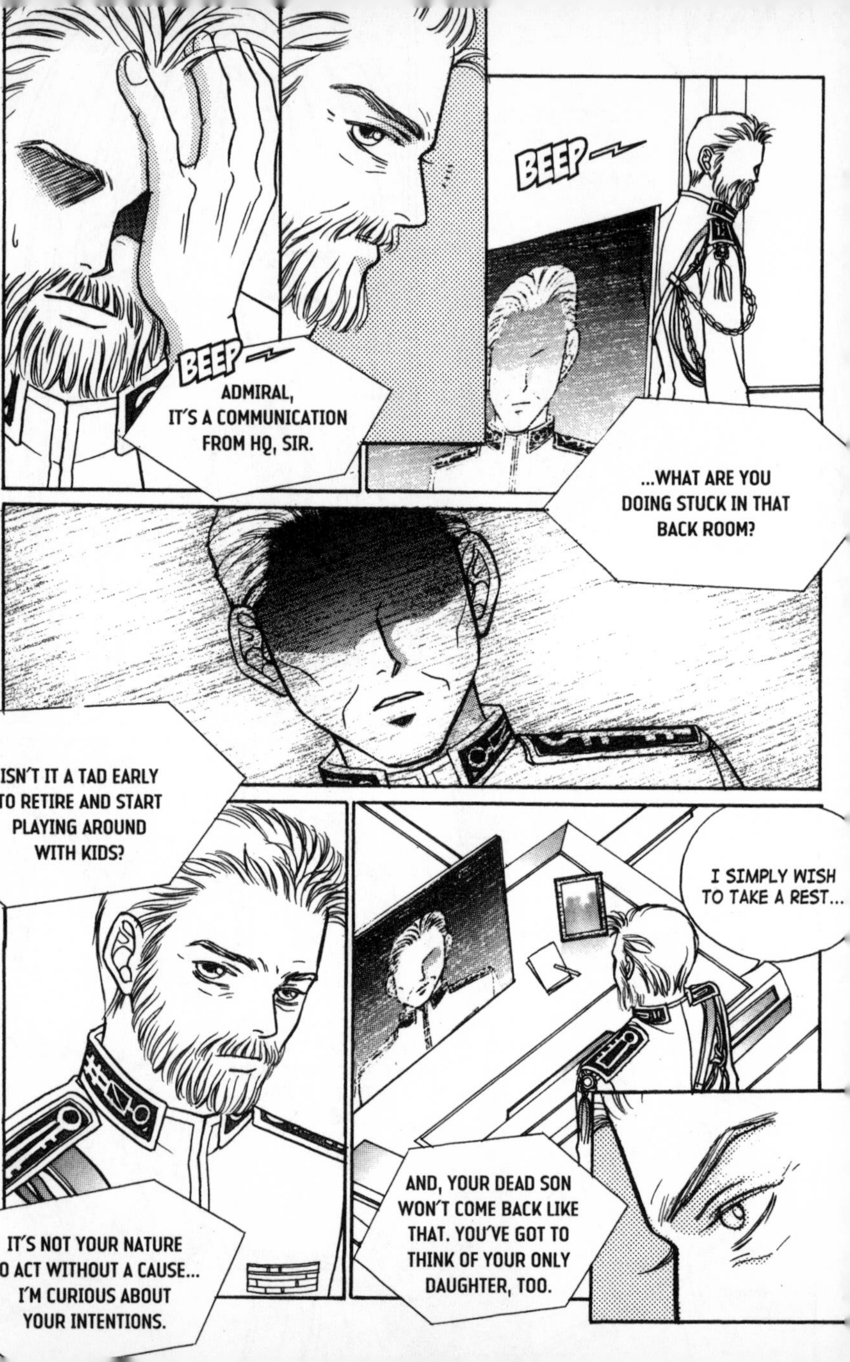
BEEP
ADMIRAL, IT'S A COMMUNICATION FROM HQ, SIR.
BEEP
...WHAT ARE YOU DOING STUCK IN THAT BACK ROOM?
ISN'T IT A TAD EARLY TO RETIRE AND START PLAYING AROUND WITH KIDS?
IT'S NOT YOUR NATURE TO ACT WITHOUT A CAUSE... I'M CURIOUS ABOUT YOUR INTENTIONS.
I SIMPLY WISH TO TAKE A REST...
AND, YOUR DEAD SON WON'T COME BACK LIKE THAT. YOU'VE GOT TO THINK OF YOUR ONLY DAUGHTER, TOO.

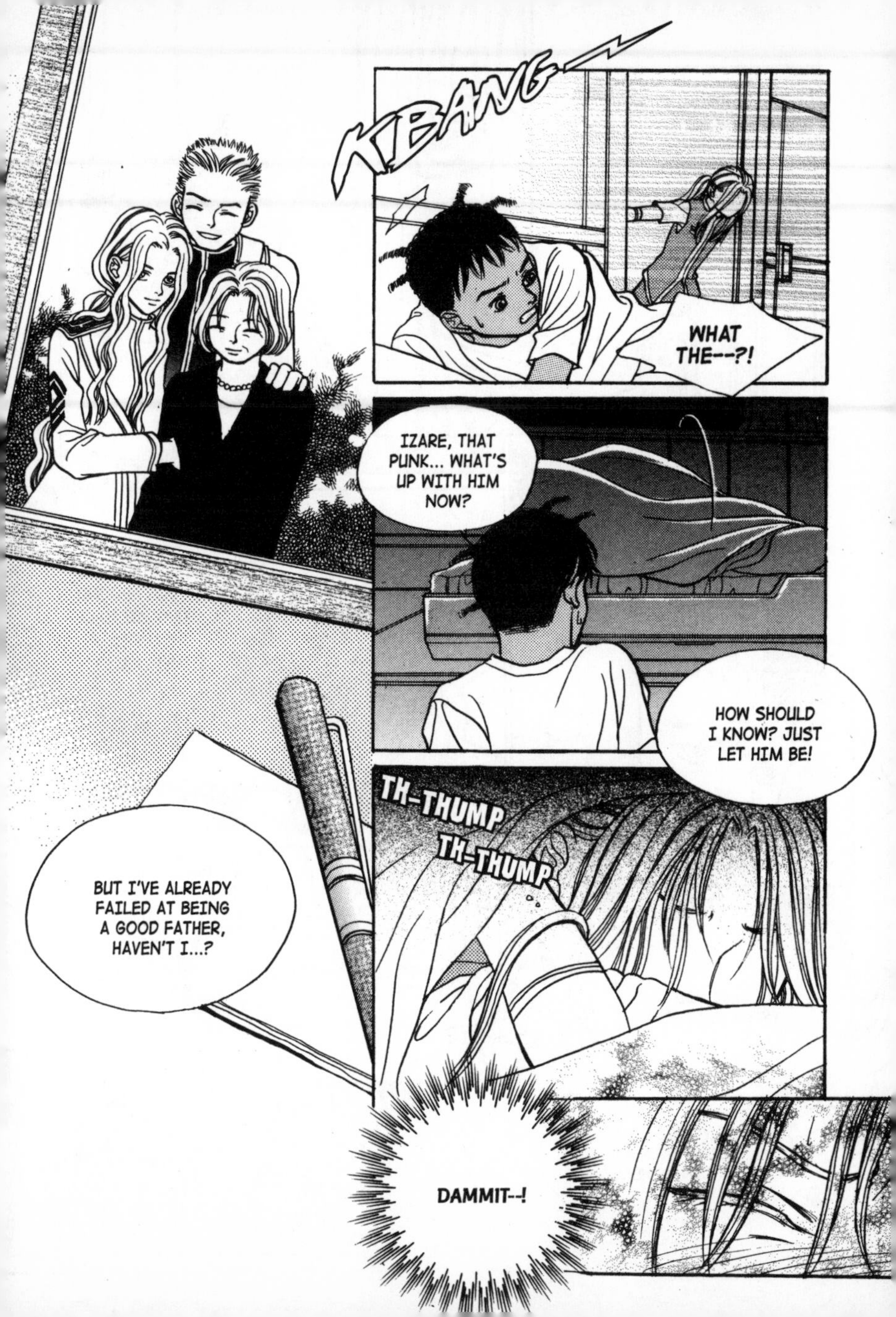
BUT I'VE ALREADY FAILED AT BEING A GOOD FATHER, HAVEN'T I...?
KBANG
WHAT THE--?!
IZARE, THAT PUNK... WHAT'S UP WITH HIM NOW?
HOW SHOULD I KNOW? JUST LET HIM BE!
TH-THUMP
TH-THUMP
DAMMIT--!

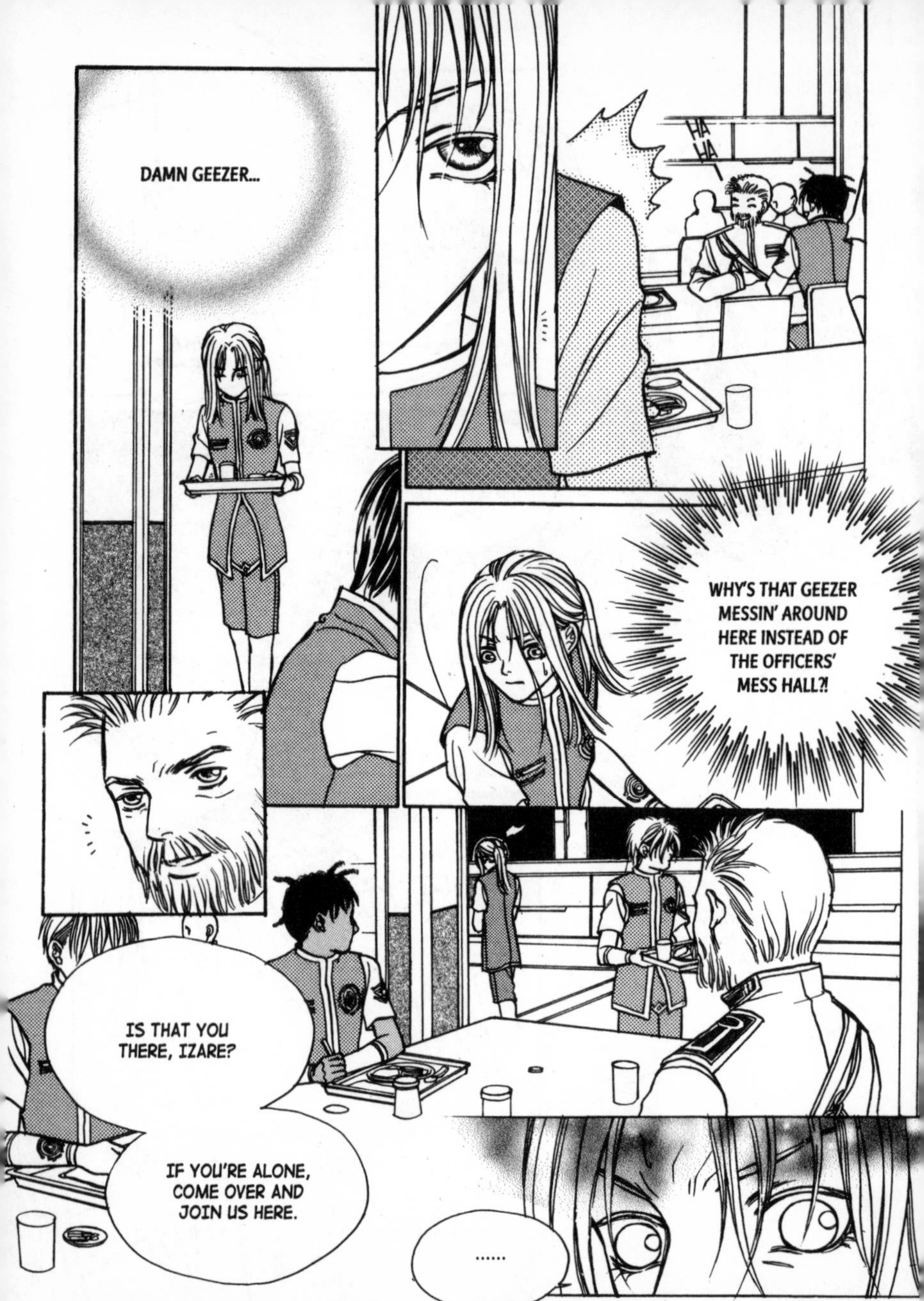
DAMN GEEZER...
HA HA
WHY'S THAT GEEZER MESSIN' AROUND HERE INSTEAD OF THE OFFICERS' MESS HALL?!
IS THAT YOU THERE, IZARE?
IF YOU'RE ALONE, COME OVER AND JOIN US HERE.
......

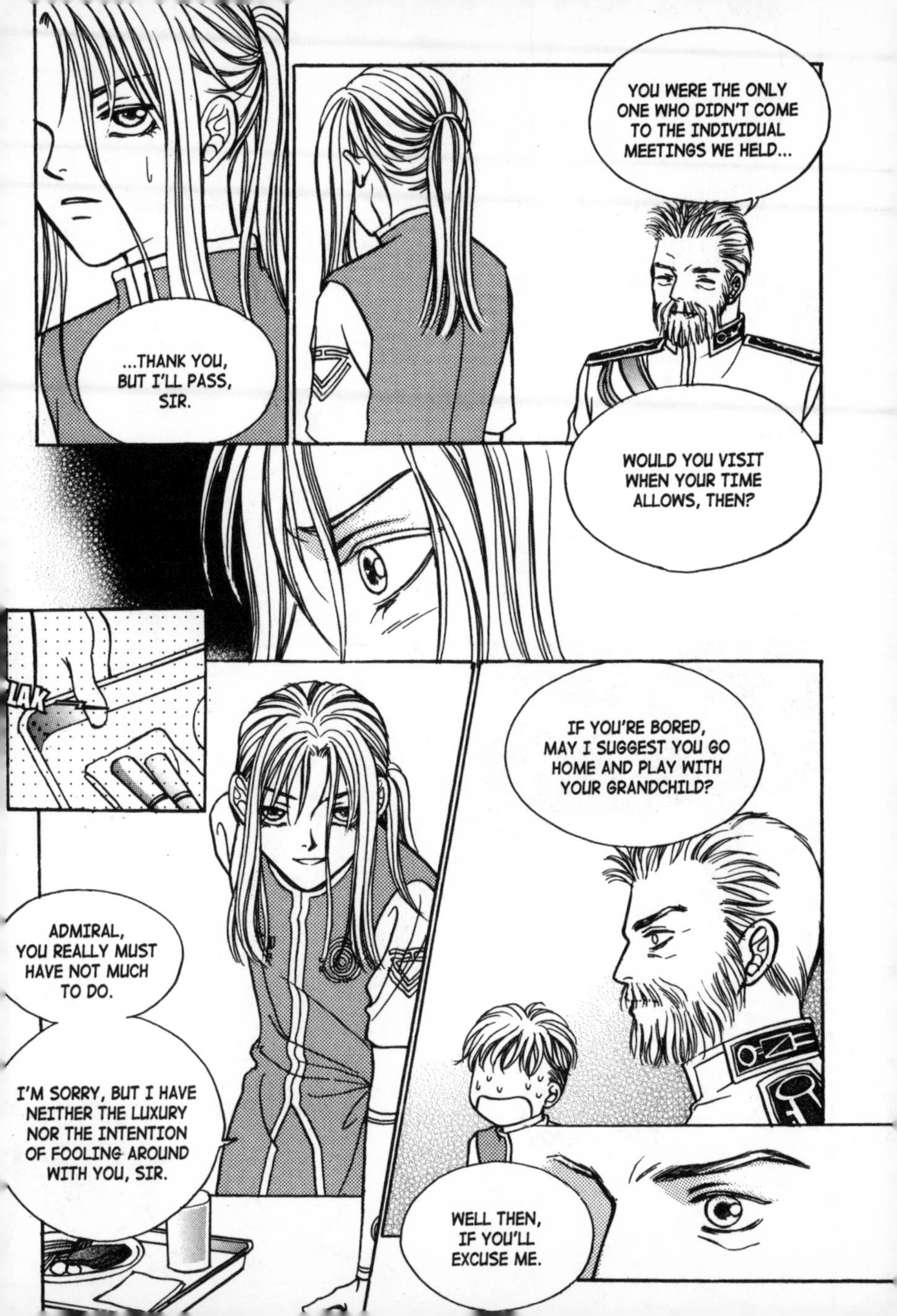
...THANK YOU, BUT I'LL PASS, SIR.
YOU WERE THE ONLY ONE WHO DIDN'T COME TO THE INDIVIDUAL MEETINGS WE HELD...
WOULD YOU VISIT WHEN YOUR TIME ALLOWS, THEN?
LAK
ADMIRAL, YOU REALLY MUST HAVE NOT MUCH TO DO.
I'M SORRY, BUT I HAVE NEITHER THE LUXURY NOR THE INTENTION OF FOOLING AROUND WITH YOU, SIR.
IF YOU'RE BORED, MAY I SUGGEST YOU GO HOME AND PLAY WITH YOUR GRANDCHILD?
WELL THEN, IF YOU'LL EXCUSE ME.

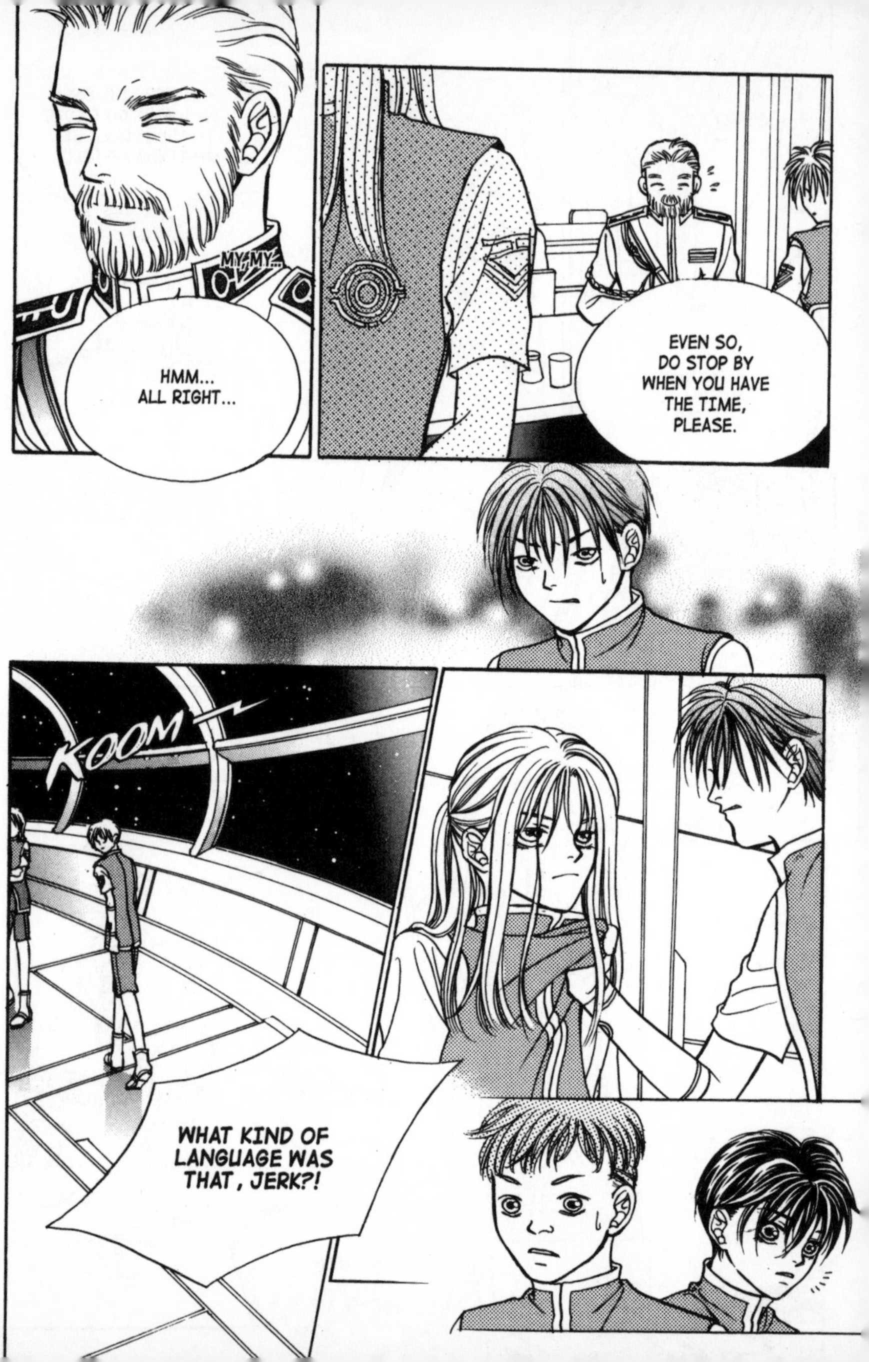
MY, MY...
HMM... ALL RIGHT...
EVEN SO, DO STOP BY WHEN YOU HAVE THE TIME, PLEASE.
KOOM
WHAT KIND OF LANGUAGE WAS THAT, JERK?!

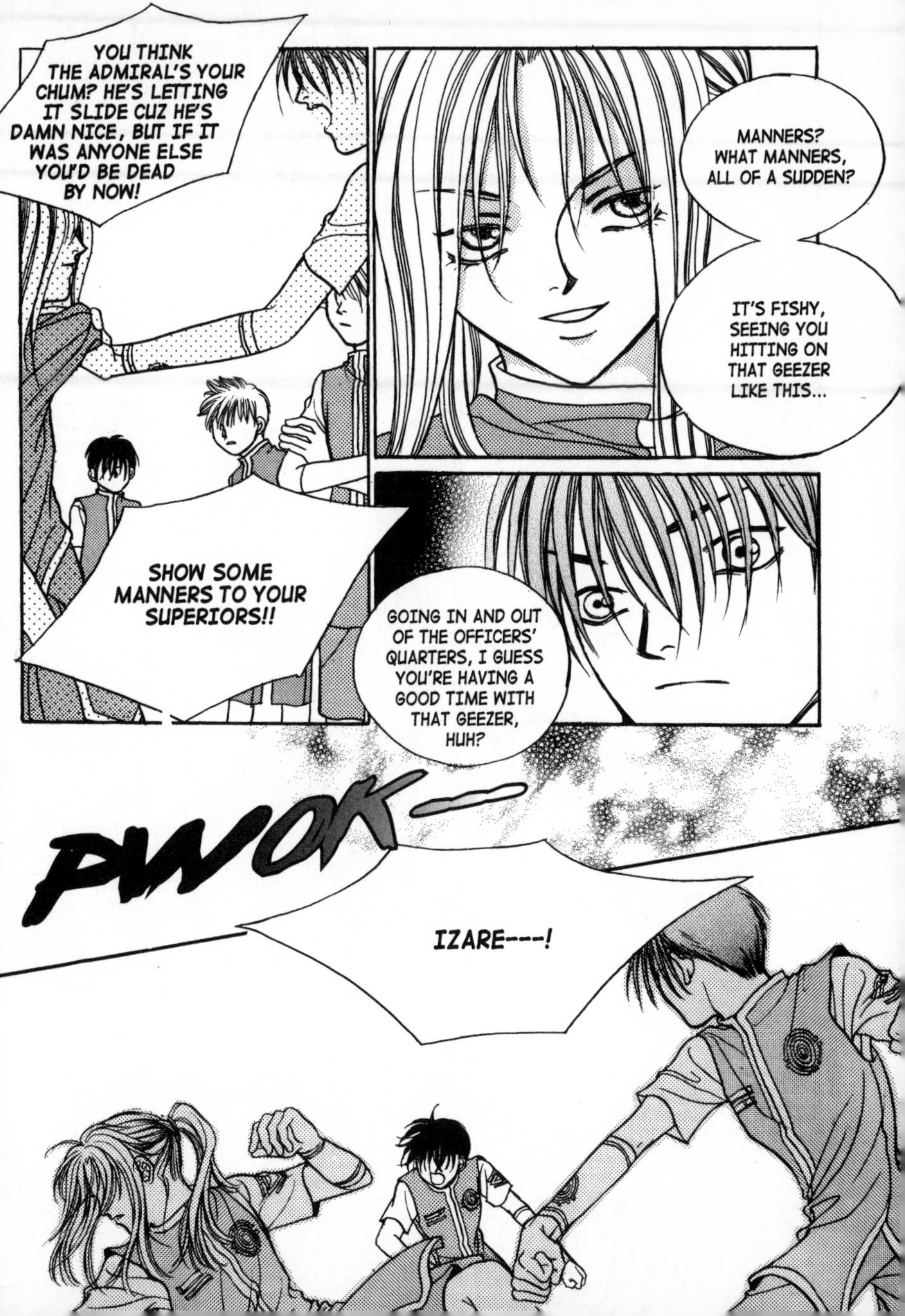
YOU THINK THE ADMIRAL'S YOUR CHUM? HE'S LETTING IT SLIDE CUZ HE'S DAMN NICE, BUT IF IT WAS ANYONE ELSE YOU'D BE DEAD BY NOW!
SHOW SOME MANNERS TO YOUR SUPERIORS!!
MANNERS? WHAT MANNERS, ALL OF A SUDDEN?
IT'S FISHY, SEEING YOU HITTING ON THAT GEEZER LIKE THIS...
GOING IN AND OUT OF THE OFFICERS' QUARTERS, I GUESS YOU'RE HAVING A GOOD TIME WITH THAT GEEZER, HUH?
PWOK---
IZARE---!

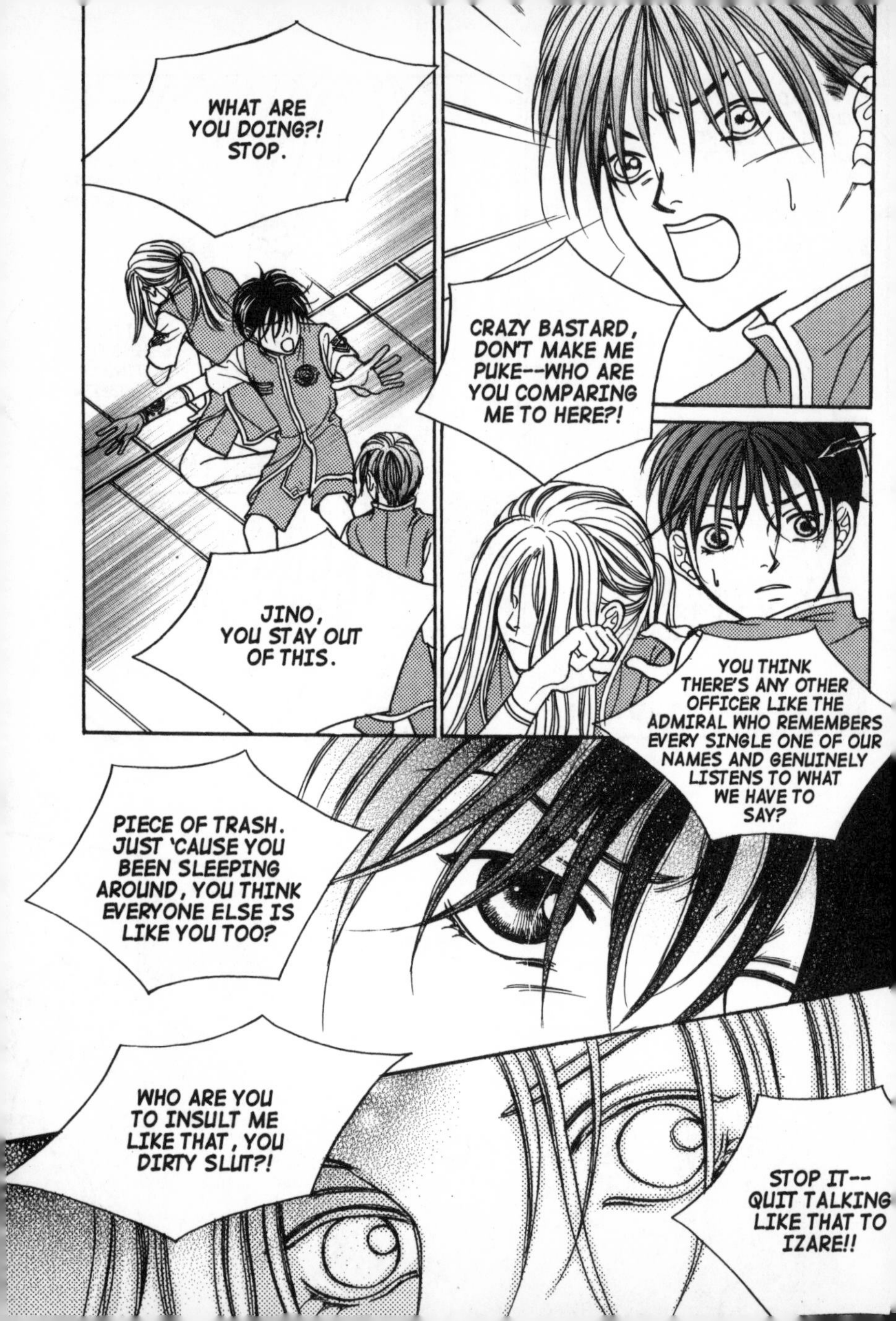
WHAT ARE YOU DOING?! STOP.
JINO, YOU STAY OUT OF THIS.
CRAZY BASTARD, DON'T MAKE ME PUKE--WHO ARE YOU COMPARING ME TO HERE?!
YOU THINK THERE'S ANY OTHER OFFICER LIKE THE ADMIRAL WHO REMEMBERS EVERY SINGLE ONE OF OUR NAMES AND GENUINELY LISTENS TO WHAT WE HAVE TO SAY?
PIECE OF TRASH. JUST 'CAUSE YOU BEEN SLEEPING AROUND, YOU THINK EVERYONE ELSE IS LIKE YOU TOO?
WHO ARE YOU TO INSULT ME LIKE THAT, YOU DIRTY SLUT?!
STOP IT--QUIT TALKING LIKE THAT TO IZARE!!

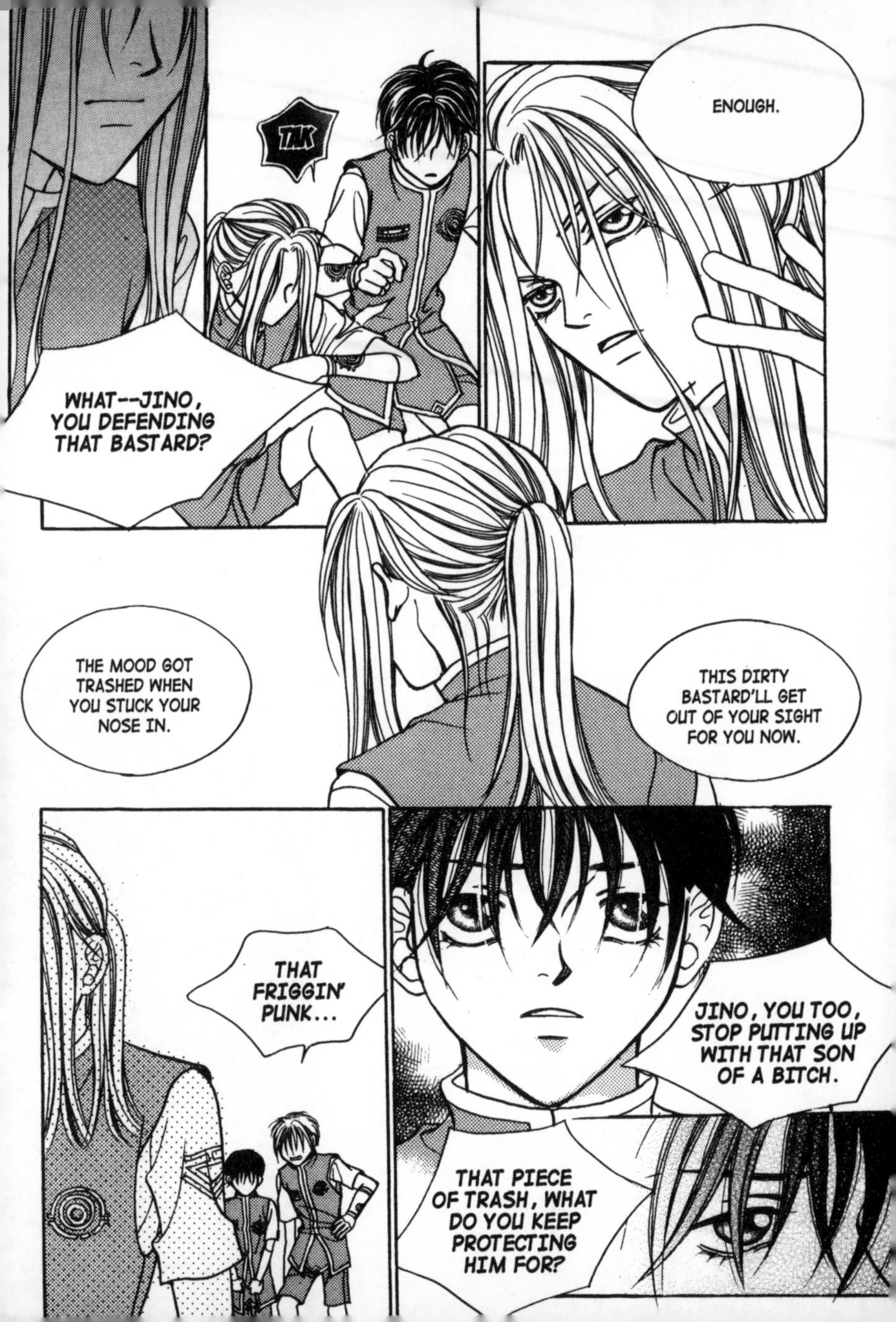
TAK
WHAT--JINO, YOU DEFENDING THAT BASTARD?
ENOUGH.
THE MOOD GOT TRASHED WHEN YOU STUCK YOUR NOSE IN.
THIS DIRTY BASTARD'LL GET OUT OF YOUR SIGHT FOR YOU NOW.
THAT FRIGGIN' PUNK...
JINO, YOU TOO, STOP PUTTING UP WITH THAT SON OF A BITCH.
THAT PIECE OF TRASH, WHAT DO YOU KEEP PROTECTING HIM FOR?

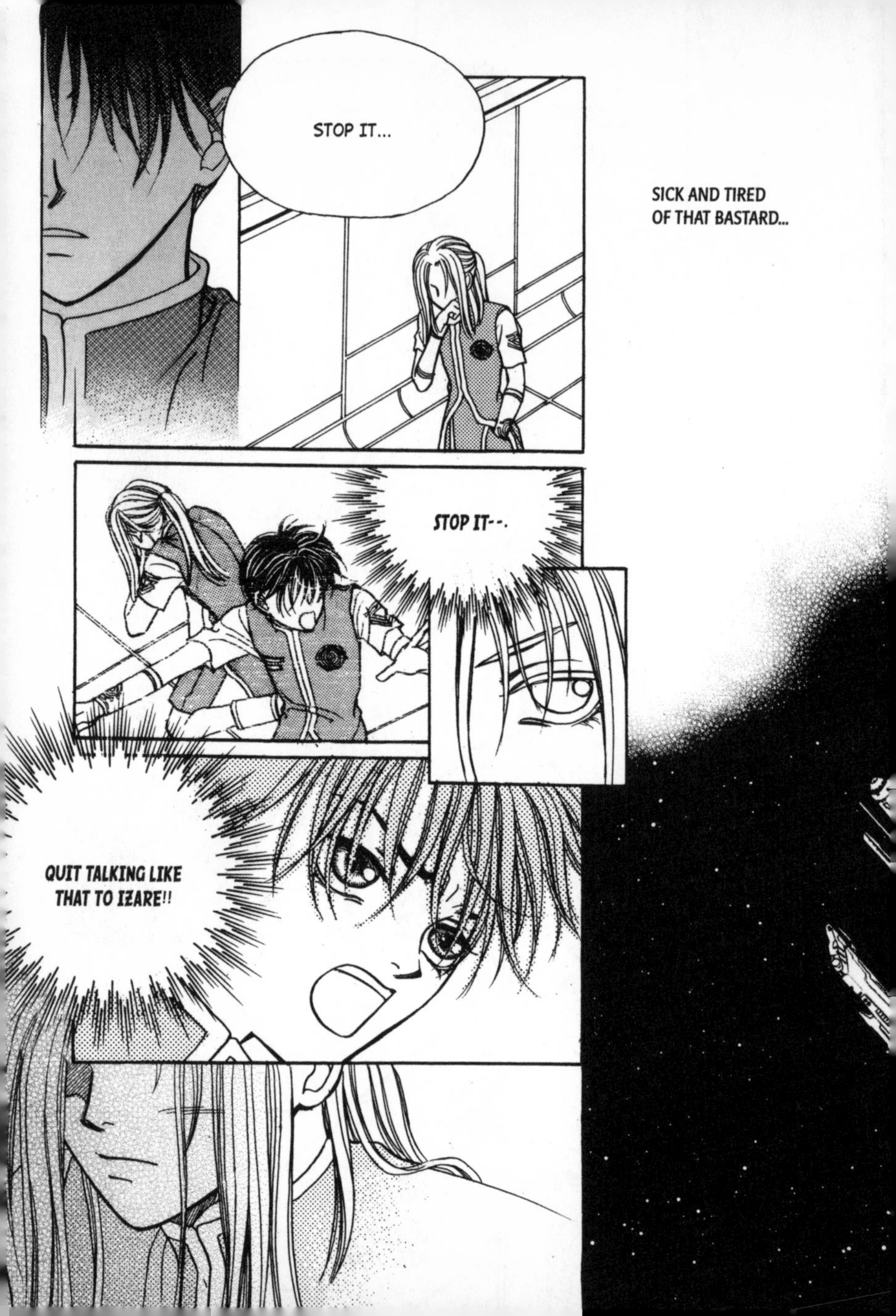
STOP IT...
SICK AND TIRED OF THAT BASTARD...
STOP IT--.
QUIT TALKING LIKE THAT TO IZARE!!

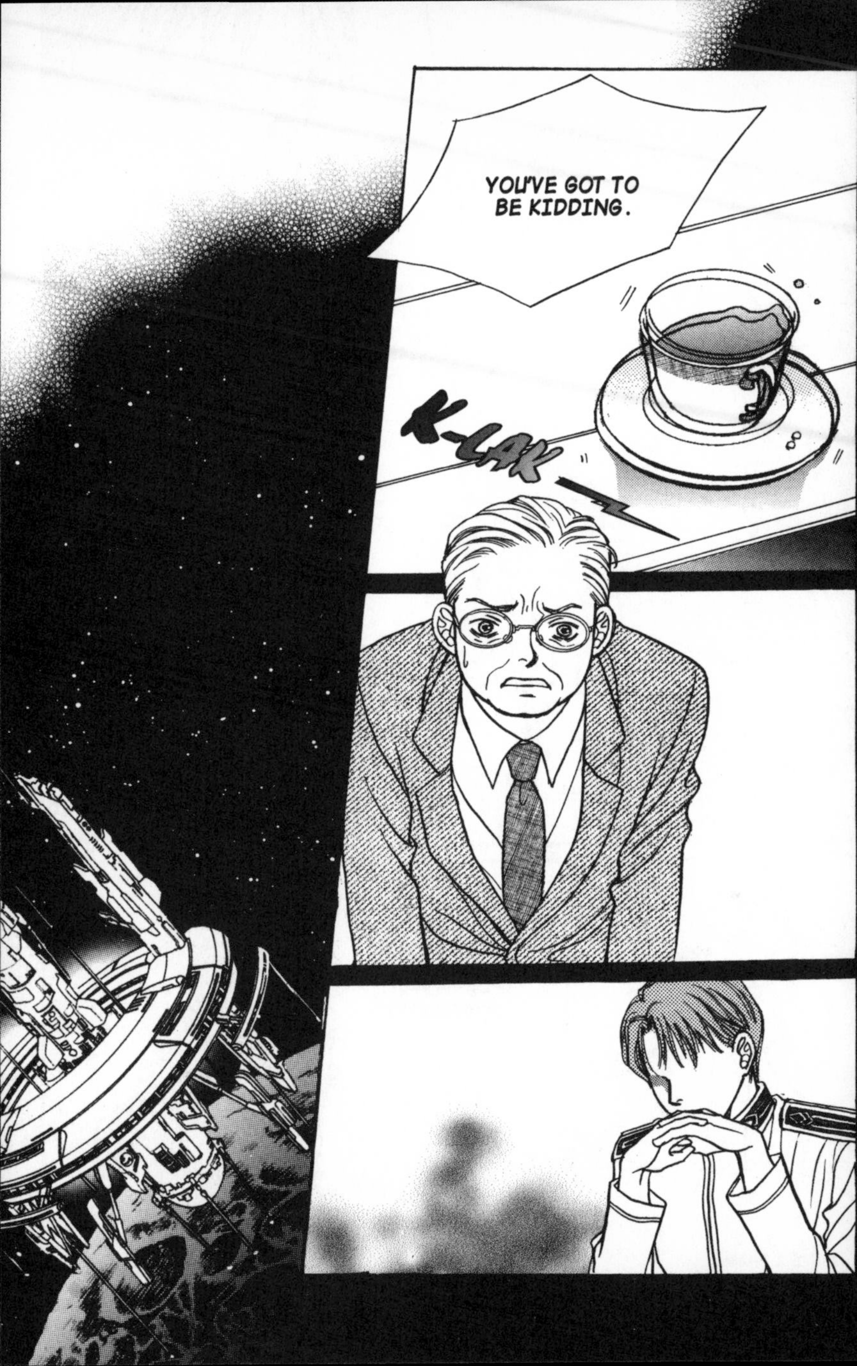
YOU'VE GOT TO BE KIDDING.
K-LAK

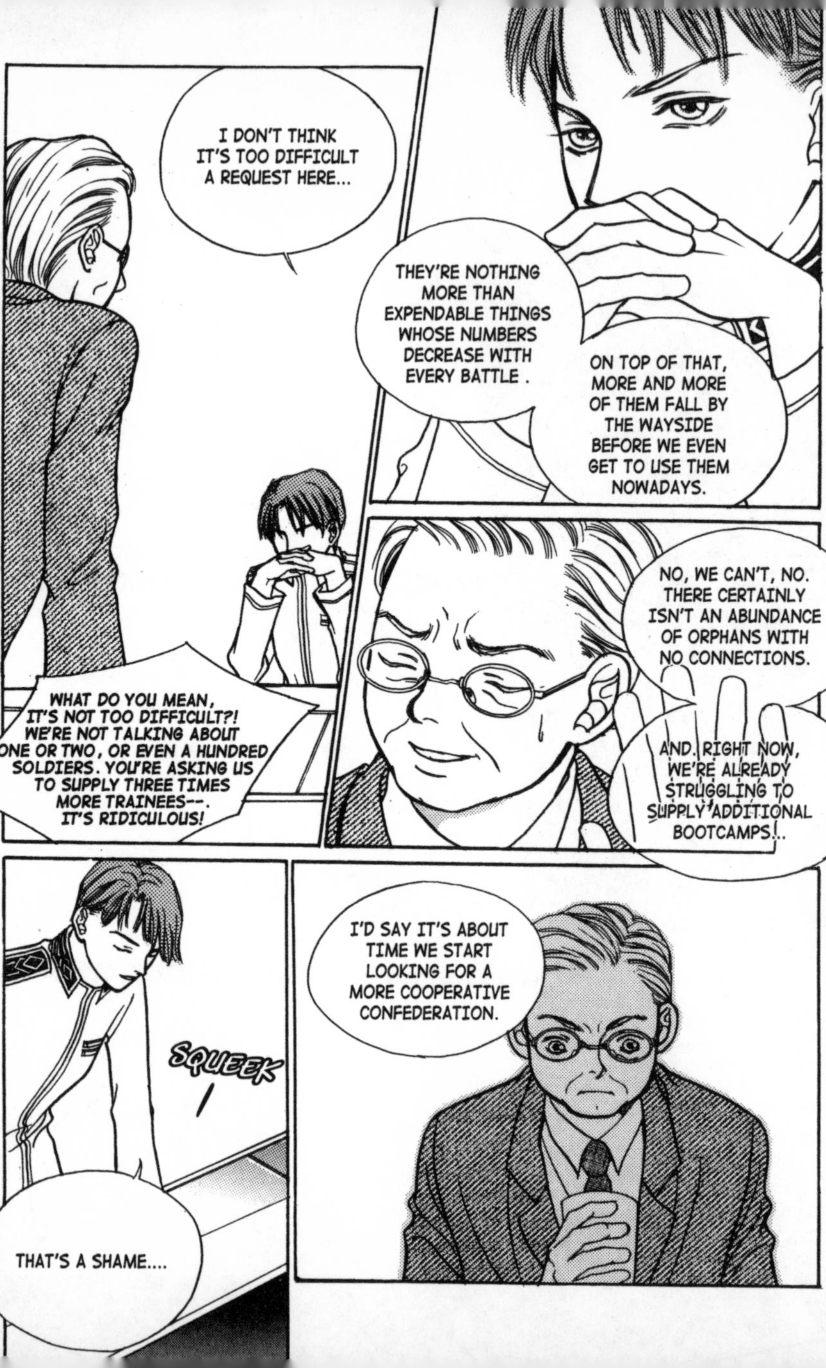
I DON'T THINK IT'S TOO DIFFICULT A REQUEST HERE...
WHAT DO YOU MEAN, IT'S NOT TOO DIFFICULT?! WE'RE NOT TALKING ABOUT ONE OR TWO, OR EVEN A HUNDRED SOLDIERS. YOU'RE ASKING US TO SUPPLY THREE TIMES MORE TRAINEES--. IT'S RIDICULOUS!
THEY'RE NOTHING MORE THAN EXPENDABLE THINGS WHOSE NUMBERS DECREASE WITH EVERY BATTLE .
ON TOP OF THAT, MORE AND MORE OF THEM FALL BY THE WAYSIDE BEFORE WE EVEN GET TO USE THEM NOWADAYS.
NO, WE CAN'T, NO. THERE CERTAINLY ISN'T AN ABUNDANCE OF ORPHANS WITH NO CONNECTIONS.
AND, RIGHT NOW, WE'RE ALREADY STRUGGLING TO SUPPLY ADDITIONAL BOOTCAMPS...
THAT'S A SHAME....
SQUEEK
I'D SAY IT'S ABOUT TIME WE START LOOKING FOR A MORE COOPERATIVE CONFEDERATION.

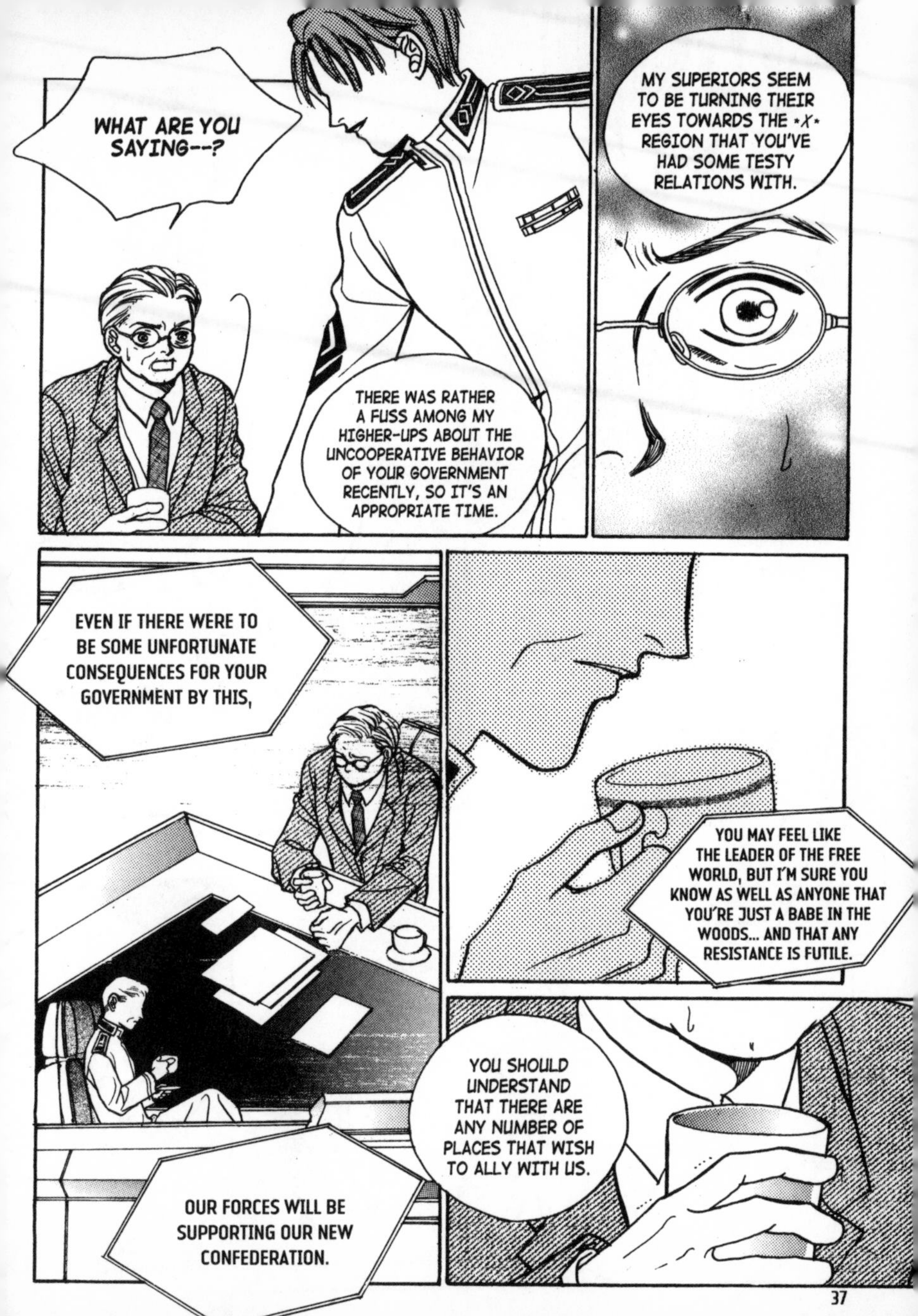
WHAT ARE YOU SAYING--?
MY SUPERIORS SEEM TO BE TURNING THEIR EYES TOWARDS THE *X* REGION THAT YOU'VE HAD SOME TESTY RELATIONS WITH.
THERE WAS RATHER A FUSS AMONG MY HIGHER-UPS ABOUT THE UNCOOPERATIVE BEHAVIOR OF YOUR GOVERNMENT RECENTLY, SO IT'S AN APPROPRIATE TIME.
EVEN IF THERE WERE TO BE SOME UNFORTUNATE CONSEQUENCES FOR YOUR GOVERNMENT BY THIS,
OUR FORCES WILL BE SUPPORTING OUR NEW CONFEDERATION.
YOU MAY FEEL LIKE THE LEADER OF THE FREE WORLD, BUT I'M SURE YOU KNOW AS WELL AS ANYONE THAT YOU'RE JUST A BABE IN THE WOODS... AND THAT ANY RESISTANCE IS FUTILE.
YOU SHOULD UNDERSTAND THAT THERE ARE ANY NUMBER OF PLACES THAT WISH TO ALLY WITH US.

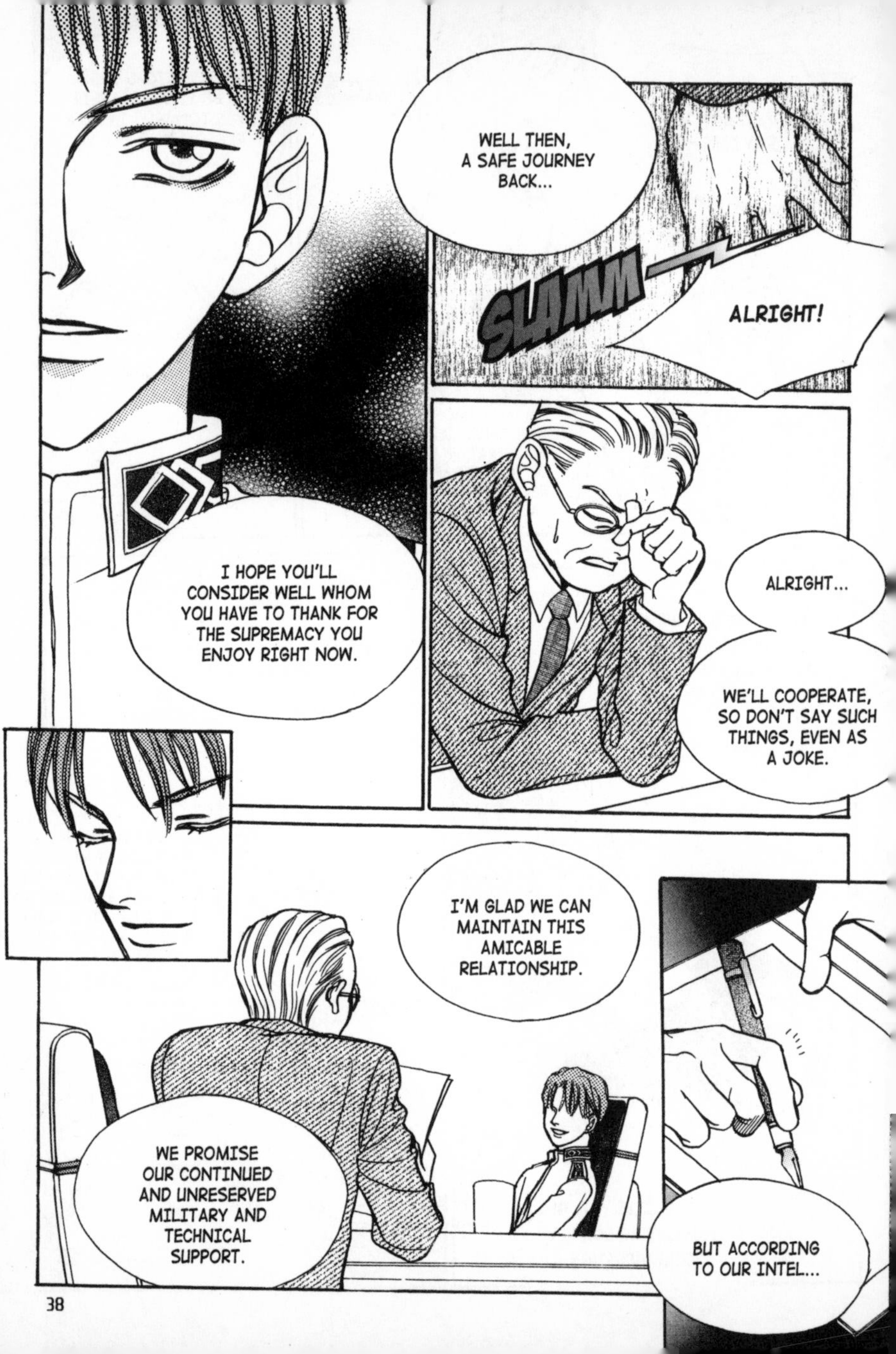
I HOPE YOU'LL CONSIDER WELL WHOM YOU HAVE TO THANK FOR THE SUPREMACY YOU ENJOY RIGHT NOW.
WELL THEN, A SAFE JOURNEY BACK...
SLAMM
ALRIGHT!
ALRIGHT...
WE'LL COOPERATE, SO DON'T SAY SUCH THINGS, EVEN AS A JOKE.
I'M GLAD WE CAN MAINTAIN THIS AMICABLE RELATIONSHIP.
WE PROMISE OUR CONTINUED AND UNRESERVED MILITARY AND TECHNICAL SUPPORT.
BUT ACCORDING TO OUR INTEL...

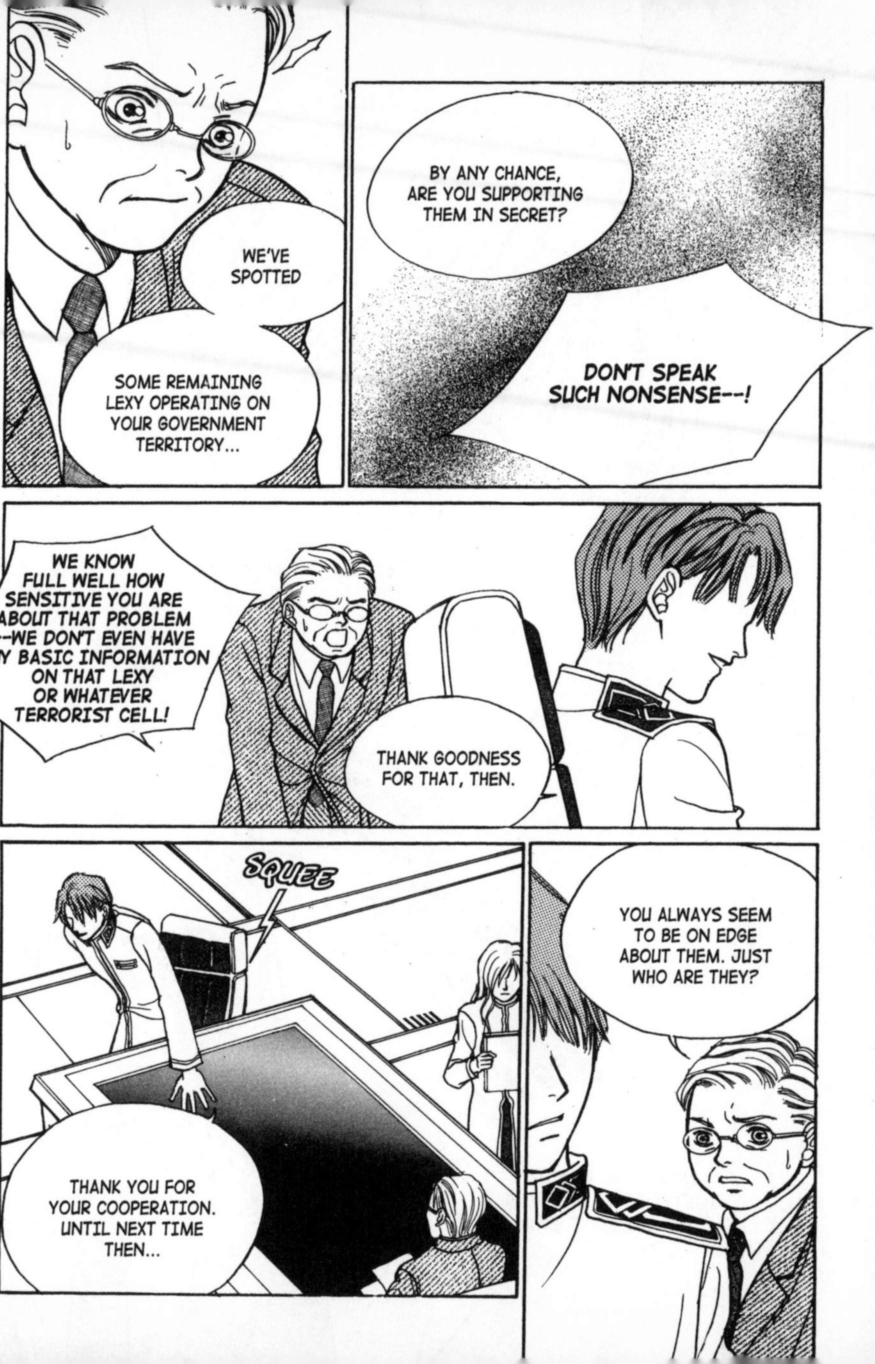
WE'VE SPOTTED
SOME REMAINING LEXY OPERATING ON YOUR GOVERNMENT TERRITORY...
BY ANY CHANCE, ARE YOU SUPPORTING THEM IN SECRET?
DON'T SPEAK SUCH NONSENSE--!
WE KNOW FULL WELL HOW SENSITIVE YOU ARE ABOUT THAT PROBLEM --WE DON'T EVEN HAVE ANY BASIC INFORMATION ON THAT LEXY OR WHATEVER TERRORIST CELL!
THANK GOODNESS FOR THAT, THEN.
SQUEE
THANK YOU FOR YOUR COOPERATION. UNTIL NEXT TIME THEN...
YOU ALWAYS SEEM TO BE ON EDGE ABOUT THEM. JUST WHO ARE THEY?

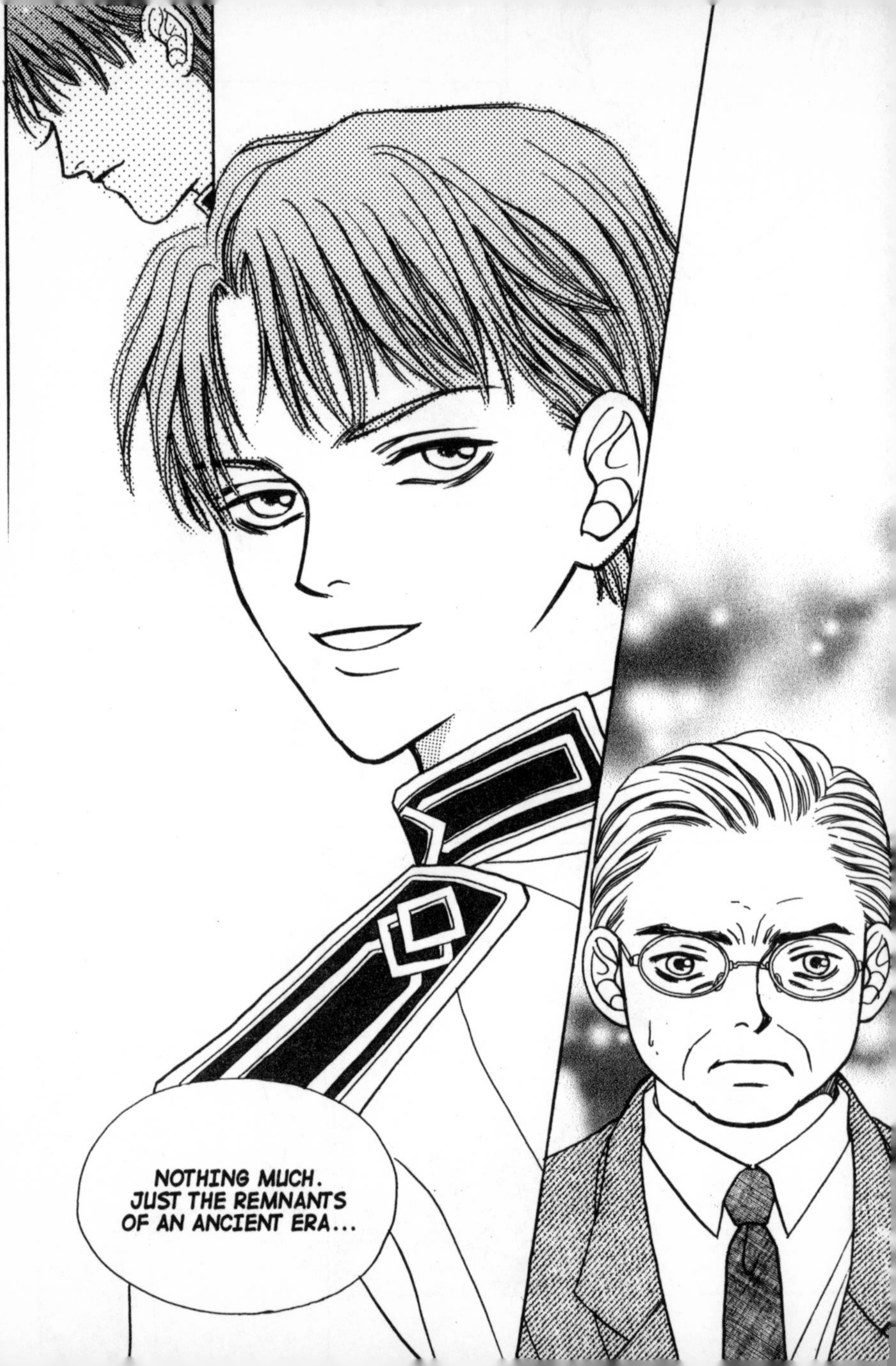
NOTHING MUCH. JUST THE REMNANTS OF AN ANCIENT ERA...

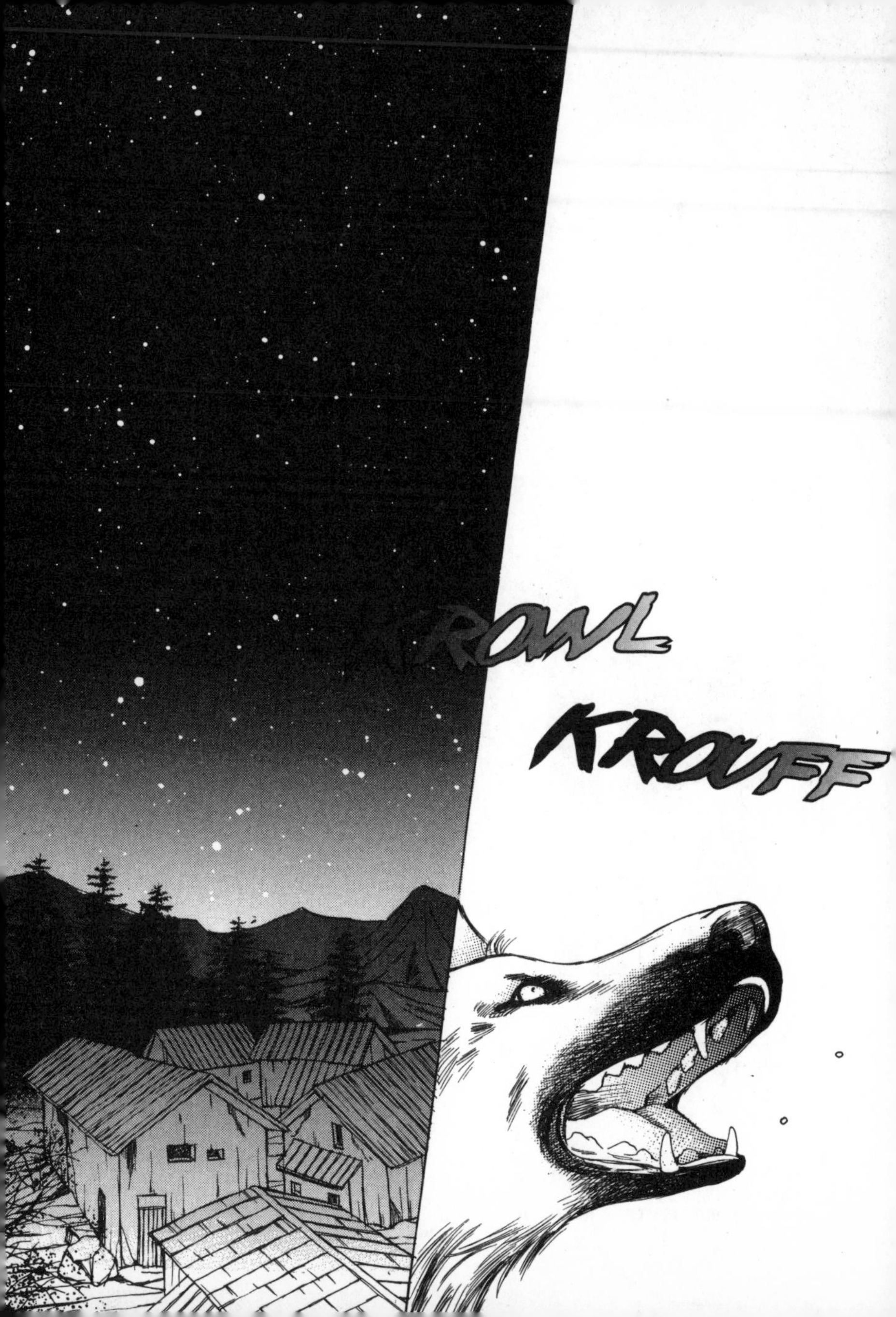
ROWL
KROUFF

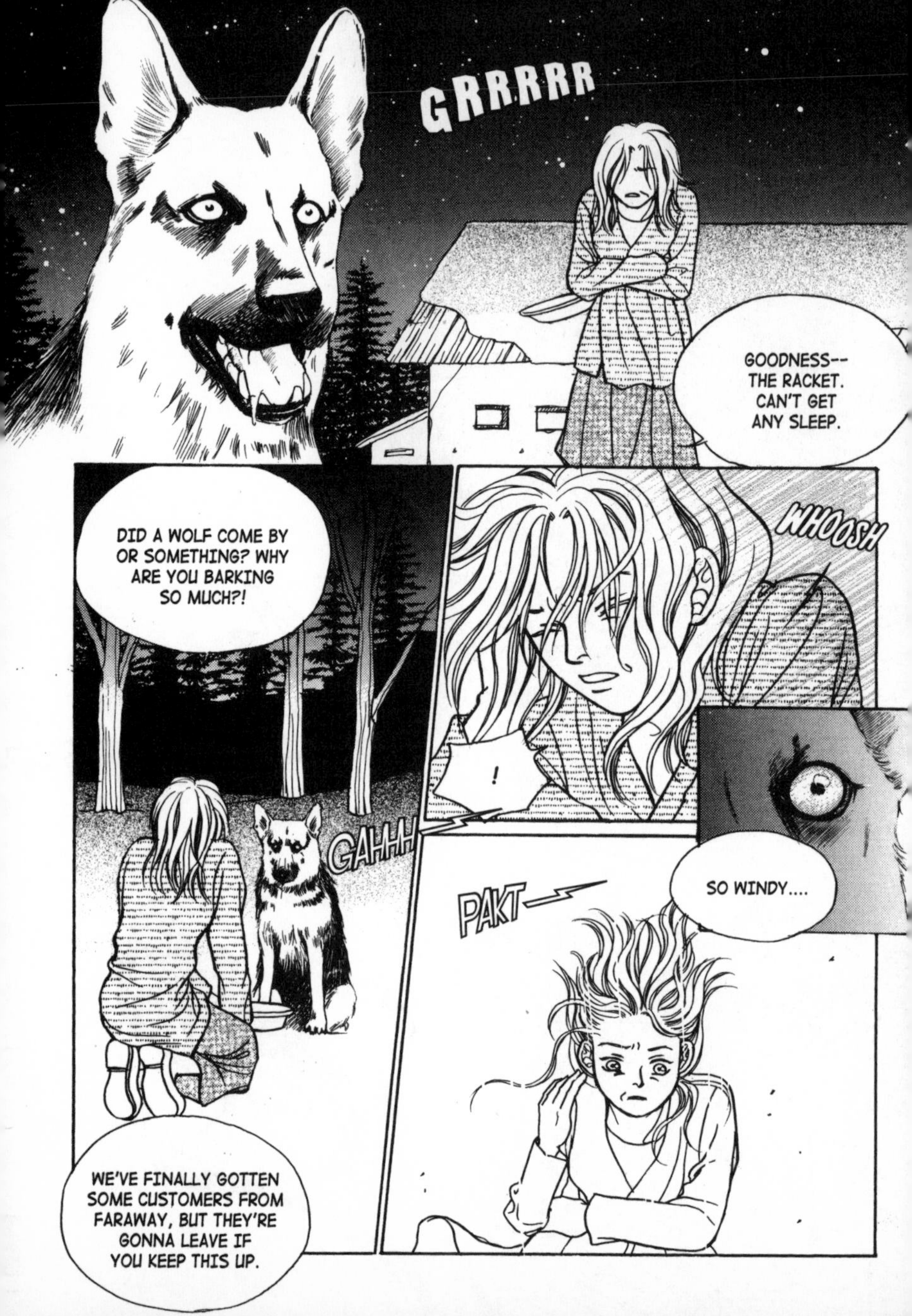
GRRRRR
GOODNESS-- THE RACKET. CAN'T GET ANY SLEEP.
DID A WOLF COME BY OR SOMETHING? WHY ARE YOU BARKING SO MUCH?!
GAHHH
WE'VE FINALLY GOTTEN SOME CUSTOMERS FROM FARAWAY, BUT THEY'RE GONNA LEAVE IF YOU KEEP THIS UP.
WHOOSH
!
PAKT
SO WINDY....

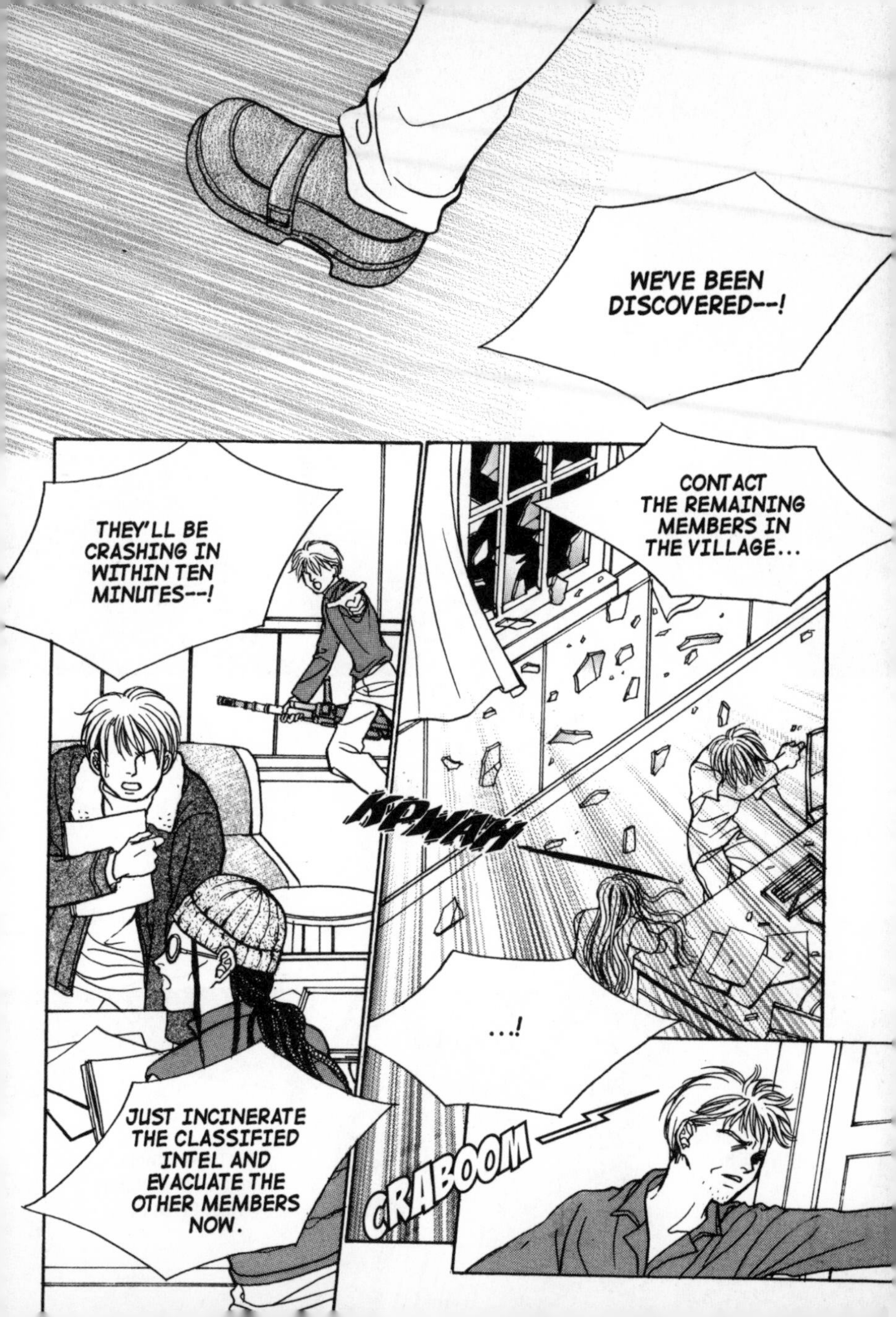
WE'VE BEEN DISCOVERED--!
THEY'LL BE CRASHING IN WITHIN TEN MINUTES--!
CONTACT THE REMAINING MEMBERS IN THE VILLAGE...
KPWAH
...!
JUST INCINERATE THE CLASSIFIED INTEL AND EVACUATE THE OTHER MEMBERS NOW.
CRABOOM

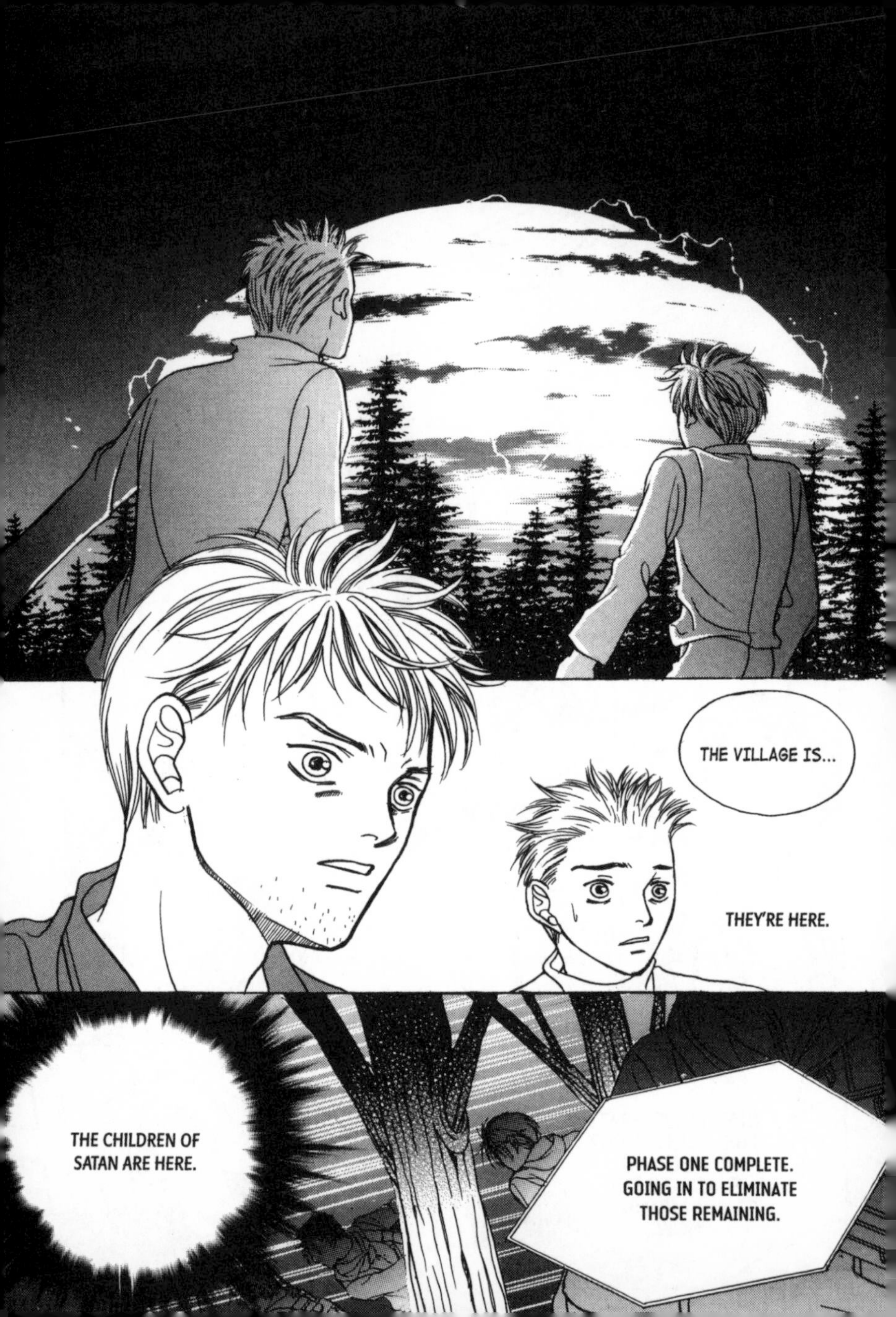
THE VILLAGE IS...
THEY'RE HERE.
PHASE ONE COMPLETE. GOING IN TO ELIMINATE THOSE REMAINING.
THE CHILDREN OF SATAN ARE HERE.

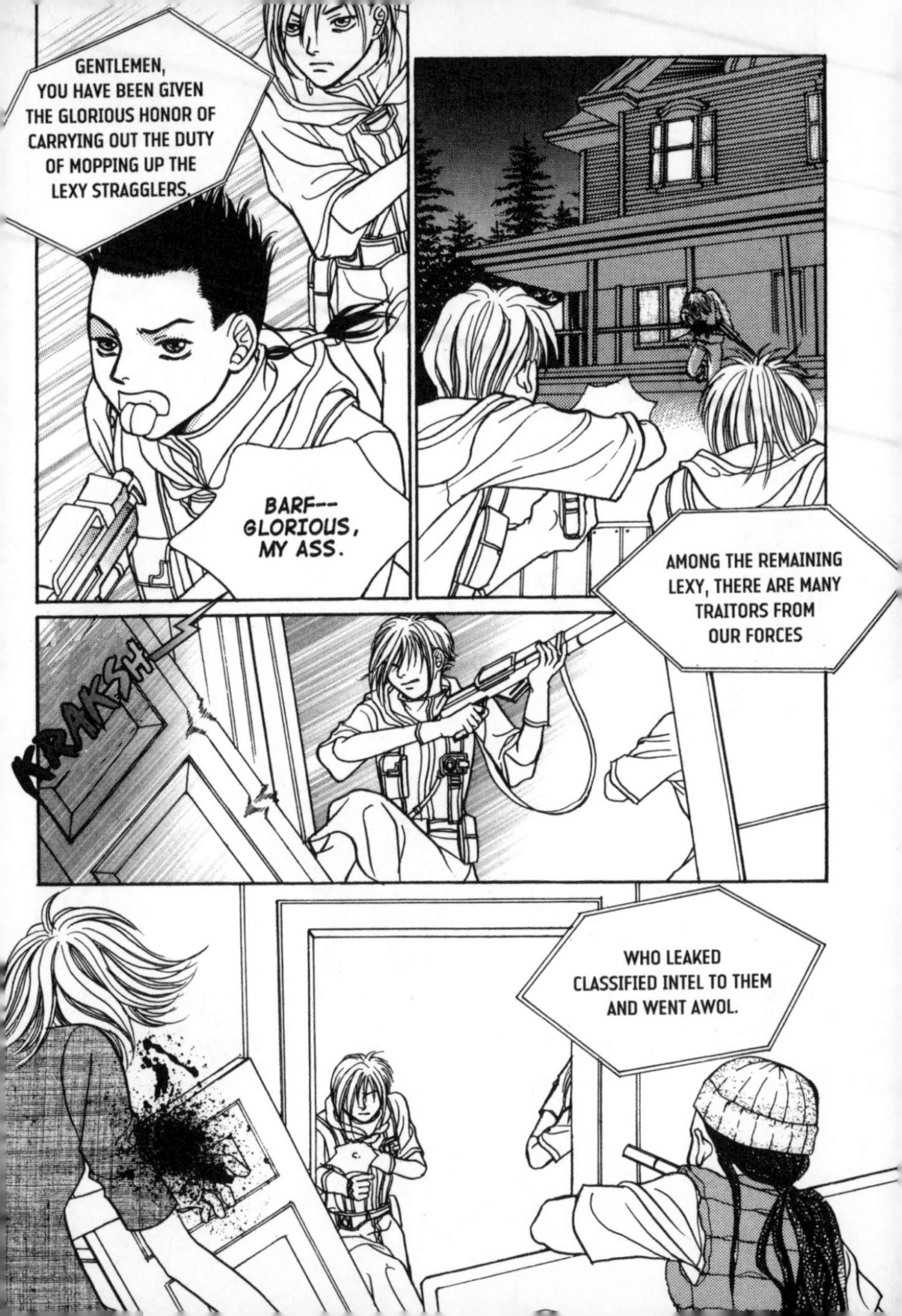
GENTLEMEN, YOU HAVE BEEN GIVEN THE GLORIOUS HONOR OF CARRYING OUT THE DUTY OF MOPPING UP THE LEXY STRAGGLERS,
BARF-- GLORIOUS, MY ASS.
AMONG THE REMAINING LEXY, THERE ARE MANY TRAITORS FROM OUR FORCES
KRAKSH
WHO LEAKED CLASSIFIED INTEL TO THEM AND WENT AWOL.

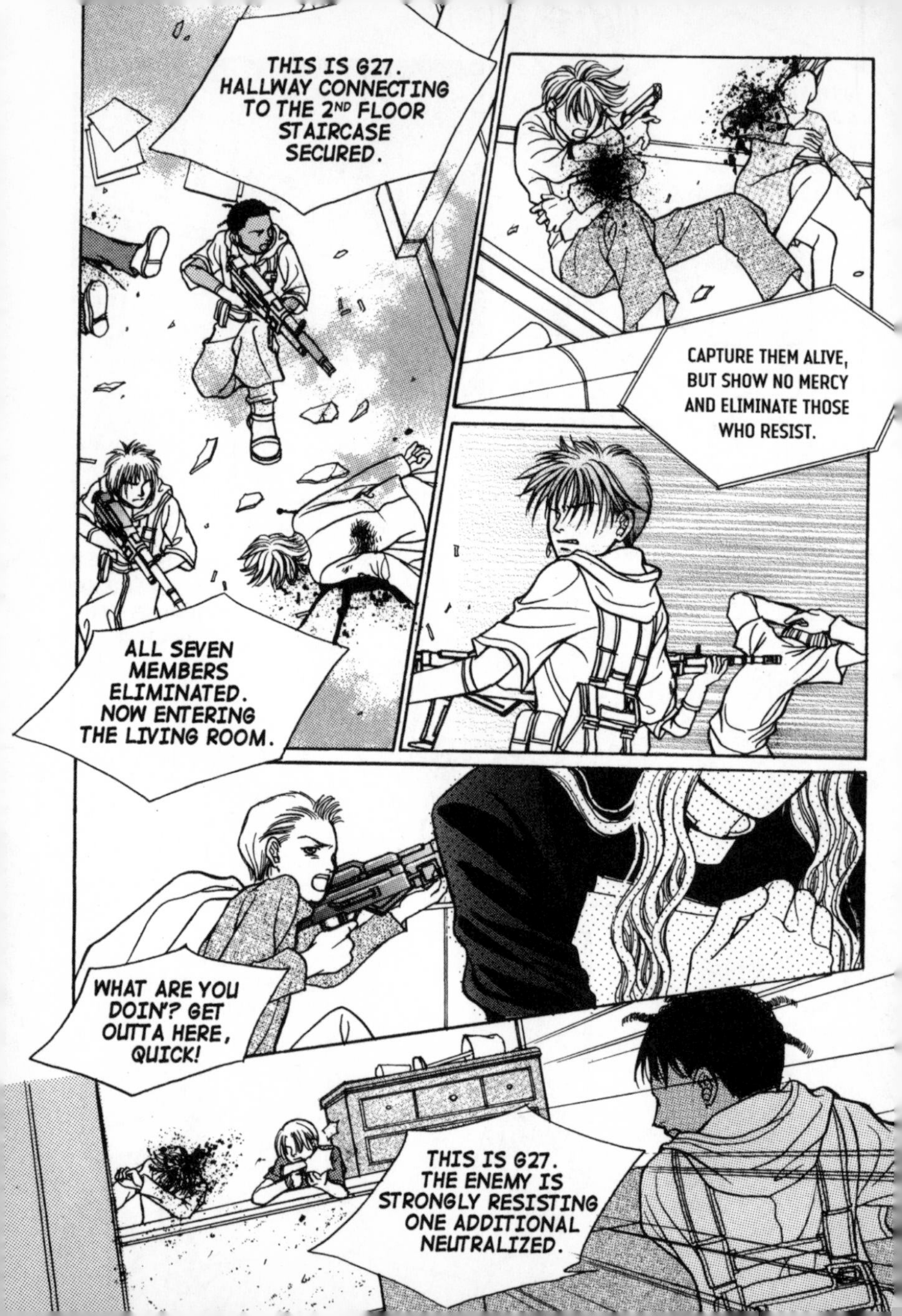

THIS IS G27. HALLWAY CONNECTING TO THE 2ND FLOOR STAIRCASE SECURED.
ALL SEVEN MEMBERS ELIMINATED. NOW ENTERING THE LIVING ROOM.
CAPTURE THEM ALIVE, BUT SHOW NO MERCY AND ELIMINATE THOSE WHO RESIST.
WHAT ARE YOU DOIN'? GET OUTTA HERE, QUICK!
THIS IS G27. THE ENEMY IS STRONGLY RESISTING ONE ADDITIONAL NEUTRALIZED.

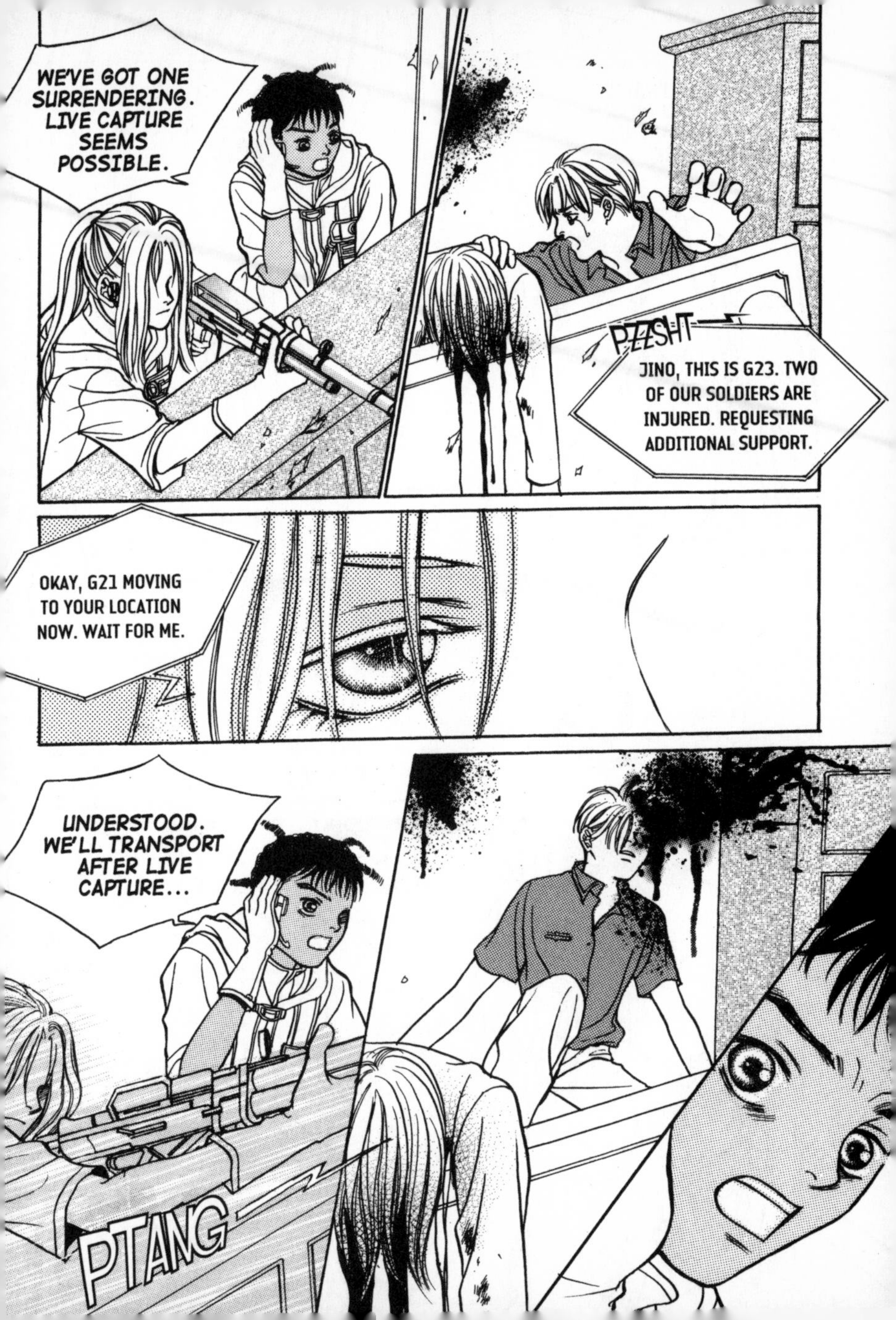
WE'VE GOT ONE SURRENDERING. LIVE CAPTURE SEEMS POSSIBLE.
PZZSHT
JINO, THIS IS G23. TWO OF OUR SOLDIERS ARE INJURED. REQUESTING ADDITIONAL SUPPORT.
OKAY, G21 MOVING TO YOUR LOCATION NOW. WAIT FOR ME.
UNDERSTOOD. WE'LL TRANSPORT AFTER LIVE CAPTURE...
PTANG

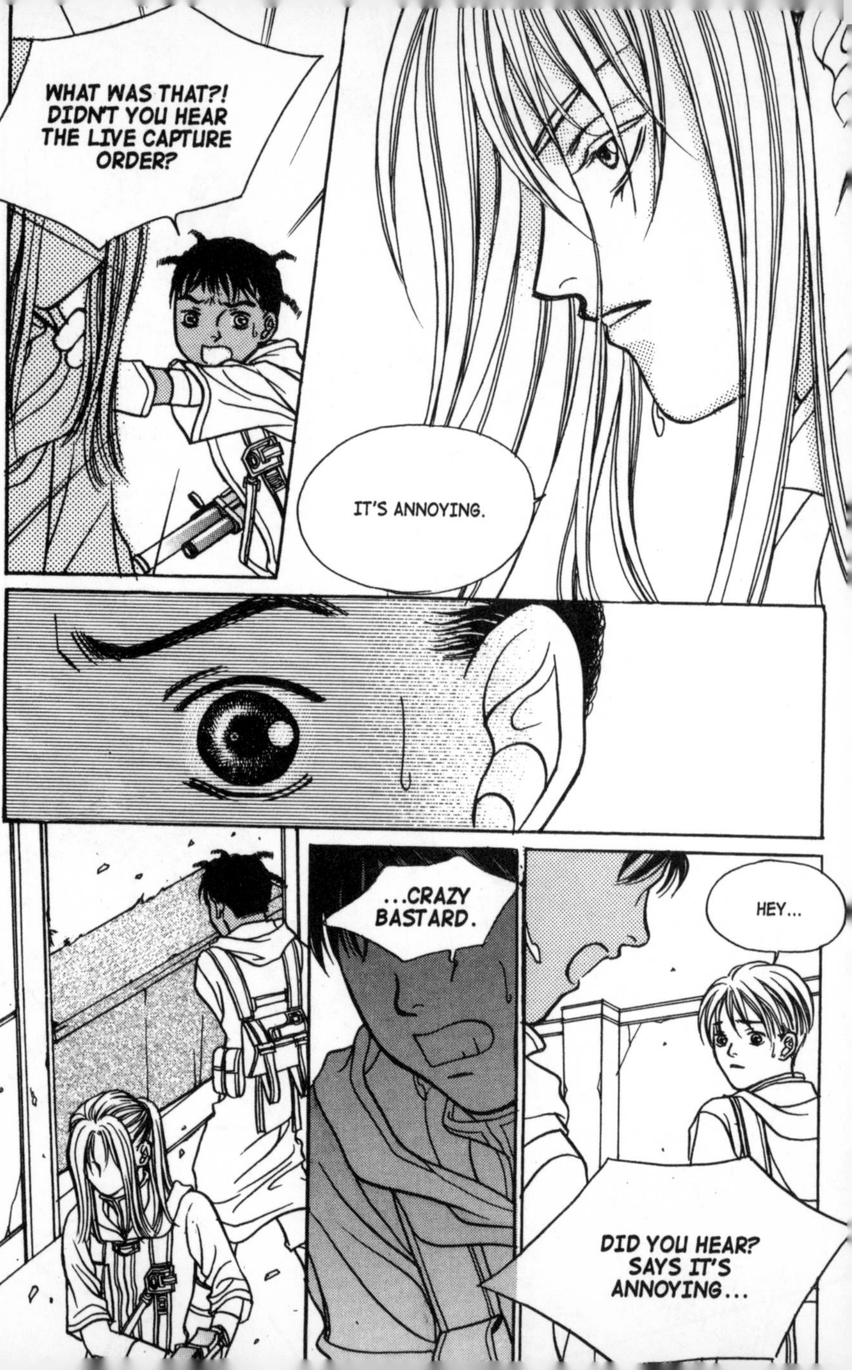
WHAT WAS THAT?! DIDN'T YOU HEAR THE LIVE CAPTURE ORDER?
IT'S ANNOYING.
...CRAZY BASTARD.
HEY...
DID YOU HEAR? SAYS IT'S ANNOYING...

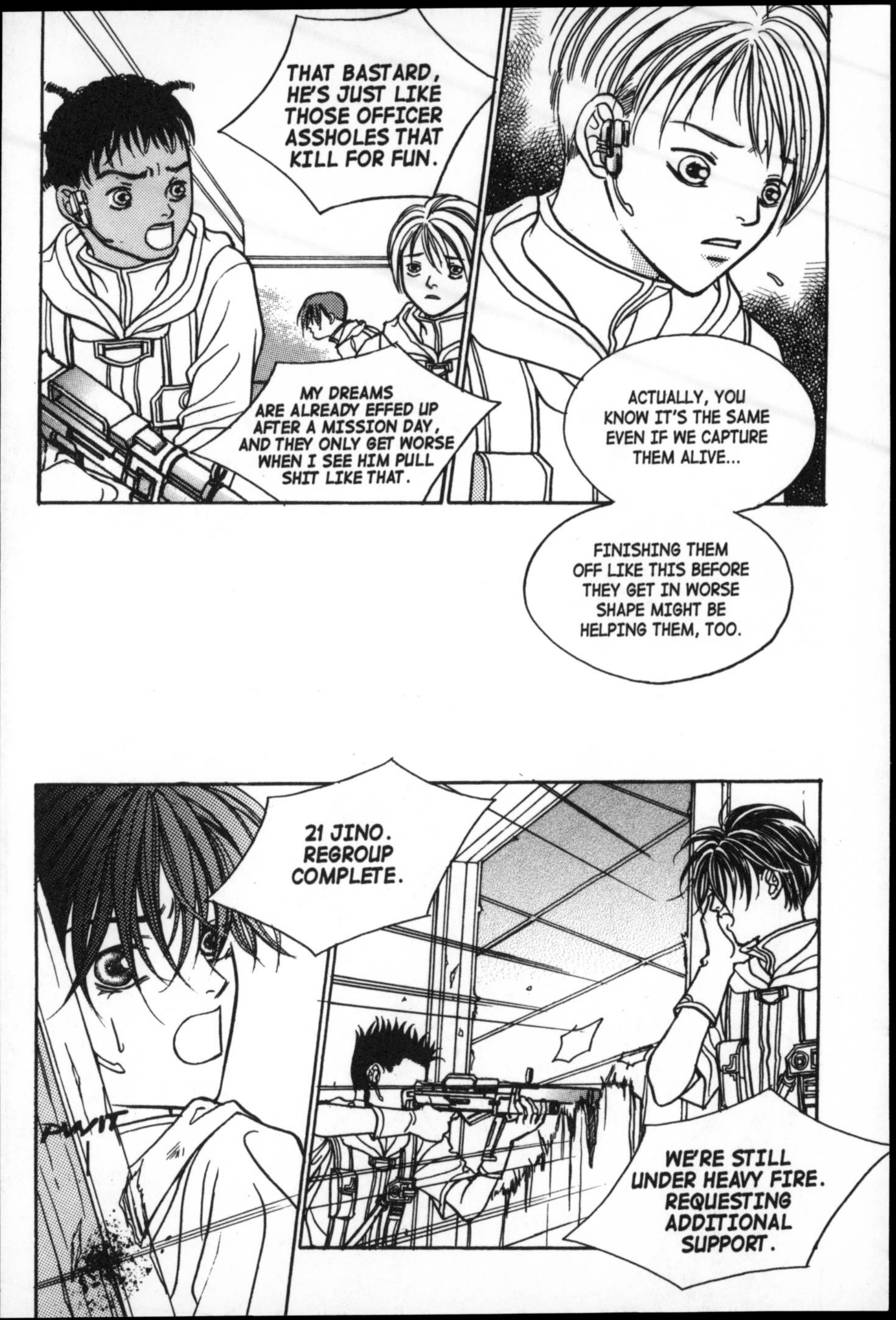
THAT BASTARD, HE'S JUST LIKE THOSE OFFICER ASSHOLES THAT KILL FOR FUN.
MY DREAMS ARE ALREADY EFFED UP AFTER A MISSION DAY, AND THEY ONLY GET WORSE WHEN I SEE HIM PULL SHIT LIKE THAT.
ACTUALLY, YOU KNOW IT'S THE SAME EVEN IF WE CAPTURE THEM ALIVE...
FINISHING THEM OFF LIKE THIS BEFORE THEY GET IN WORSE SHAPE MIGHT BE HELPING THEM, TOO.
21 JINO. REGROUP COMPLETE.
PWIT
WE'RE STILL UNDER HEAVY FIRE. REQUESTING ADDITIONAL SUPPORT.

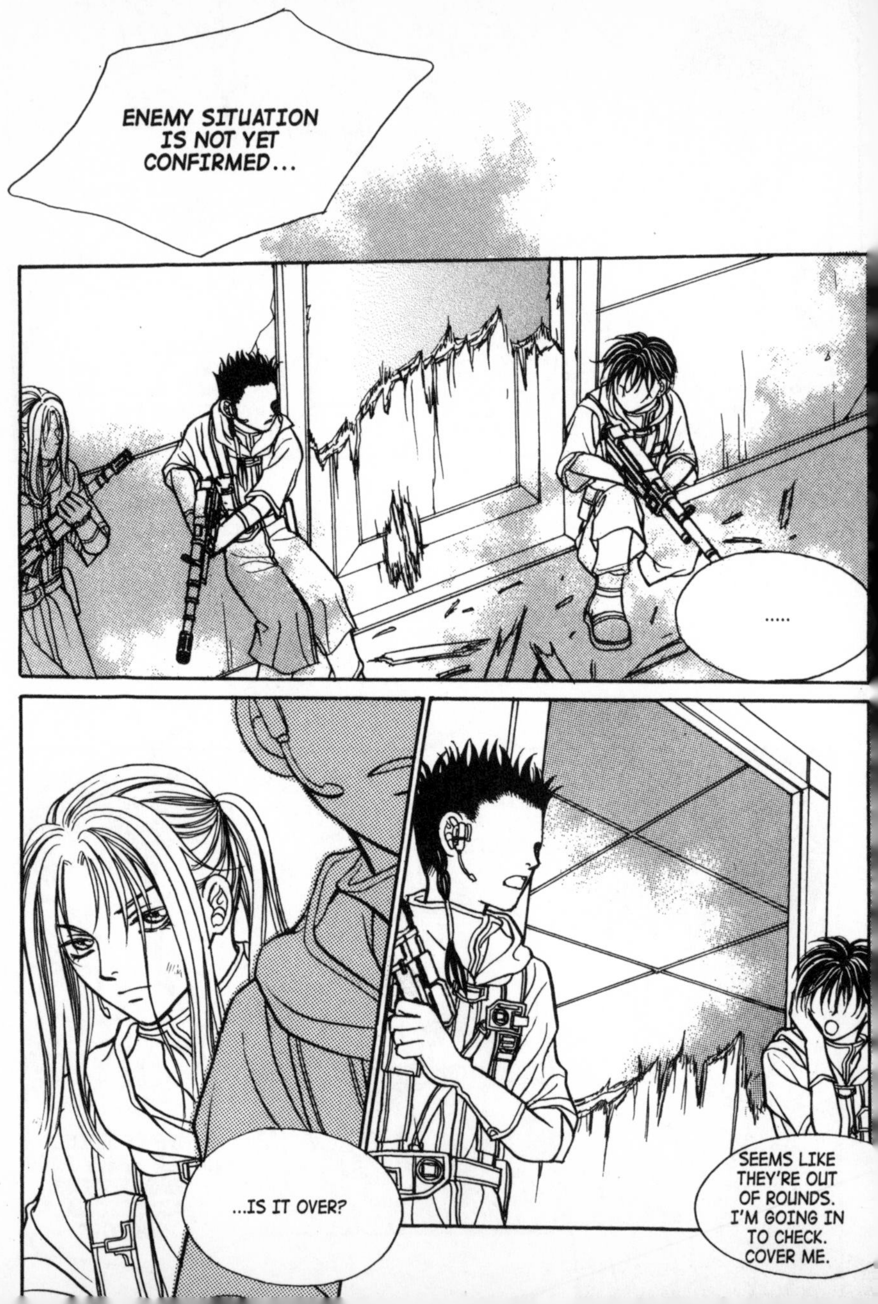
ENEMY SITUATION IS NOT YET CONFIRMED...
.....
...IS IT OVER?
SEEMS LIKE THEY'RE OUT OF ROUNDS. I'M GOING IN TO CHECK. COVER ME.

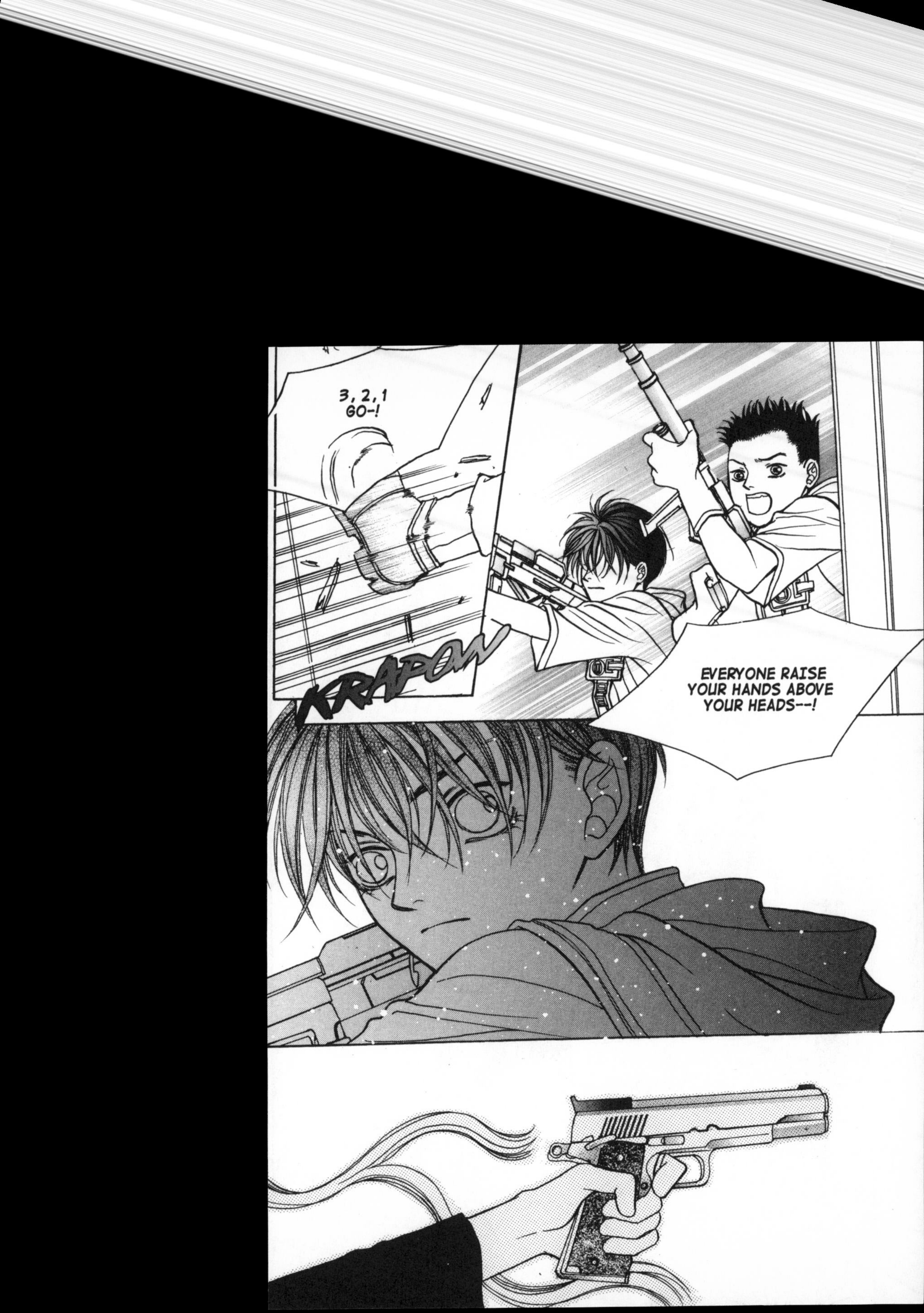
3, 2, 1 GO-!
KRAPOW
EVERYONE RAISE YOUR HANDS ABOVE YOUR HEADS--!

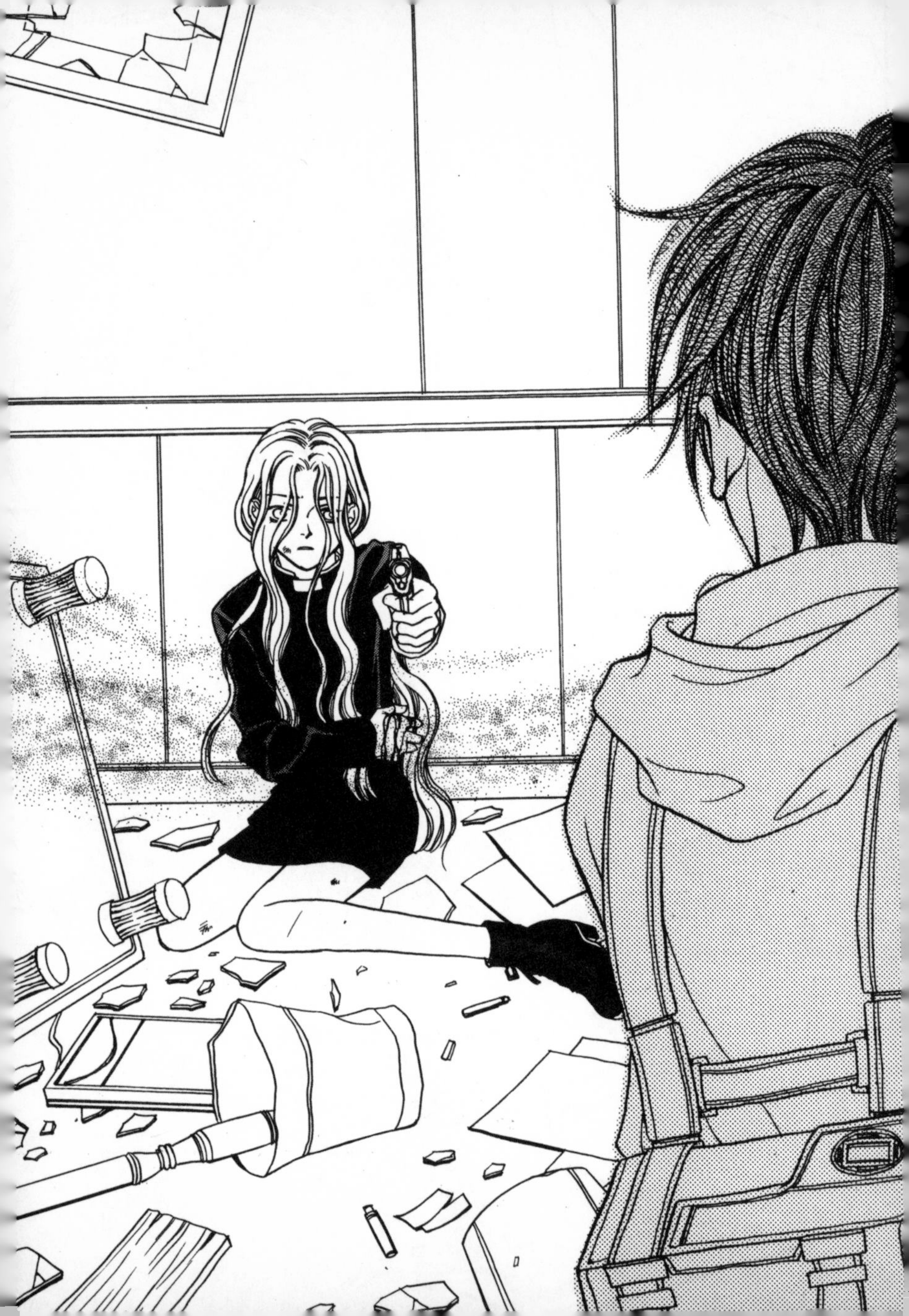

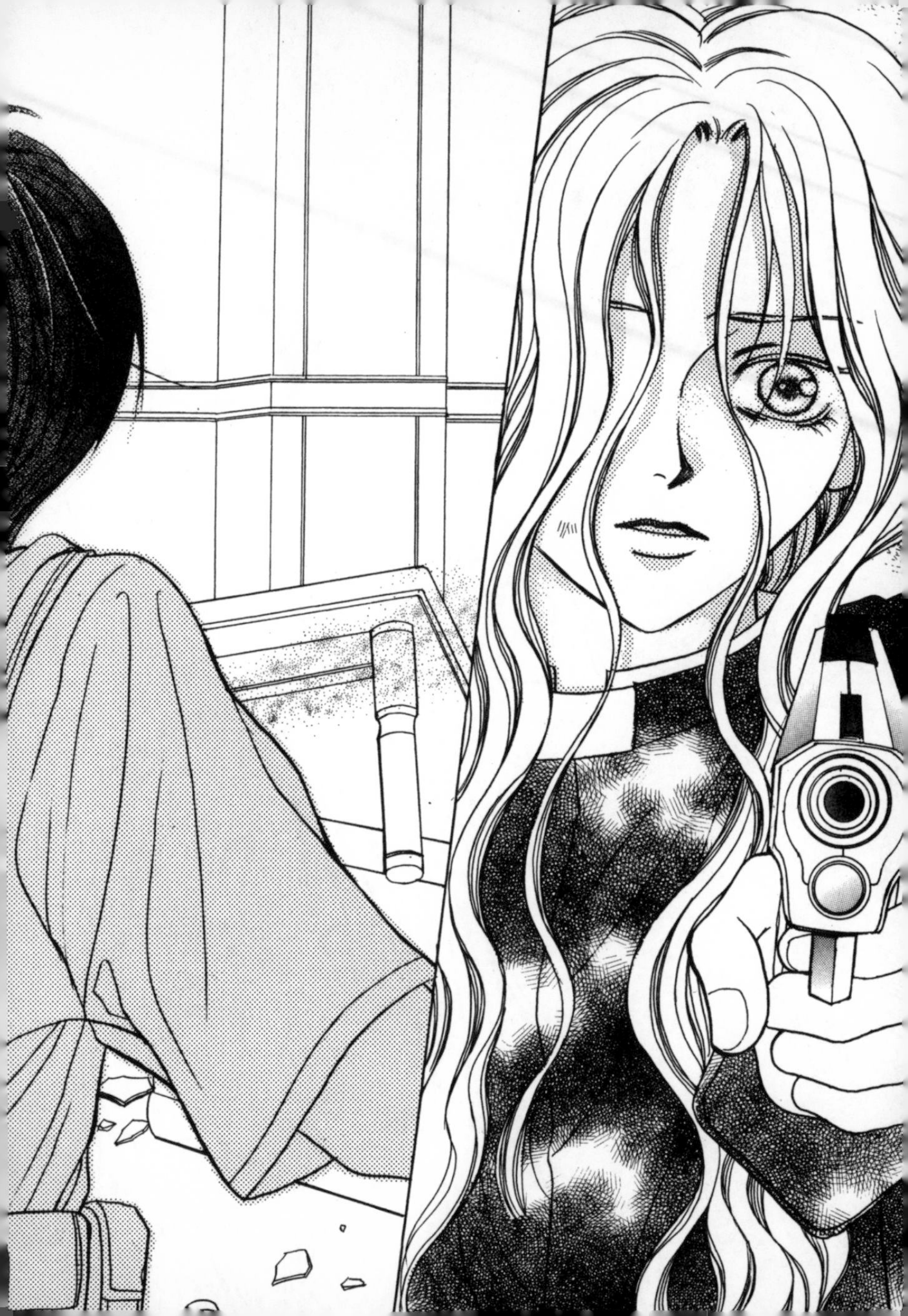

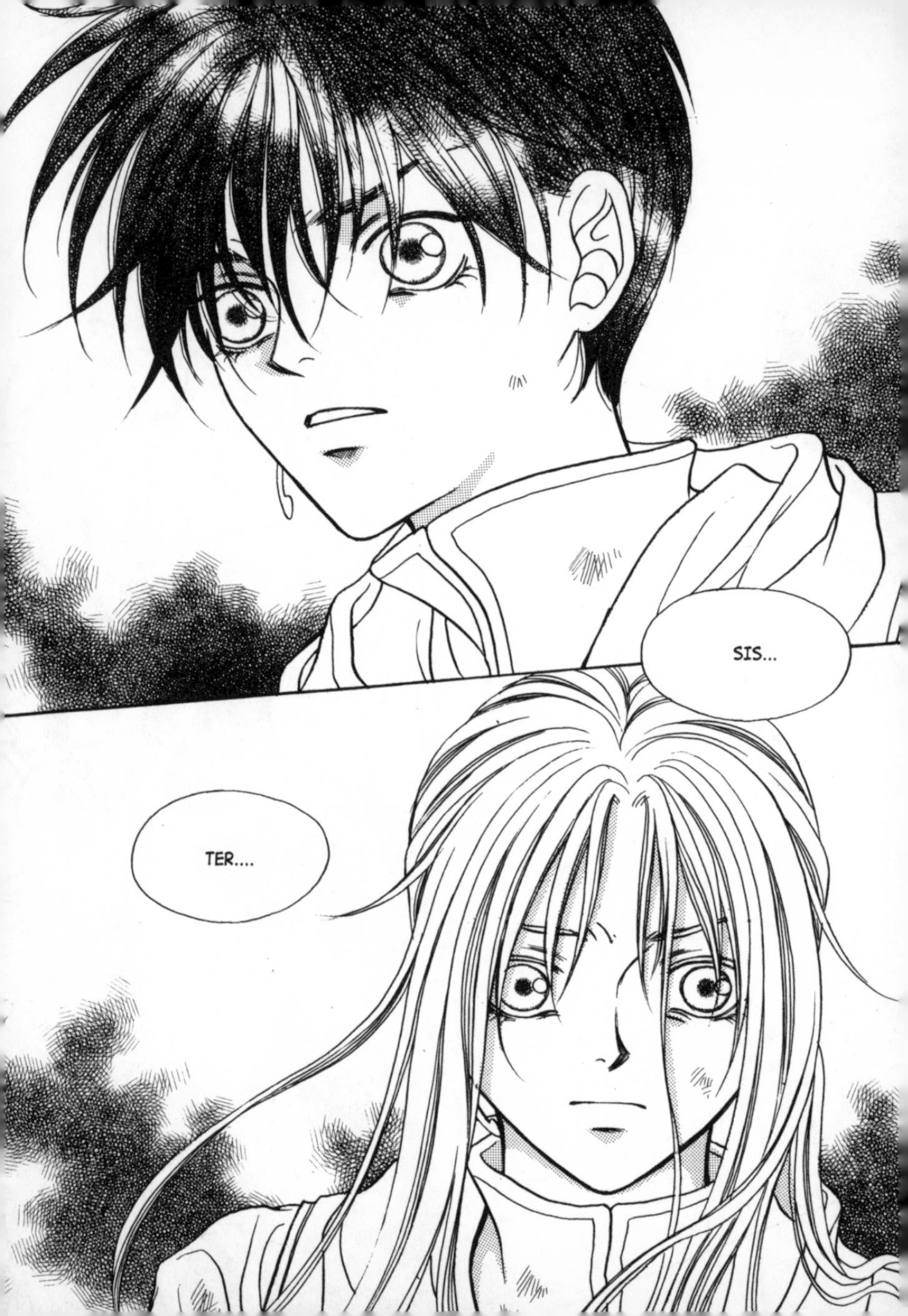
SIS...
TER....

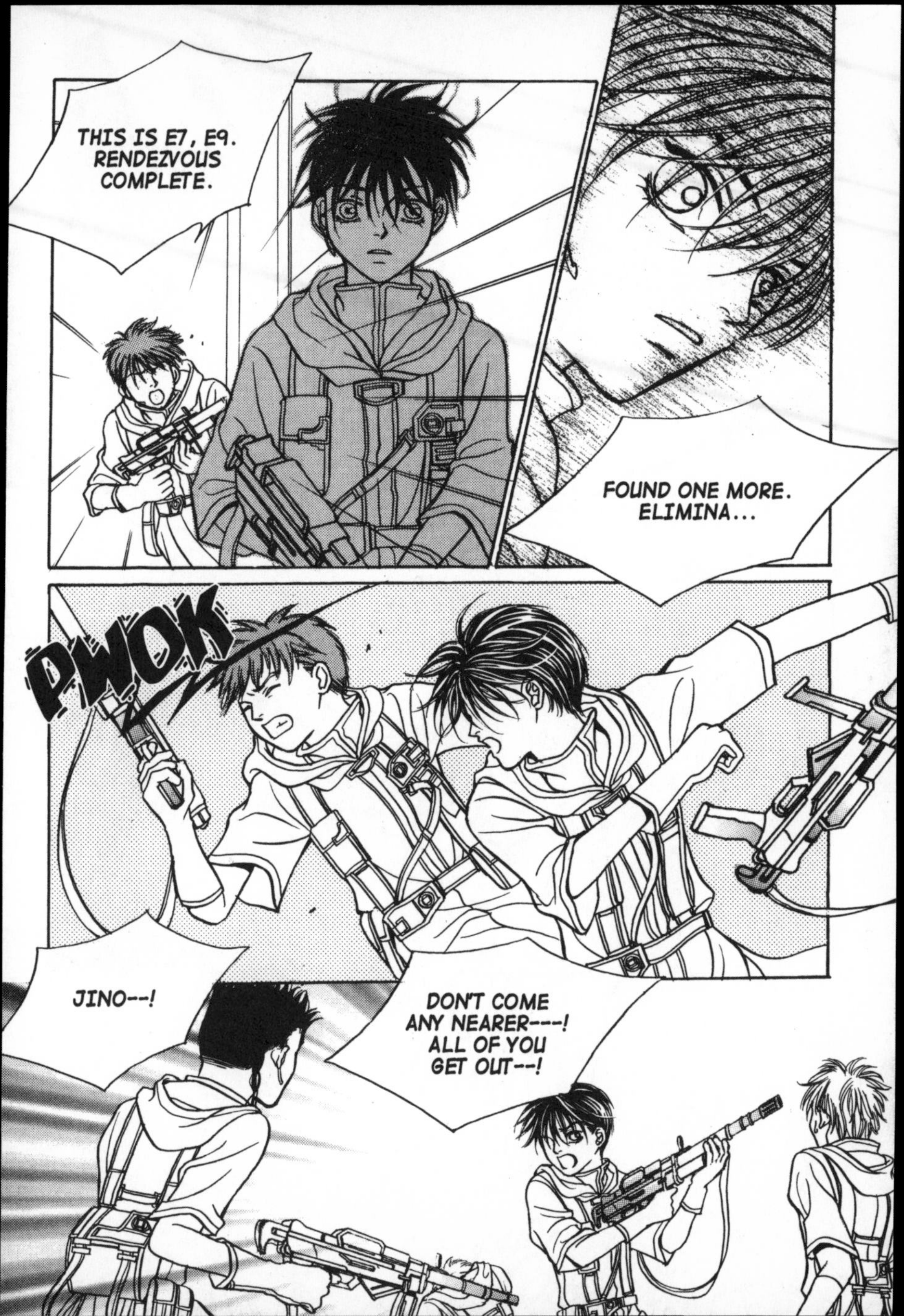
THIS IS E7, E9. RENDEZVOUS COMPLETE.
FOUND ONE MORE. ELIMINA...
PWOK
JINO--!
DON'T COME ANY NEARER---! ALL OF YOU GET OUT--!

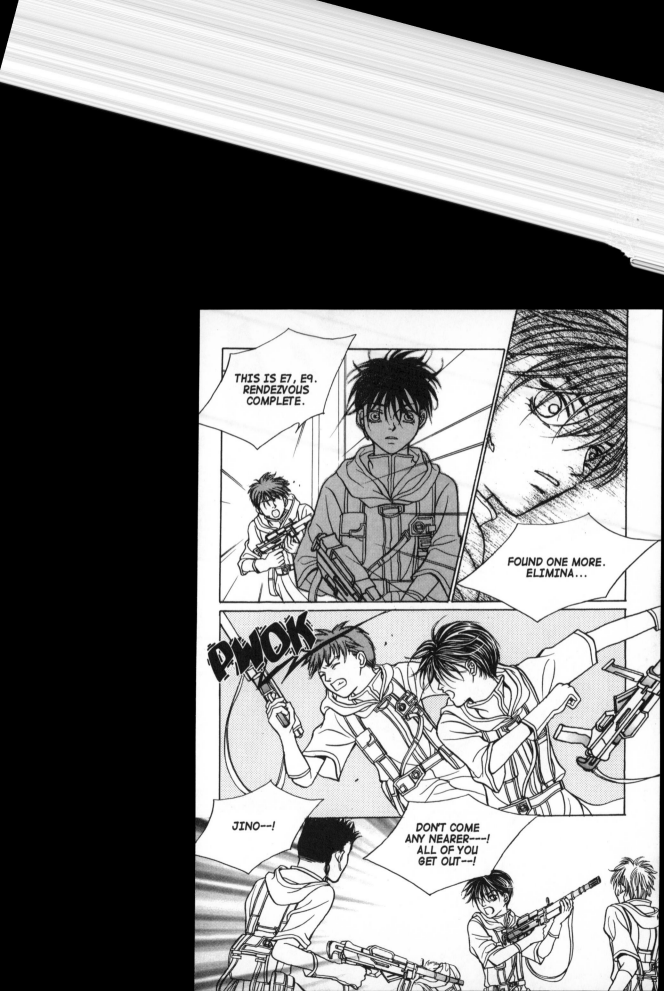

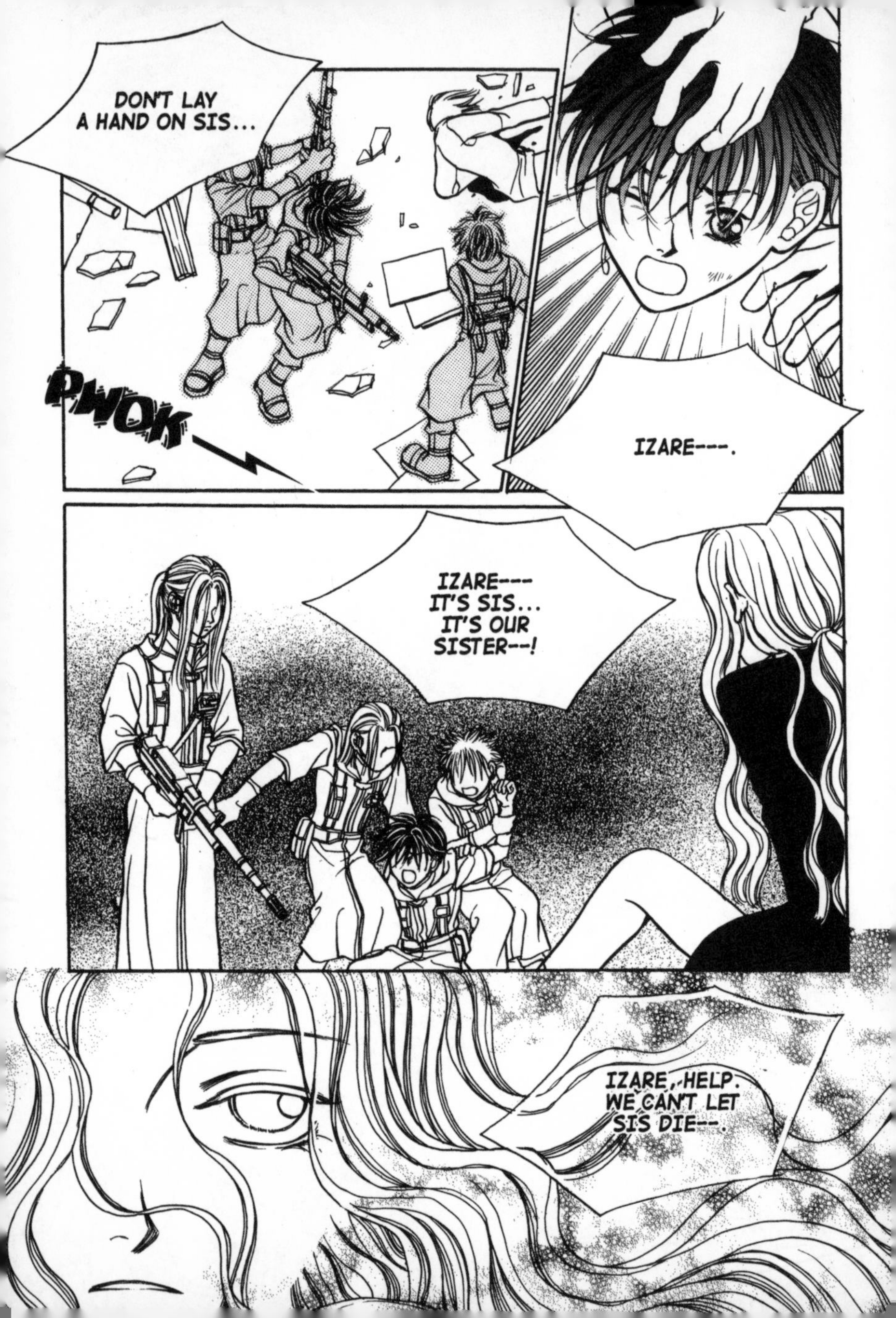
DON'T LAY A HAND ON SIS...
PWOK
IZARE---.
IZARE--- IT'S SIS... IT'S OUR SISTER--!
IZARE, HELP. WE CAN'T LET SIS DIE--.

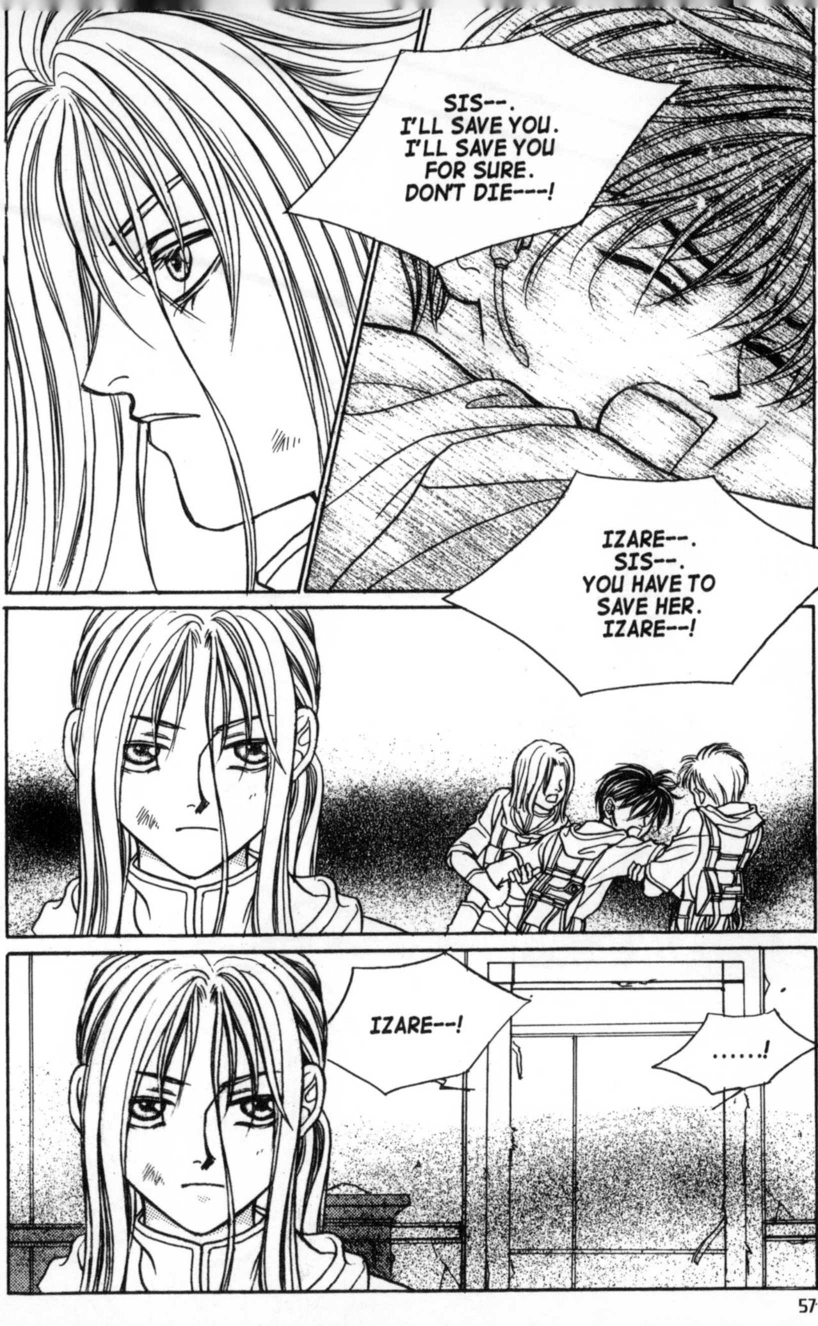
SIS--. I'LL SAVE YOU. I'LL SAVE YOU FOR SURE. DON'T DIE---!
IZARE--. SIS--. YOU HAVE TO SAVE HER. IZARE--!
IZARE--!
......!

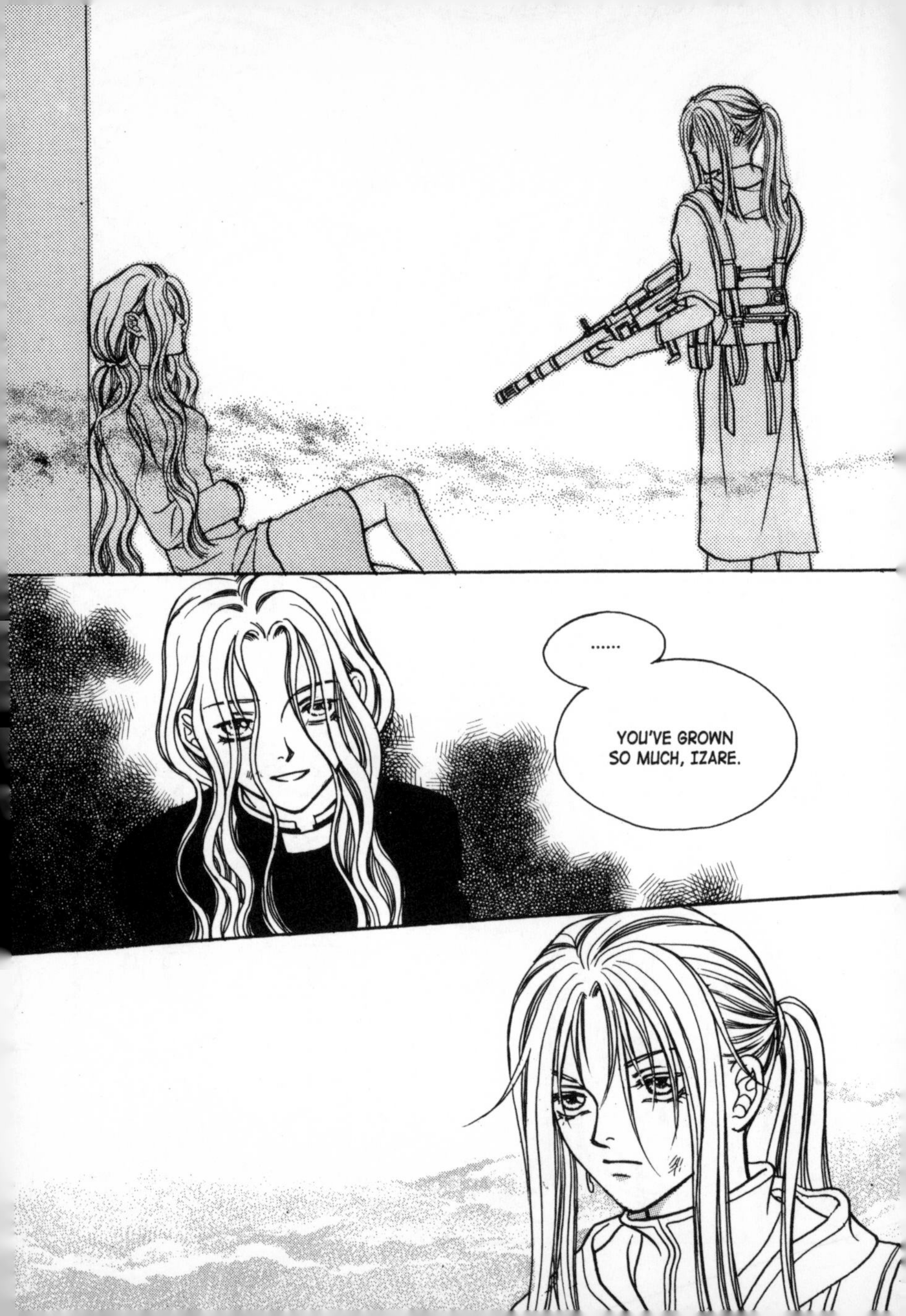
......
YOU'VE GROWN SO MUCH, IZARE.

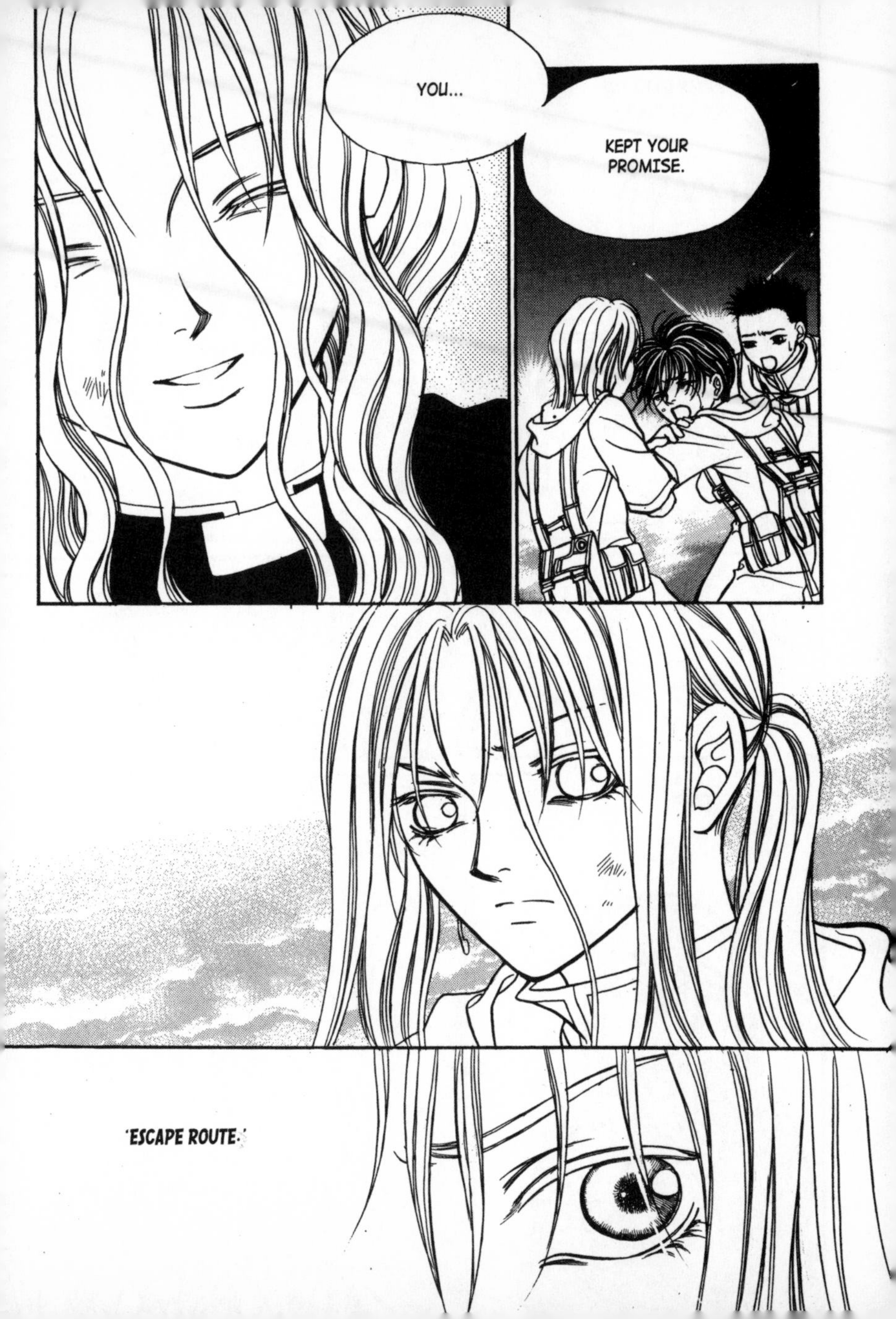
YOU...
KEPT YOUR PROMISE.
ESCAPE ROUTE

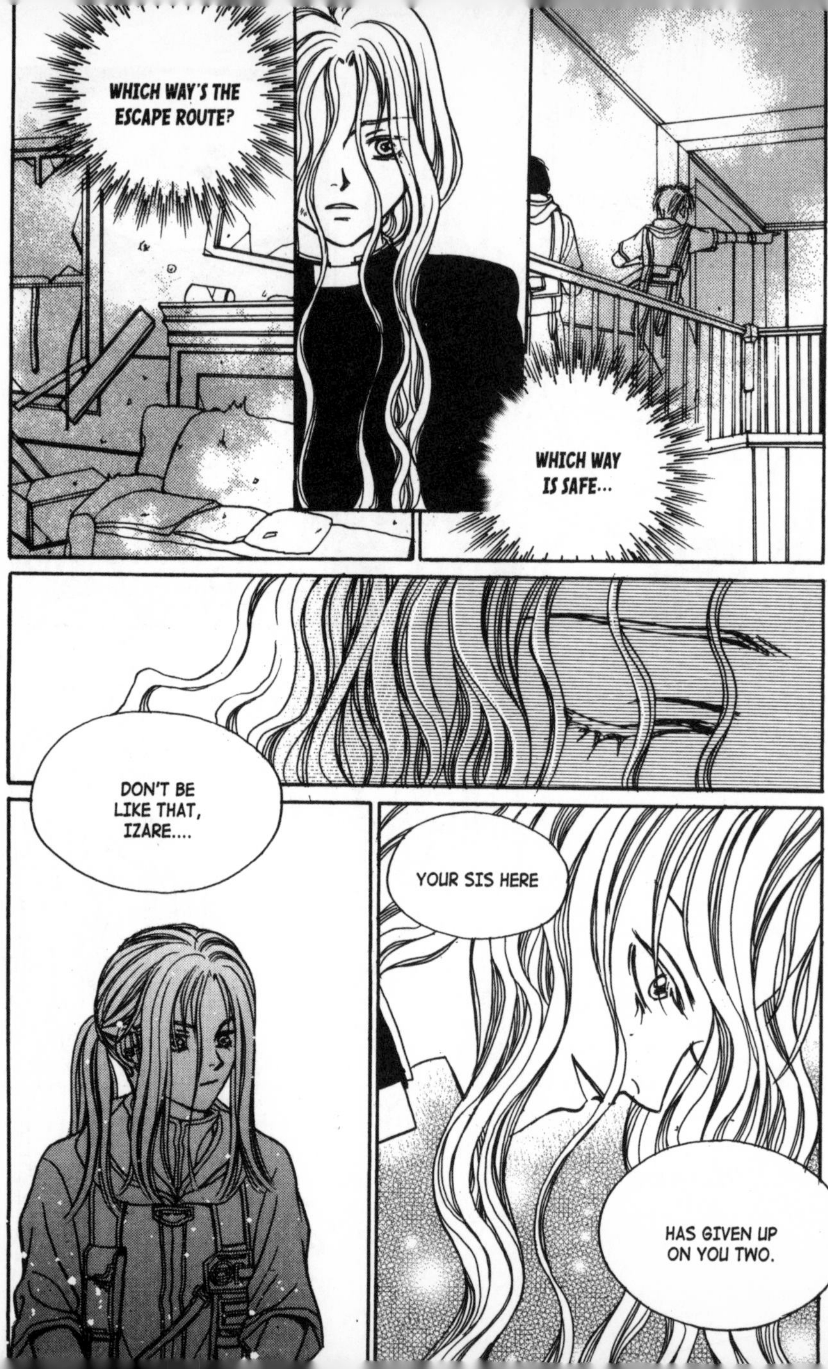
WHICH WAY'S THE ESCAPE ROUTE?
WHICH WAY IS SAFE...
DON'T BE LIKE THAT, IZARE....
YOUR SIS HERE
HAS GIVEN UP ON YOU TWO.

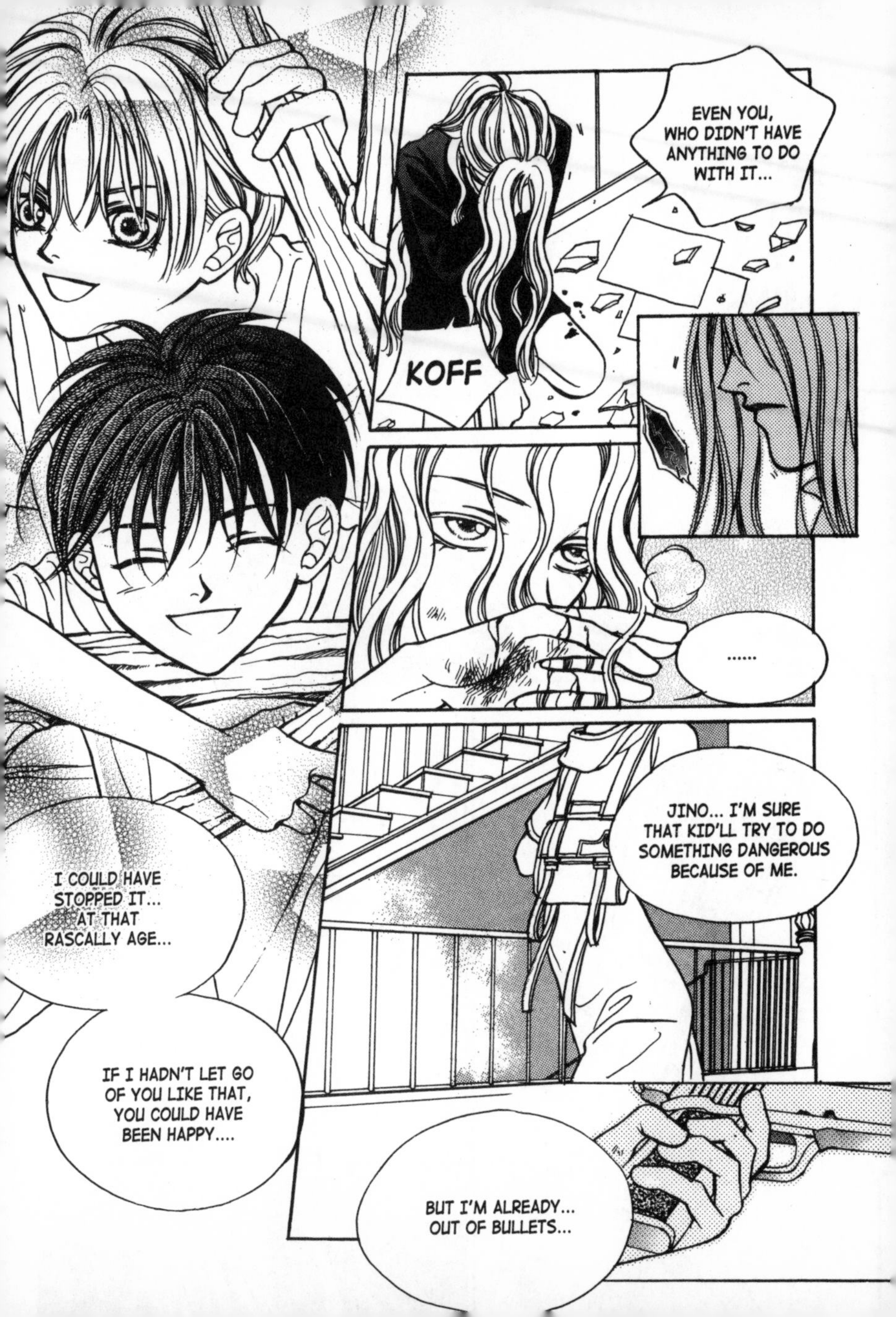
I COULD HAVE STOPPED IT... AT THAT RASCALLY AGE...
IF I HADN'T LET GO OF YOU LIKE THAT, YOU COULD HAVE BEEN HAPPY....
EVEN YOU, WHO DIDN'T HAVE ANYTHING TO DO WITH IT...
KOFF
......
JINO... I'M SURE THAT KID'LL TRY TO DO SOMETHING DANGEROUS BECAUSE OF ME.
BUT I'M ALREADY... OUT OF BULLETS...

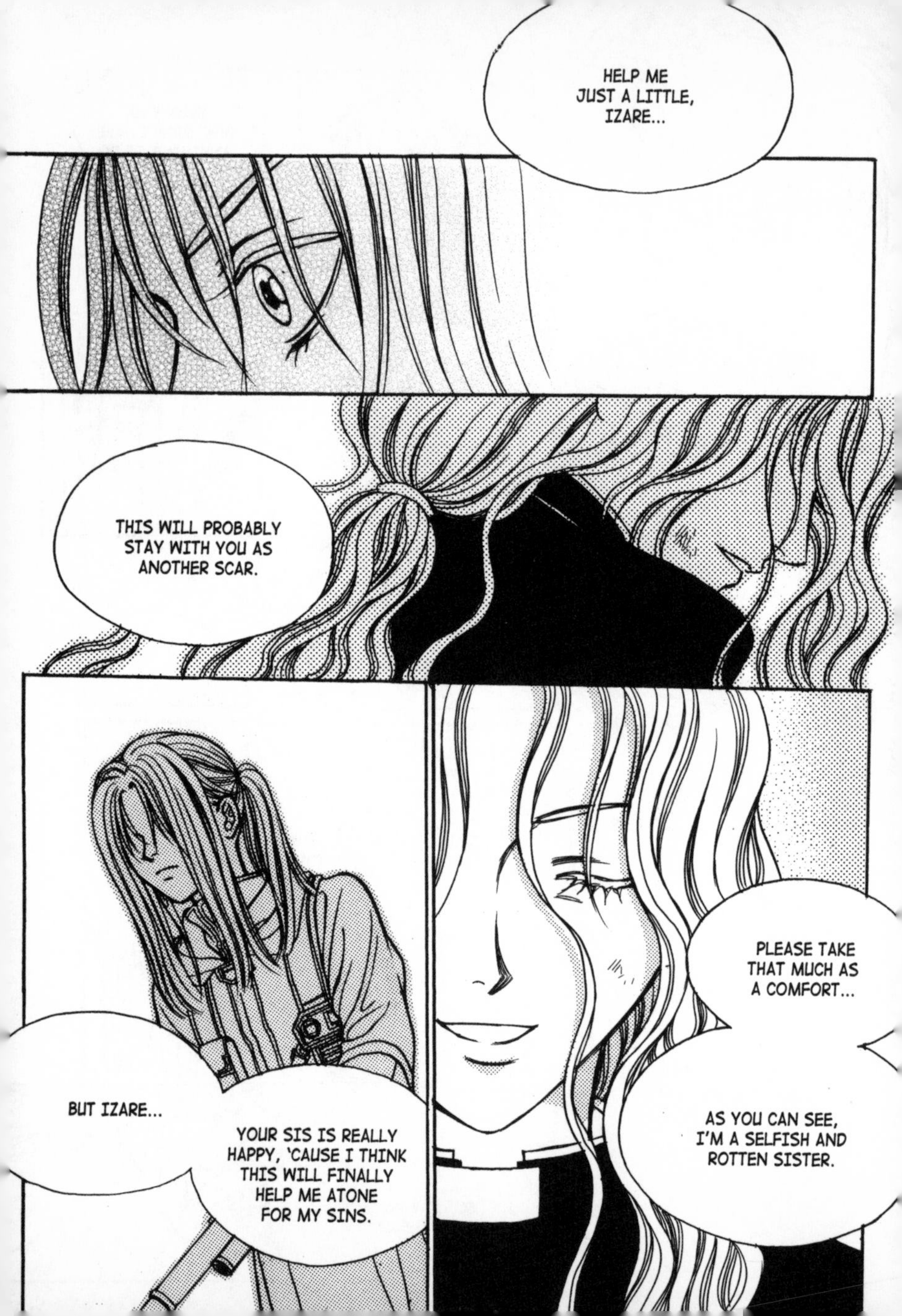
HELP ME JUST A LITTLE, IZARE...
THIS WILL PROBABLY STAY WITH YOU AS ANOTHER SCAR.
BUT IZARE...
YOUR SIS IS REALLY HAPPY, 'CAUSE I THINK THIS WILL FINALLY HELP ME ATONE FOR MY SINS.
PLEASE TAKE THAT MUCH AS A COMFORT...
AS YOU CAN SEE, I'M A SELFISH AND ROTTEN SISTER.

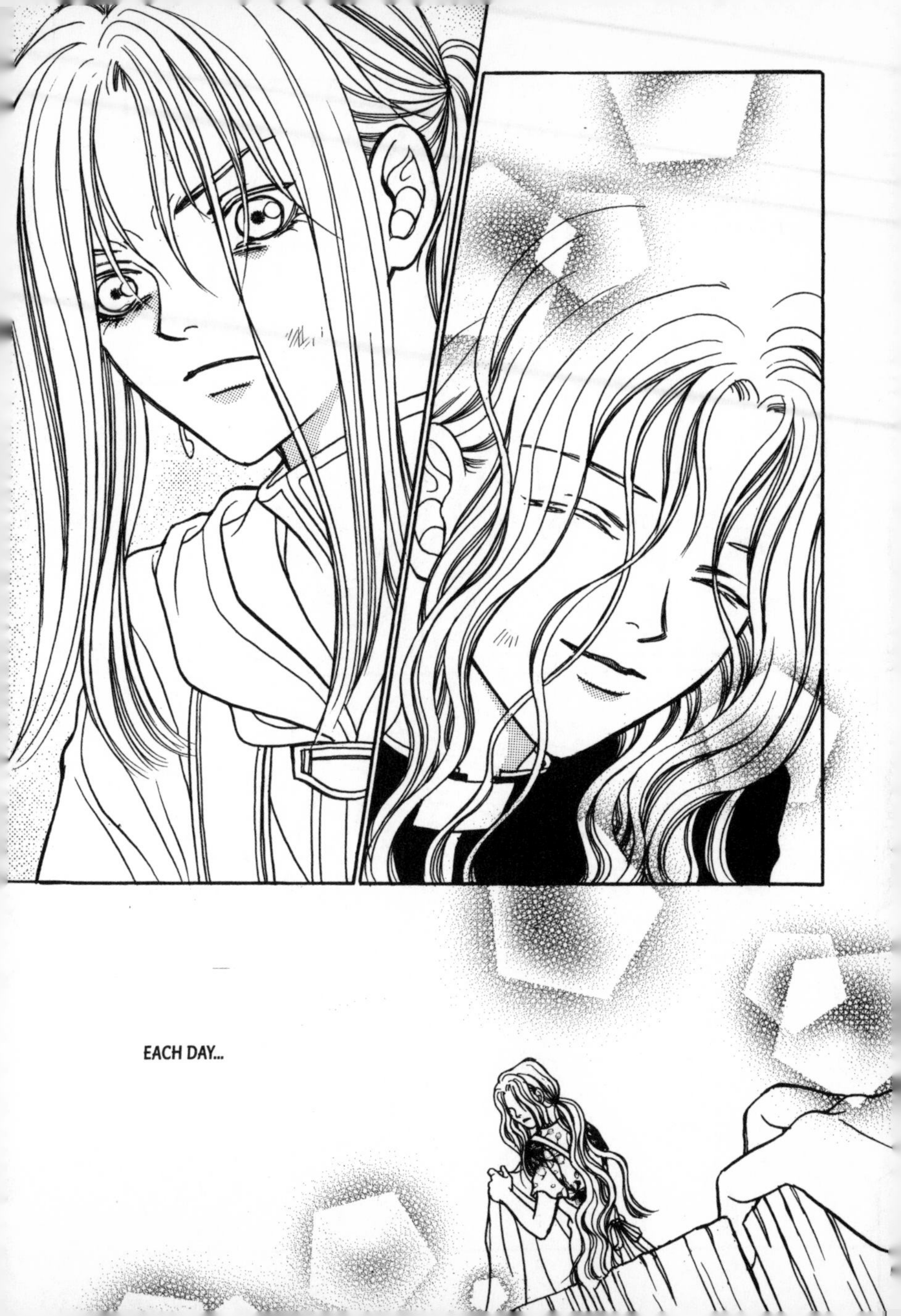
EACH DAY...

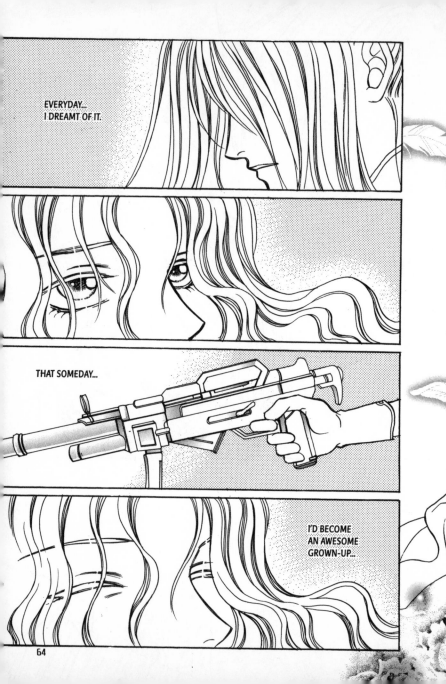

EVERYDAY...
I DREAMT OF IT.

THAT SOMEDAY...

I'D BECOME
AN AWESOME
GROWN-UP...

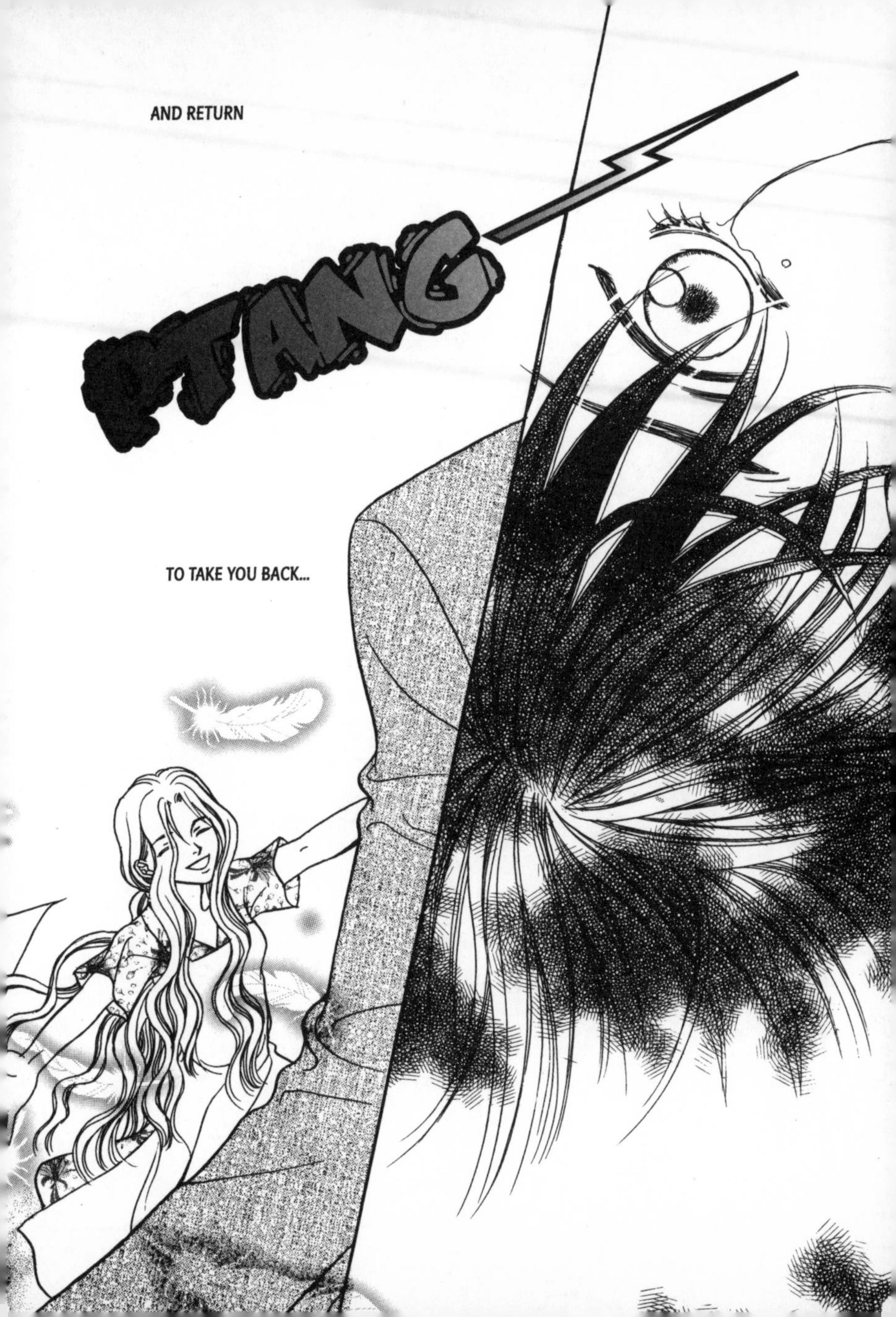
AND RETURN
PTANG
TO TAKE YOU BACK...

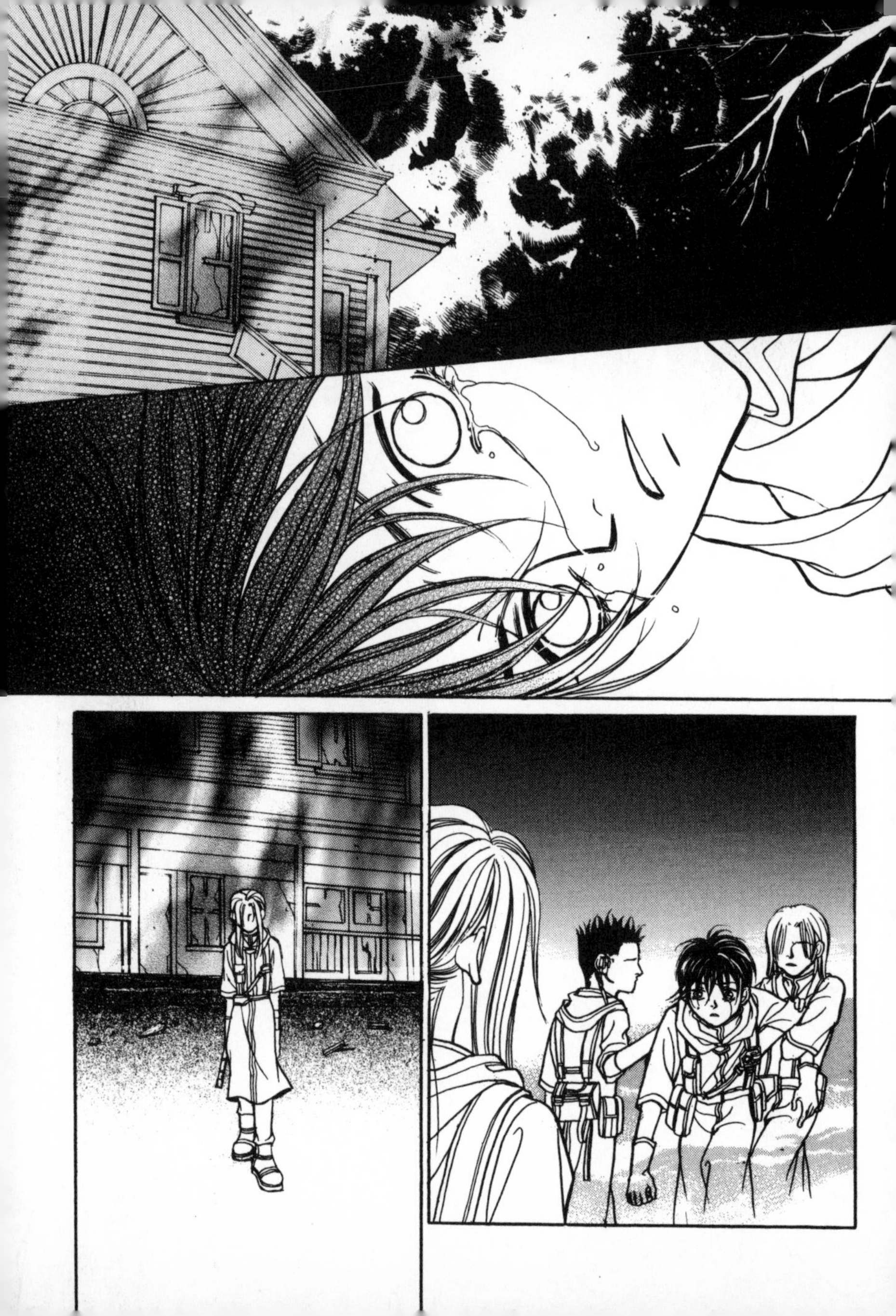

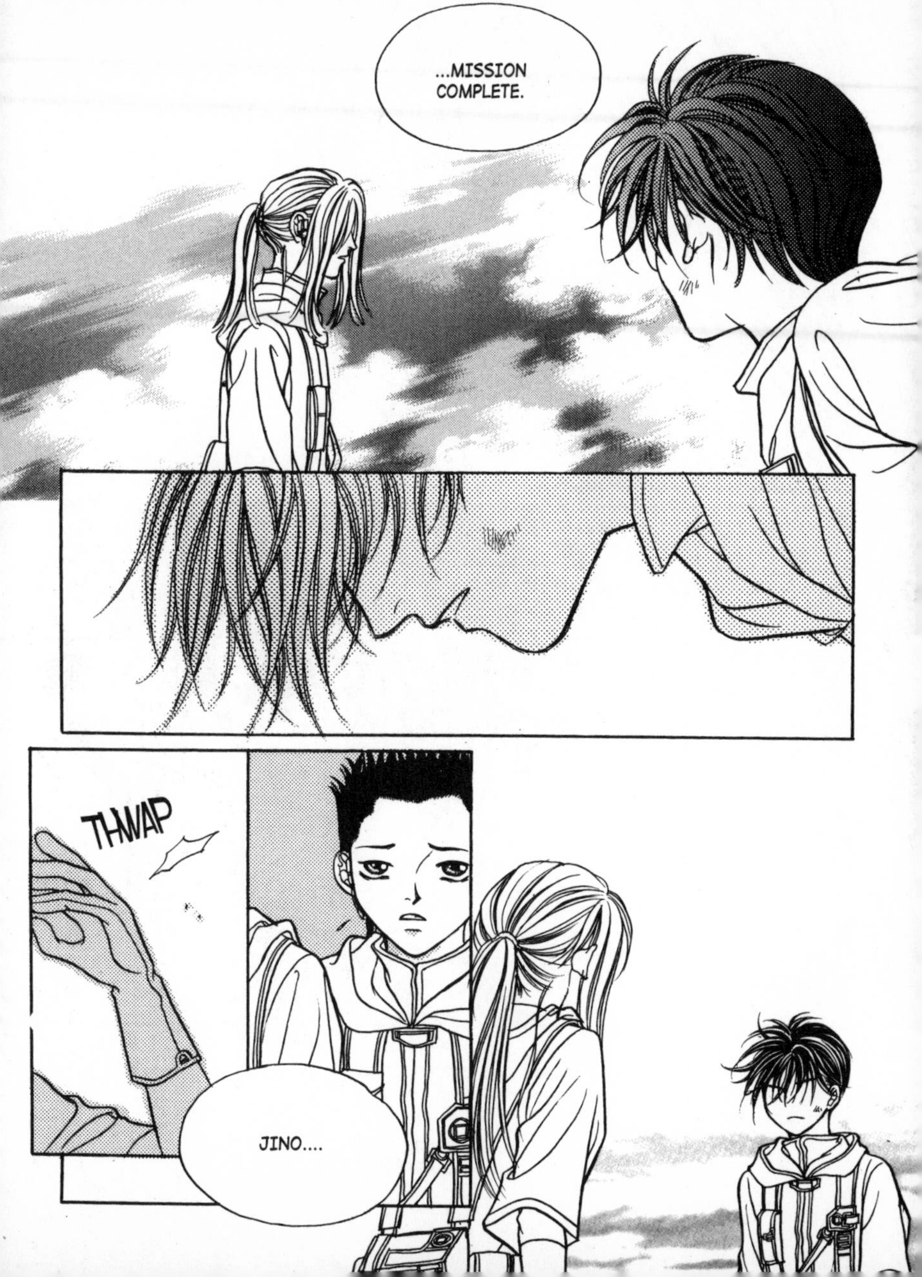
...MISSION COMPLETE.
THWAP
JINO....

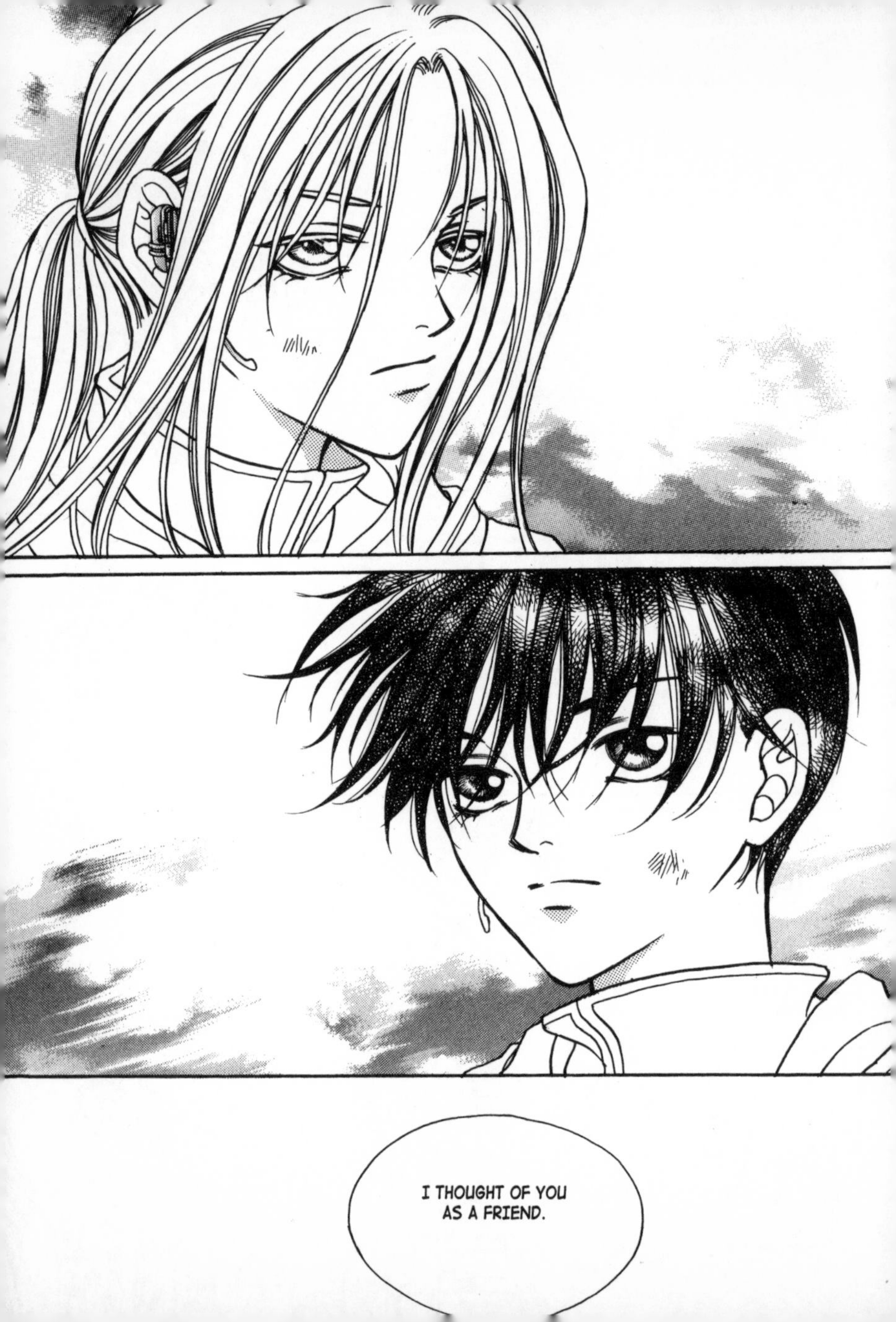
I THOUGHT OF YOU AS A FRIEND.

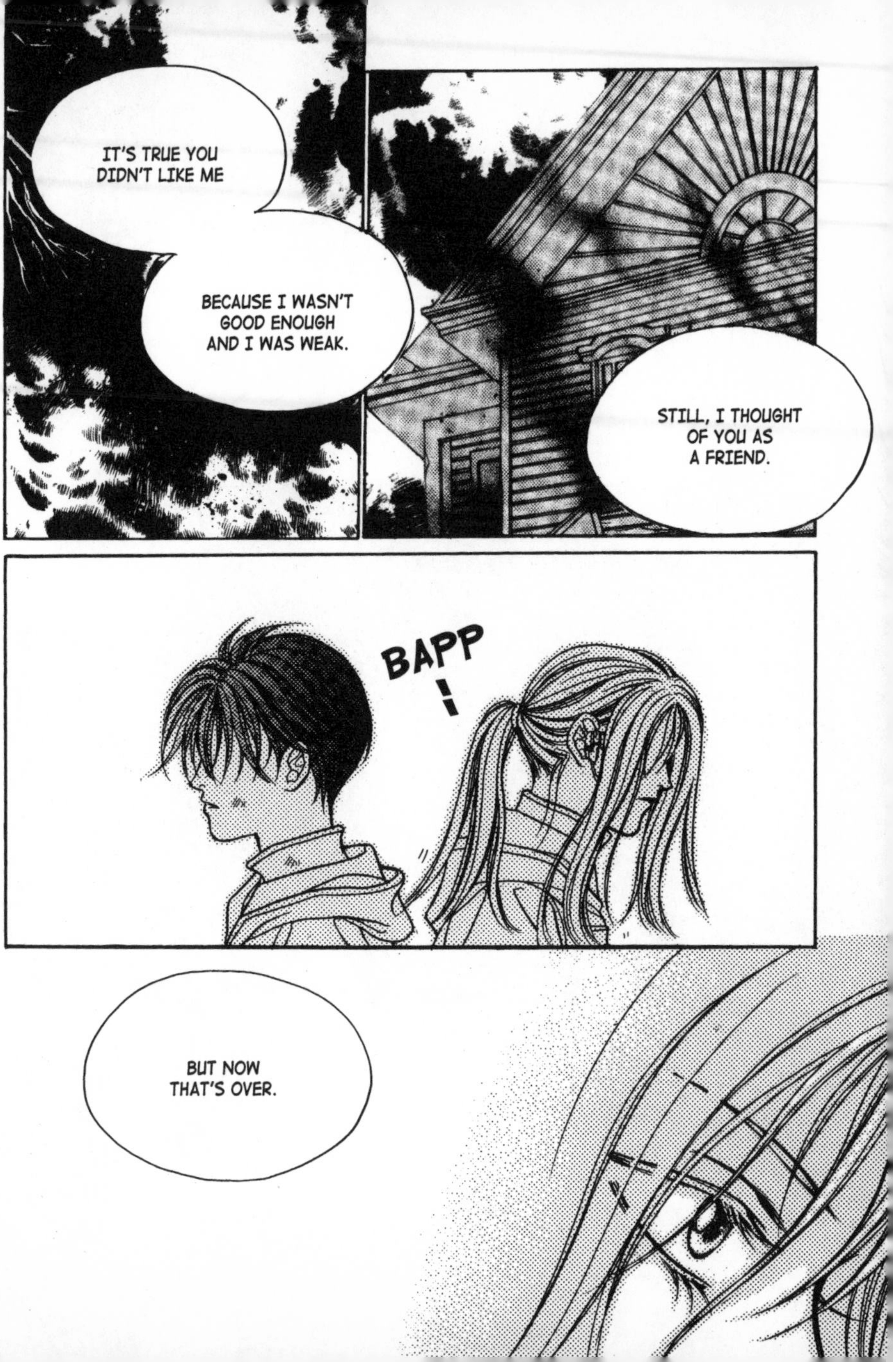
IT'S TRUE YOU DIDN'T LIKE ME
BECAUSE I WASN'T GOOD ENOUGH AND I WAS WEAK.
STILL, I THOUGHT OF YOU AS A FRIEND.
BAPP
BUT NOW THAT'S OVER.

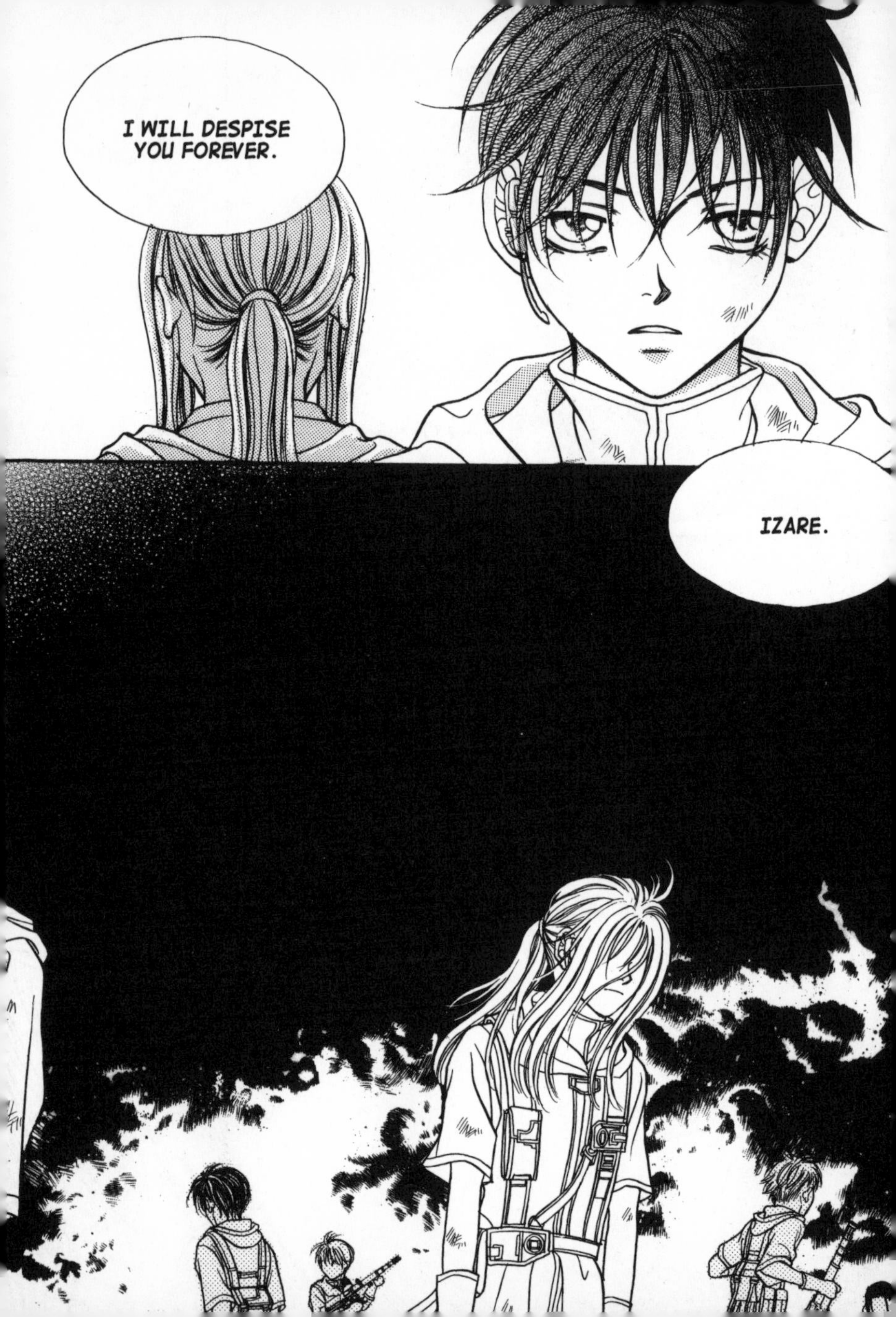
I WILL DESPISE YOU FOREVER.
IZARE.

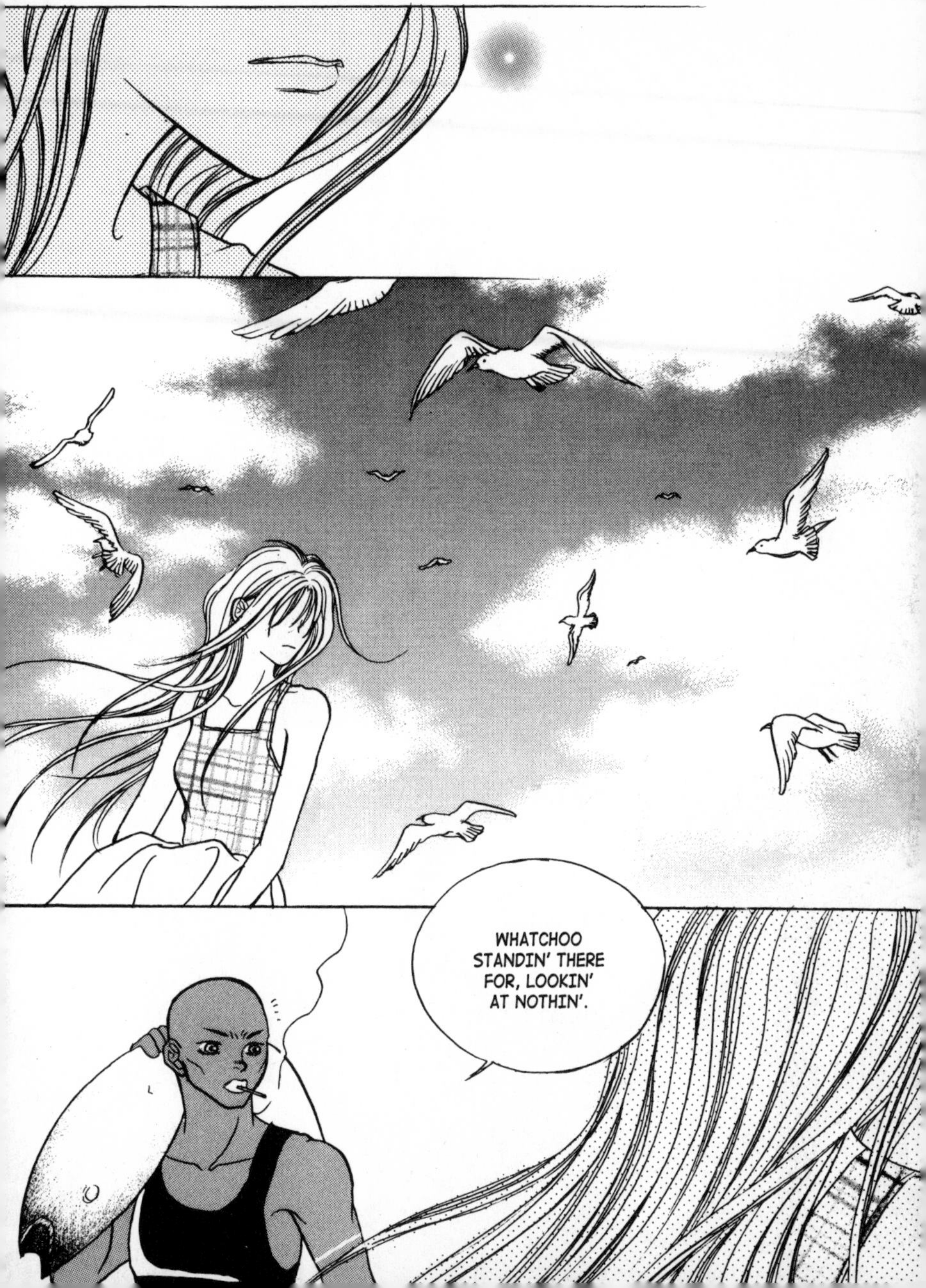
WHATCHOO STANDIN' THERE FOR, LOOKIN' AT NOTHIN'.

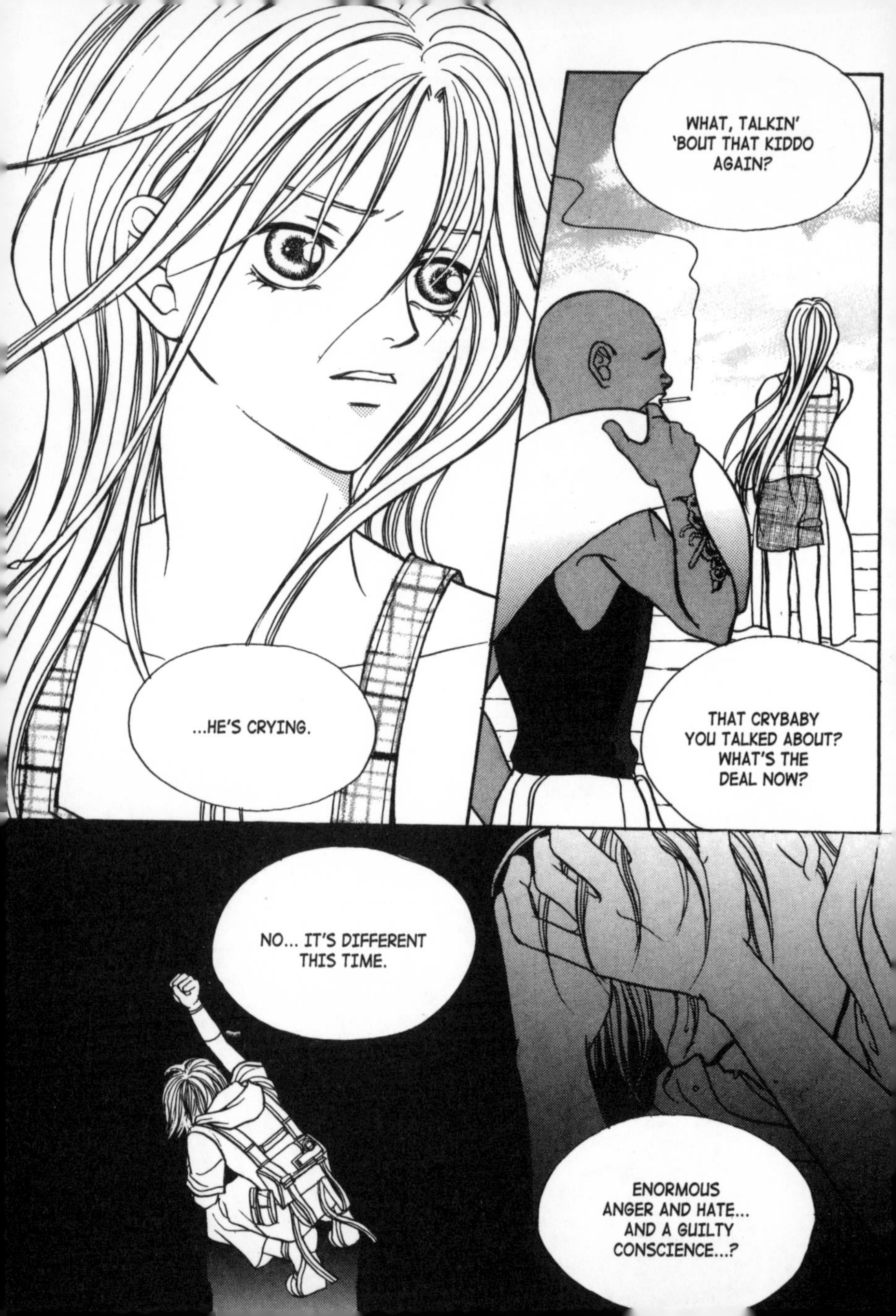

...HE'S CRYING.
WHAT, TALKIN' 'BOUT THAT KIDDO AGAIN?
THAT CRYBABY YOU TALKED ABOUT? WHAT'S THE DEAL NOW?
NO... IT'S DIFFERENT THIS TIME.
ENORMOUS ANGER AND HATE... AND A GUILTY CONSCIENCE...?

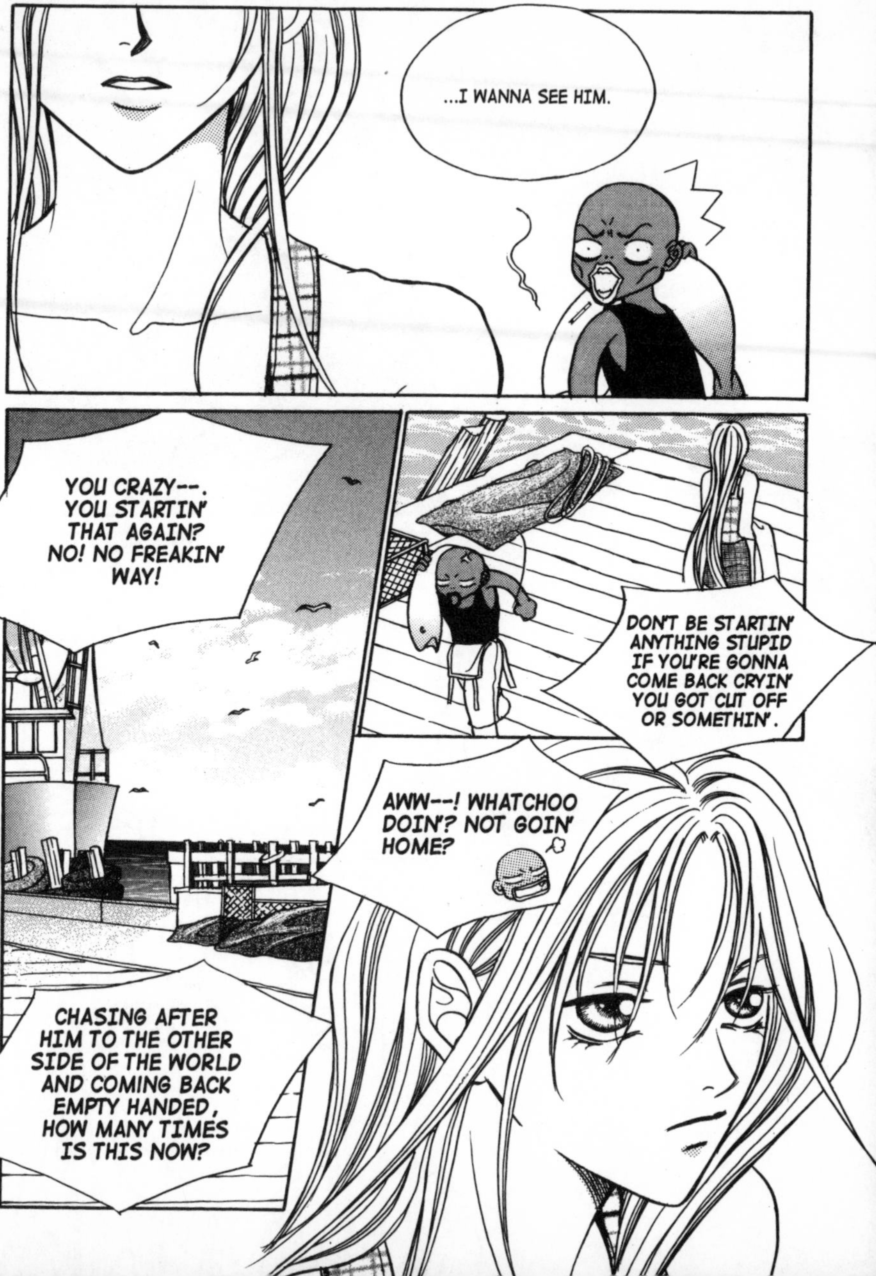
...I WANNA SEE HIM.
YOU CRAZY--. YOU STARTIN' THAT AGAIN? NO! NO FREAKIN' WAY!
CHASING AFTER HIM TO THE OTHER SIDE OF THE WORLD AND COMING BACK EMPTY HANDED, HOW MANY TIMES IS THIS NOW?
DON'T BE STARTIN' ANYTHING STUPID IF YOU'RE GONNA COME BACK CRYIN' YOU GOT CUT OFF OR SOMETHIN'.
AWW--! WHATCHOO DOIN'? NOT GOIN' HOME?

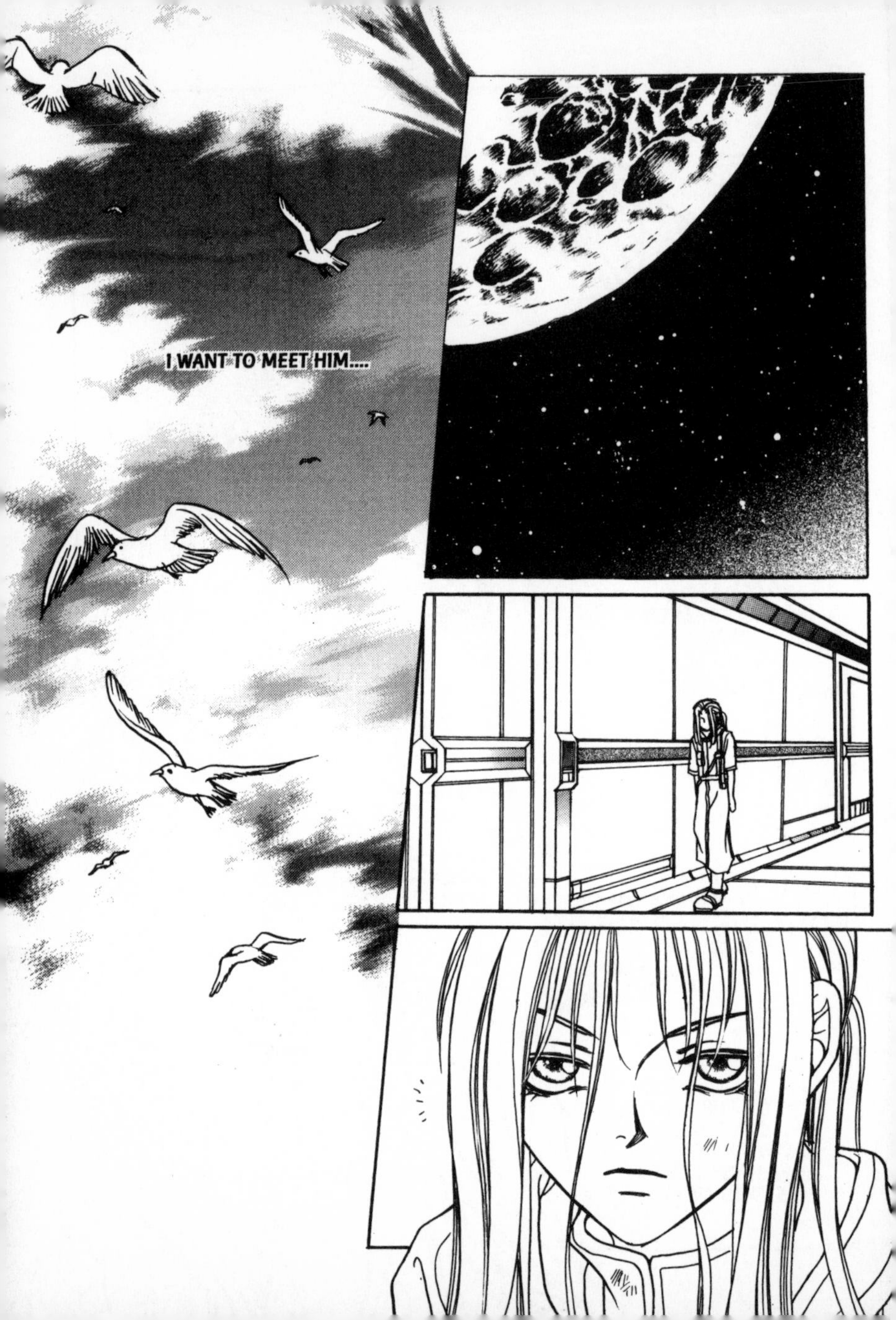
I WANT TO MEET HIM....

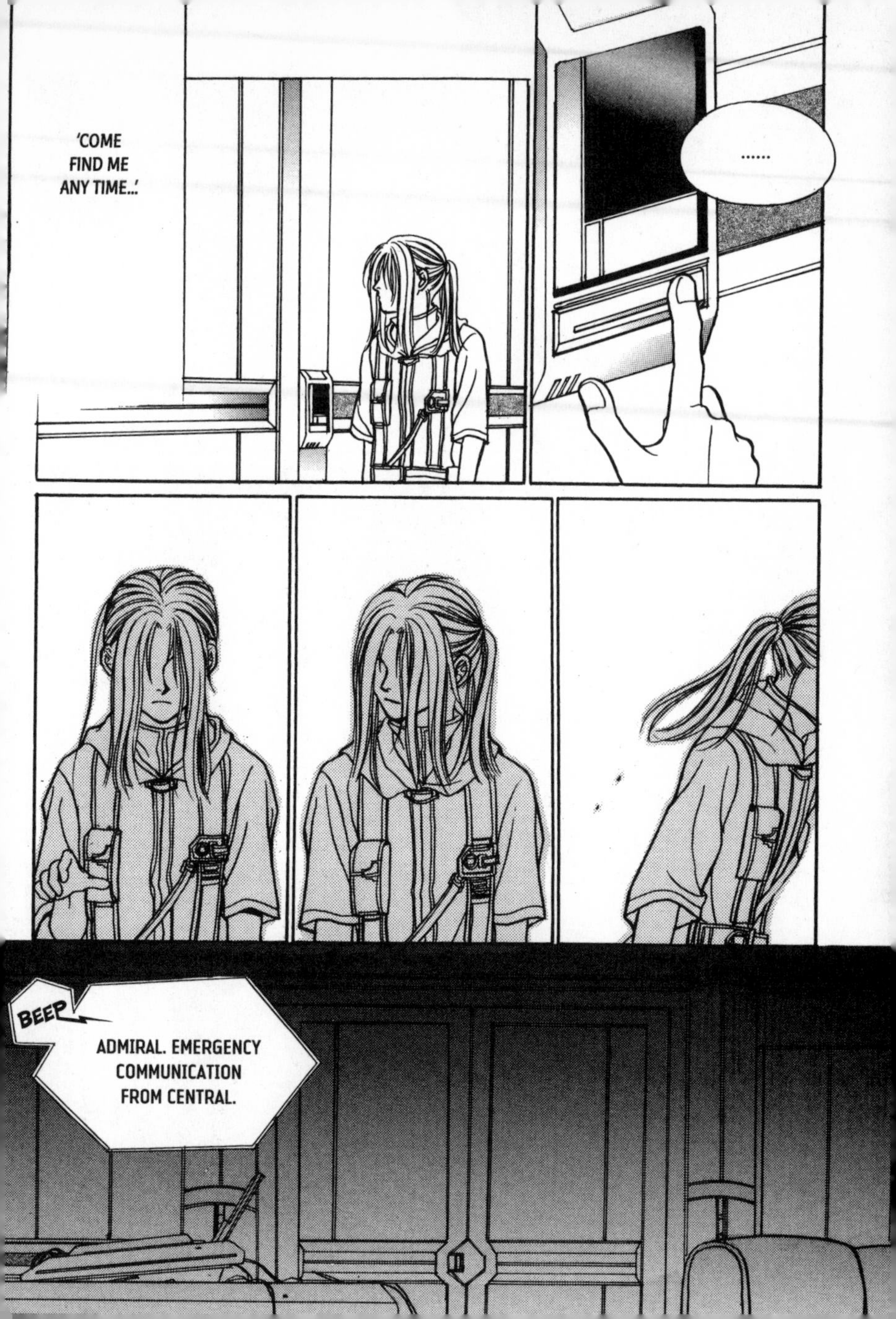
'COME FIND ME ANY TIME...'
......
BEEP
ADMIRAL. EMERGENCY COMMUNICATION FROM CENTRAL.

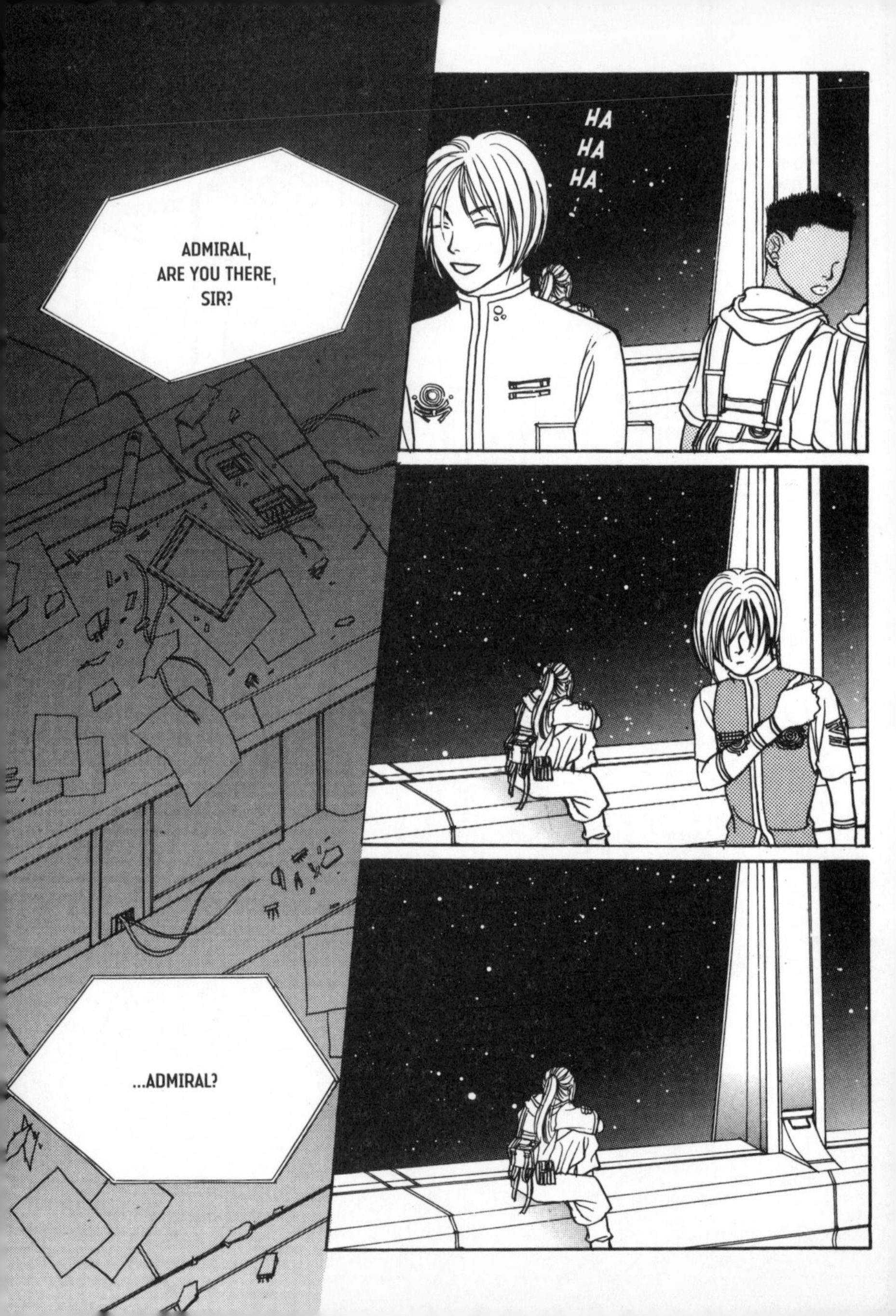
ADMIRAL, ARE YOU THERE, SIR?
...ADMIRAL?
HA HA HA!

SIS....

I DID WELL, RIGHT?

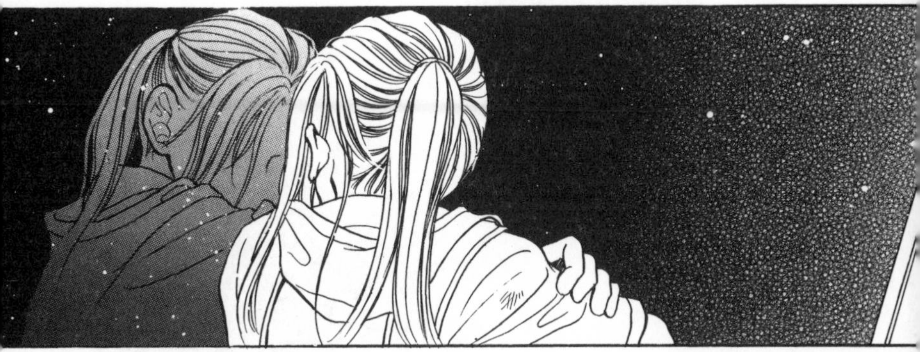

I'M DOING GOOD, RIGHT?

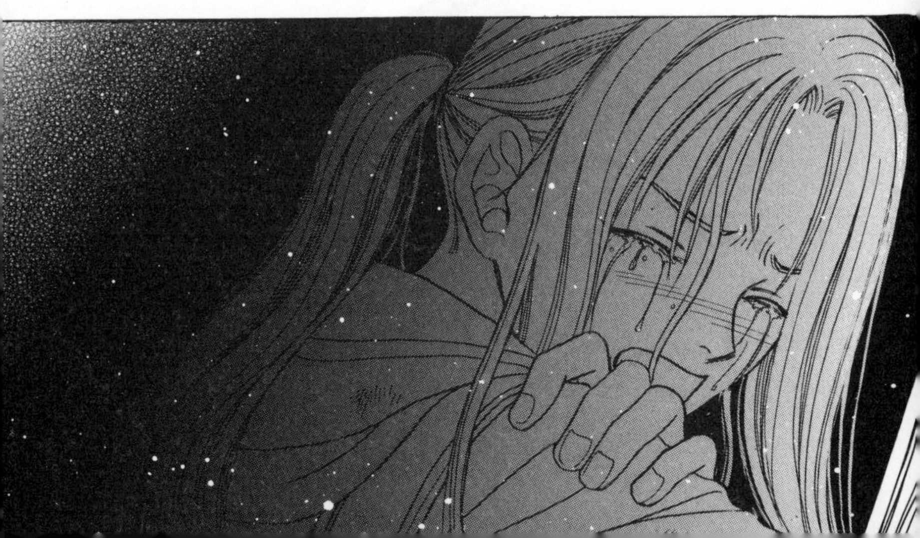

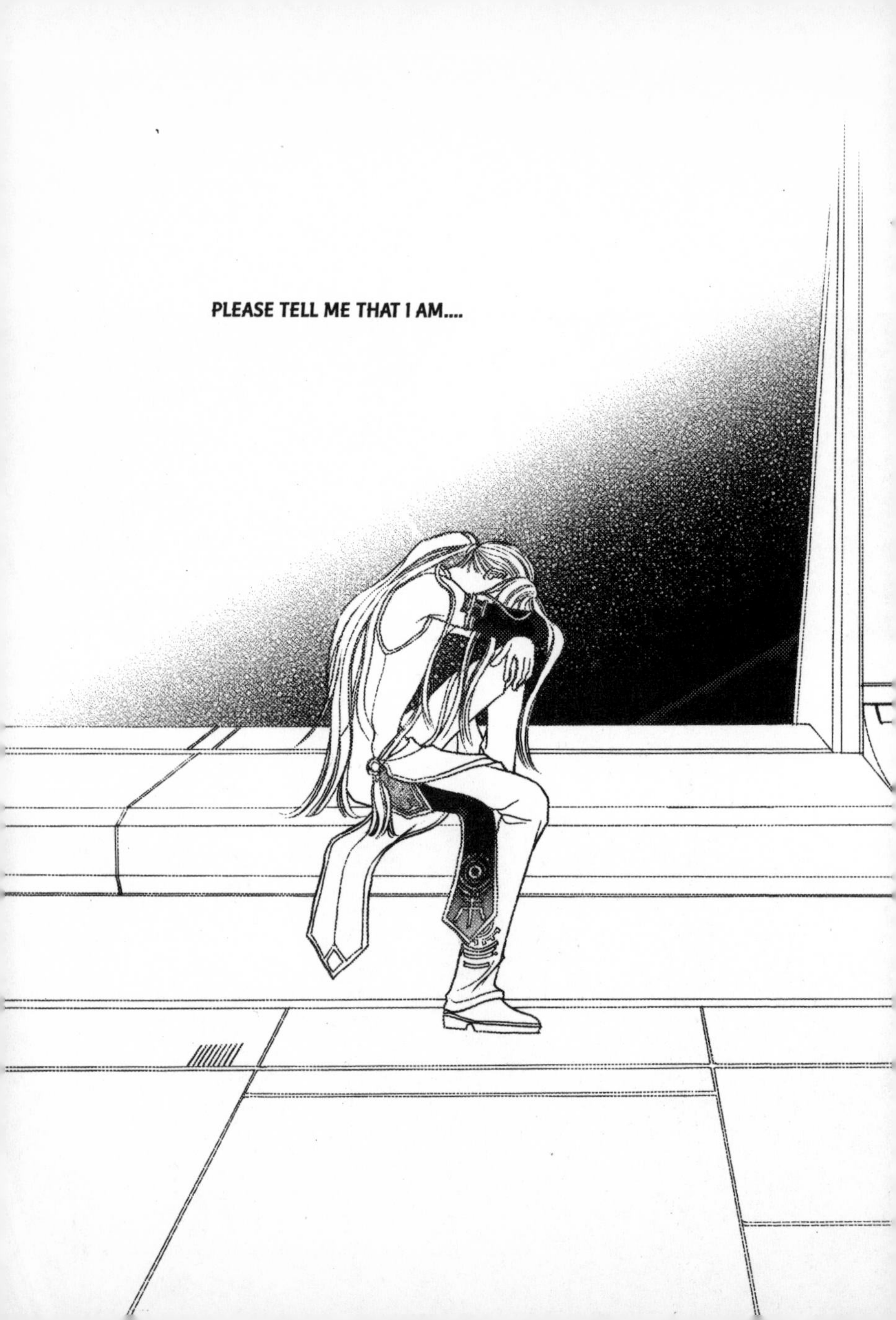
PLEASE TELL ME THAT I AM....

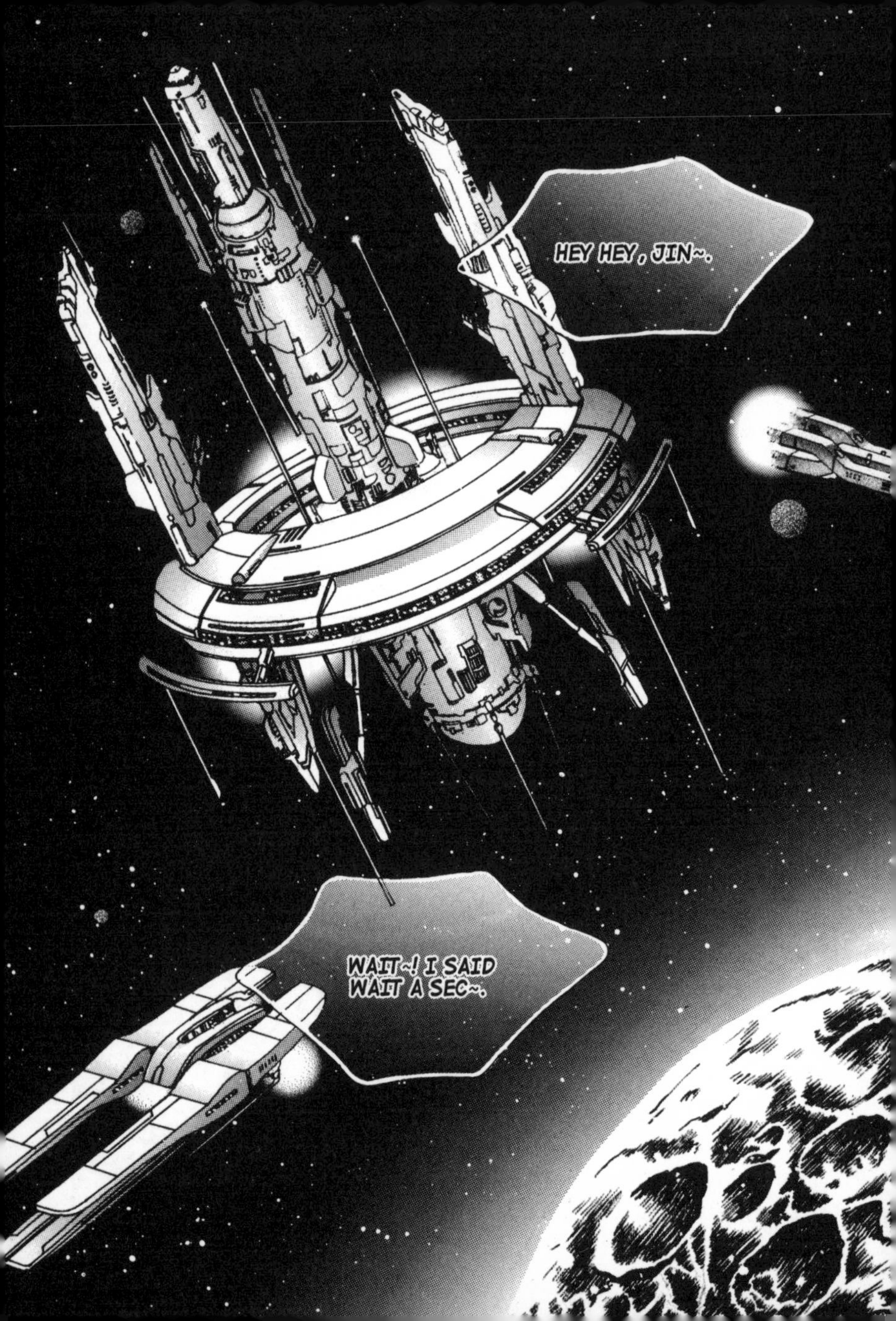

HEY HEY, JIN~.
WAIT~! I SAID WAIT A SEC~.

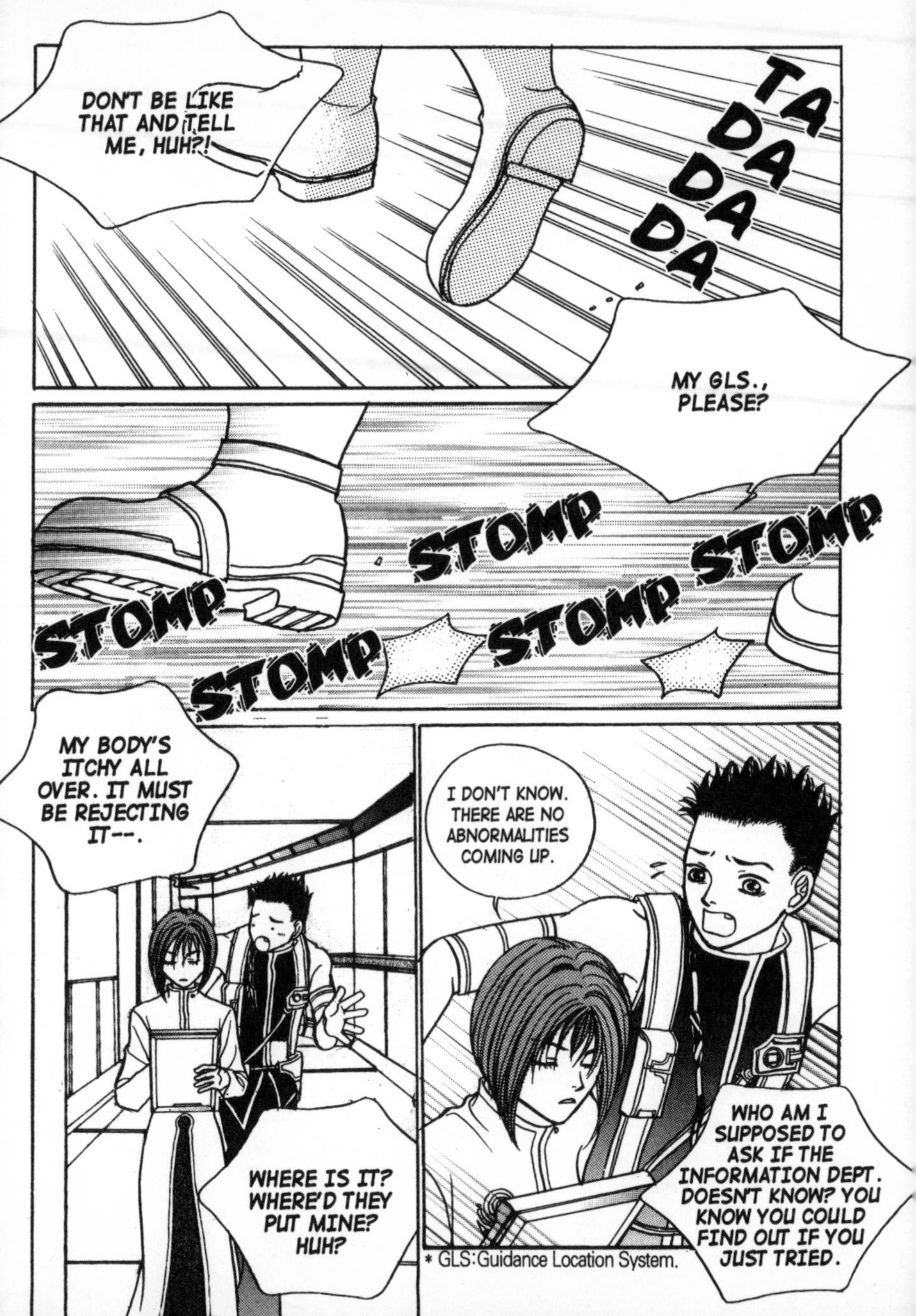
DON'T BE LIKE THAT AND TELL ME, HUH?!
TA DA DA DA DA
MY GLS., PLEASE?
STOMP STOMP STOMP STOMP STOMP STOMP
MY BODY'S ITCHY ALL OVER. IT MUST BE REJECTING IT--.
WHERE IS IT? WHERE'D THEY PUT MINE? HUH?
I DON'T KNOW. THERE ARE NO ABNORMALITIES COMING UP.
WHO AM I SUPPOSED TO ASK IF THE INFORMATION DEPT. DOESN'T KNOW? YOU KNOW YOU COULD FIND OUT IF YOU JUST TRIED.

* GLS: Guidance Location System.

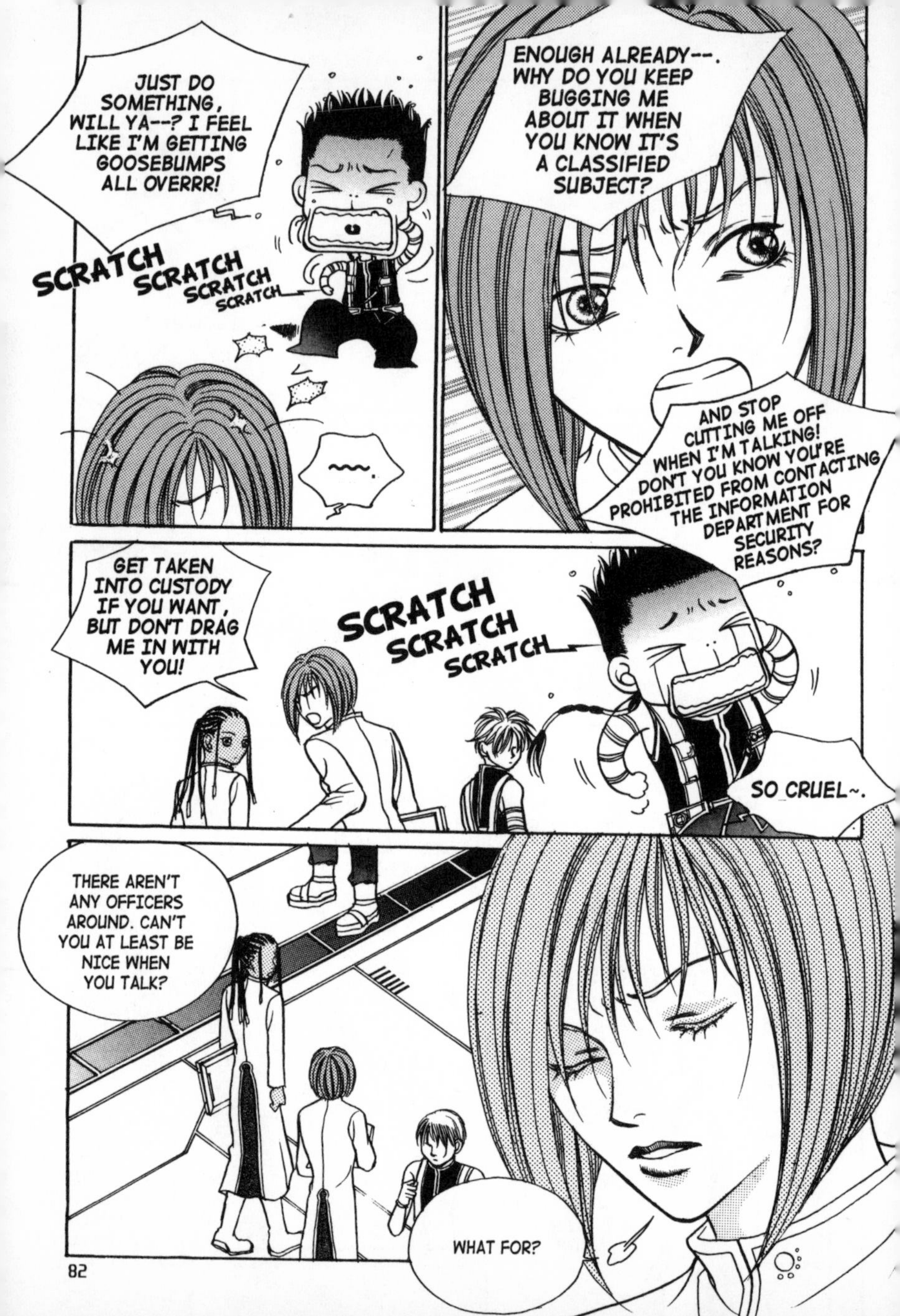
JUST DO SOMETHING, WILL YA--? I FEEL LIKE I'M GETTING GOOSEBUMPS ALL OVERRR!
SCRATCH SCRATCH SCRATCH SCRATCH
~~~.
ENOUGH ALREADY--. WHY DO YOU KEEP BUGGING ME ABOUT IT WHEN YOU KNOW IT'S A CLASSIFIED SUBJECT?
AND STOP CUTTING ME OFF WHEN I'M TALKING! DON'T YOU KNOW YOU'RE PROHIBITED FROM CONTACTING THE INFORMATION DEPARTMENT FOR SECURITY REASONS?
GET TAKEN INTO CUSTODY IF YOU WANT, BUT DON'T DRAG ME IN WITH YOU!
SCRATCH SCRATCH SCRATCH
SO CRUEL~.
THERE AREN'T ANY OFFICERS AROUND. CAN'T YOU AT LEAST BE NICE WHEN YOU TALK?
WHAT FOR?
~~~

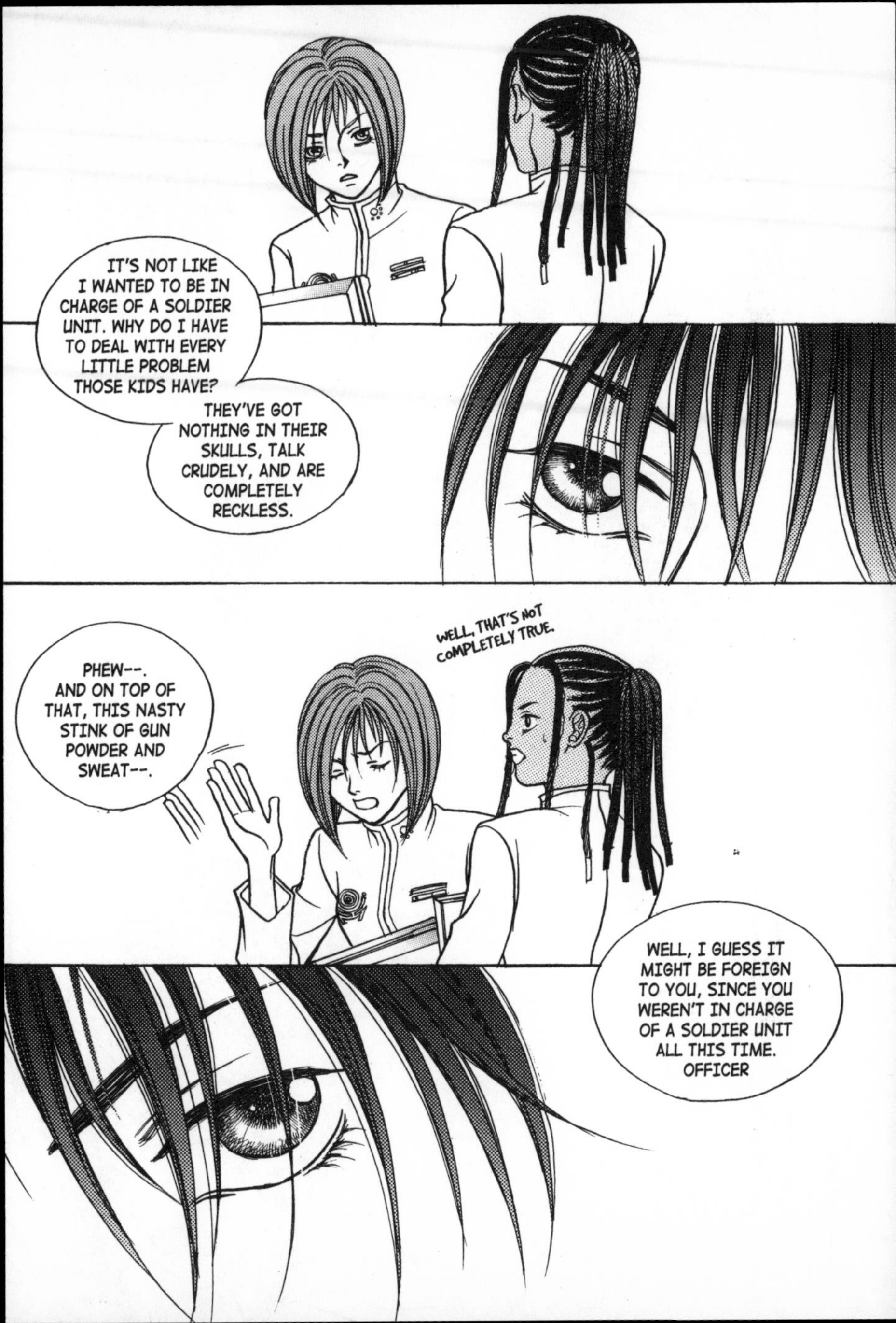
IT'S NOT LIKE I WANTED TO BE IN CHARGE OF A SOLDIER UNIT. WHY DO I HAVE TO DEAL WITH EVERY LITTLE PROBLEM THOSE KIDS HAVE?
THEY'VE GOT NOTHING IN THEIR SKULLS, TALK CRUDELY, AND ARE COMPLETELY RECKLESS.
PHEW--. AND ON TOP OF THAT, THIS NASTY STINK OF GUN POWDER AND SWEAT--.
WELL, THAT'S NOT COMPLETELY TRUE.
WELL, I GUESS IT MIGHT BE FOREIGN TO YOU, SINCE YOU WEREN'T IN CHARGE OF A SOLDIER UNIT ALL THIS TIME. OFFICER

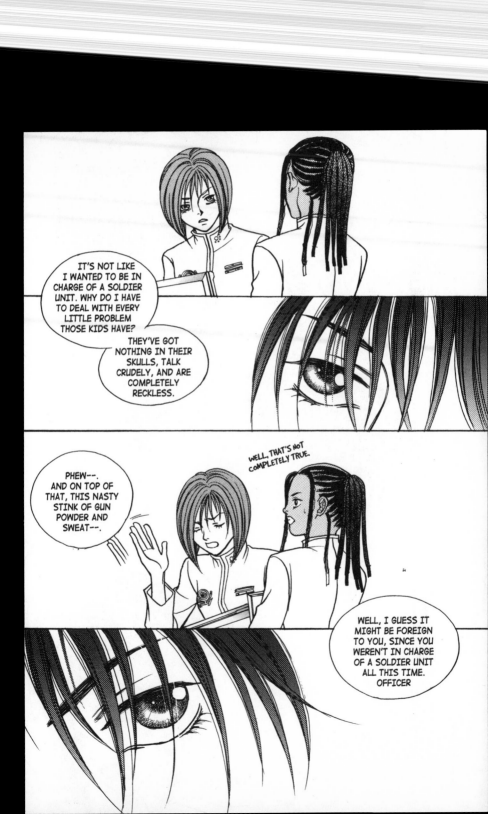

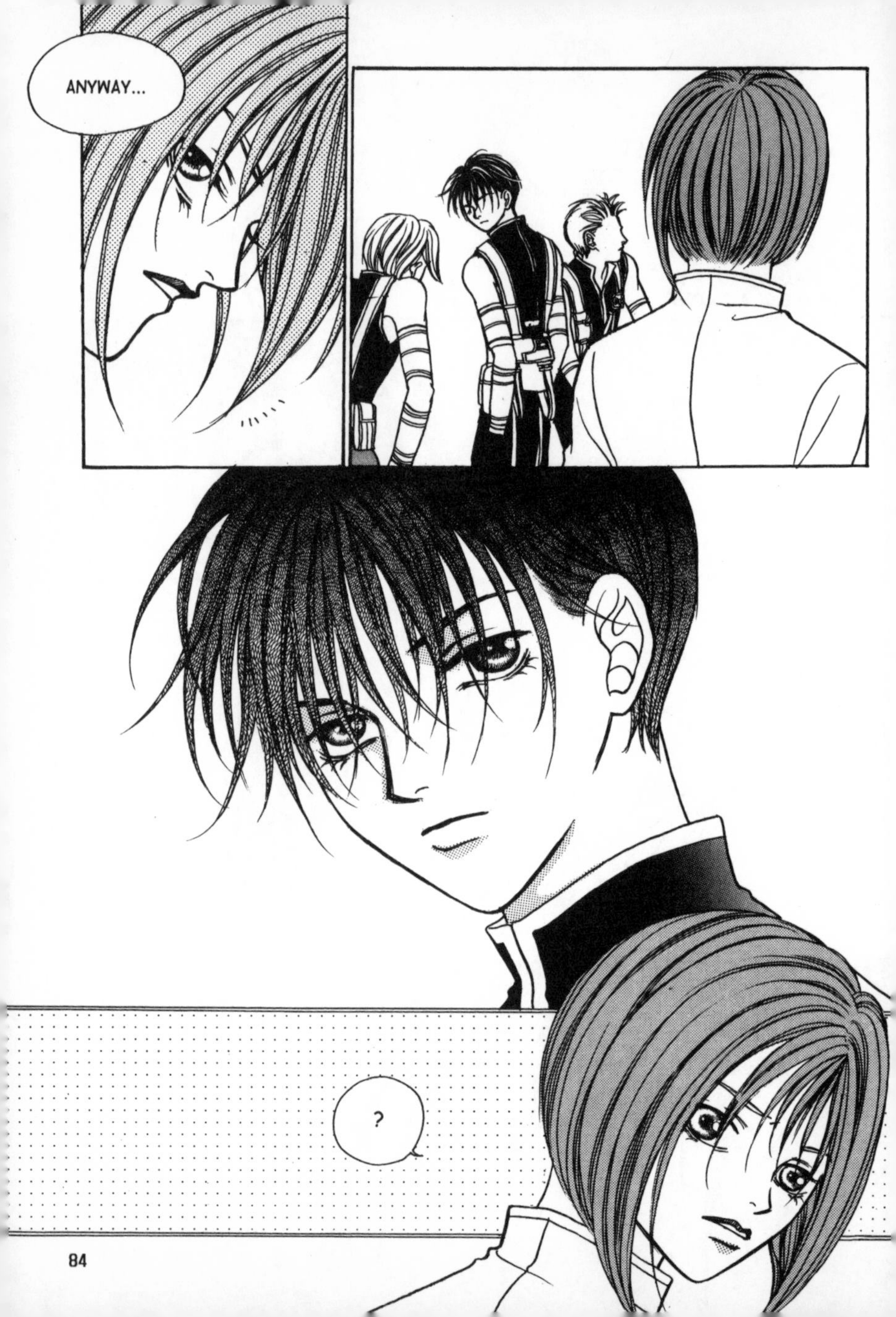
ANYWAY...
?

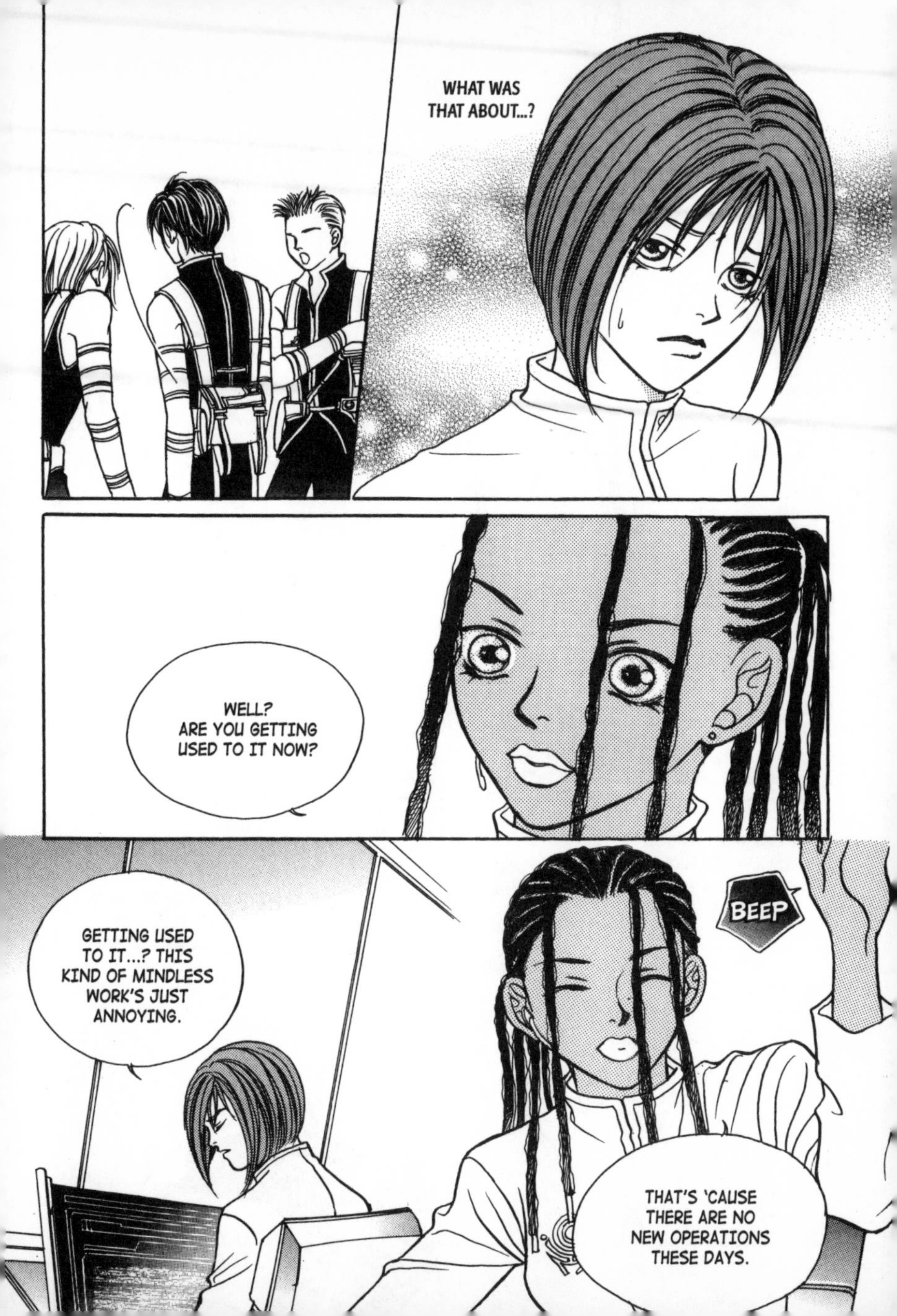
WHAT WAS THAT ABOUT...?
WELL? ARE YOU GETTING USED TO IT NOW?
GETTING USED TO IT...? THIS KIND OF MINDLESS WORK'S JUST ANNOYING.
BEEP
THAT'S 'CAUSE THERE ARE NO NEW OPERATIONS THESE DAYS.

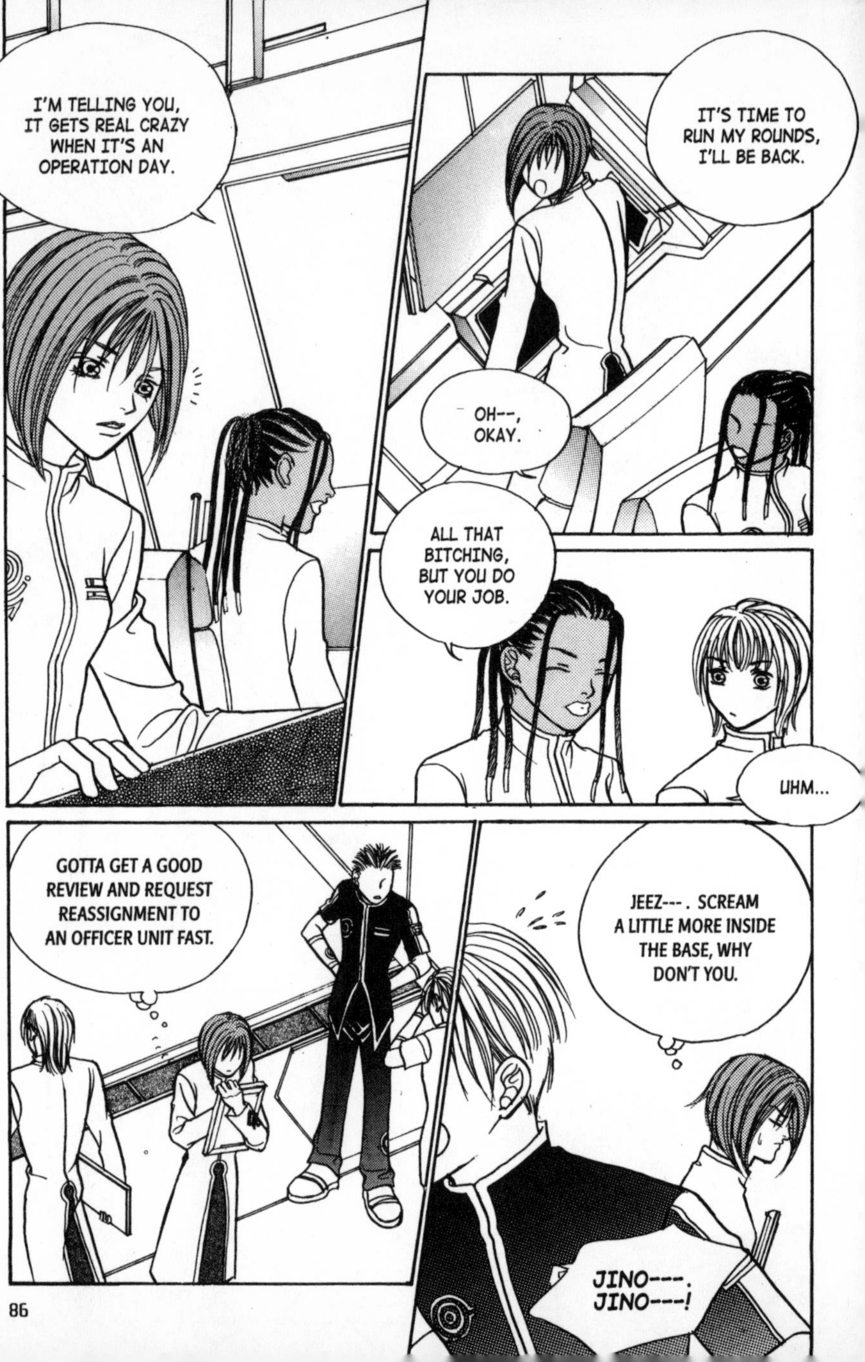
I'M TELLING YOU, IT GETS REAL CRAZY WHEN IT'S AN OPERATION DAY.
IT'S TIME TO RUN MY ROUNDS, I'LL BE BACK.
OH--, OKAY.
ALL THAT BITCHING, BUT YOU DO YOUR JOB.
UHM...
GOTTA GET A GOOD REVIEW AND REQUEST REASSIGNMENT TO AN OFFICER UNIT FAST.
JEEZ---. SCREAM A LITTLE MORE INSIDE THE BASE, WHY DON'T YOU.
JINO---. JINO---!

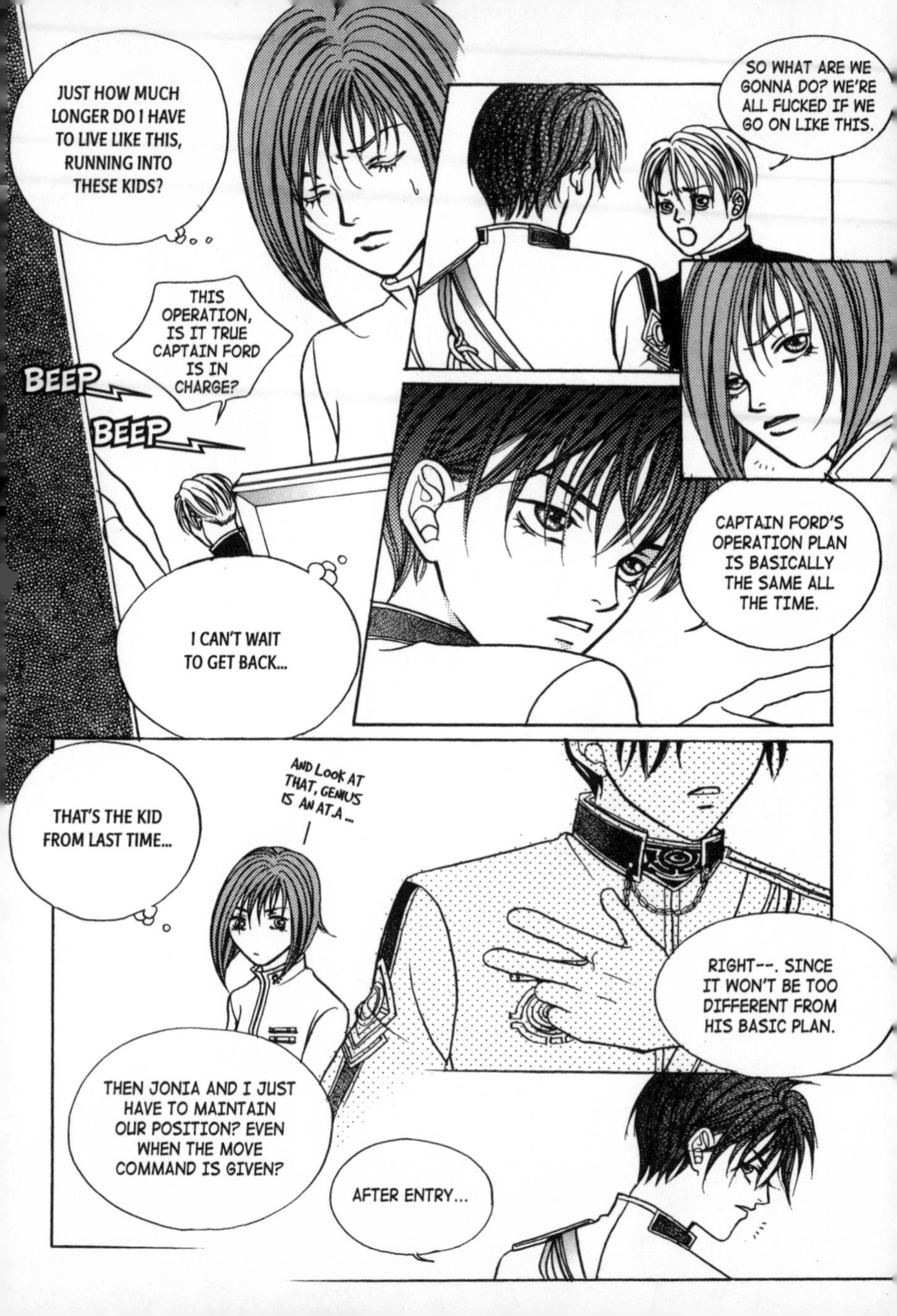
JUST HOW MUCH LONGER DO I HAVE TO LIVE LIKE THIS, RUNNING INTO THESE KIDS?
THIS OPERATION, IS IT TRUE CAPTAIN FORD IS IN CHARGE?
BEEP
BEEP
I CAN'T WAIT TO GET BACK...
SO WHAT ARE WE GONNA DO? WE'RE ALL FUCKED IF WE GO ON LIKE THIS.
CAPTAIN FORD'S OPERATION PLAN IS BASICALLY THE SAME ALL THE TIME.
THAT'S THE KID FROM LAST TIME...
AND LOOK AT THAT, GENIUS IS AN AT.A ...
RIGHT--. SINCE IT WON'T BE TOO DIFFERENT FROM HIS BASIC PLAN.
THEN JONIA AND I JUST HAVE TO MAINTAIN OUR POSITION? EVEN WHEN THE MOVE COMMAND IS GIVEN?
AFTER ENTRY...

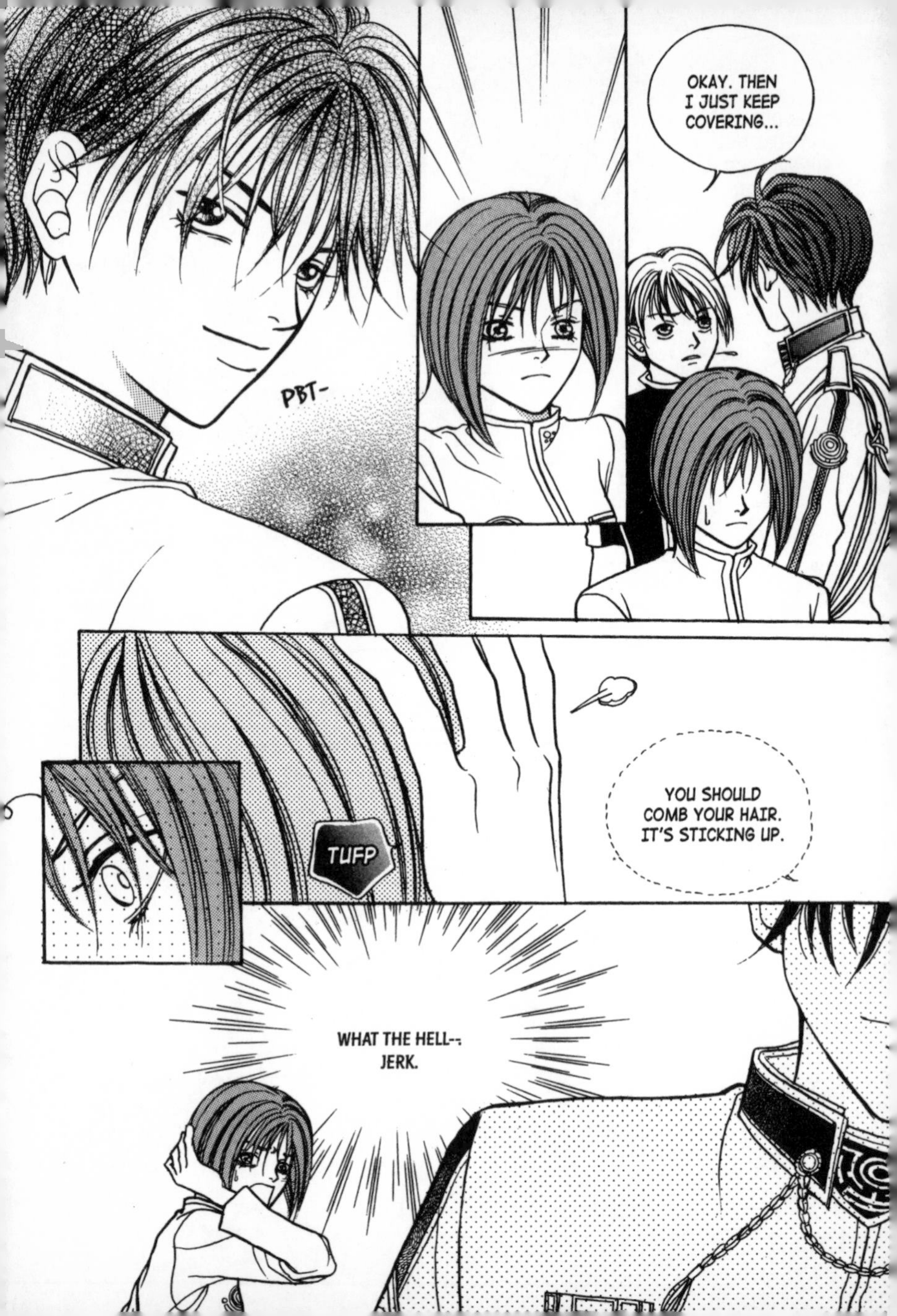
PBT-
OKAY. THEN I JUST KEEP COVERING...
TUFP
YOU SHOULD COMB YOUR HAIR. IT'S STICKING UP.
WHAT THE HELL--: JERK.

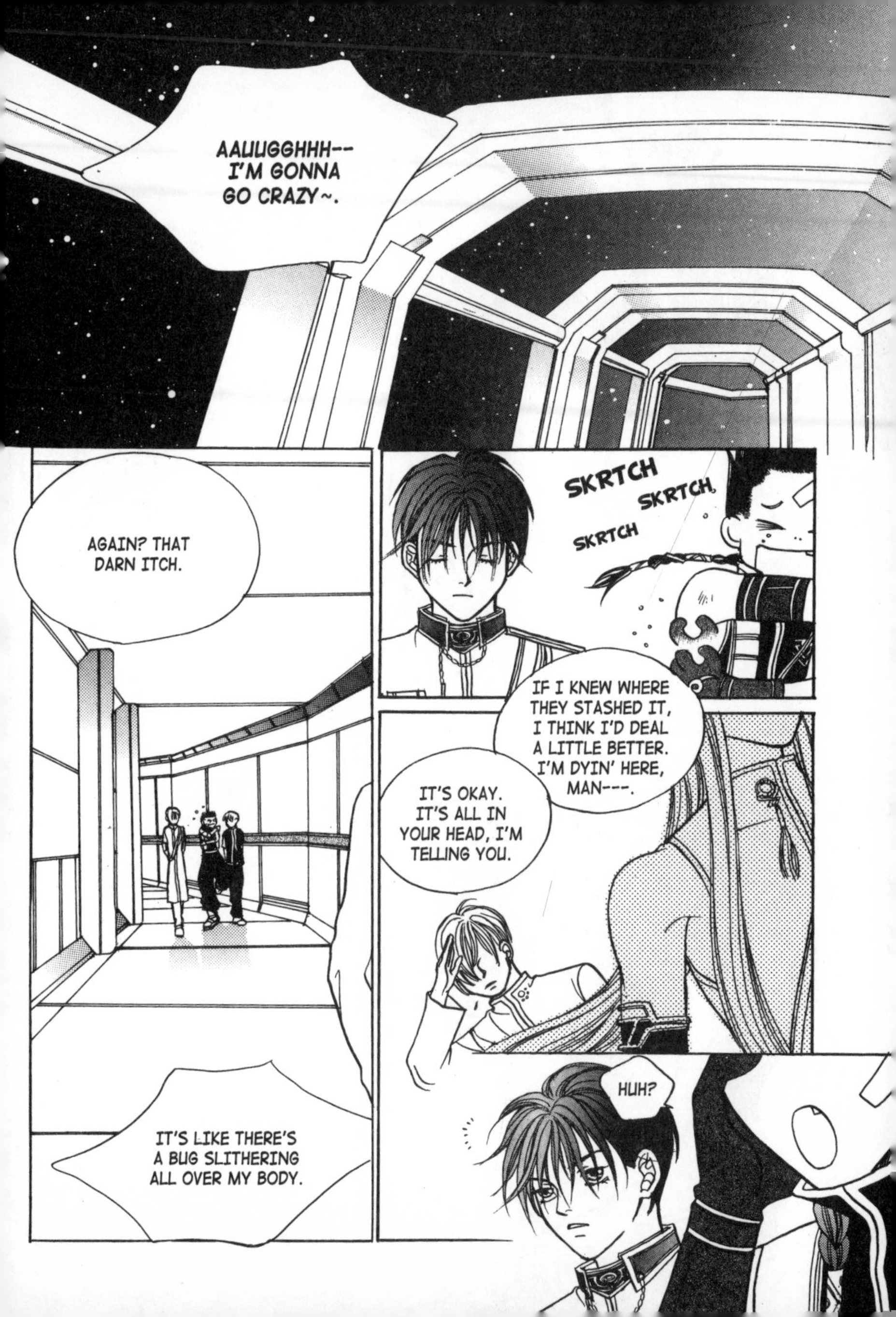
AAUUGGHHH-- I'M GONNA GO CRAZY~.
AGAIN? THAT DARN ITCH.
IT'S LIKE THERE'S A BUG SLITHERING ALL OVER MY BODY.
SKRTCH
SKRTCH
SKRTCH
IF I KNEW WHERE THEY STASHED IT, I THINK I'D DEAL A LITTLE BETTER. I'M DYIN' HERE, MAN---.
IT'S OKAY. IT'S ALL IN YOUR HEAD, I'M TELLING YOU.
HUH?

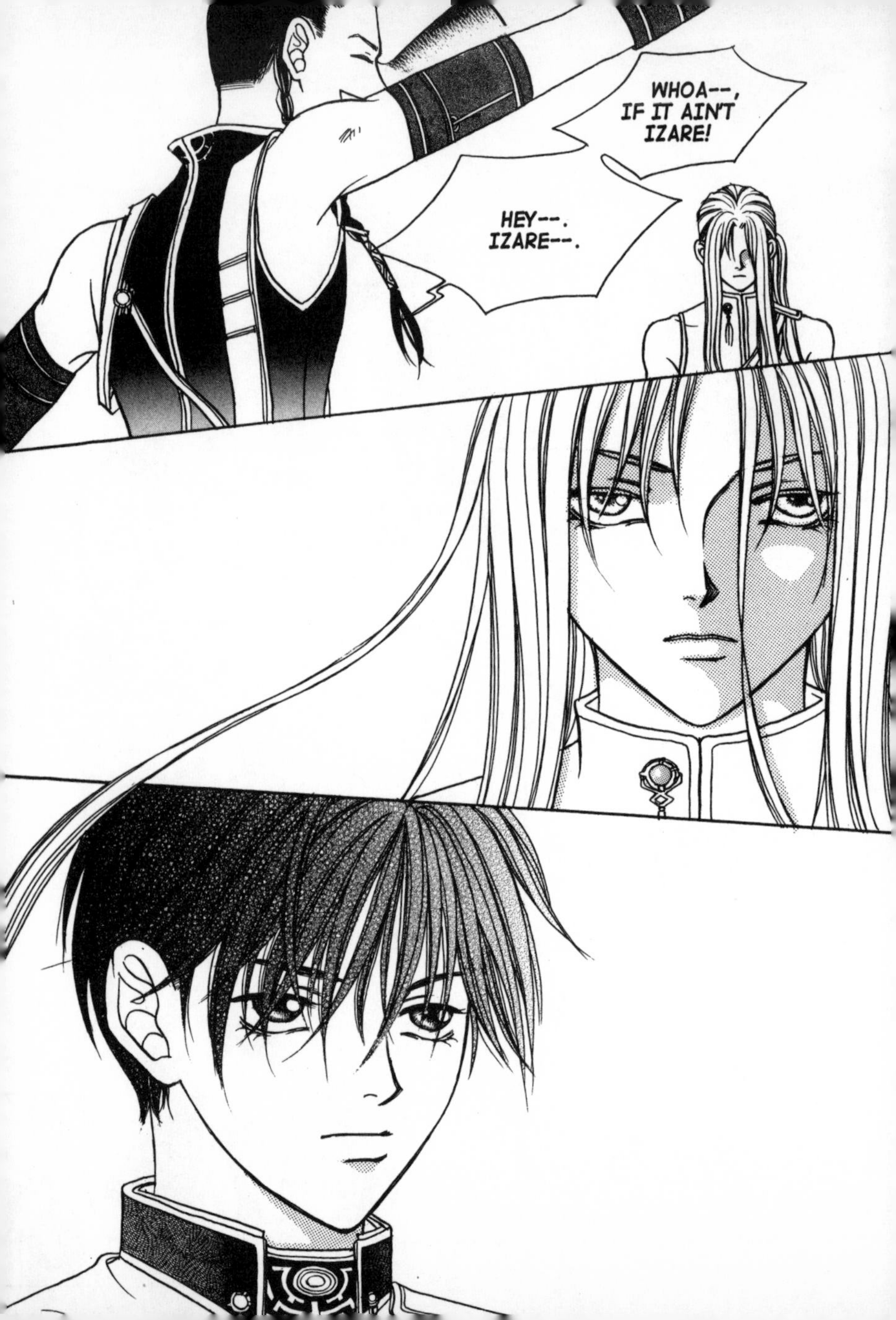
WHOA--, IF IT AIN'T IZARE!
HEY--. IZARE--.

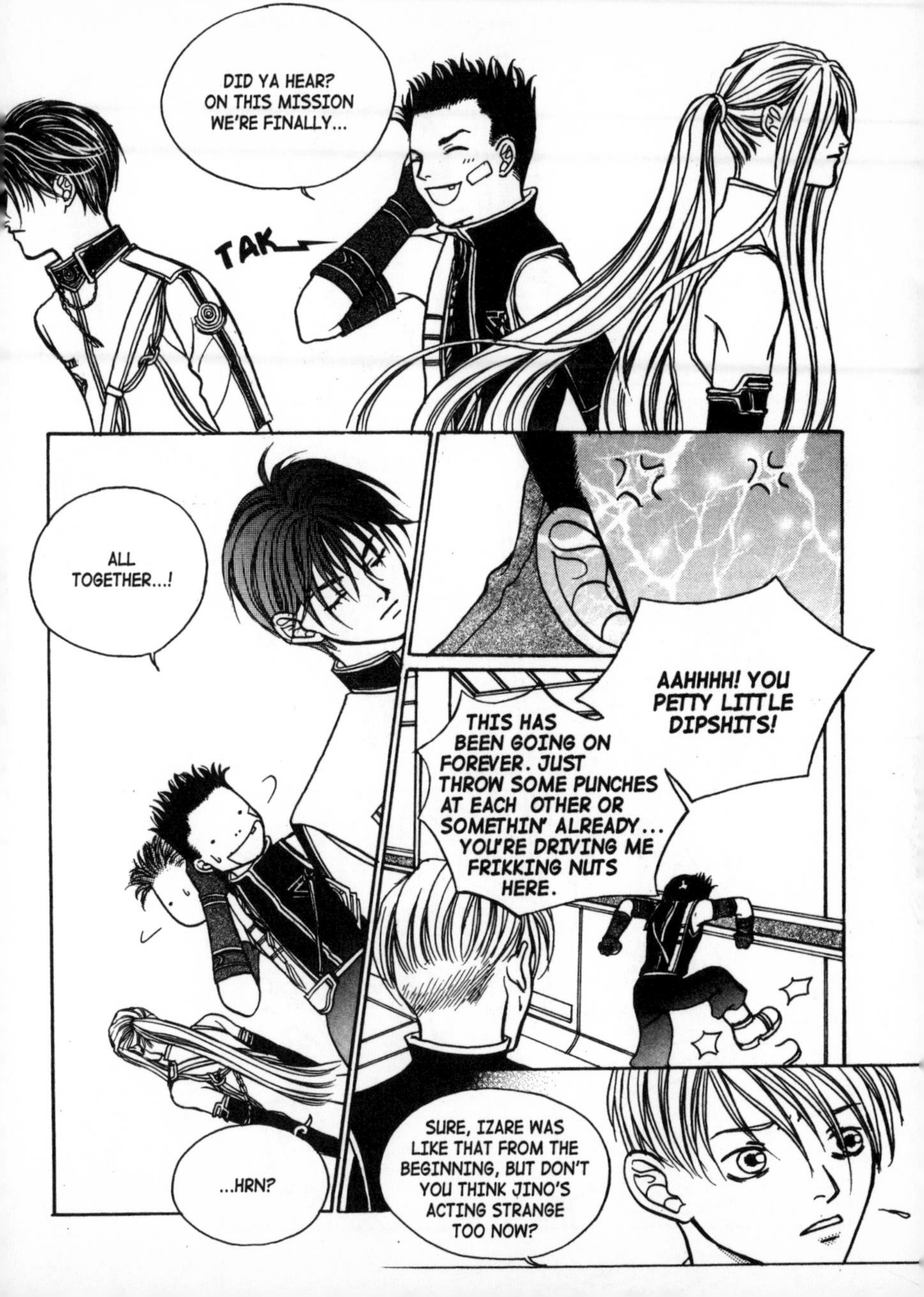

DID YA HEAR? ON THIS MISSION WE'RE FINALLY...
TAK
ALL TOGETHER...!
...HRN?
AAHHHH! YOU PETTY LITTLE DIPSHITS!
THIS HAS BEEN GOING ON FOREVER. JUST THROW SOME PUNCHES AT EACH OTHER OR SOMETHIN' ALREADY... YOU'RE DRIVING ME FRIKKING NUTS HERE.
SURE, IZARE WAS LIKE THAT FROM THE BEGINNING, BUT DON'T YOU THINK JINO'S ACTING STRANGE TOO NOW?

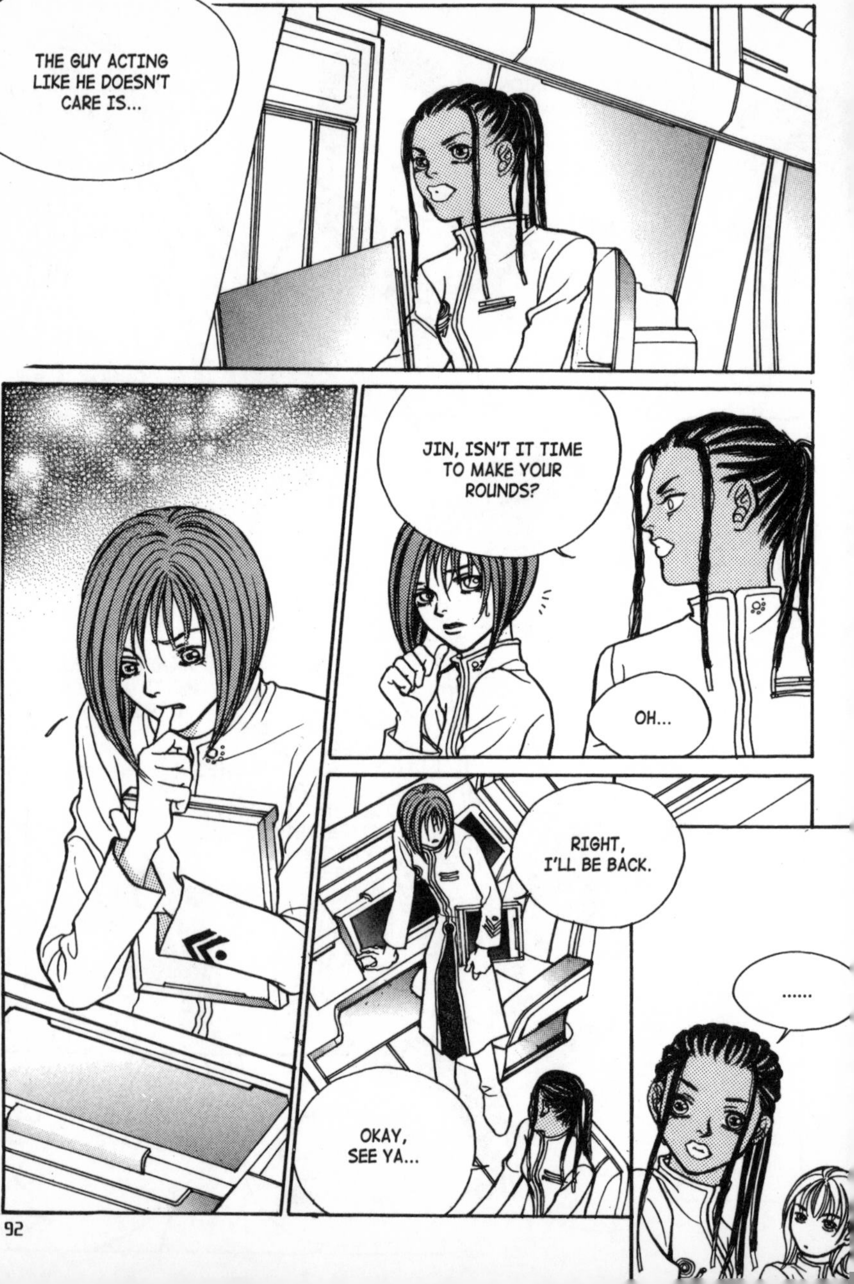
THE GUY ACTING LIKE HE DOESN'T CARE IS...
JIN, ISN'T IT TIME TO MAKE YOUR ROUNDS?
OH...
RIGHT, I'LL BE BACK.
OKAY, SEE YA...
......

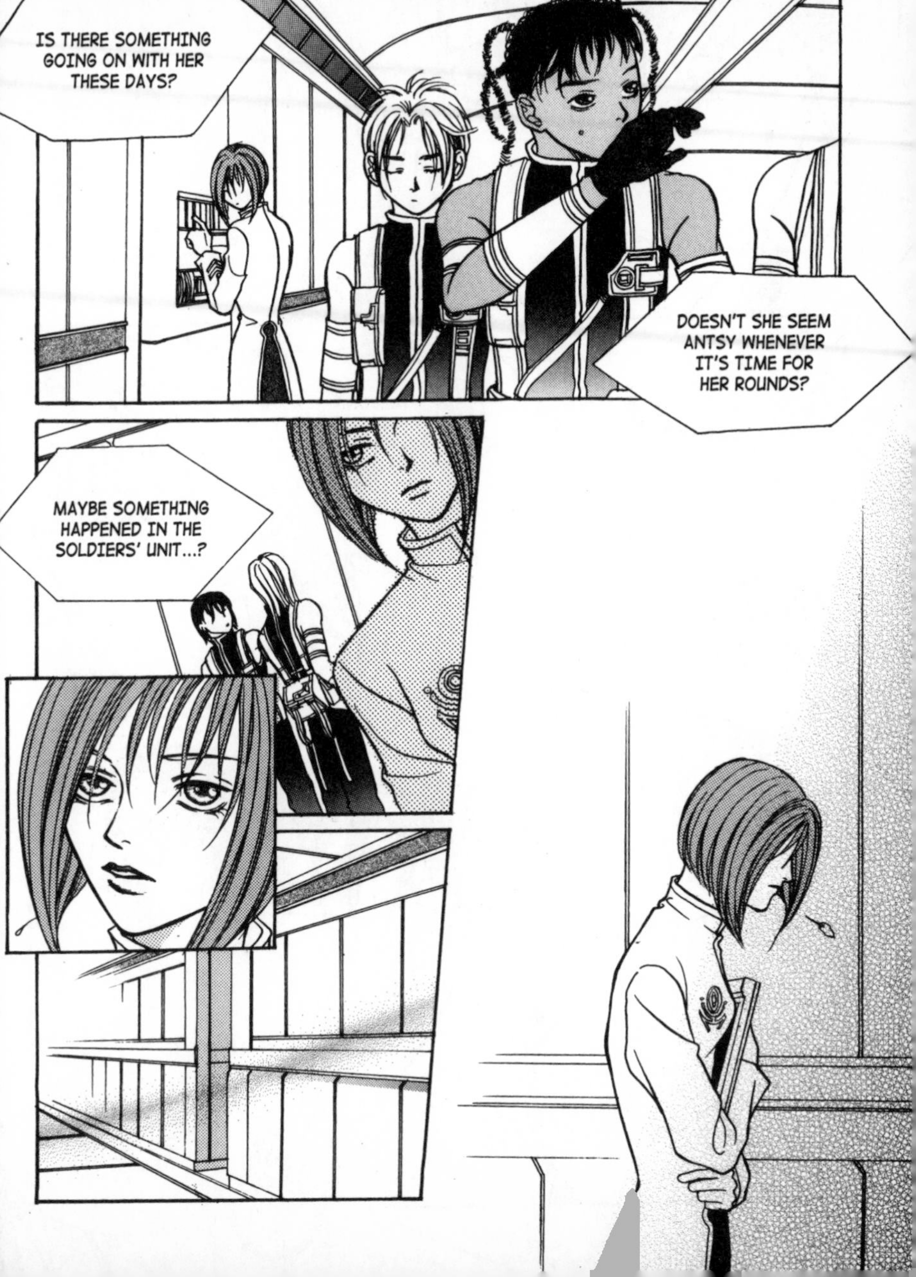
IS THERE SOMETHING GOING ON WITH HER THESE DAYS?
DOESN'T SHE SEEM ANTSY WHENEVER IT'S TIME FOR HER ROUNDS?
MAYBE SOMETHING HAPPENED IN THE SOLDIERS' UNIT...?

WHO IS IT YOU'RE AFTER SO BAD?

!

D...DON'T MAKE ME LAUGH. WHO'D BE LOOKING FOR SOMEONE LIKE--!

AHA--. WERE YOU LOOKING FOR ME BY ANY CHANCE?

THAT'S A SHAME. I MADE IT OUT HERE JUST IN TIME TO MEET YOU.

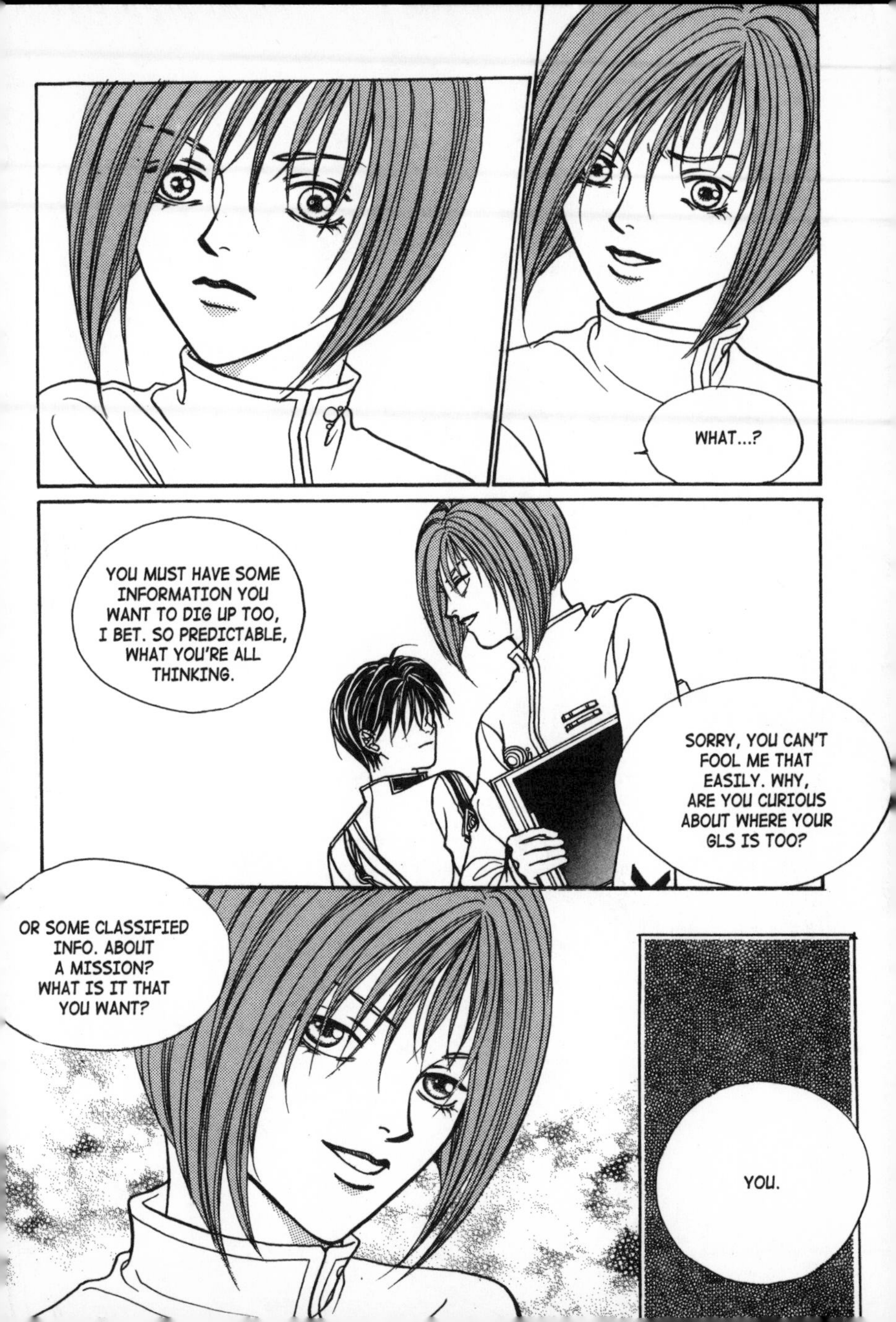
WHAT...?
YOU MUST HAVE SOME INFORMATION YOU WANT TO DIG UP TOO, I BET. SO PREDICTABLE, WHAT YOU'RE ALL THINKING.
SORRY, YOU CAN'T FOOL ME THAT EASILY. WHY, ARE YOU CURIOUS ABOUT WHERE YOUR GLS IS TOO?
OR SOME CLASSIFIED INFO. ABOUT A MISSION? WHAT IS IT THAT YOU WANT?
YOU.

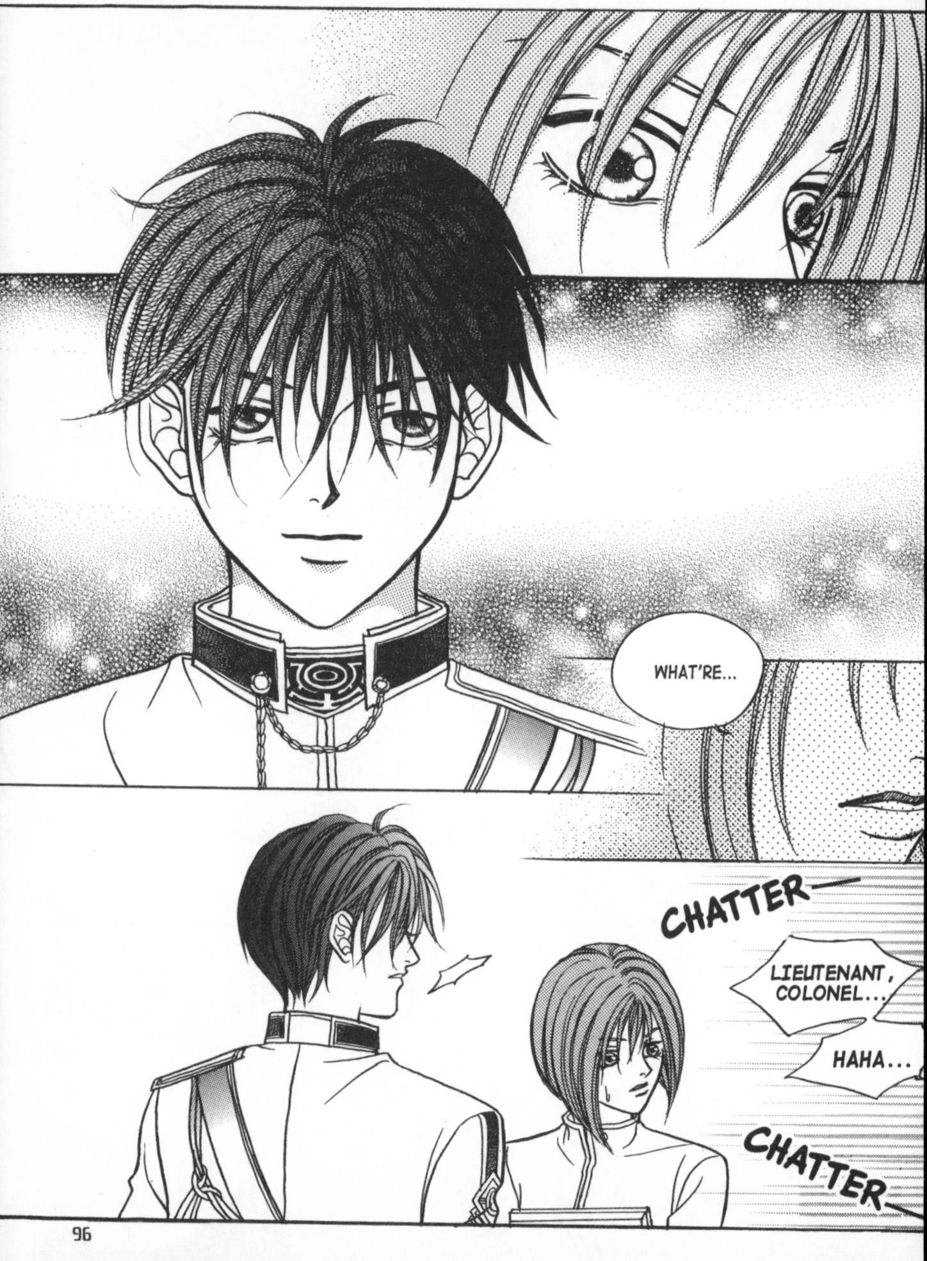
WHAT'RE...
CHATTER—
LIEUTENANT, COLONEL...
HAHA...
CHATTER—

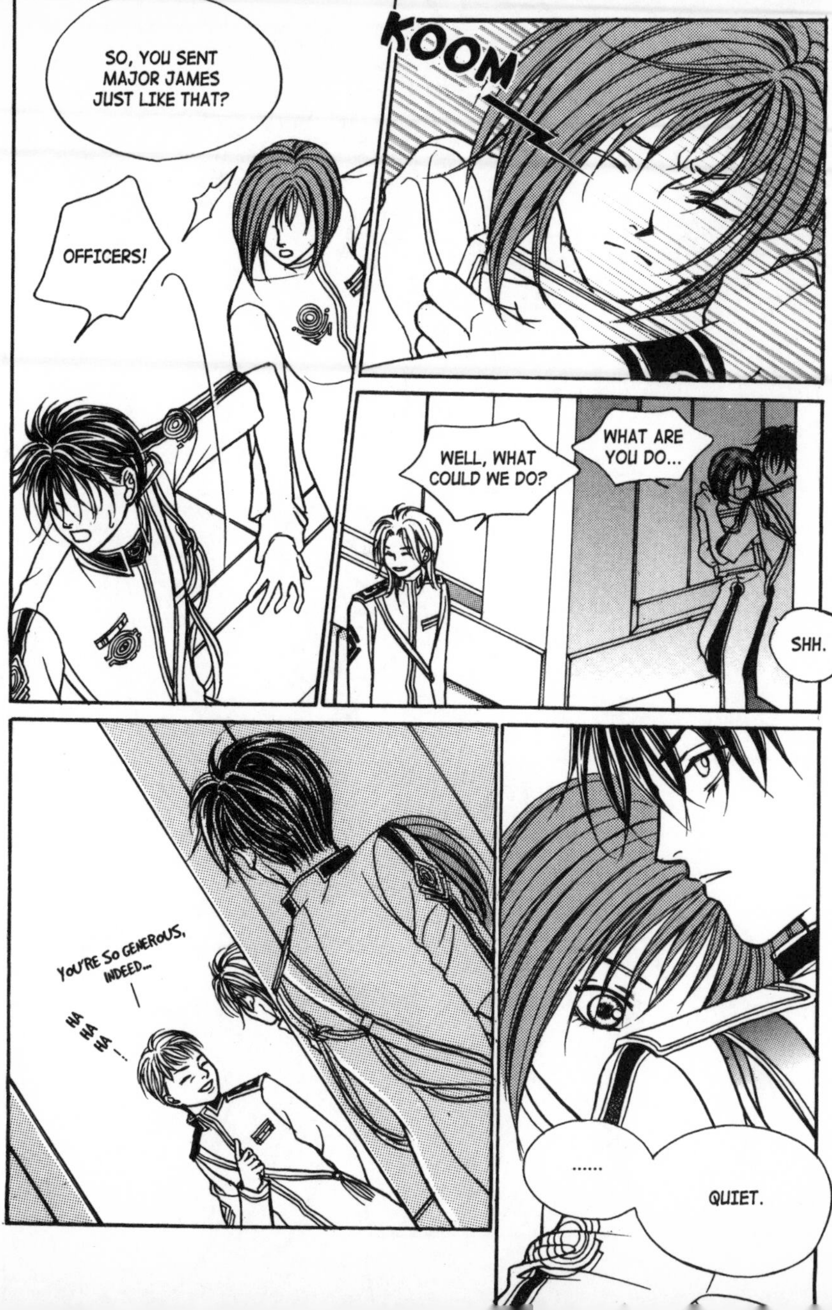
SO, YOU SENT MAJOR JAMES JUST LIKE THAT?
OFFICERS!
KOOM
WELL, WHAT COULD WE DO?
WHAT ARE YOU DO...
SHH.
YOU'RE SO GENEROUS, INDEED...
HA HA HA...
......
QUIET.

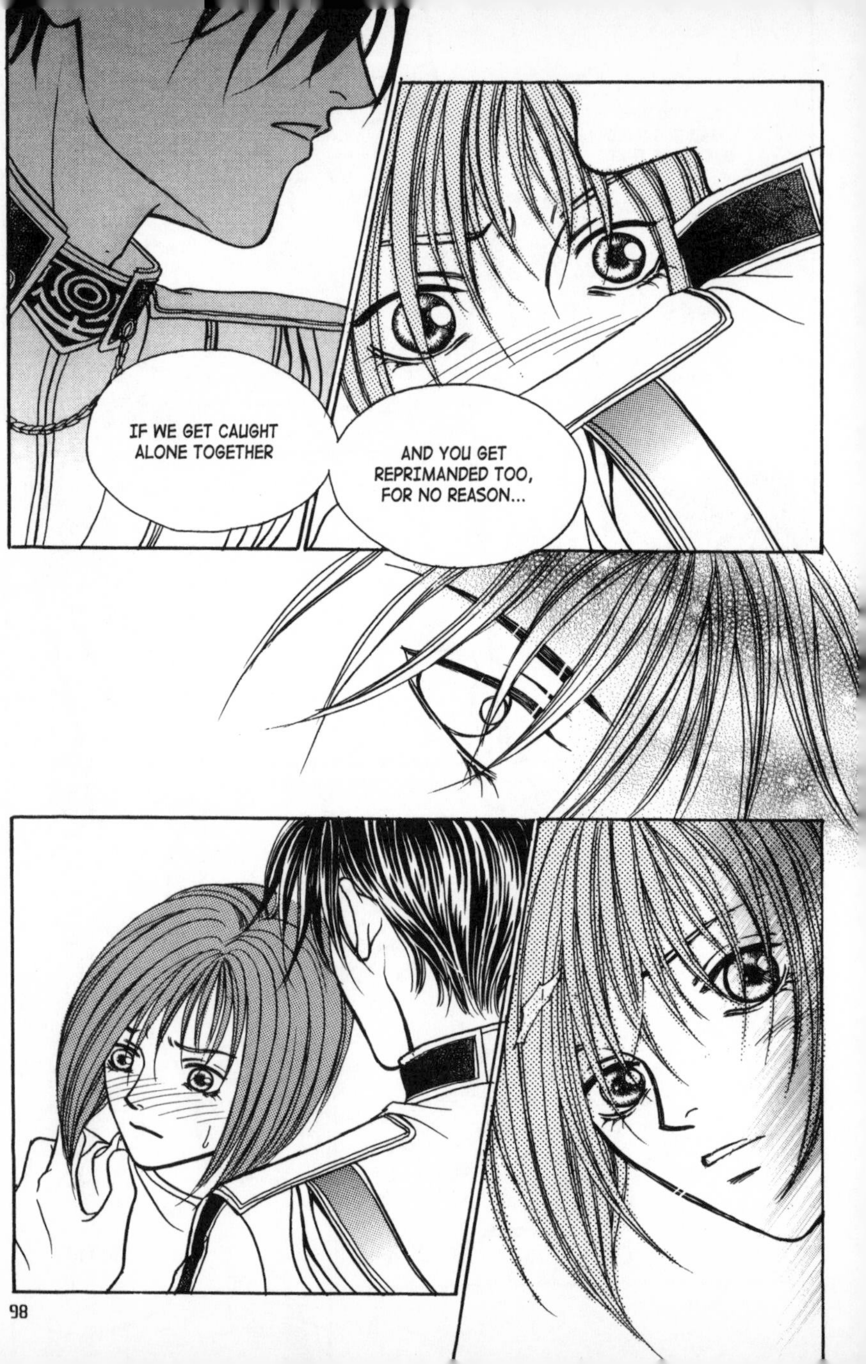
IF WE GET CAUGHT ALONE TOGETHER
AND YOU GET REPRIMANDED TOO, FOR NO REASON...

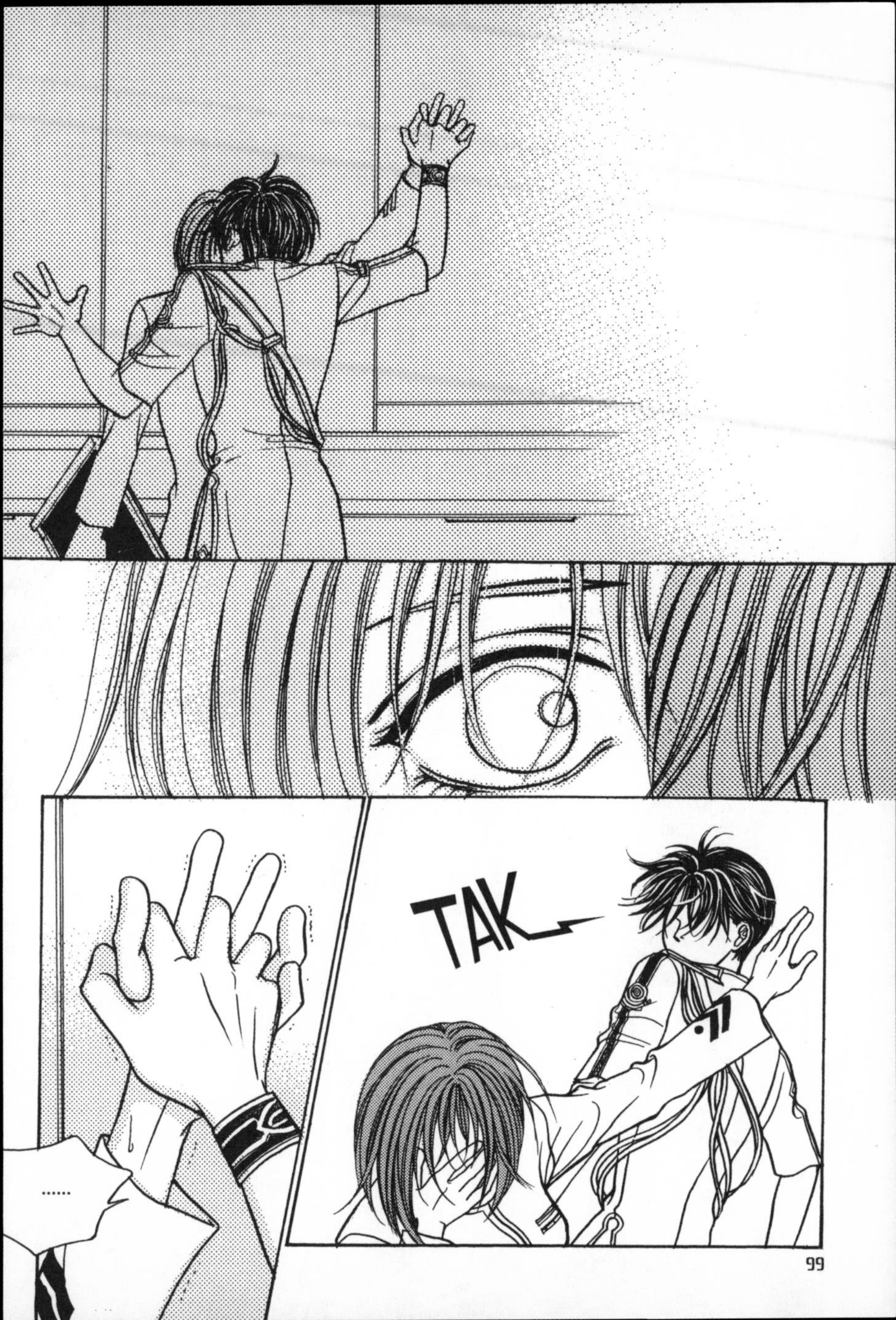
......
TAK

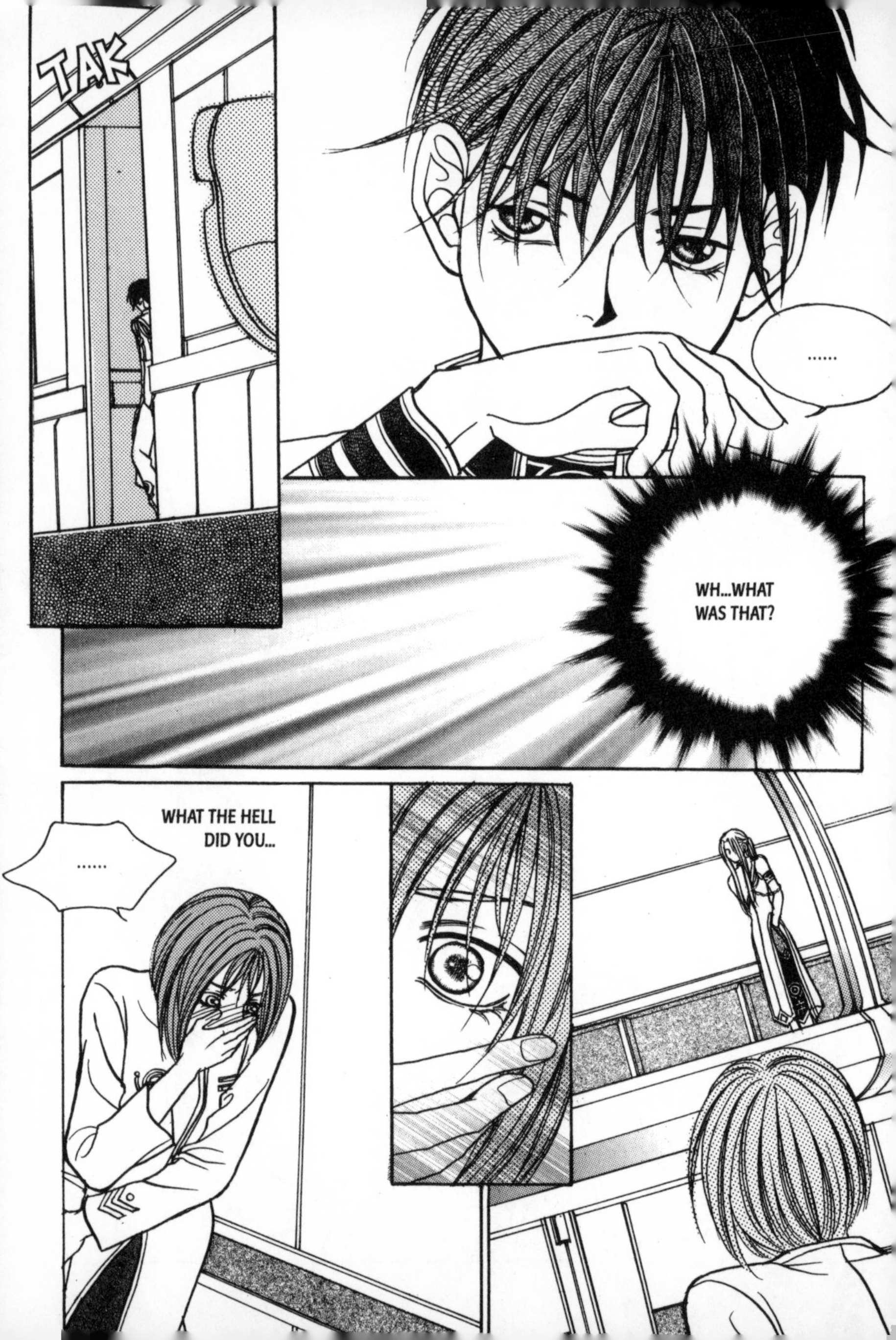
TAK
......
WH...WHAT
WAS THAT?
WHAT THE HELL
DID YOU...
......

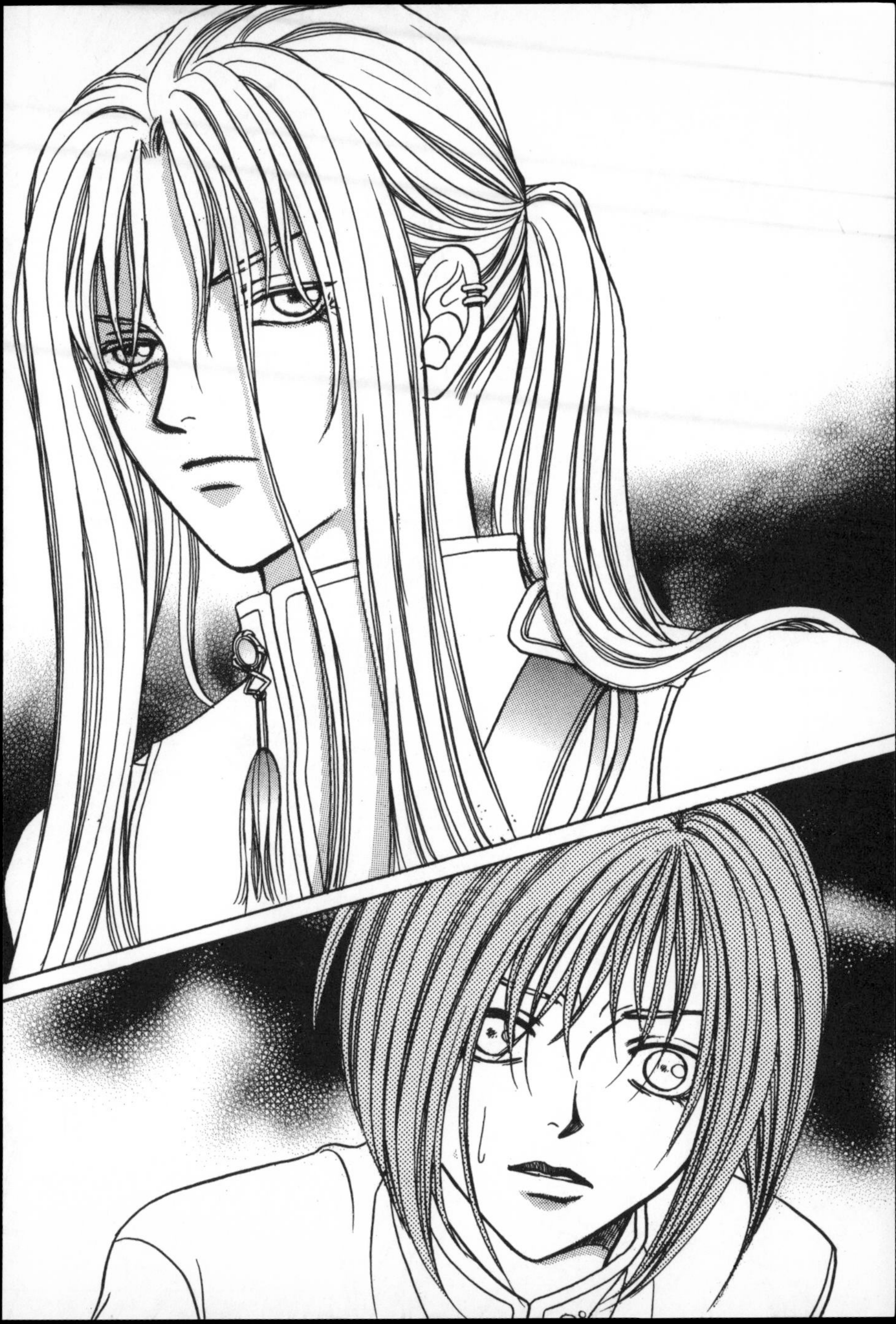

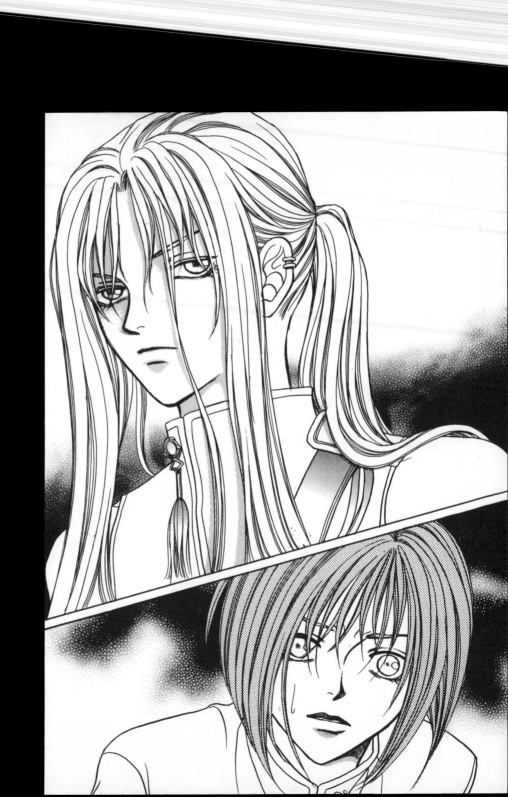

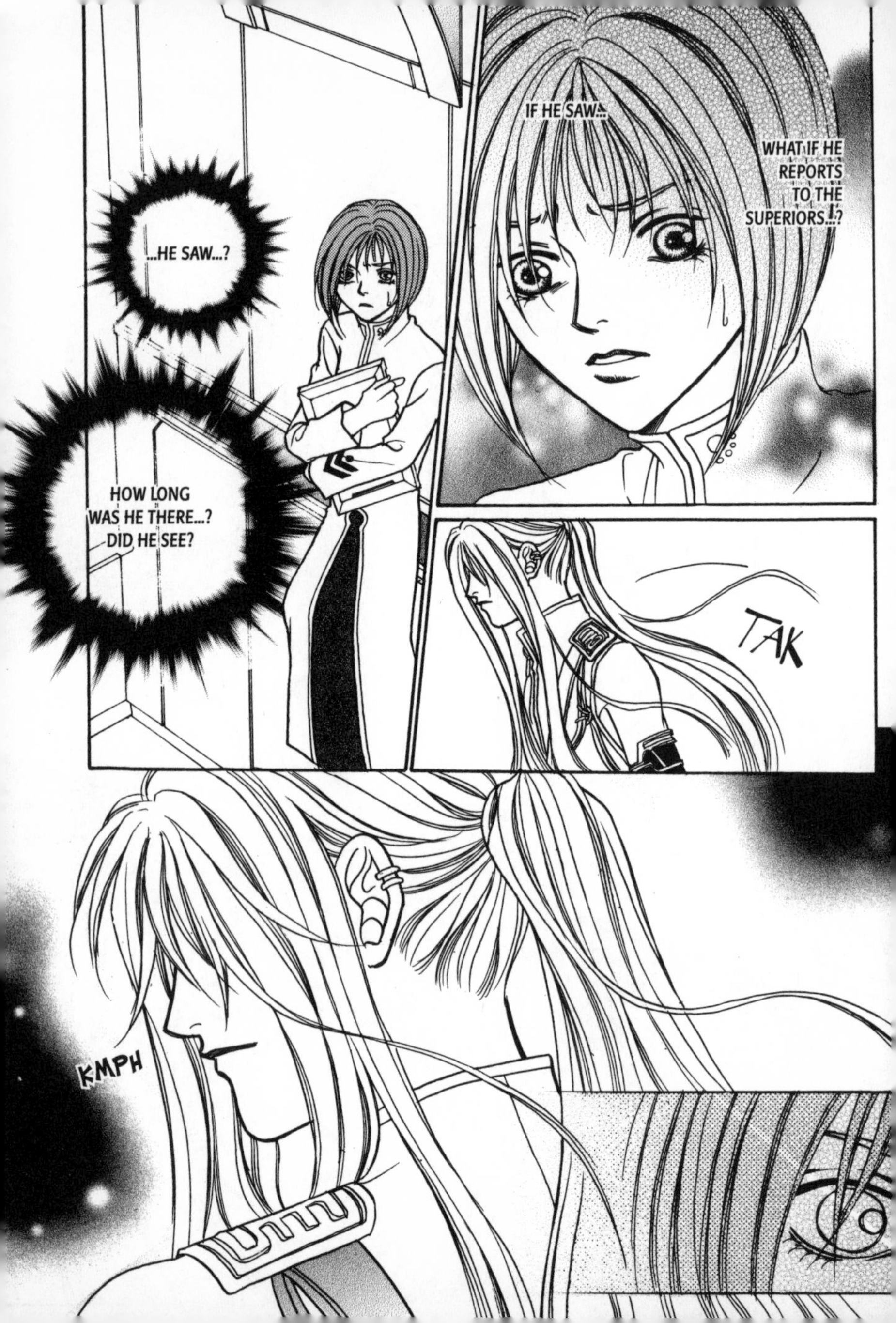
...HE SAW...?
HOW LONG WAS HE THERE...? DID HE SEE?
IF HE SAW...
WHAT IF HE REPORTS TO THE SUPERIORS...?
TAK
KMPH

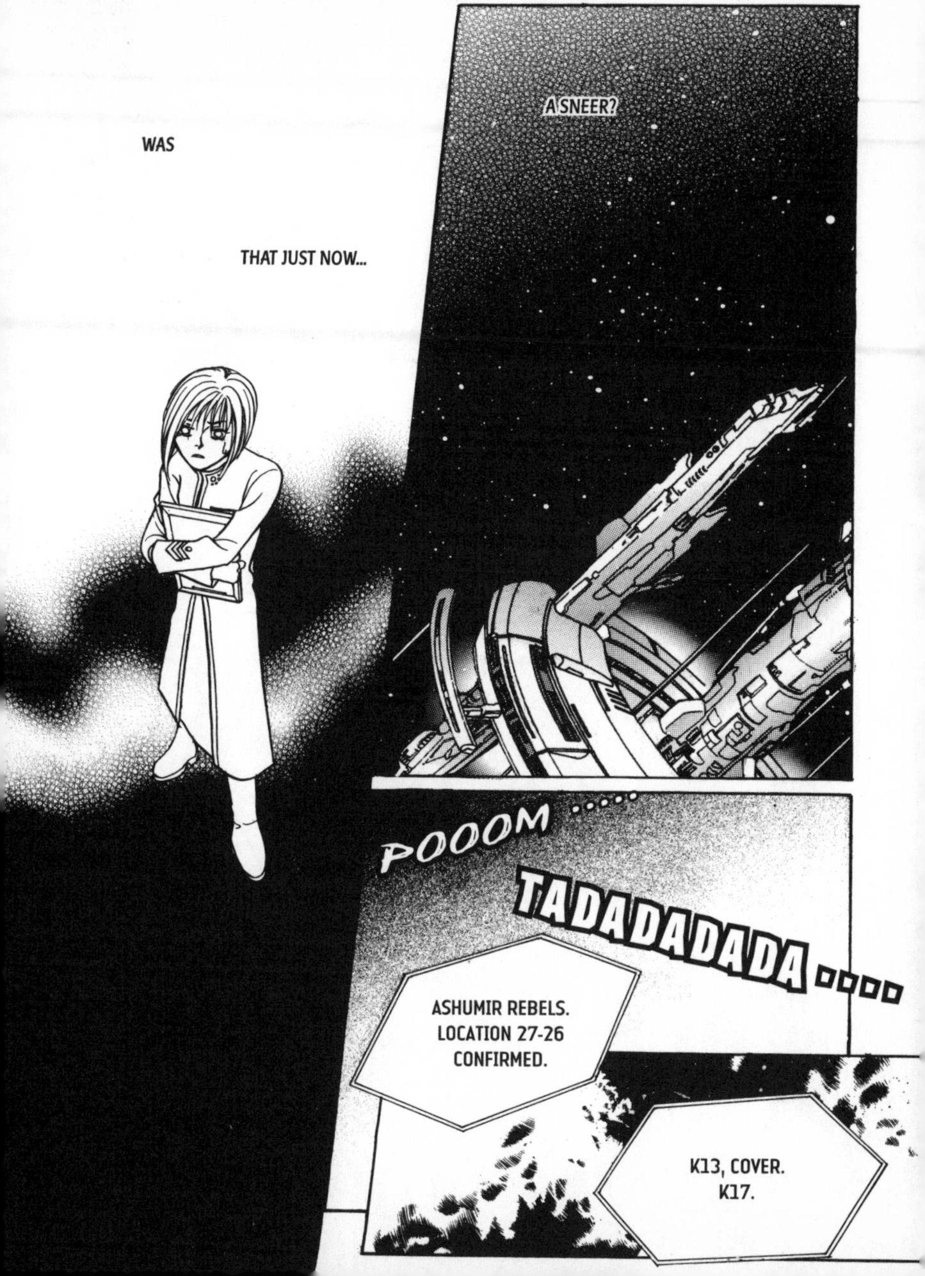
WAS
THAT JUST NOW...
A SNEER?
POOOM .....
TADADADADA ....
ASHUMIR REBELS. LOCATION 27-26 CONFIRMED.
K13, COVER. K17.

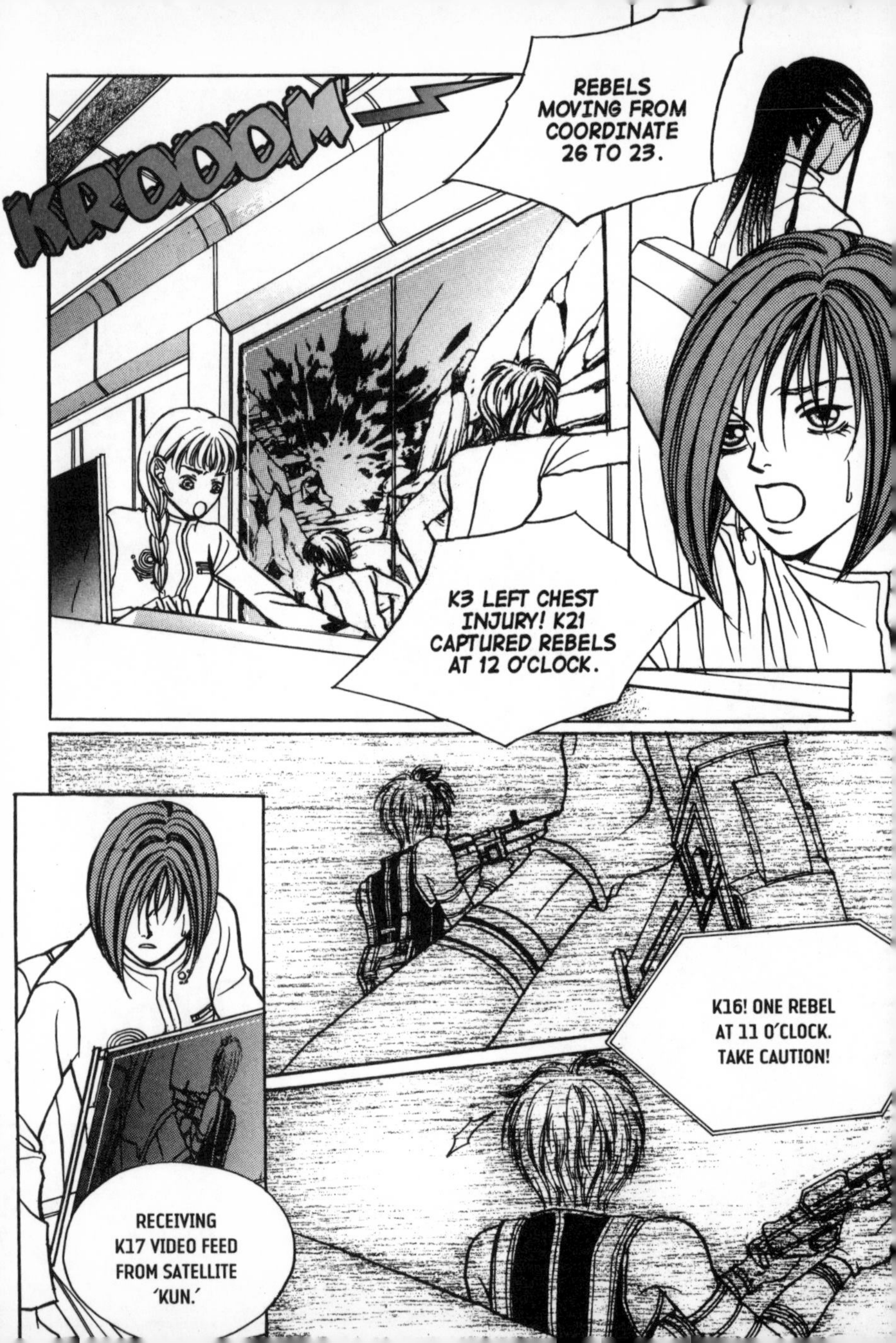
KROOOM
REBELS MOVING FROM COORDINATE 26 TO 23.
K3 LEFT CHEST INJURY! K21 CAPTURED REBELS AT 12 O'CLOCK.
RECEIVING K17 VIDEO FEED FROM SATELLITE 'KUN.'
K16! ONE REBEL AT 11 O'CLOCK. TAKE CAUTION!

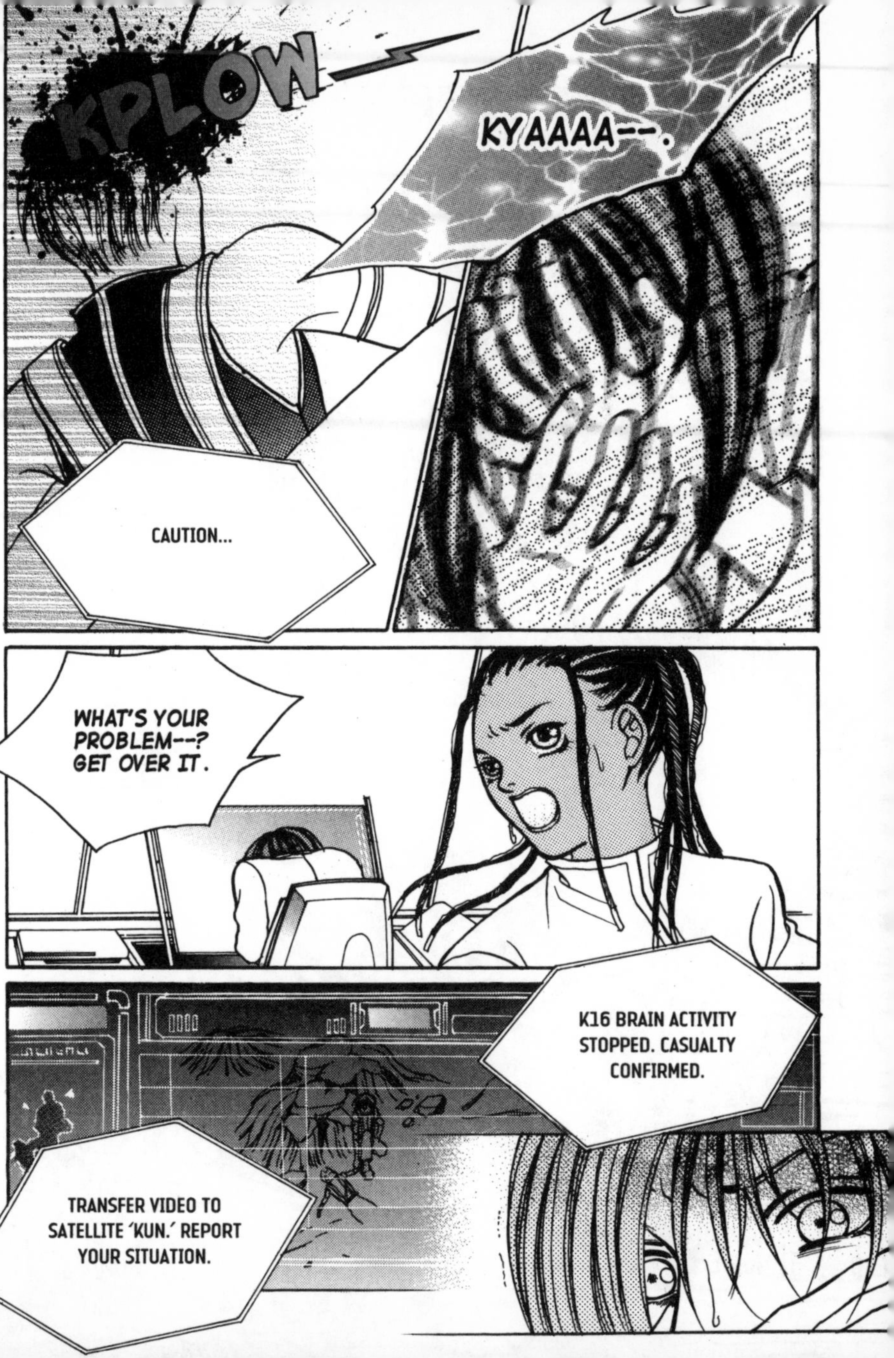
KPLOW
KYAAAA--.
CAUTION...
WHAT'S YOUR PROBLEM--? GET OVER IT.
K16 BRAIN ACTIVITY STOPPED. CASUALTY CONFIRMED.
TRANSFER VIDEO TO SATELLITE 'KUN.' REPORT YOUR SITUATION.

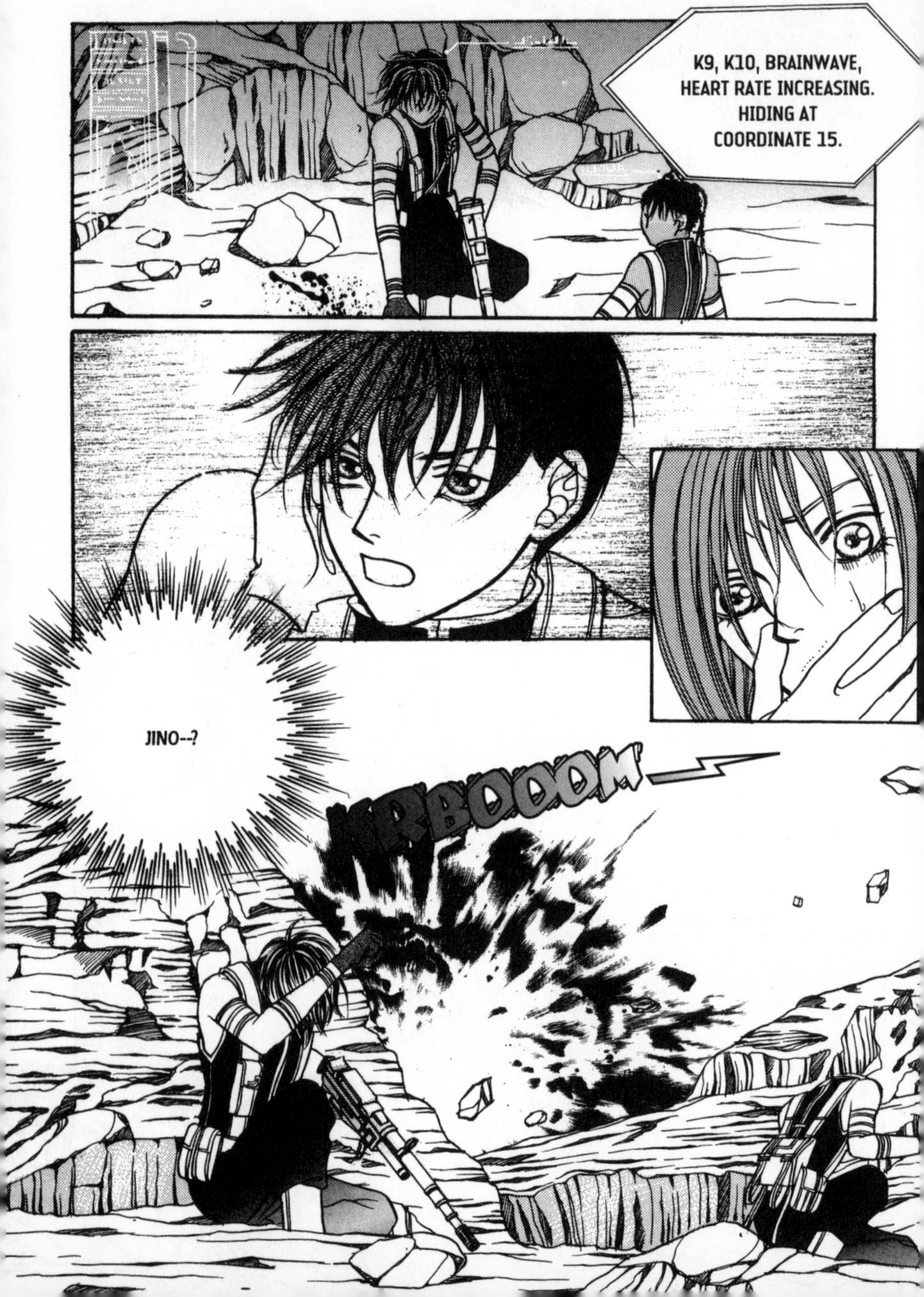
K9, K10, BRAINWAVE, HEART RATE INCREASING. HIDING AT COORDINATE 15.
JINO--?
KRBOOOM

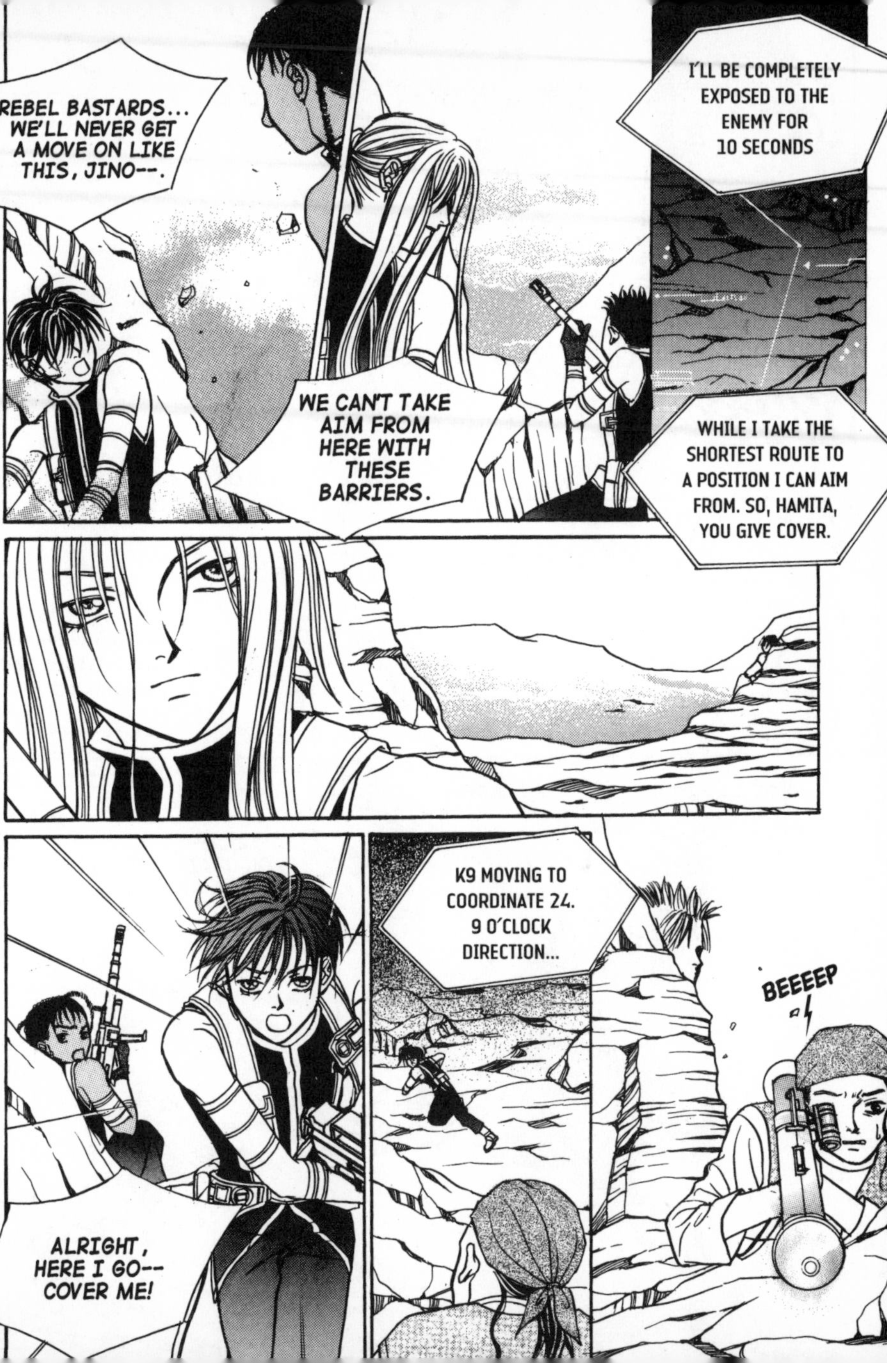
REBEL BASTARDS... WE'LL NEVER GET A MOVE ON LIKE THIS, JINO--.
WE CAN'T TAKE AIM FROM HERE WITH THESE BARRIERS.
I'LL BE COMPLETELY EXPOSED TO THE ENEMY FOR 10 SECONDS
WHILE I TAKE THE SHORTEST ROUTE TO A POSITION I CAN AIM FROM. SO, HAMITA, YOU GIVE COVER.
ALRIGHT, HERE I GO-- COVER ME!
K9 MOVING TO COORDINATE 24. 9 O'CLOCK DIRECTION...
BEEEEP

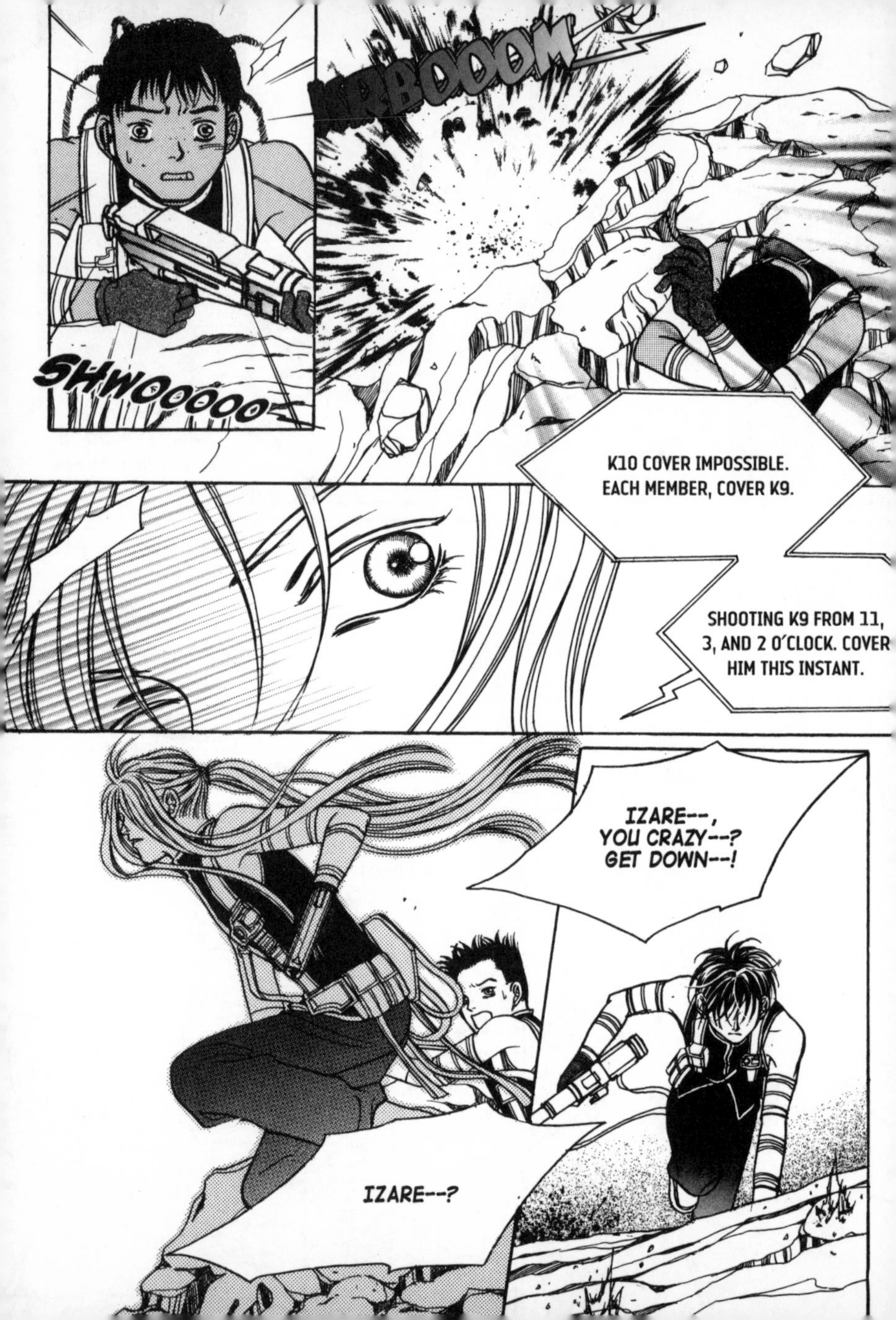
SHWOOOOO
KRBOOOM
K10 COVER IMPOSSIBLE. EACH MEMBER, COVER K9.
SHOOTING K9 FROM 11, 3, AND 2 O'CLOCK. COVER HIM THIS INSTANT.
IZARE--?
IZARE--, YOU CRAZY--? GET DOWN--!

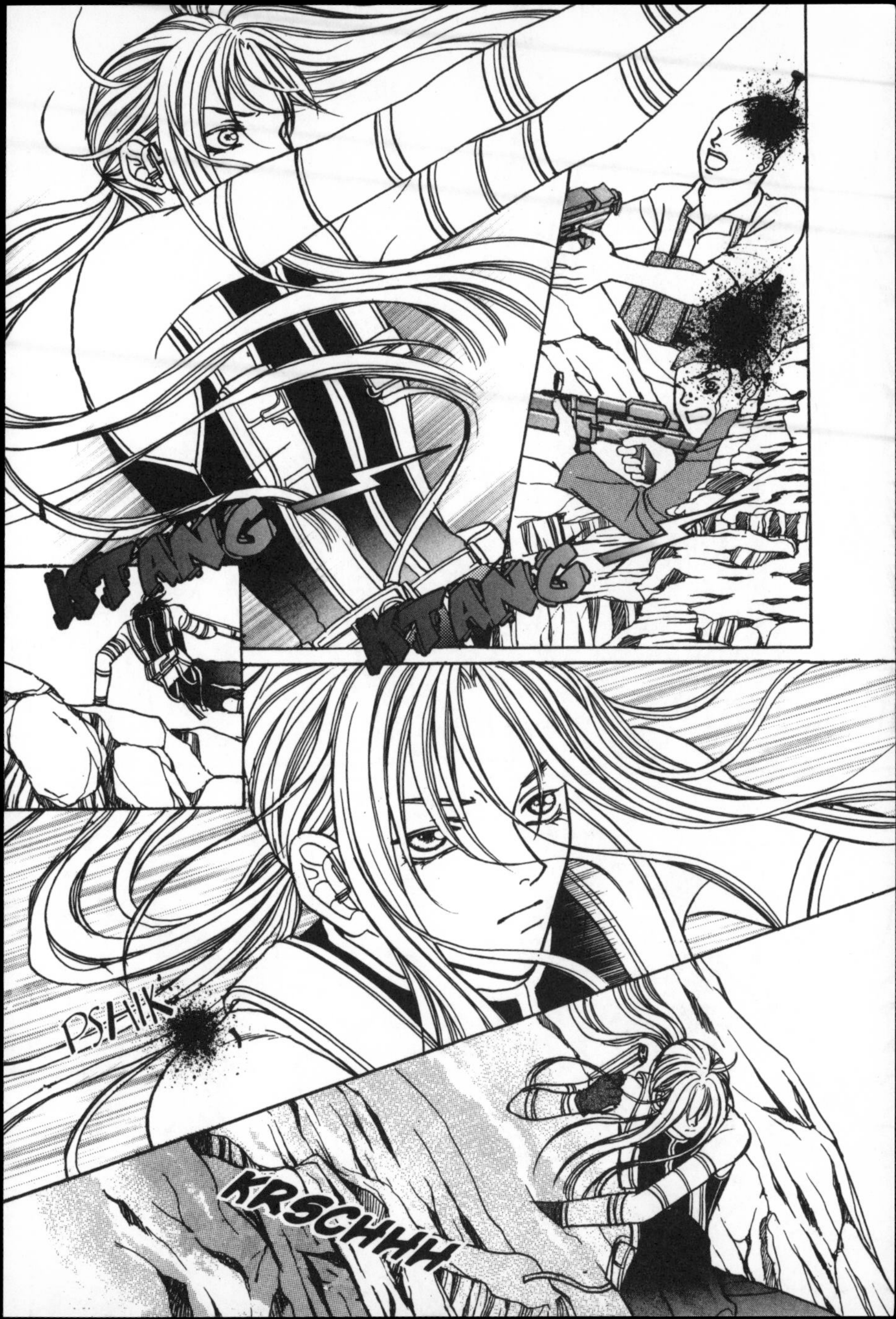
KTANG
KTANG
PSHIK
KRSCHHH

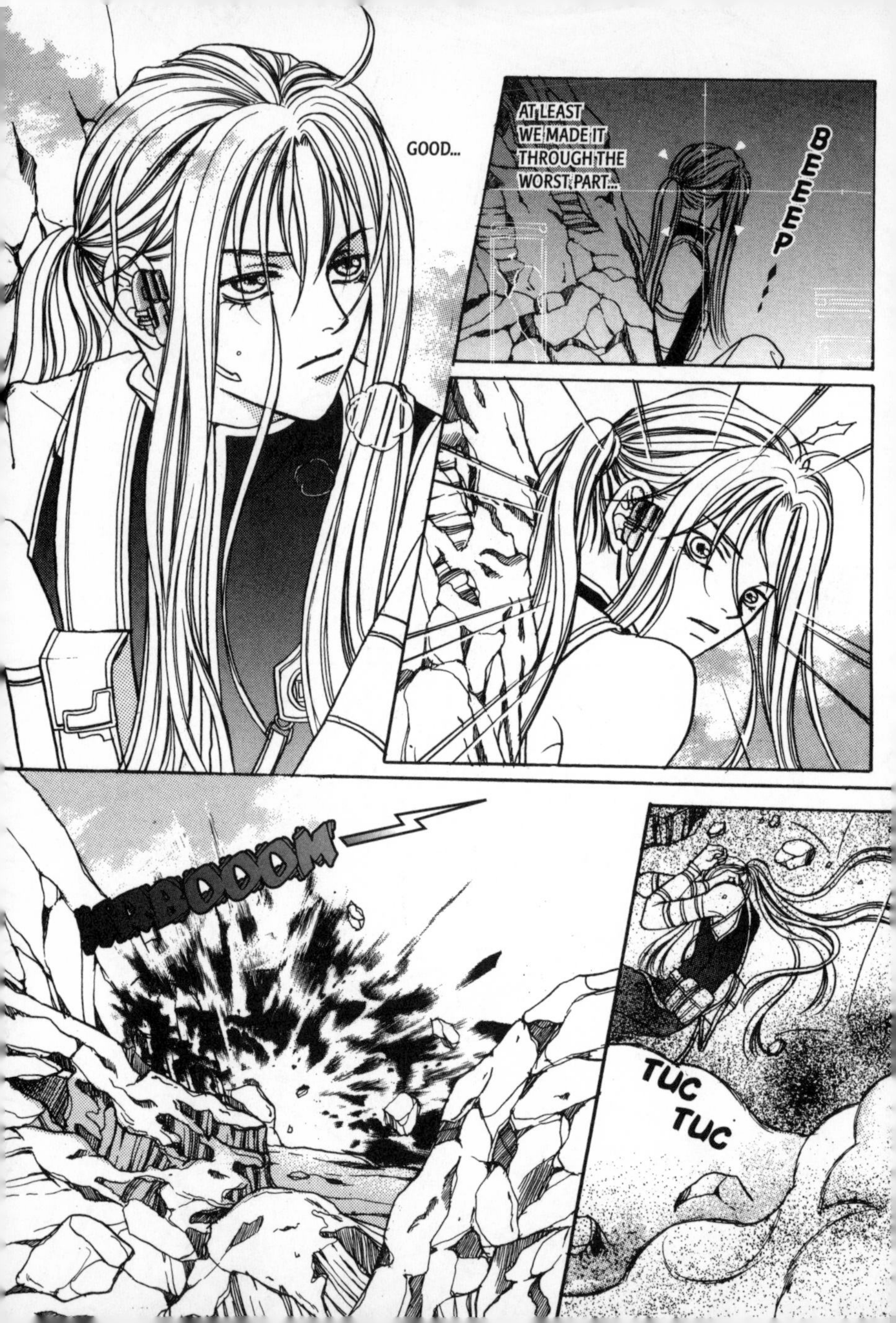
GOOD...
AT LEAST WE MADE IT THROUGH THE WORST PART...
BEEEEP...
BOOOM
TUC TUC

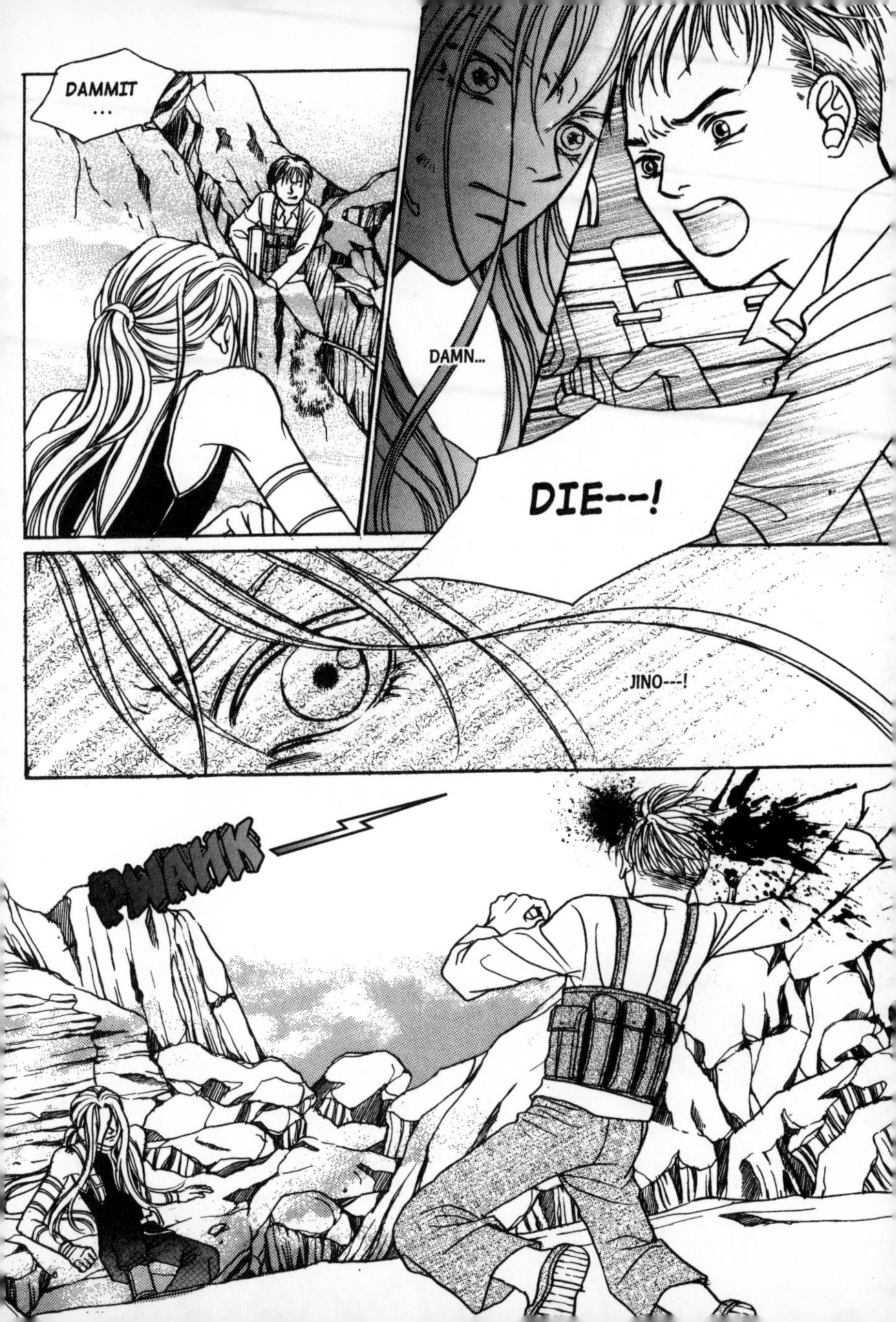
DAMMIT
...
DAMN...
DIE---!
JINO---!
PWAHK

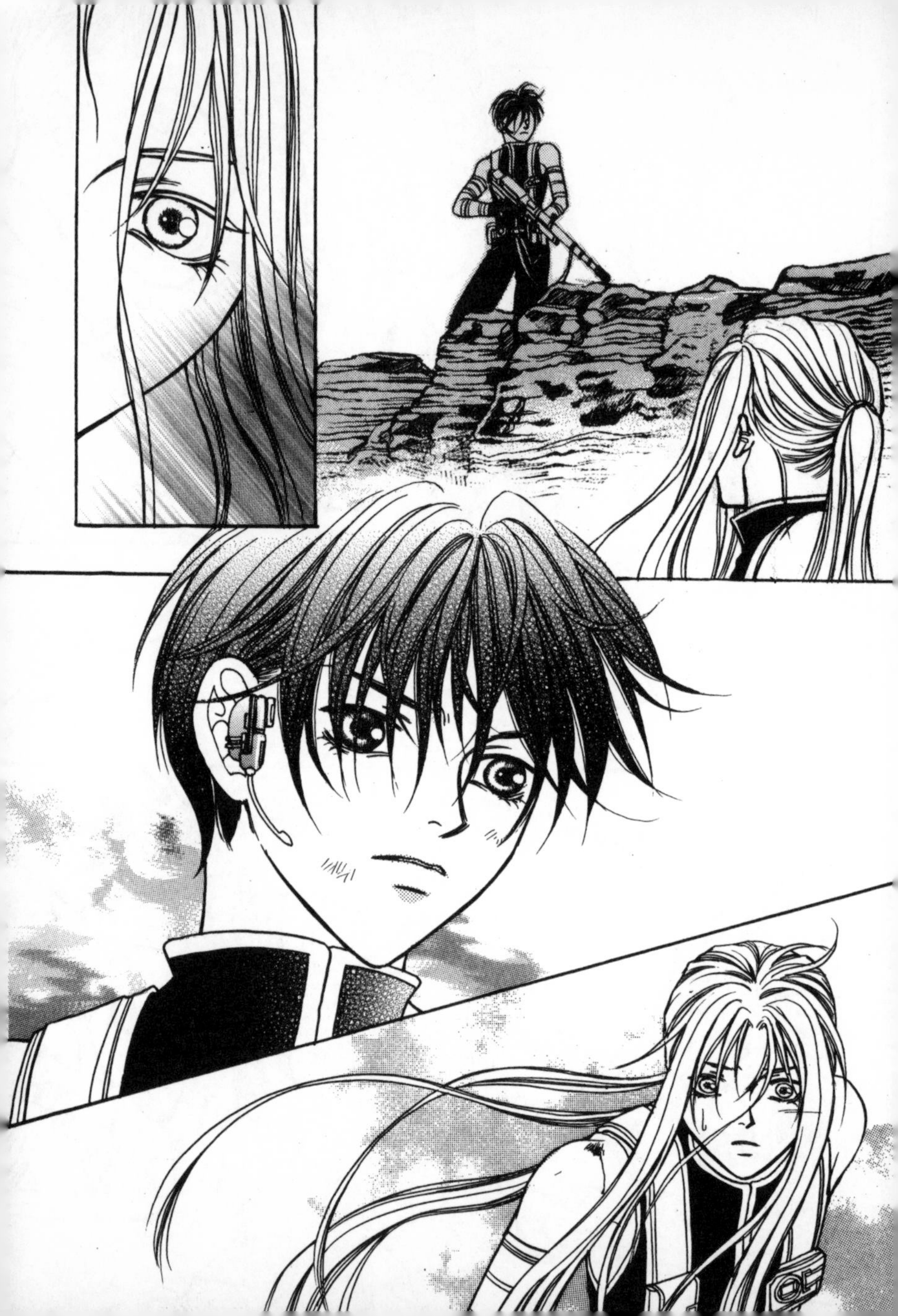

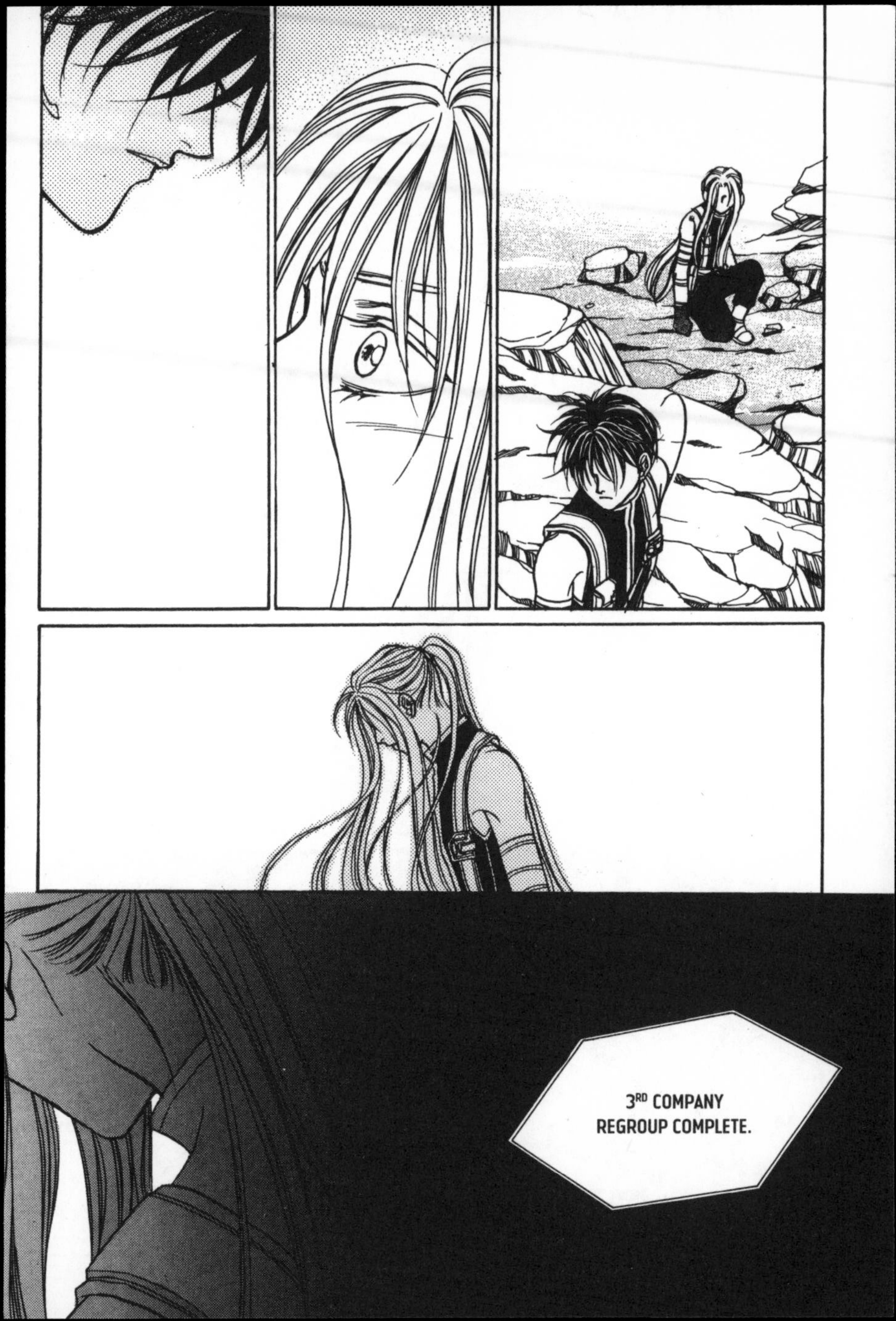
3RD COMPANY
REGROUP COMPLETE.

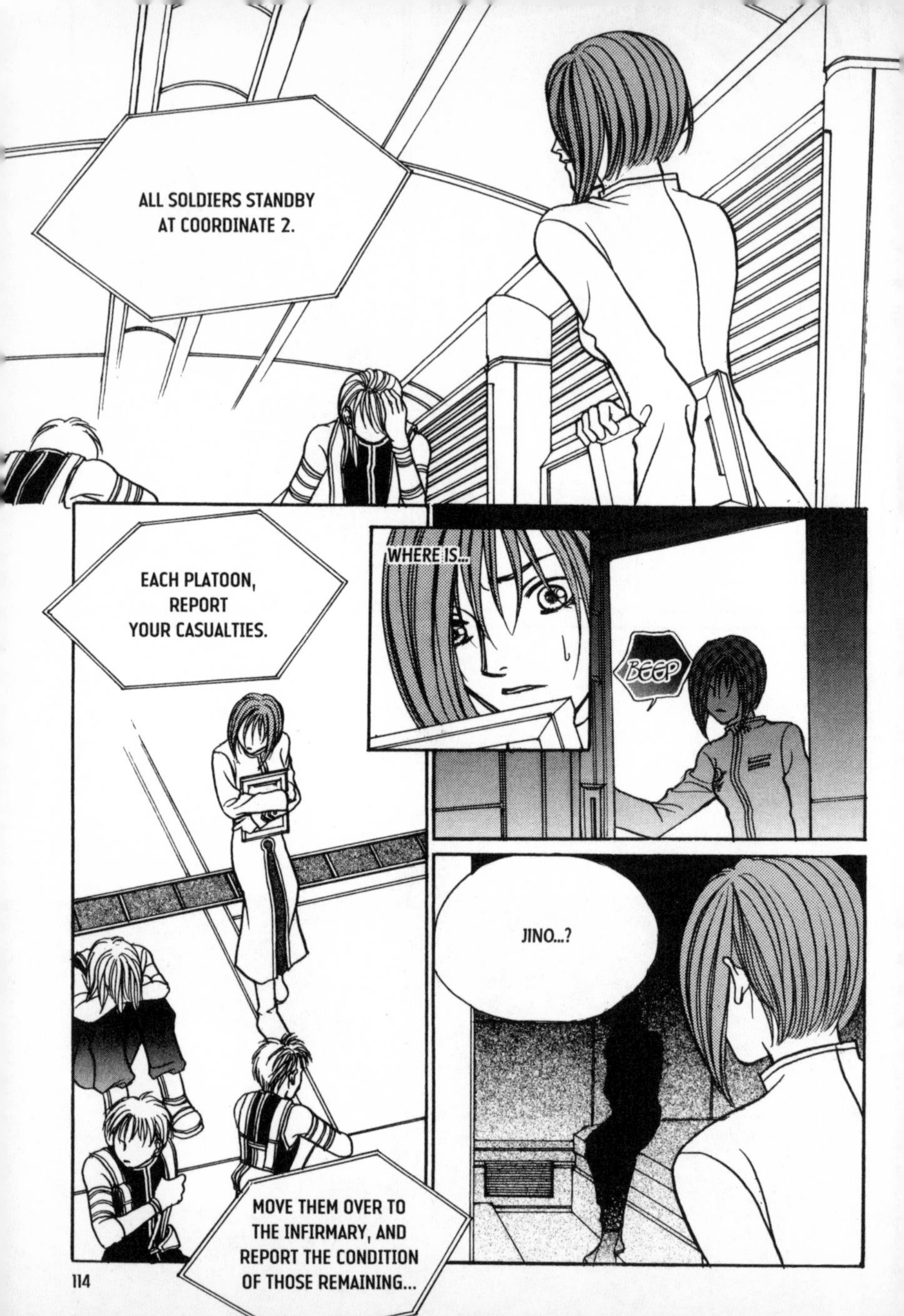
ALL SOLDIERS STANDBY AT COORDINATE 2.
EACH PLATOON, REPORT YOUR CASUALTIES.
MOVE THEM OVER TO THE INFIRMARY, AND REPORT THE CONDITION OF THOSE REMAINING...
WHERE IS...
BEEP
JINO...?

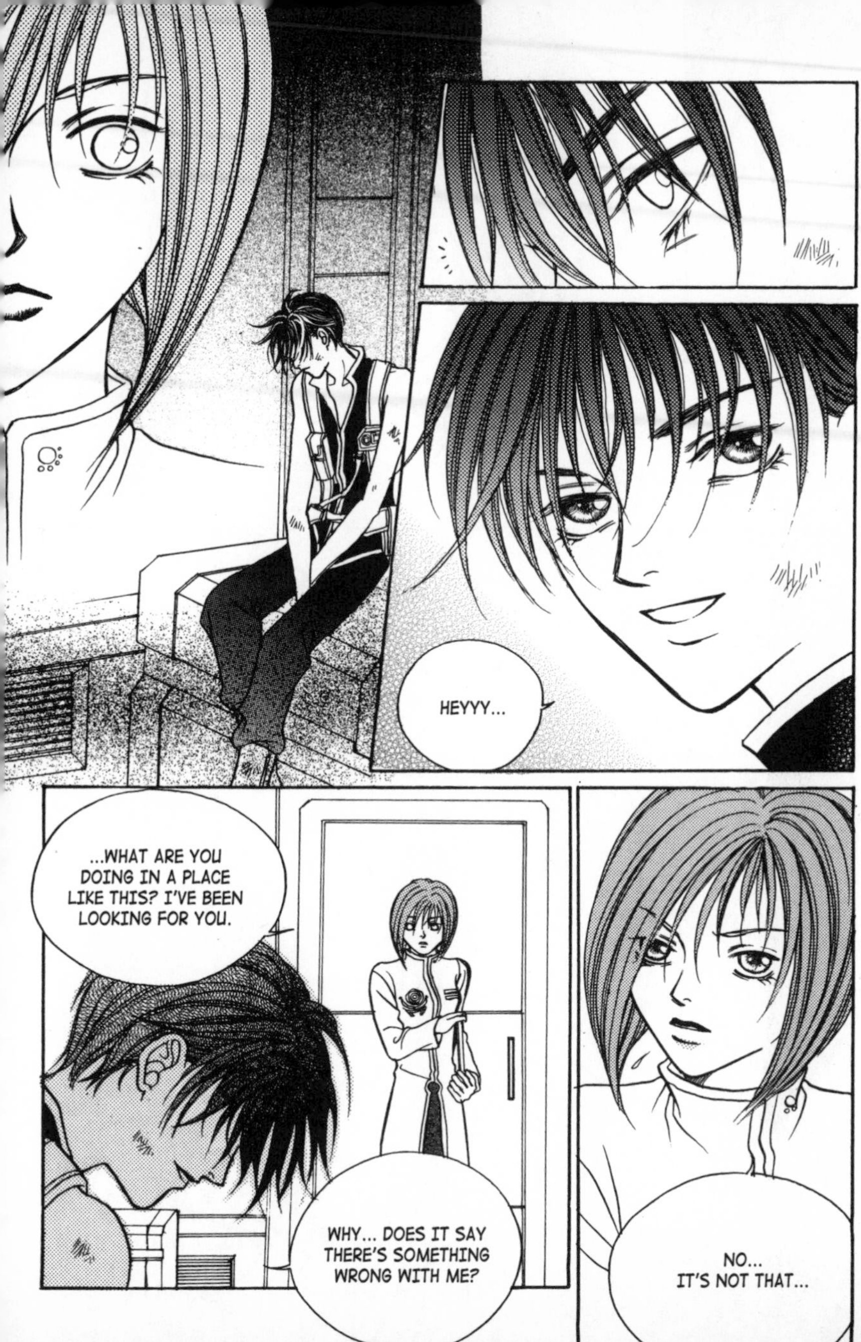
HEYYY...
...WHAT ARE YOU DOING IN A PLACE LIKE THIS? I'VE BEEN LOOKING FOR YOU.
WHY... DOES IT SAY THERE'S SOMETHING WRONG WITH ME?
NO... IT'S NOT THAT...

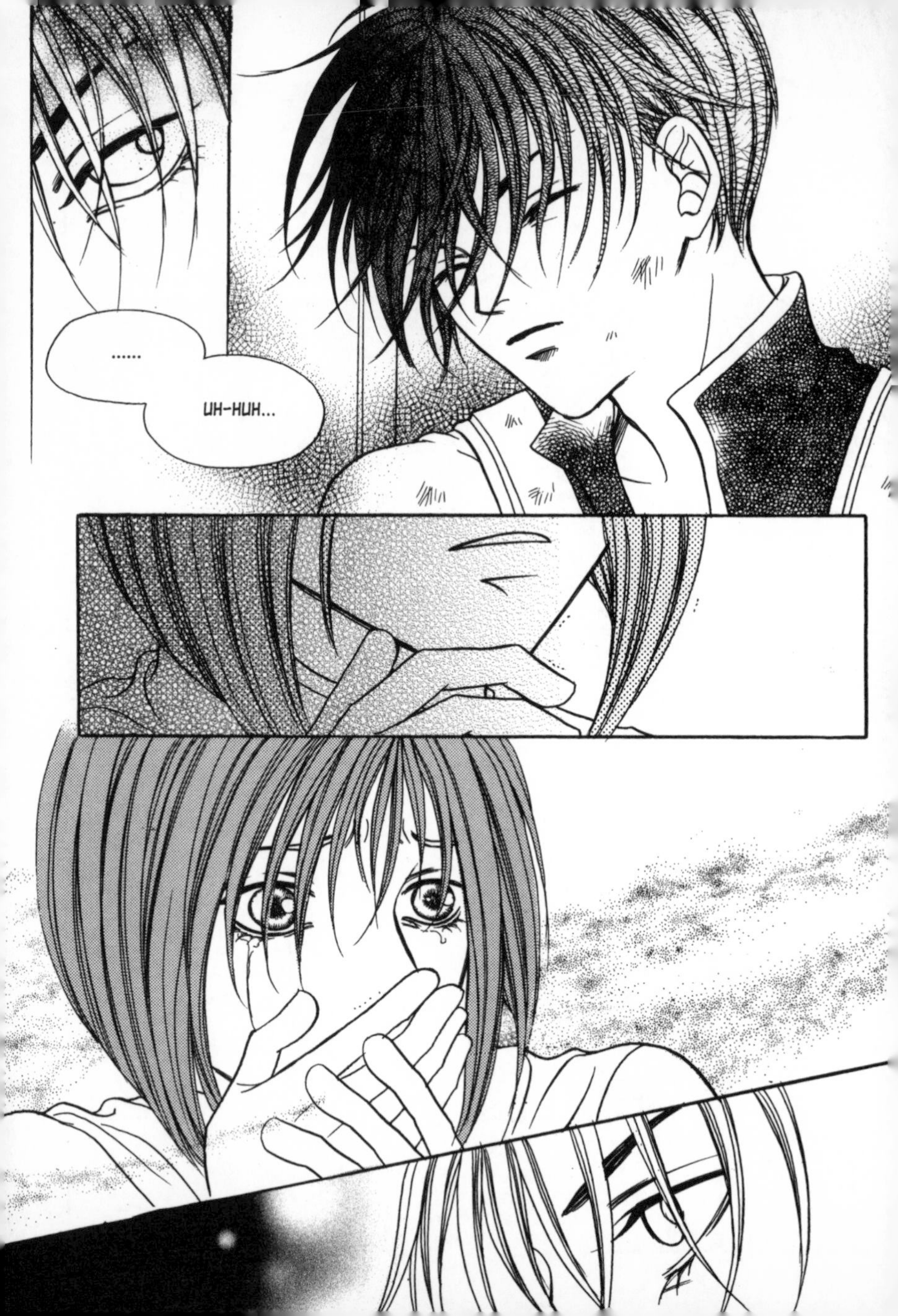
......
UH-HUH...

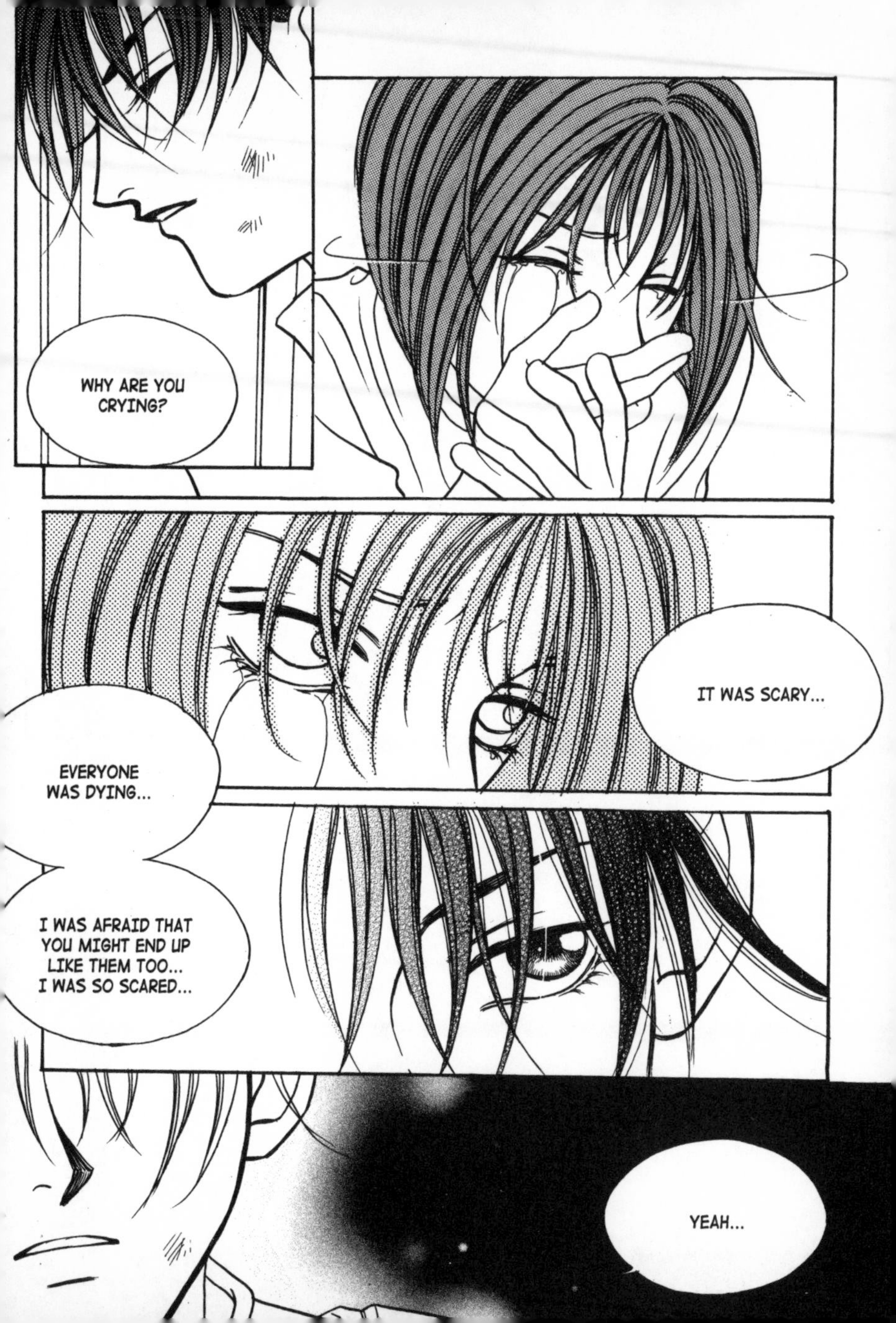
WHY ARE YOU CRYING?
EVERYONE WAS DYING...
IT WAS SCARY...
I WAS AFRAID THAT YOU MIGHT END UP LIKE THEM TOO... I WAS SO SCARED...
YEAH...

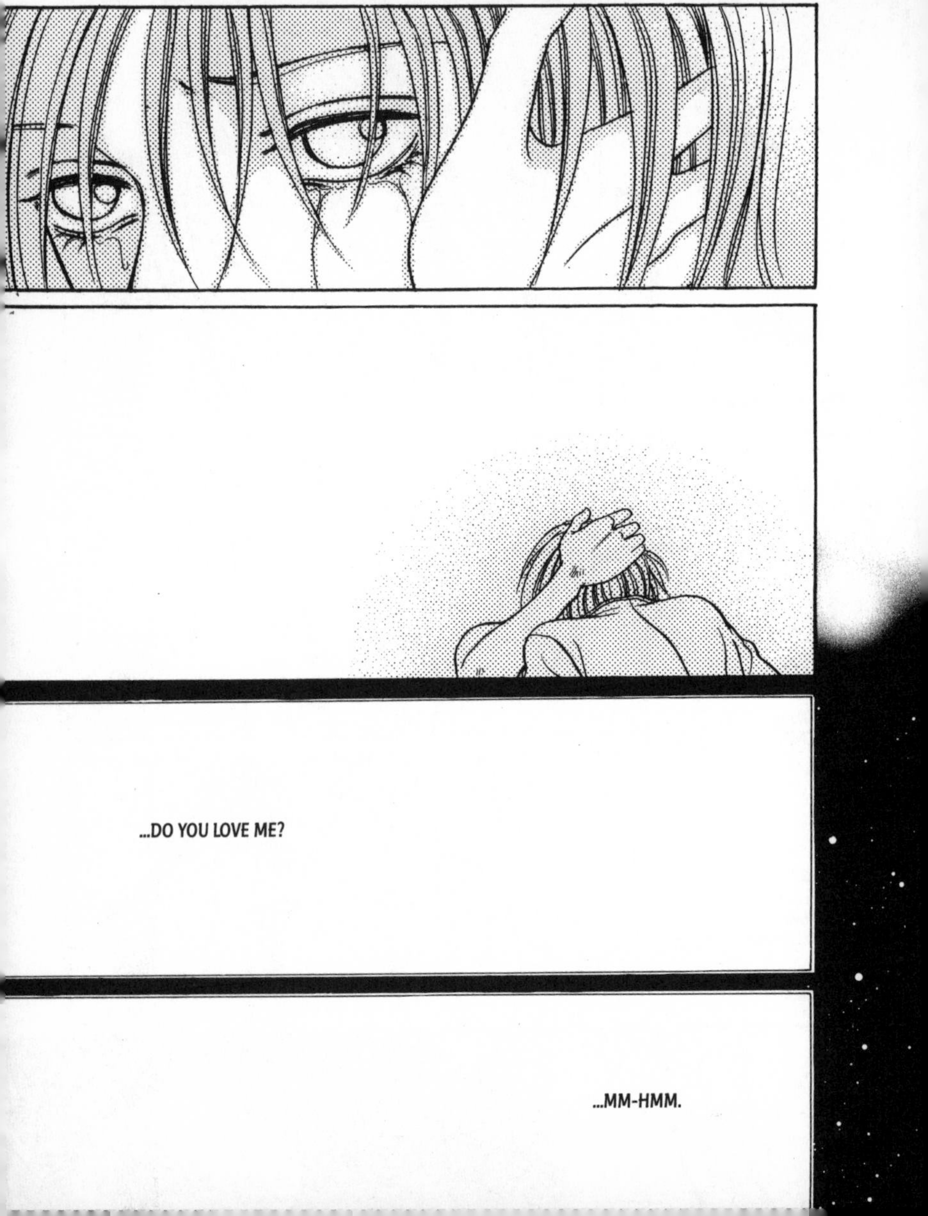
...DO YOU LOVE ME?
...MM-HMM.

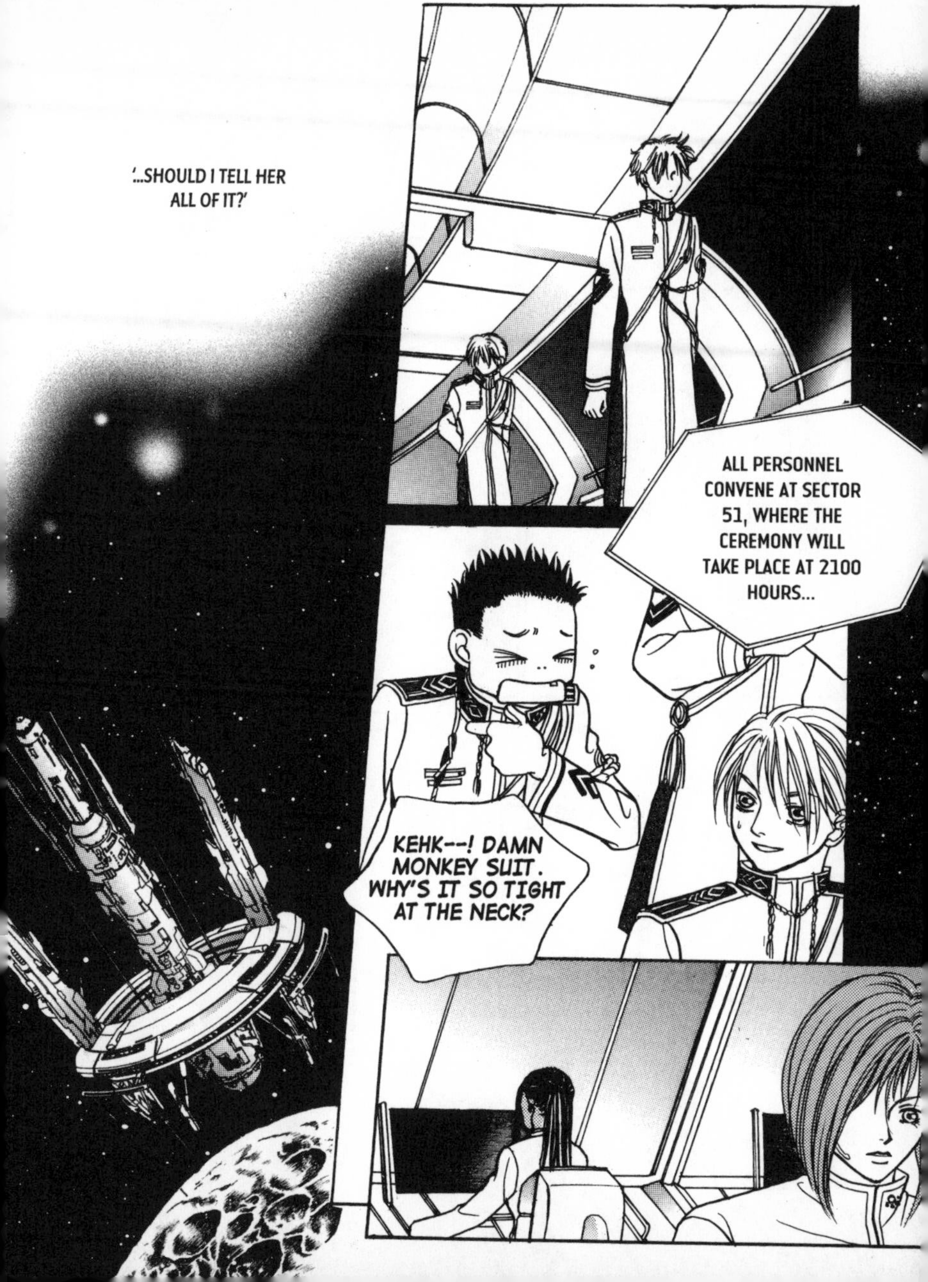
'...SHOULD I TELL HER ALL OF IT?'
ALL PERSONNEL CONVENE AT SECTOR 51, WHERE THE CEREMONY WILL TAKE PLACE AT 2100 HOURS...
KEHK--! DAMN MONKEY SUIT. WHY'S IT SO TIGHT AT THE NECK?

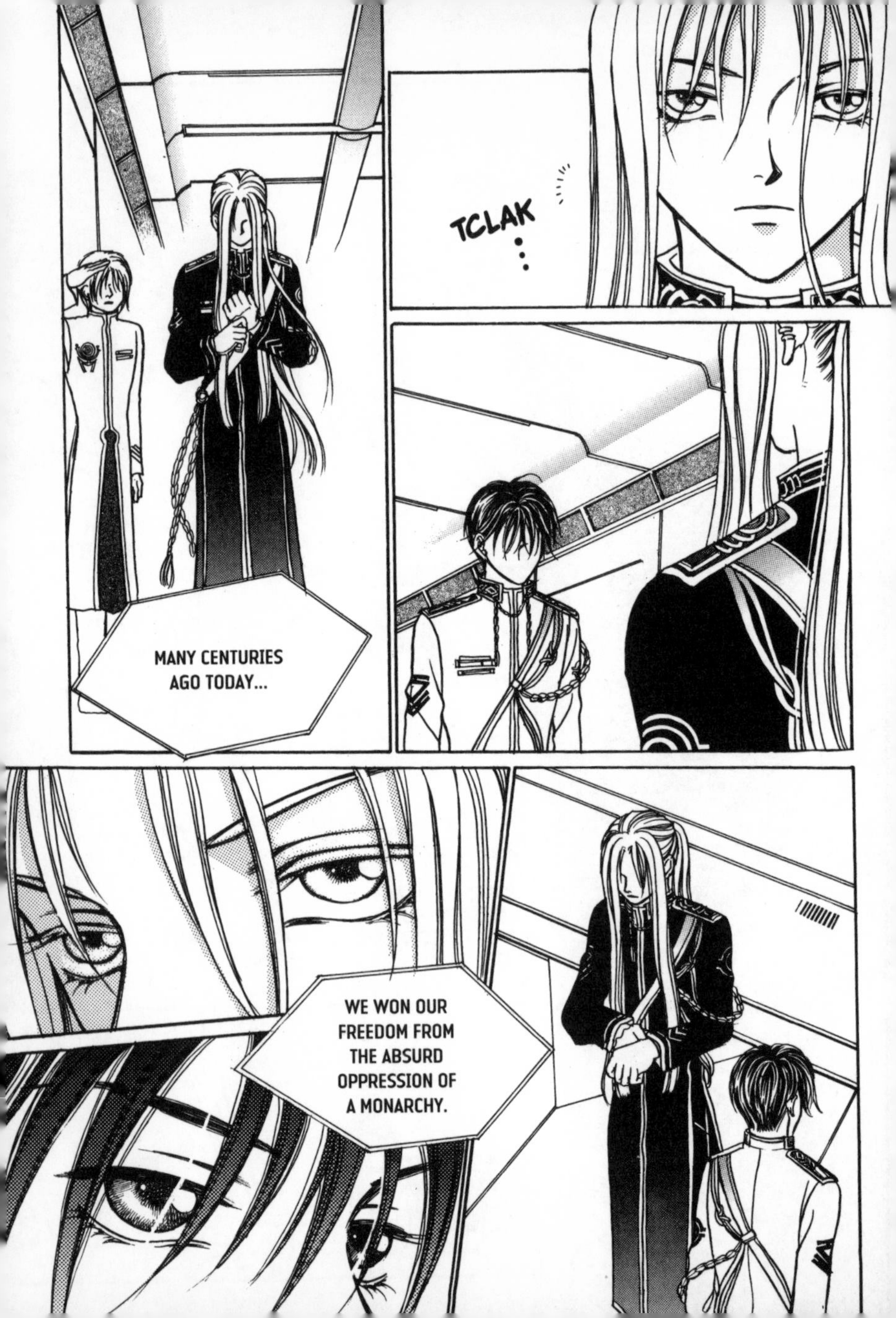
TCLAK...
MANY CENTURIES AGO TODAY...
WE WON OUR FREEDOM FROM THE ABSURD OPPRESSION OF A MONARCHY.

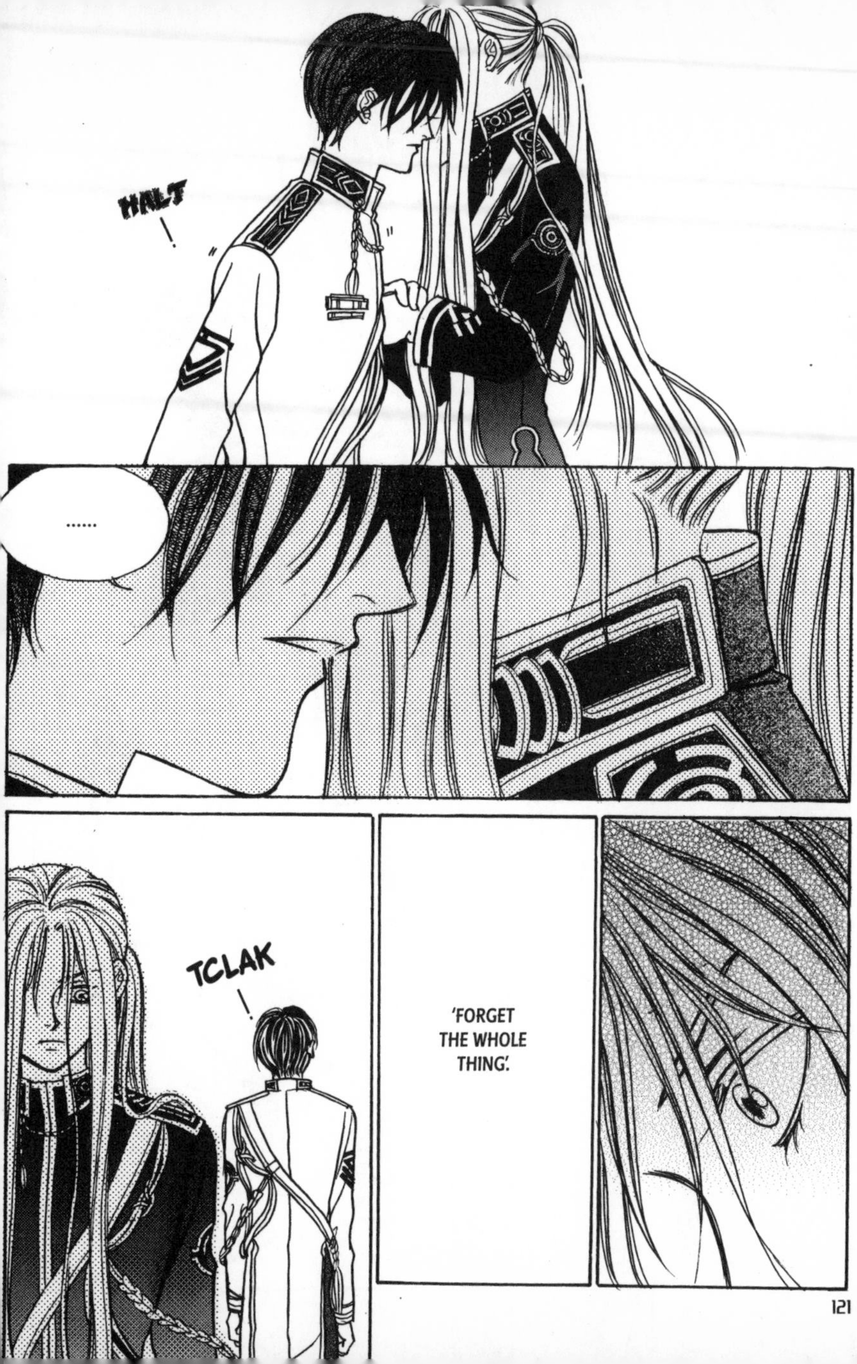

HALT
......
TCLAK
'FORGET THE WHOLE THING'.

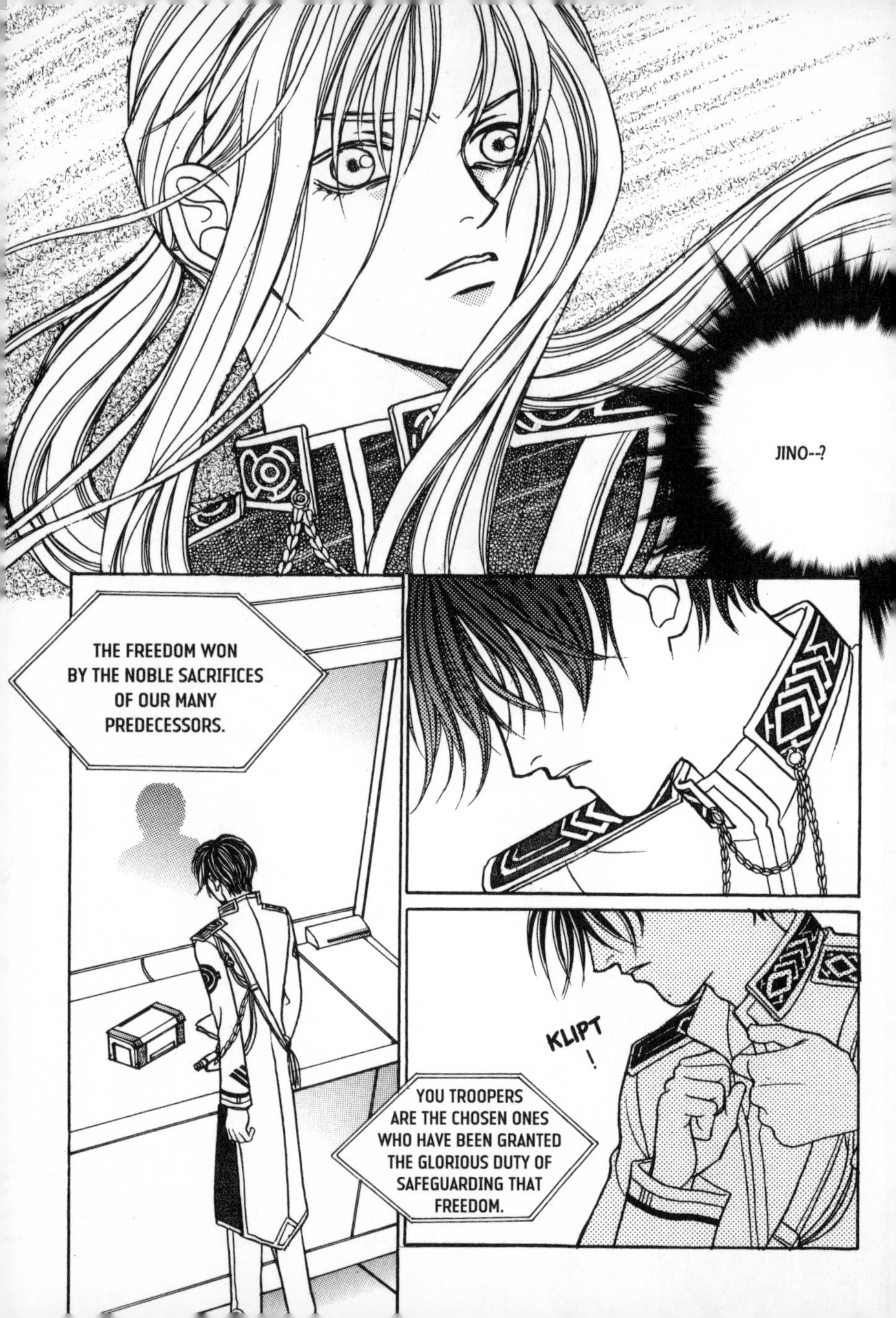
JINO--?
THE FREEDOM WON BY THE NOBLE SACRIFICES OF OUR MANY PREDECESSORS.
KLIPT !
YOU TROOPERS ARE THE CHOSEN ONES WHO HAVE BEEN GRANTED THE GLORIOUS DUTY OF SAFEGUARDING THAT FREEDOM.

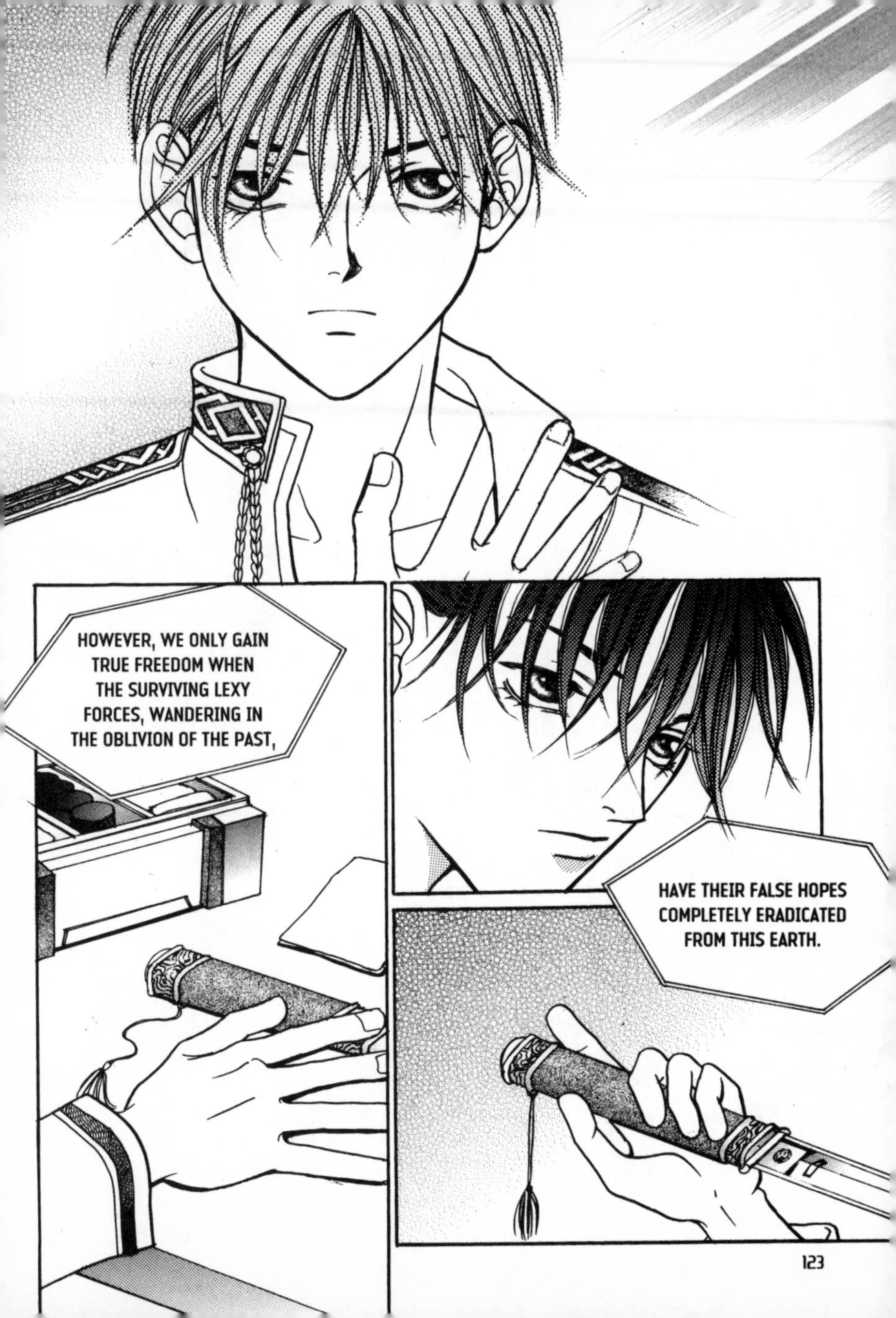
HOWEVER, WE ONLY GAIN TRUE FREEDOM WHEN THE SURVIVING LEXY FORCES, WANDERING IN THE OBLIVION OF THE PAST,
HAVE THEIR FALSE HOPES COMPLETELY ERADICATED FROM THIS EARTH.

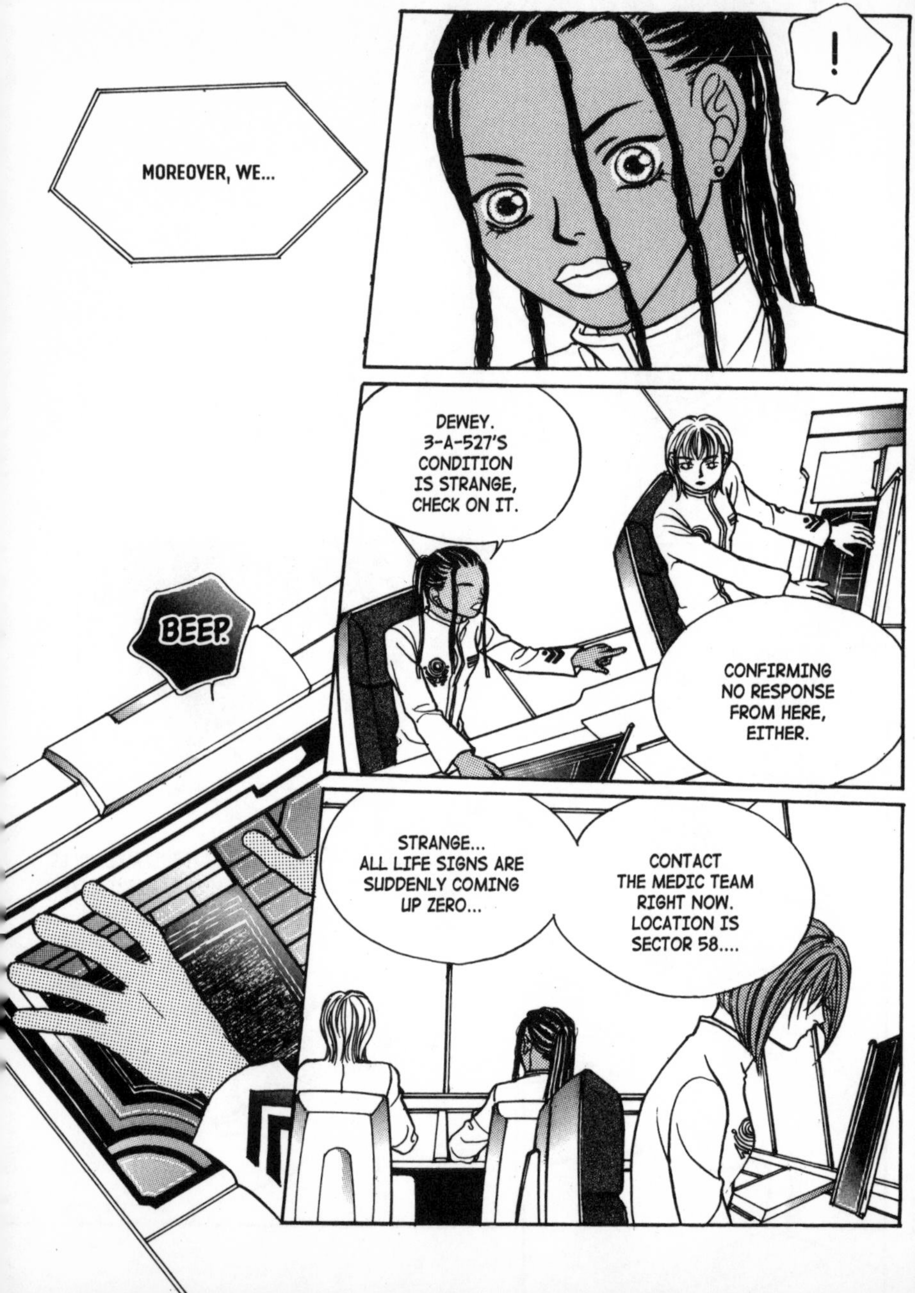

MOREOVER, WE...
!
BEEP.
DEWEY. 3-A-527'S CONDITION IS STRANGE, CHECK ON IT.
CONFIRMING NO RESPONSE FROM HERE, EITHER.
STRANGE... ALL LIFE SIGNS ARE SUDDENLY COMING UP ZERO...
CONTACT THE MEDIC TEAM RIGHT NOW. LOCATION IS SECTOR 58....

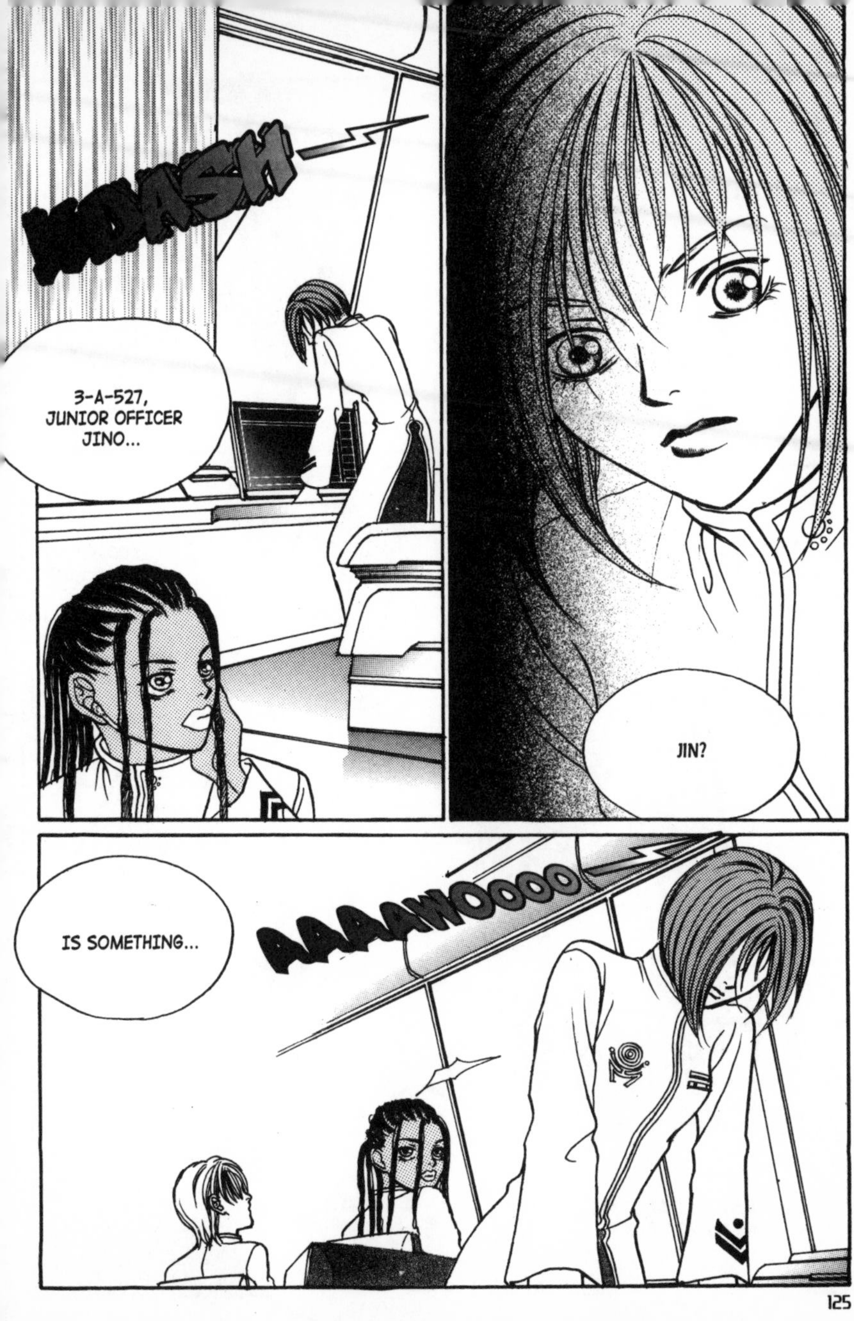
WHASH
3-A-527, JUNIOR OFFICER JINO...
JIN?
IS SOMETHING...
AAAAWOOOO

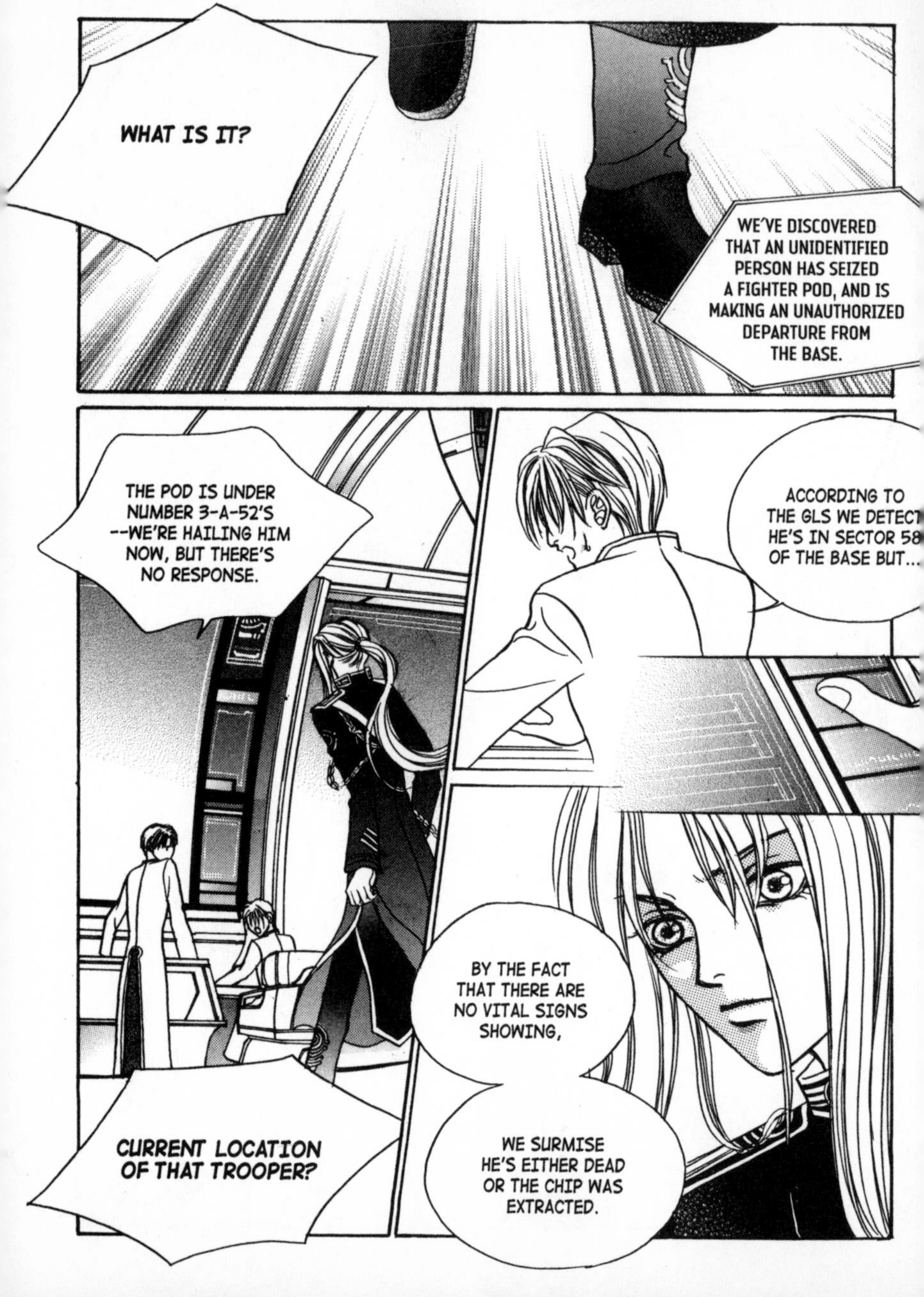
WHAT IS IT?
WE'VE DISCOVERED THAT AN UNIDENTIFIED PERSON HAS SEIZED A FIGHTER POD, AND IS MAKING AN UNAUTHORIZED DEPARTURE FROM THE BASE.
THE POD IS UNDER NUMBER 3-A-52'S --WE'RE HAILING HIM NOW, BUT THERE'S NO RESPONSE.
CURRENT LOCATION OF THAT TROOPER?
ACCORDING TO THE GLS WE DETECT HE'S IN SECTOR 58 OF THE BASE BUT...
BY THE FACT THAT THERE ARE NO VITAL SIGNS SHOWING,
WE SURMISE HE'S EITHER DEAD OR THE CHIP WAS EXTRACTED.

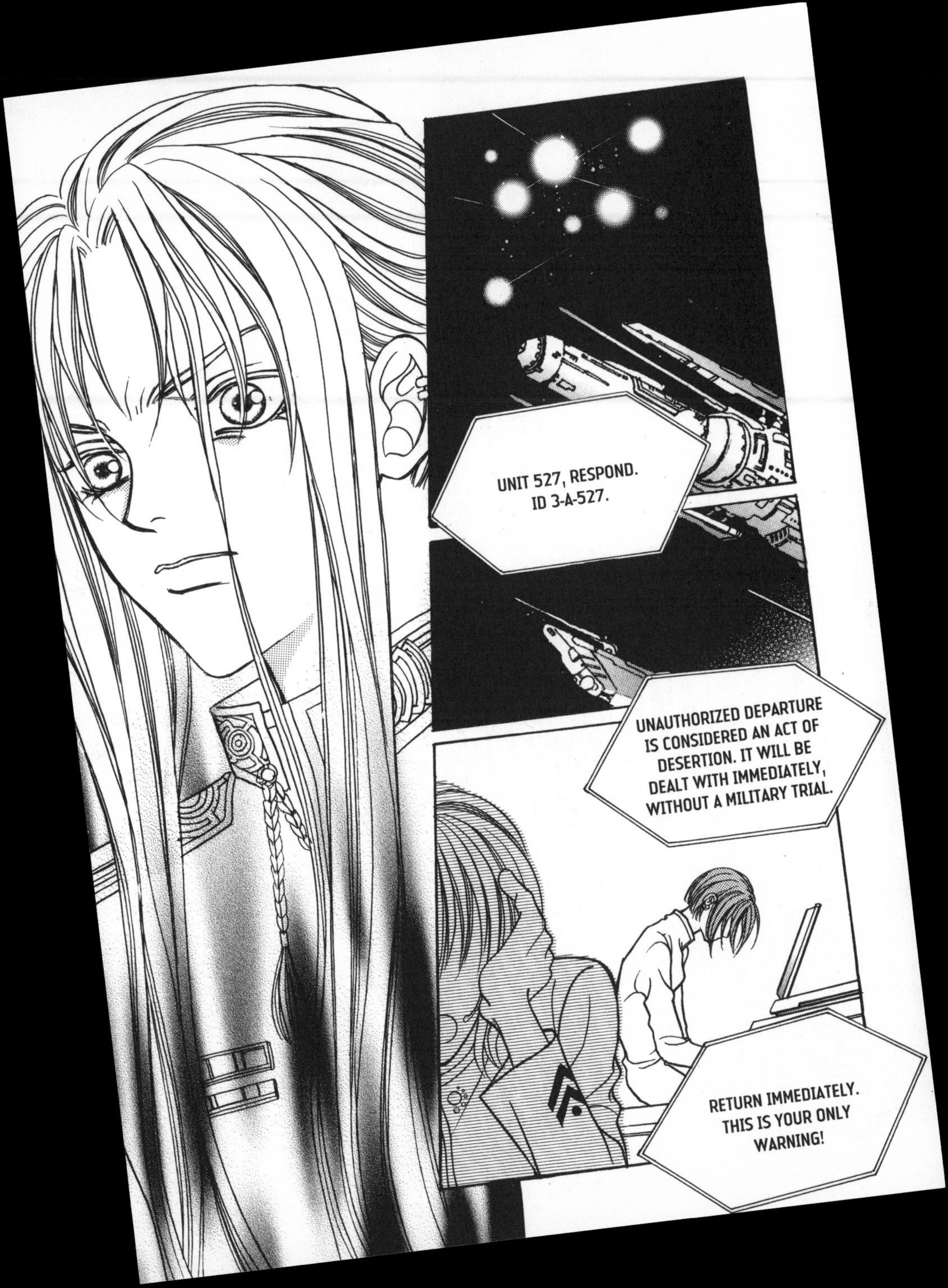
UNIT 527, RESPOND. ID 3-A-527.
UNAUTHORIZED DEPARTURE IS CONSIDERED AN ACT OF DESERTION. IT WILL BE DEALT WITH IMMEDIATELY, WITHOUT A MILITARY TRIAL.
RETURN IMMEDIATELY. THIS IS YOUR ONLY WARNING!

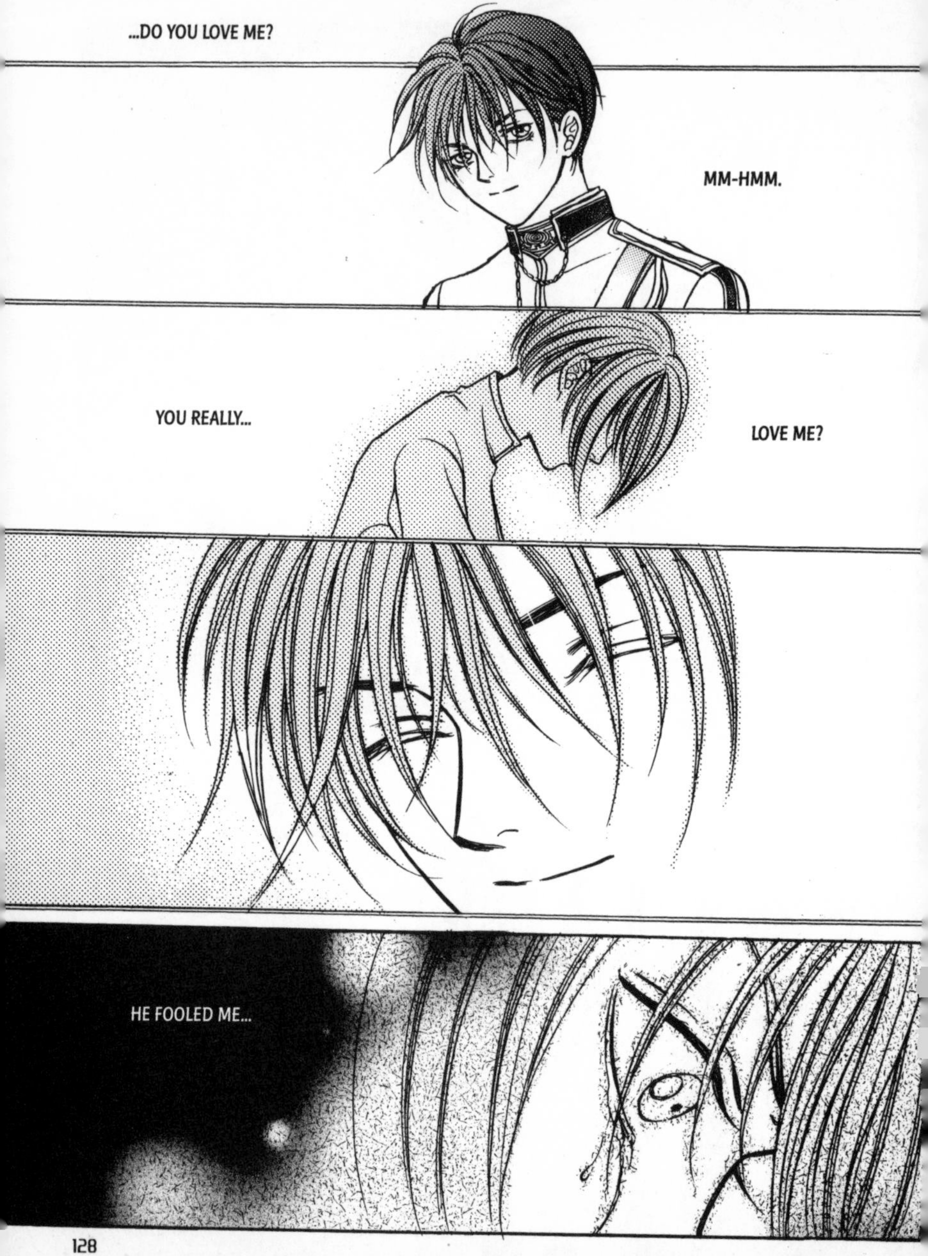
...DO YOU LOVE ME?
MM-HMM.
YOU REALLY...
LOVE ME?
HE FOOLED ME...

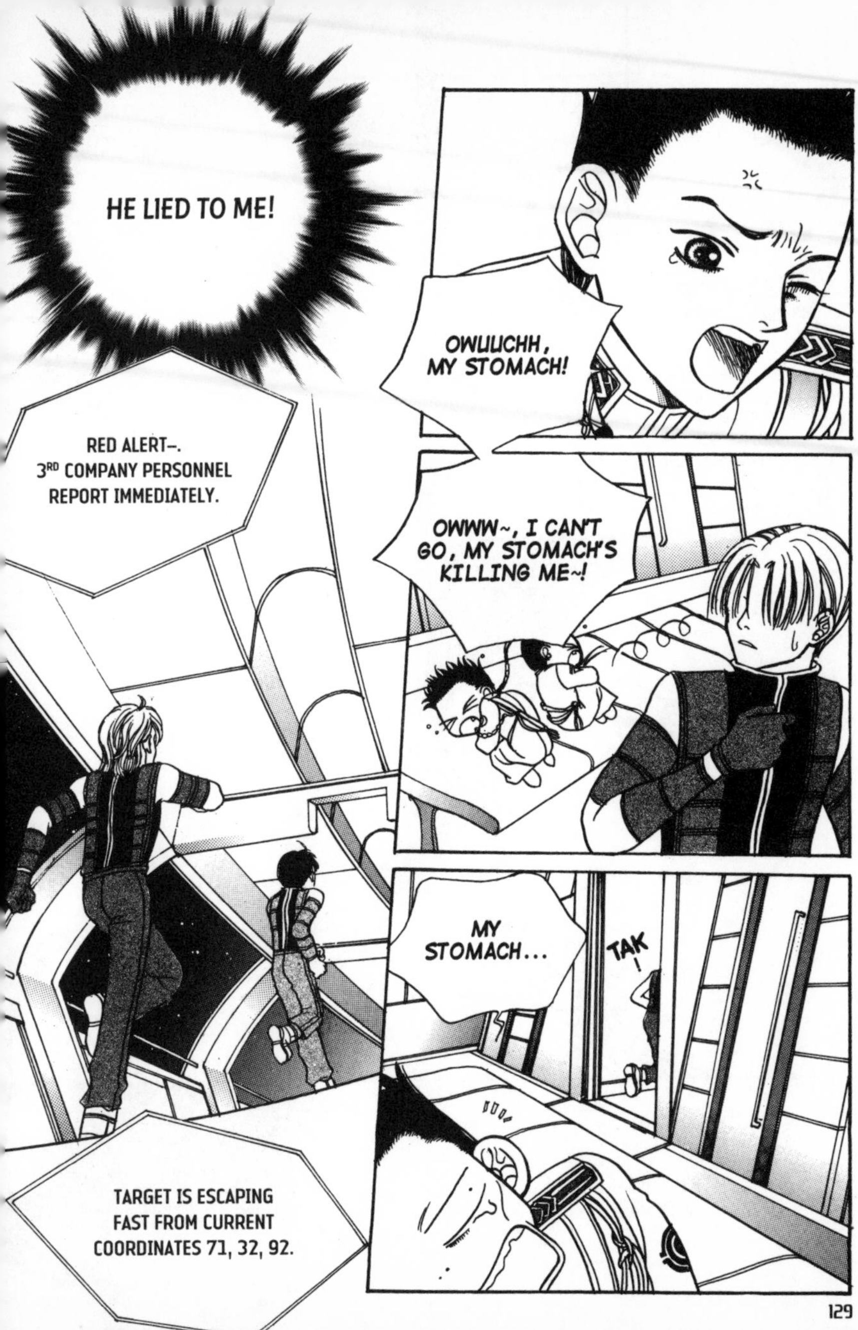
HE LIED TO ME!
OWUUCHH, MY STOMACH!
RED ALERT–. 3RD COMPANY PERSONNEL REPORT IMMEDIATELY.
TARGET IS ESCAPING FAST FROM CURRENT COORDINATES 71, 32, 92.
OWWW~, I CAN'T GO, MY STOMACH'S KILLING ME~!
MY STOMACH...
TAK!

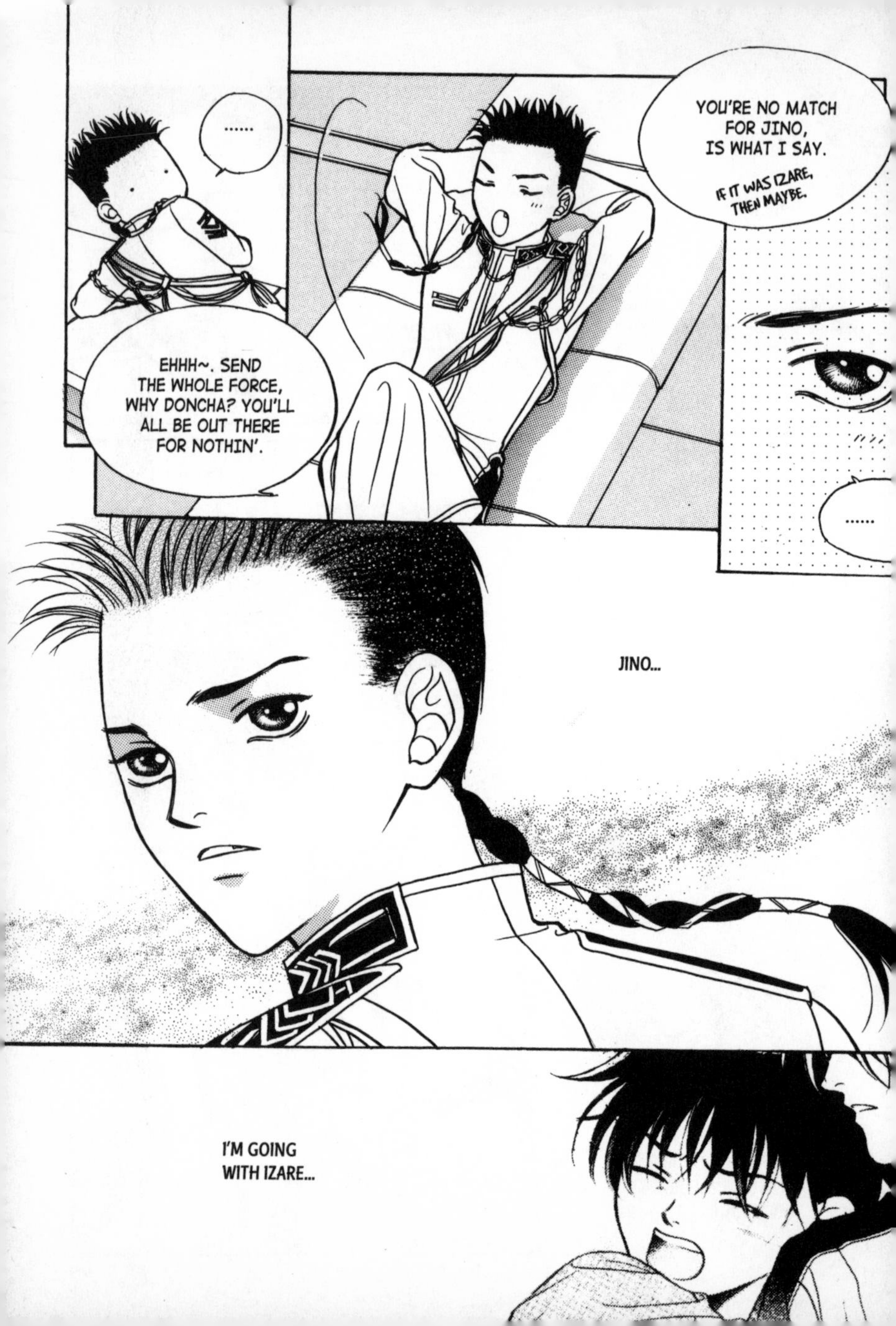

......
EHHH~. SEND THE WHOLE FORCE, WHY DONCHA? YOU'LL ALL BE OUT THERE FOR NOTHIN'.
YOU'RE NO MATCH FOR JINO, IS WHAT I SAY.
IF IT WAS IZARE, THEN MAYBE.
......
JINO...
I'M GOING WITH IZARE...

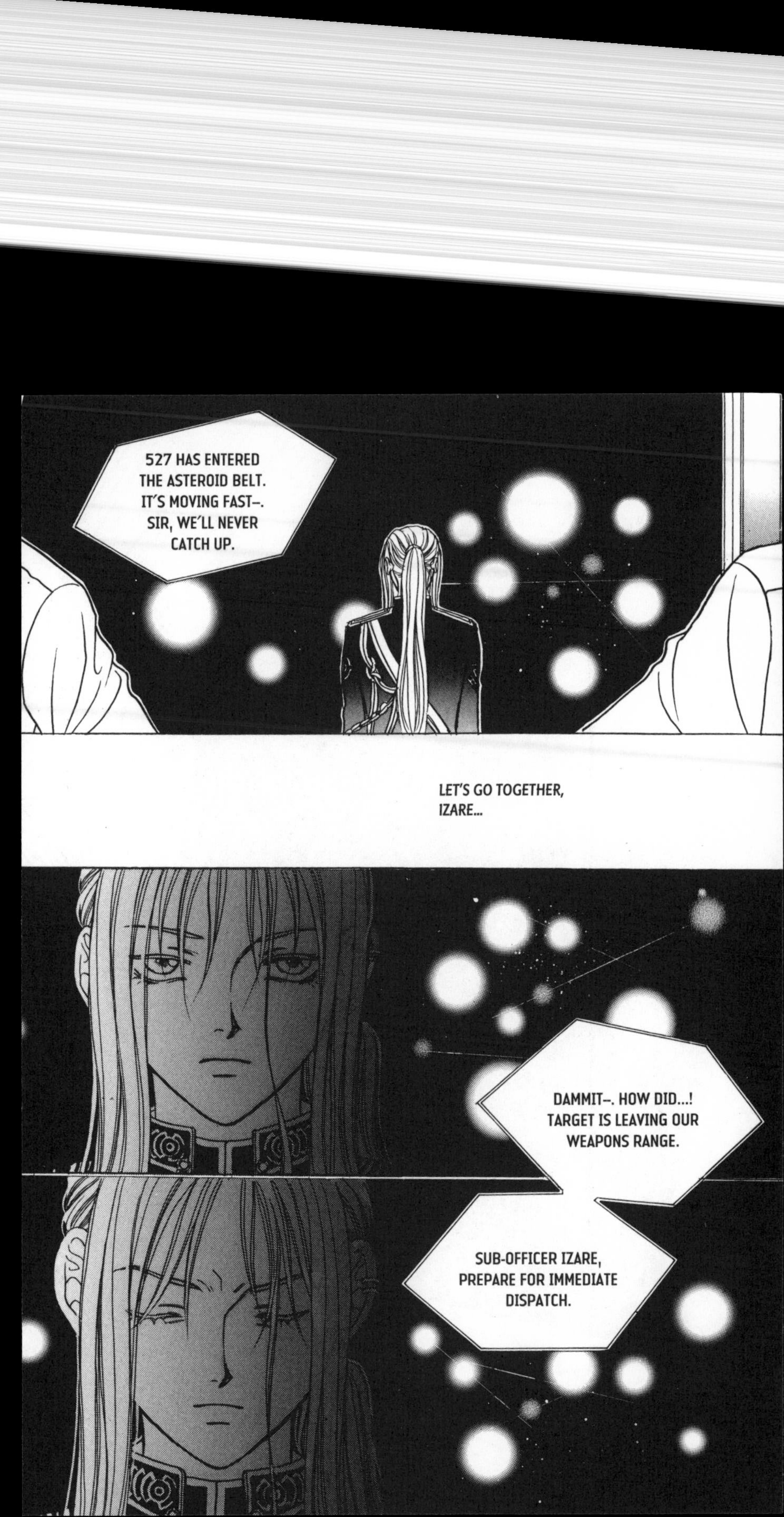
527 HAS ENTERED THE ASTEROID BELT. IT'S MOVING FAST–. SIR, WE'LL NEVER CATCH UP.
LET'S GO TOGETHER, IZARE...
DAMMIT–. HOW DID...! TARGET IS LEAVING OUR WEAPONS RANGE.
SUB-OFFICER IZARE, PREPARE FOR IMMEDIATE DISPATCH.

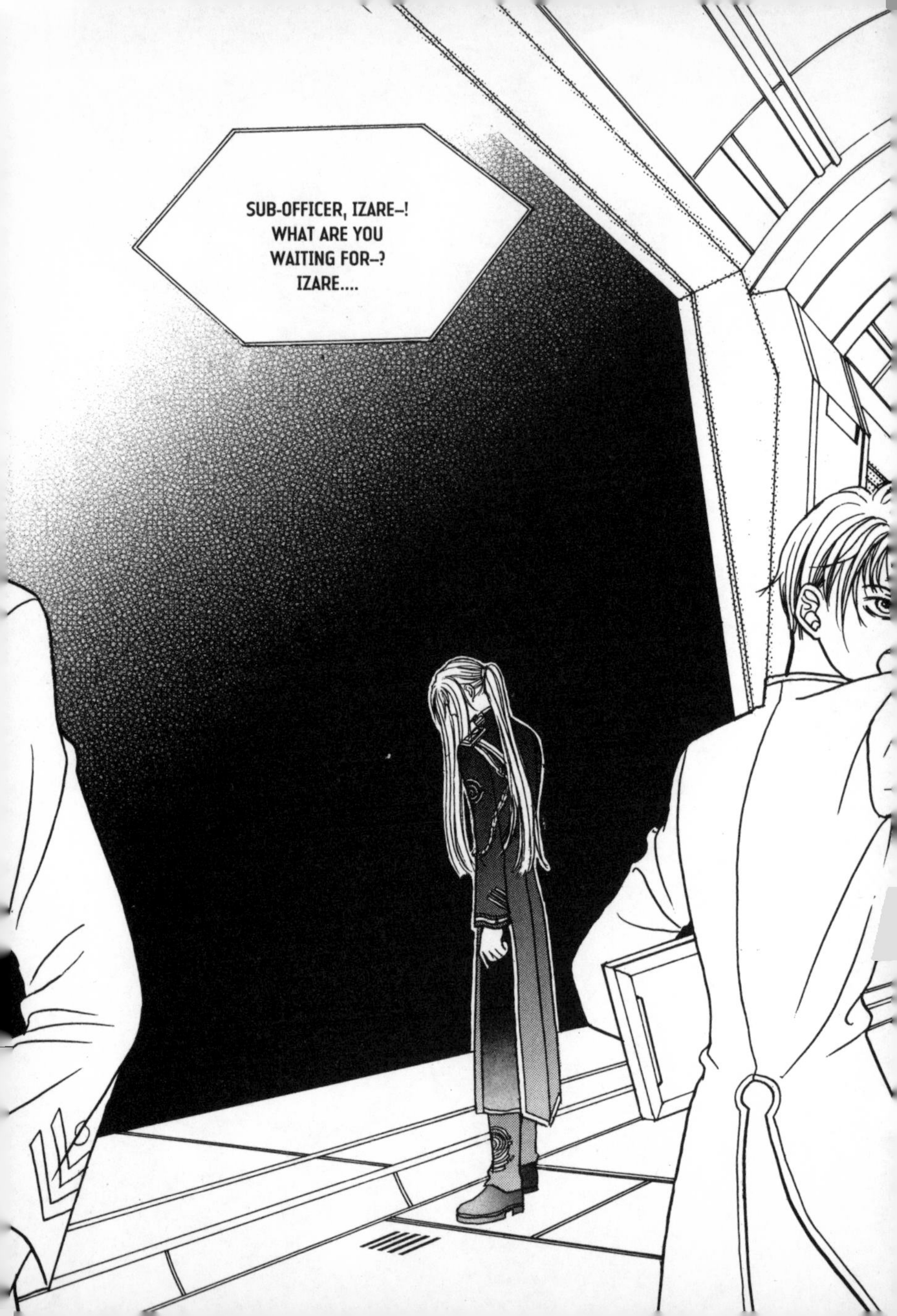
SUB-OFFICER, IZARE–! WHAT ARE YOU WAITING FOR–? IZARE....

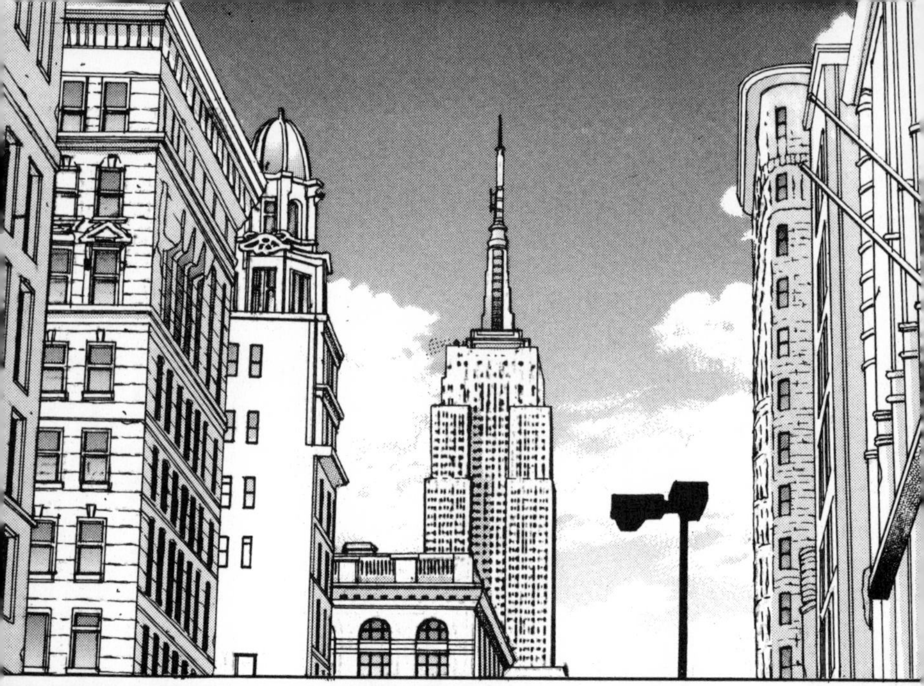

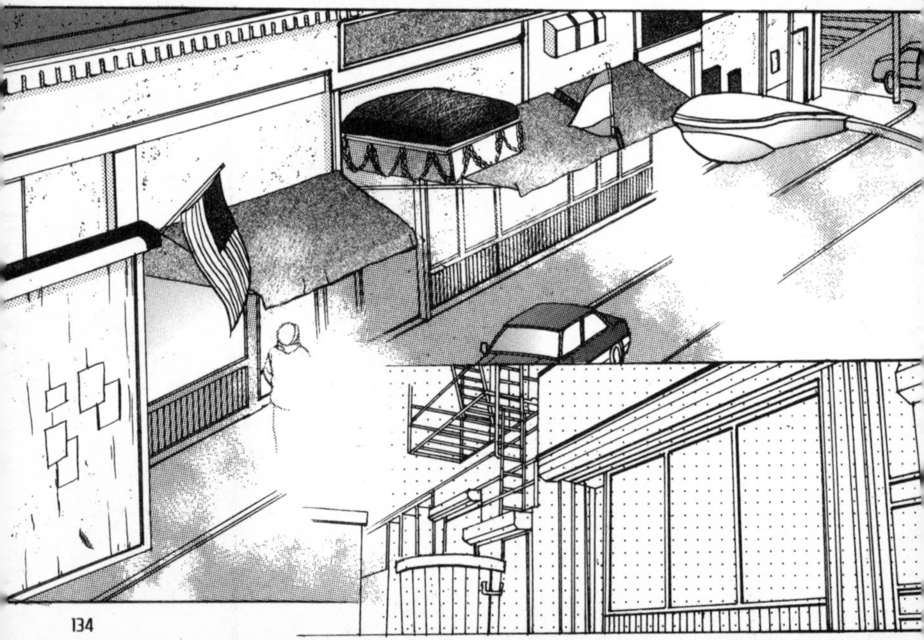

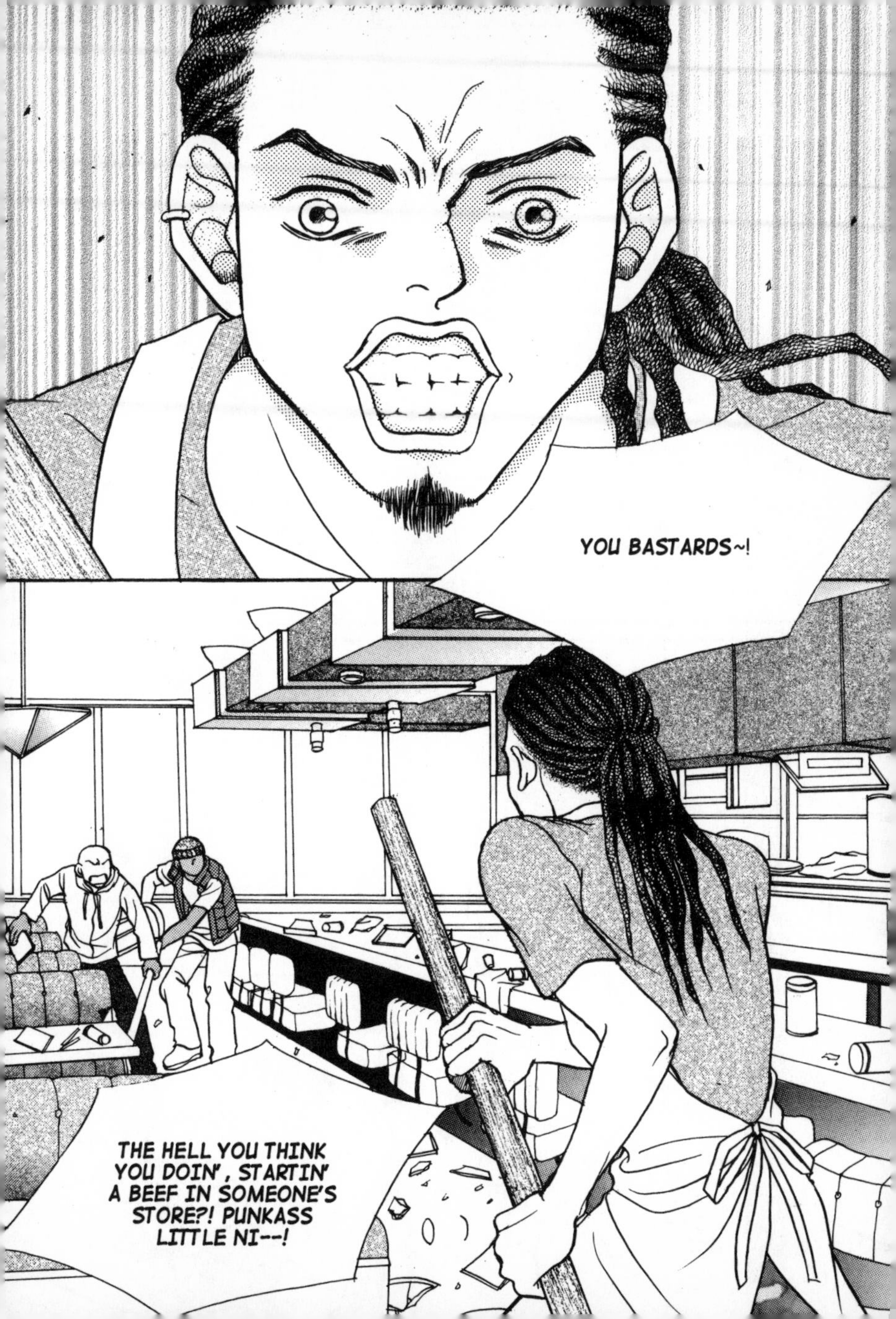
YOU BASTARDS~!
THE HELL YOU THINK YOU DOIN', STARTIN' A BEEF IN SOMEONE'S STORE?! PUNKASS LITTLE NI--!

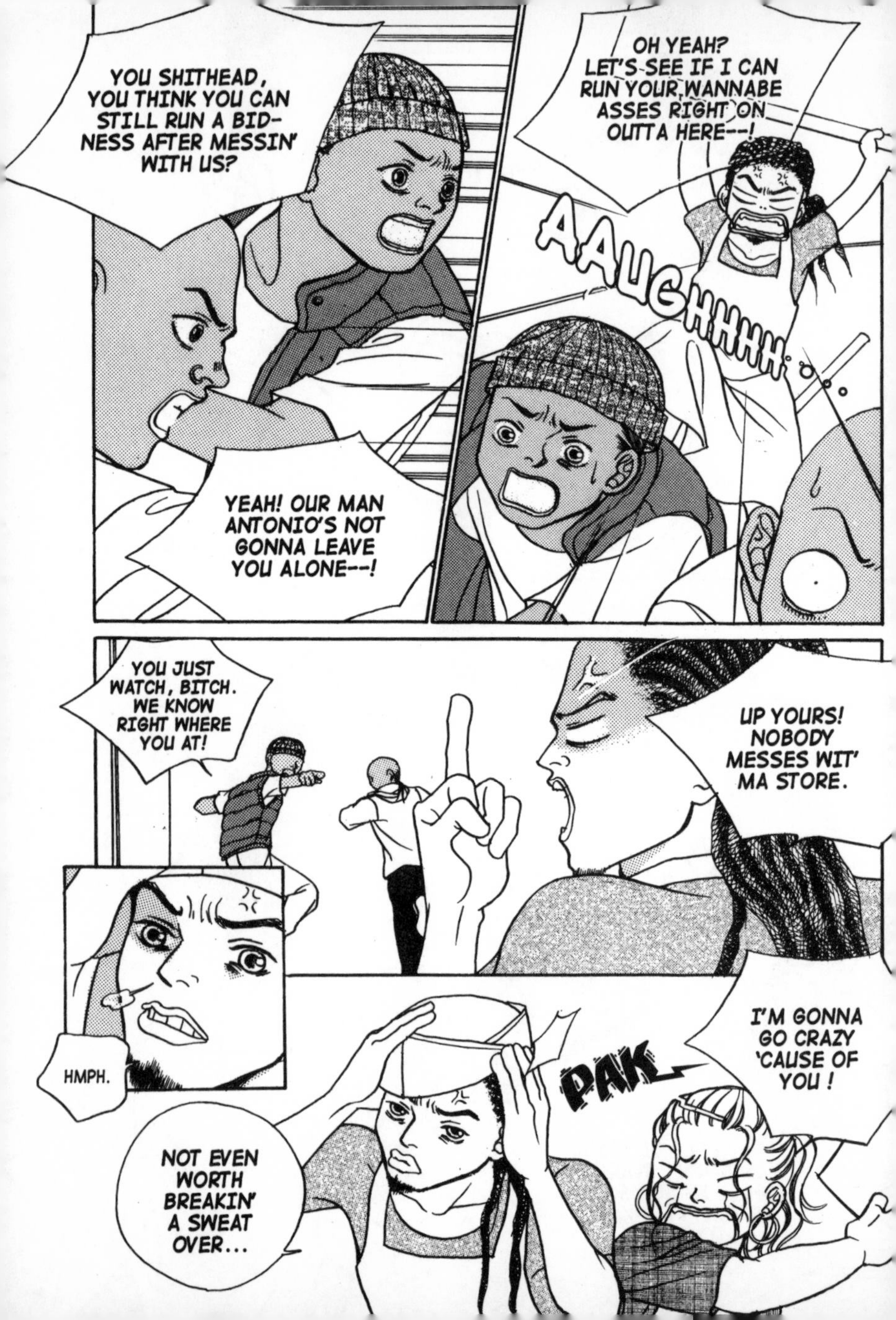
YOU SHITHEAD, YOU THINK YOU CAN STILL RUN A BID- NESS AFTER MESSIN' WITH US?
YEAH! OUR MAN ANTONIO'S NOT GONNA LEAVE YOU ALONE--!
OH YEAH? LET'S SEE IF I CAN RUN YOUR WANNABE ASSES RIGHT ON OUTTA HERE--!
AAUGHHHHH...
YOU JUST WATCH, BITCH. WE KNOW RIGHT WHERE YOU AT!
UP YOURS! NOBODY MESSES WIT' MA STORE.
HMPH.
NOT EVEN WORTH BREAKIN' A SWEAT OVER...
PAK
I'M GONNA GO CRAZY 'CAUSE OF YOU !

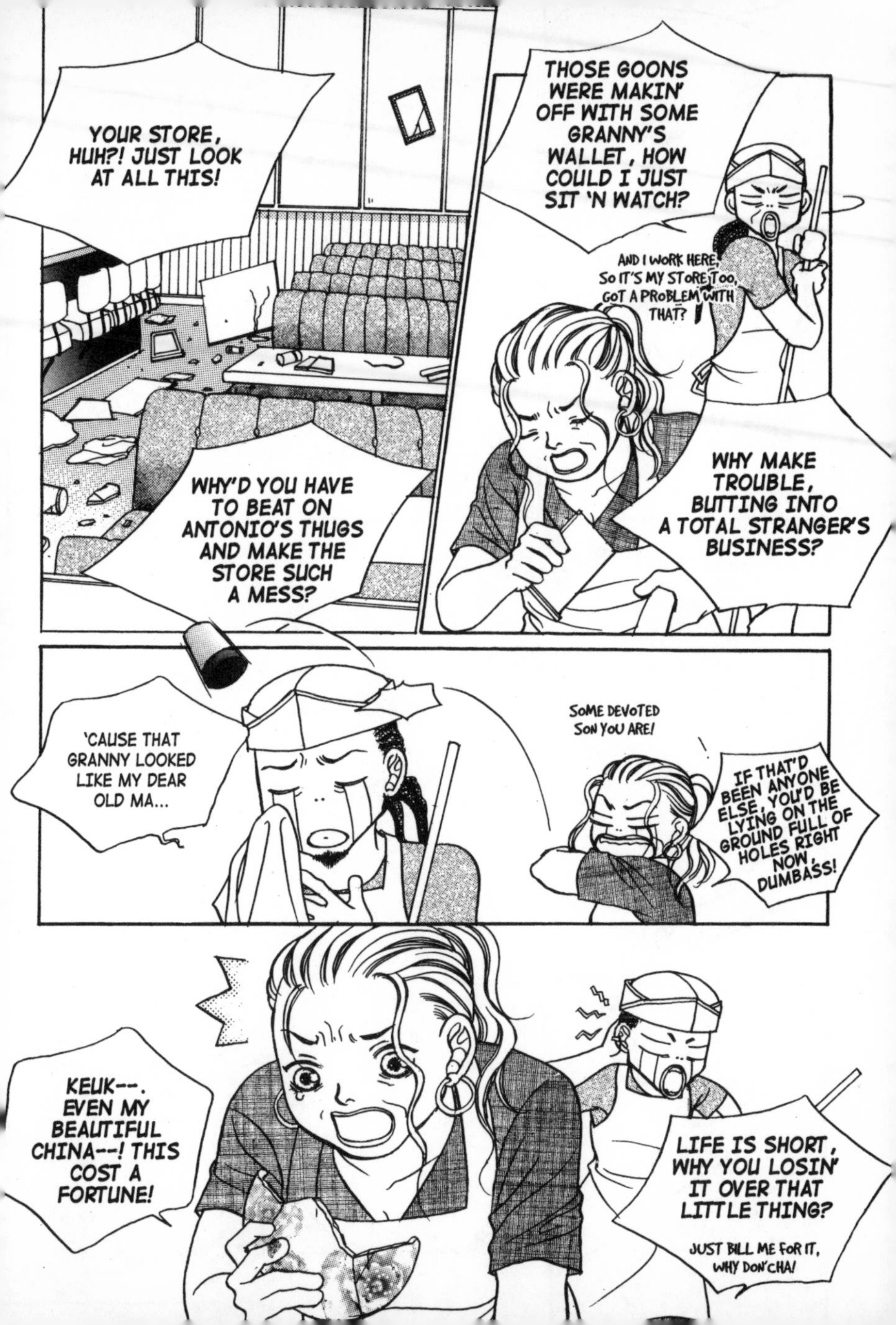
YOUR STORE, HUH?! JUST LOOK AT ALL THIS!
WHY'D YOU HAVE TO BEAT ON ANTONIO'S THUGS AND MAKE THE STORE SUCH A MESS?
THOSE GOONS WERE MAKIN' OFF WITH SOME GRANNY'S WALLET, HOW COULD I JUST SIT 'N WATCH?
AND I WORK HERE, SO IT'S MY STORE TOO, GOT A PROBLEM WITH THAT?
WHY MAKE TROUBLE, BUTTING INTO A TOTAL STRANGER'S BUSINESS?
'CAUSE THAT GRANNY LOOKED LIKE MY DEAR OLD MA...
SOME DEVOTED SON YOU ARE!
IF THAT'D BEEN ANYONE ELSE, YOU'D BE LYING ON THE GROUND FULL OF HOLES RIGHT NOW, DUMBASS!
KEUK--. EVEN MY BEAUTIFUL CHINA--! THIS COST A FORTUNE!
LIFE IS SHORT, WHY YOU LOSIN' IT OVER THAT LITTLE THING?
JUST BILL ME FOR IT, WHY DON'CHA!

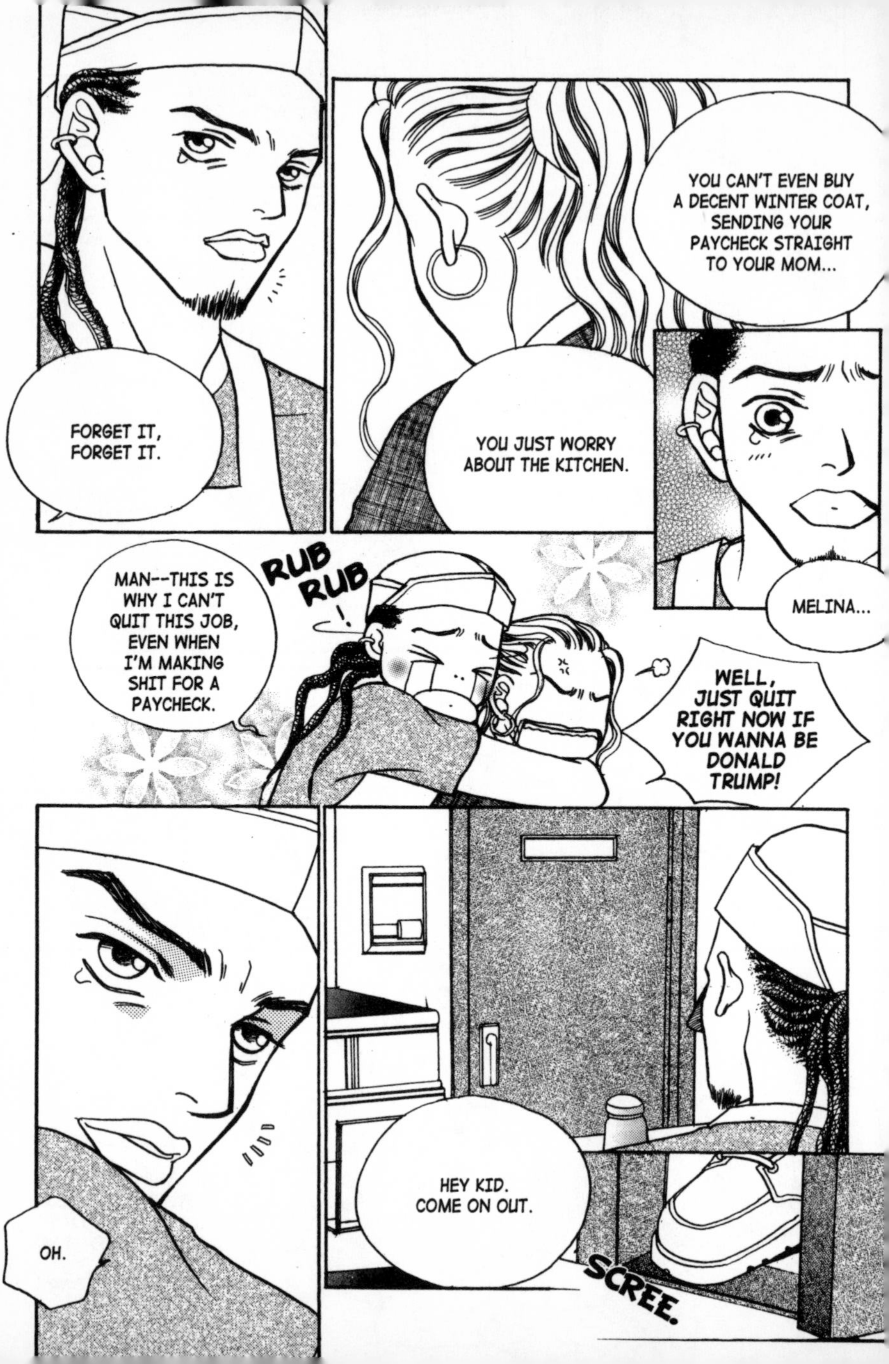
FORGET IT, FORGET IT.
YOU CAN'T EVEN BUY A DECENT WINTER COAT, SENDING YOUR PAYCHECK STRAIGHT TO YOUR MOM...
YOU JUST WORRY ABOUT THE KITCHEN.
MELINA...
MAN--THIS IS WHY I CAN'T QUIT THIS JOB, EVEN WHEN I'M MAKING SHIT FOR A PAYCHECK.
RUB RUB
WELL, JUST QUIT RIGHT NOW IF YOU WANNA BE DONALD TRUMP!
OH.
HEY KID. COME ON OUT.
SCREE.

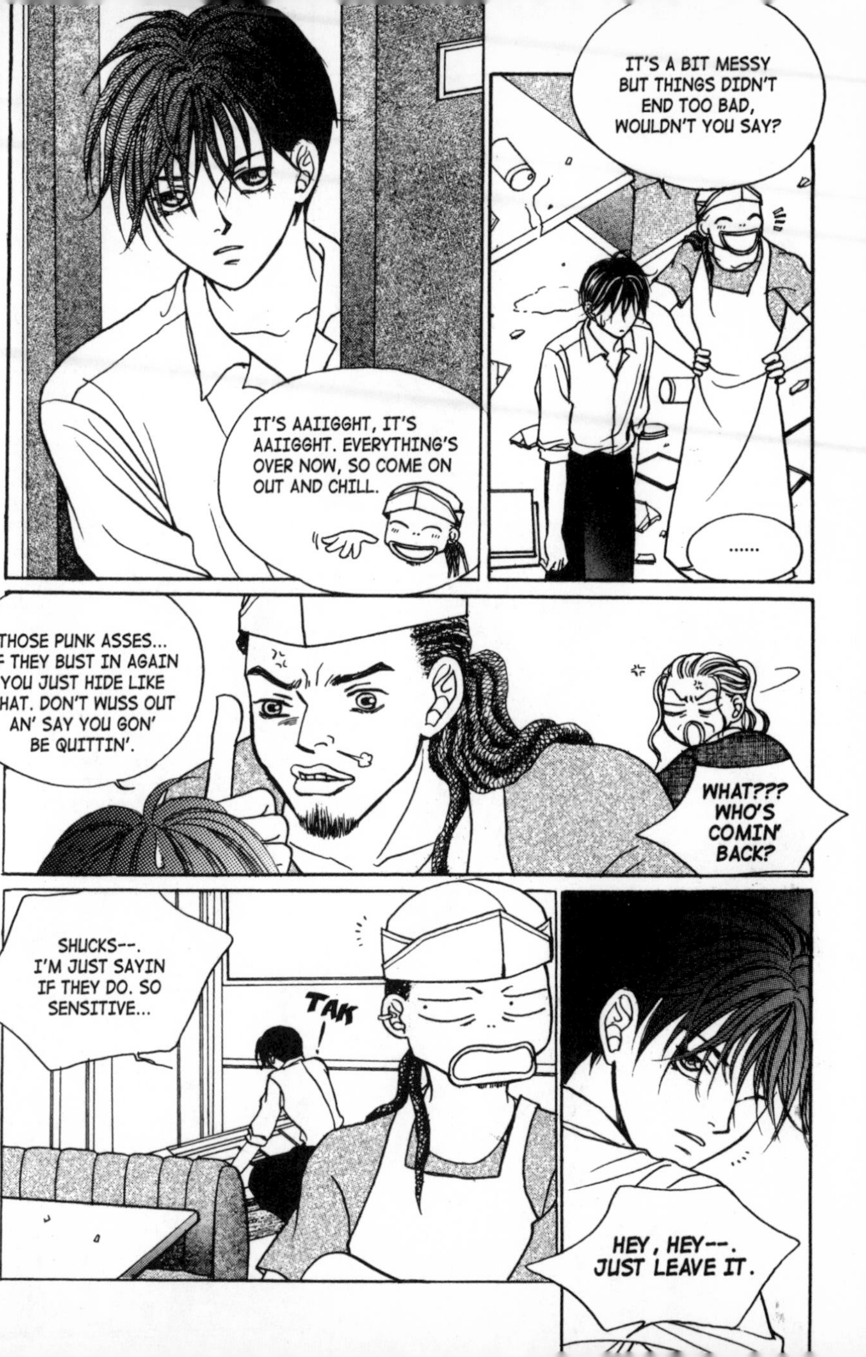
IT'S AAIIGGHT, IT'S AAIIGGHT. EVERYTHING'S OVER NOW, SO COME ON OUT AND CHILL.
IT'S A BIT MESSY BUT THINGS DIDN'T END TOO BAD, WOULDN'T YOU SAY?
......
THOSE PUNK ASSES... IF THEY BUST IN AGAIN YOU JUST HIDE LIKE THAT. DON'T WUSS OUT AN' SAY YOU GON' BE QUITTIN'.
WHAT??? WHO'S COMIN' BACK?
SHUCKS--. I'M JUST SAYIN IF THEY DO. SO SENSITIVE...
TAK
HEY, HEY--. JUST LEAVE IT.

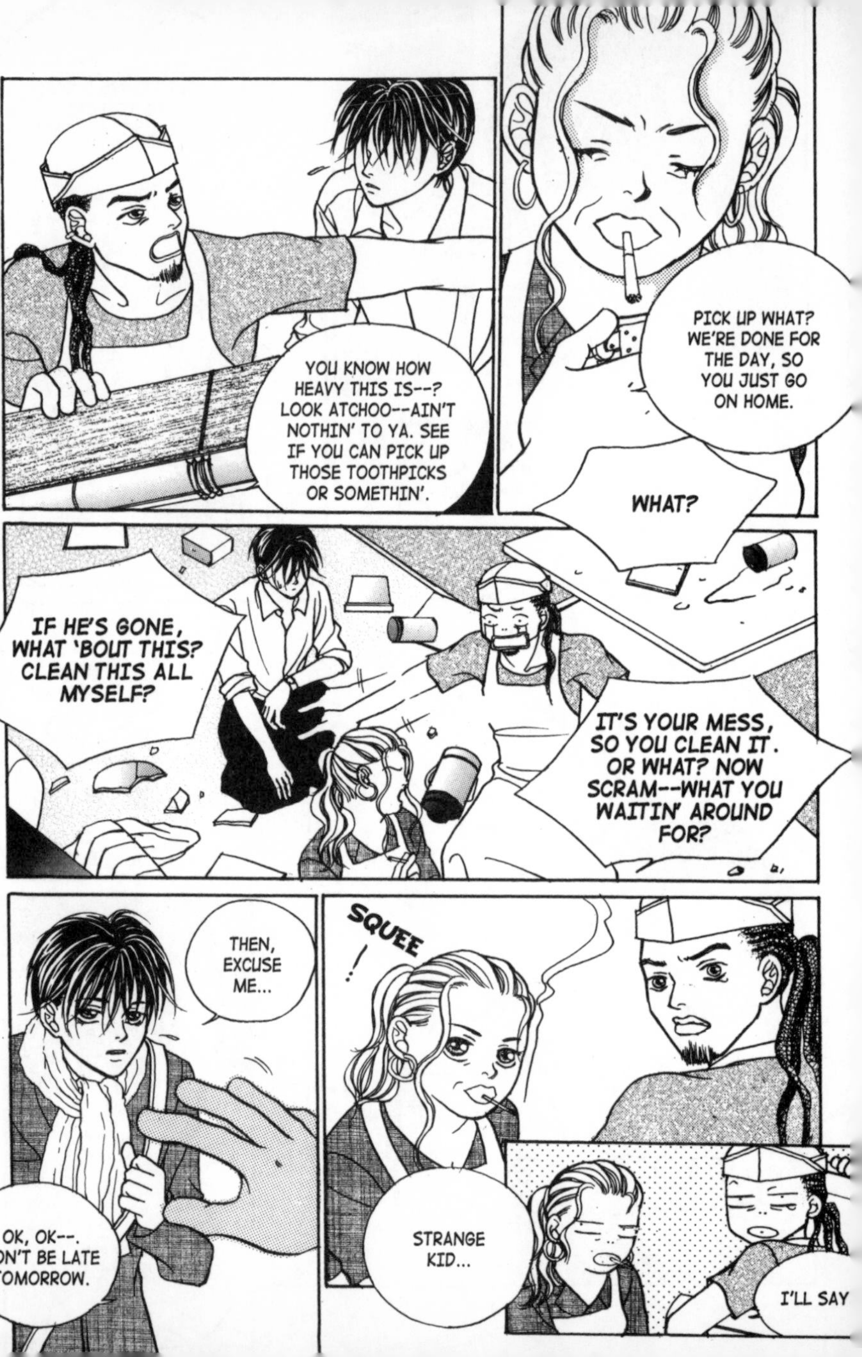
YOU KNOW HOW HEAVY THIS IS--? LOOK ATCHOO--AIN'T NOTHIN' TO YA. SEE IF YOU CAN PICK UP THOSE TOOTHPICKS OR SOMETHIN'.
PICK UP WHAT? WE'RE DONE FOR THE DAY, SO YOU JUST GO ON HOME.
WHAT?
IF HE'S GONE, WHAT 'BOUT THIS? CLEAN THIS ALL MYSELF?
IT'S YOUR MESS, SO YOU CLEAN IT. OR WHAT? NOW SCRAM--WHAT YOU WAITIN' AROUND FOR?
THEN, EXCUSE ME...
OK, OK--. DON'T BE LATE TOMORROW.
SQUEE
STRANGE KID...
I'LL SAY

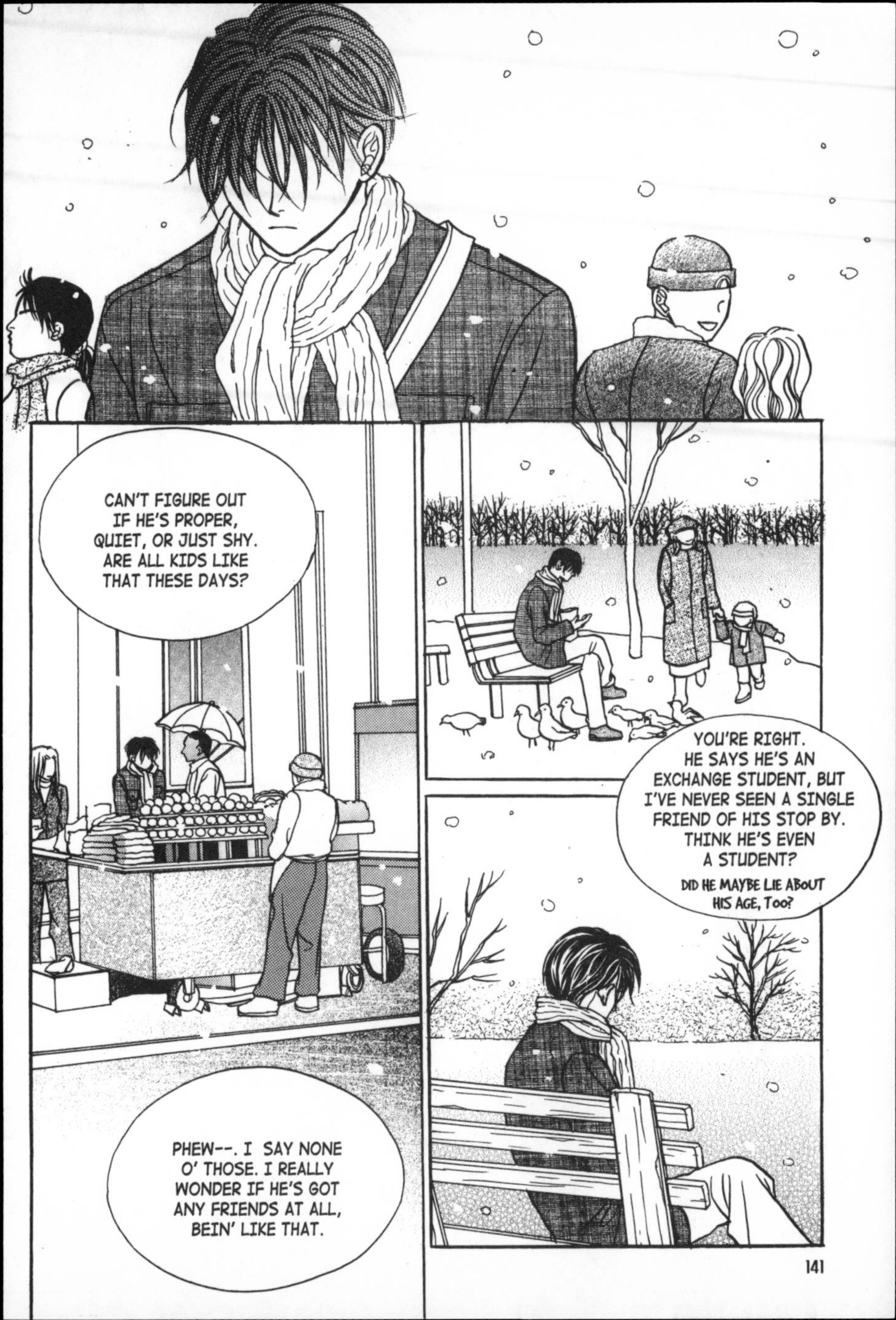
CAN'T FIGURE OUT IF HE'S PROPER, QUIET, OR JUST SHY. ARE ALL KIDS LIKE THAT THESE DAYS?
PHEW--. I SAY NONE O' THOSE. I REALLY WONDER IF HE'S GOT ANY FRIENDS AT ALL, BEIN' LIKE THAT.
YOU'RE RIGHT. HE SAYS HE'S AN EXCHANGE STUDENT, BUT I'VE NEVER SEEN A SINGLE FRIEND OF HIS STOP BY. THINK HE'S EVEN A STUDENT?
DID HE MAYBE LIE ABOUT HIS AGE, TOO?

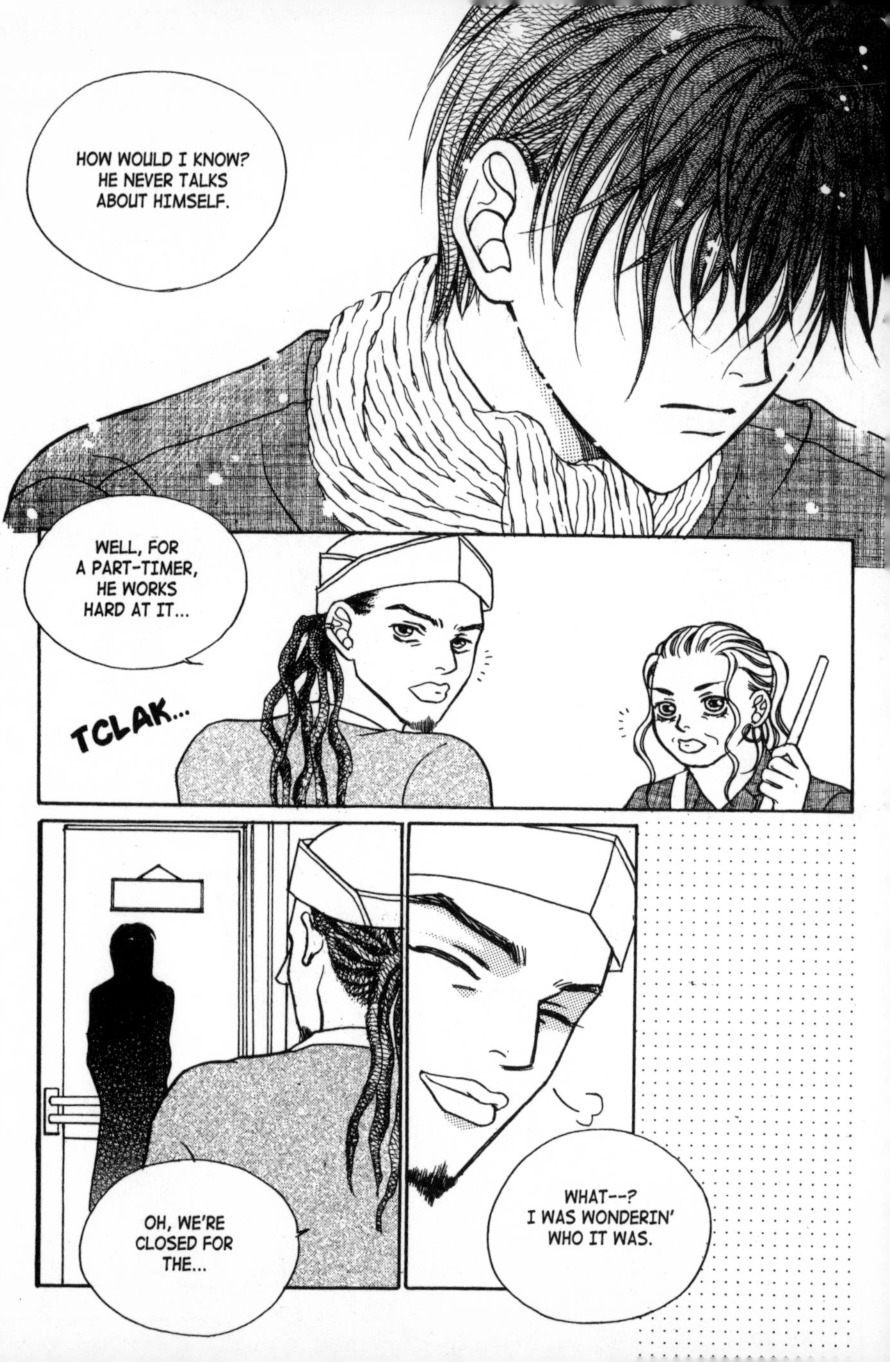
HOW WOULD I KNOW? HE NEVER TALKS ABOUT HIMSELF.
WELL, FOR A PART-TIMER, HE WORKS HARD AT IT...
TCLAK...
OH, WE'RE CLOSED FOR THE...
WHAT--? I WAS WONDERIN' WHO IT WAS.

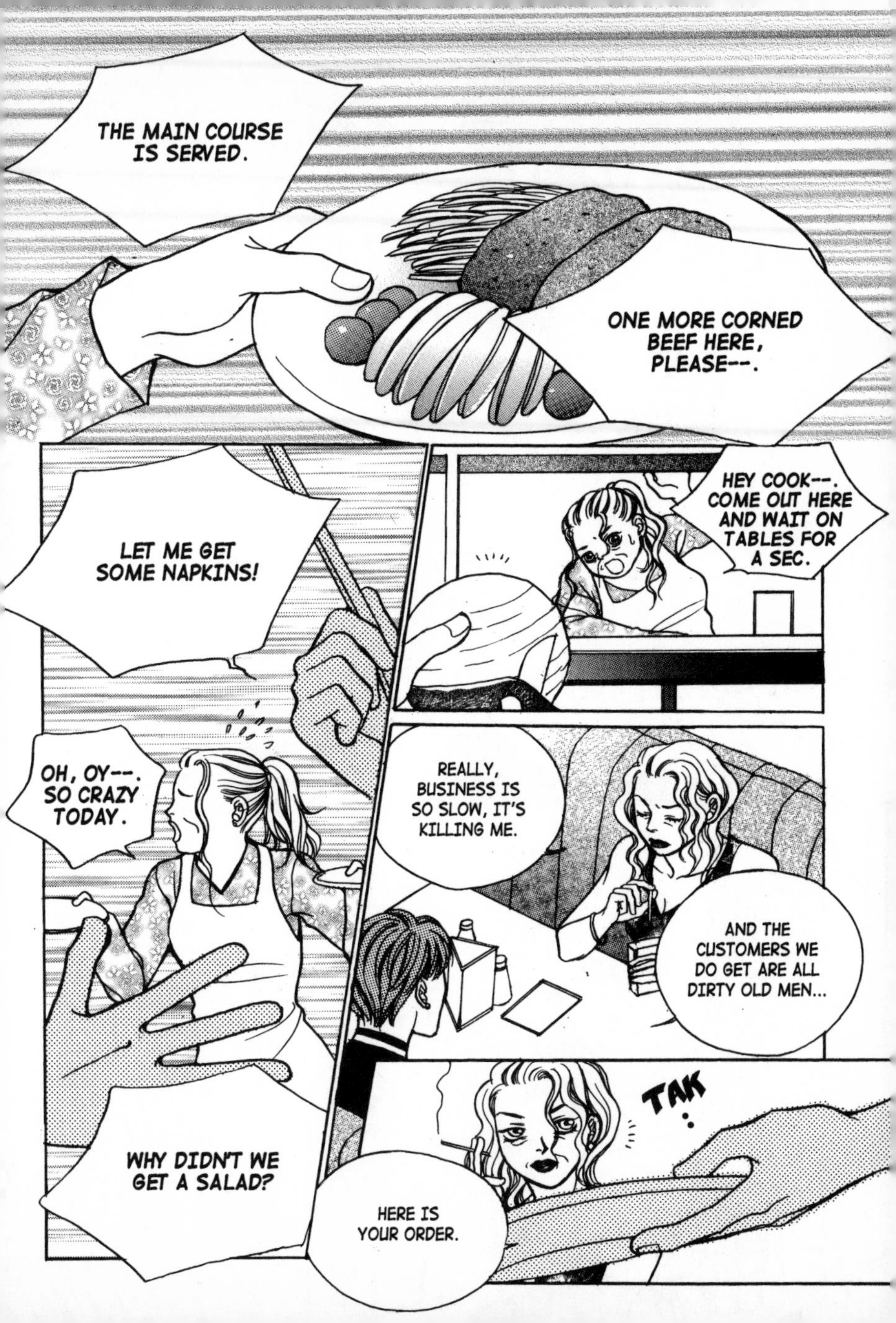
THE MAIN COURSE IS SERVED.
ONE MORE CORNED BEEF HERE, PLEASE--.
LET ME GET SOME NAPKINS!
OH, OY--. SO CRAZY TODAY.
WHY DIDN'T WE GET A SALAD?
HEY COOK--. COME OUT HERE AND WAIT ON TABLES FOR A SEC.
REALLY, BUSINESS IS SO SLOW, IT'S KILLING ME.
AND THE CUSTOMERS WE DO GET ARE ALL DIRTY OLD MEN...
TAK
HERE IS YOUR ORDER.

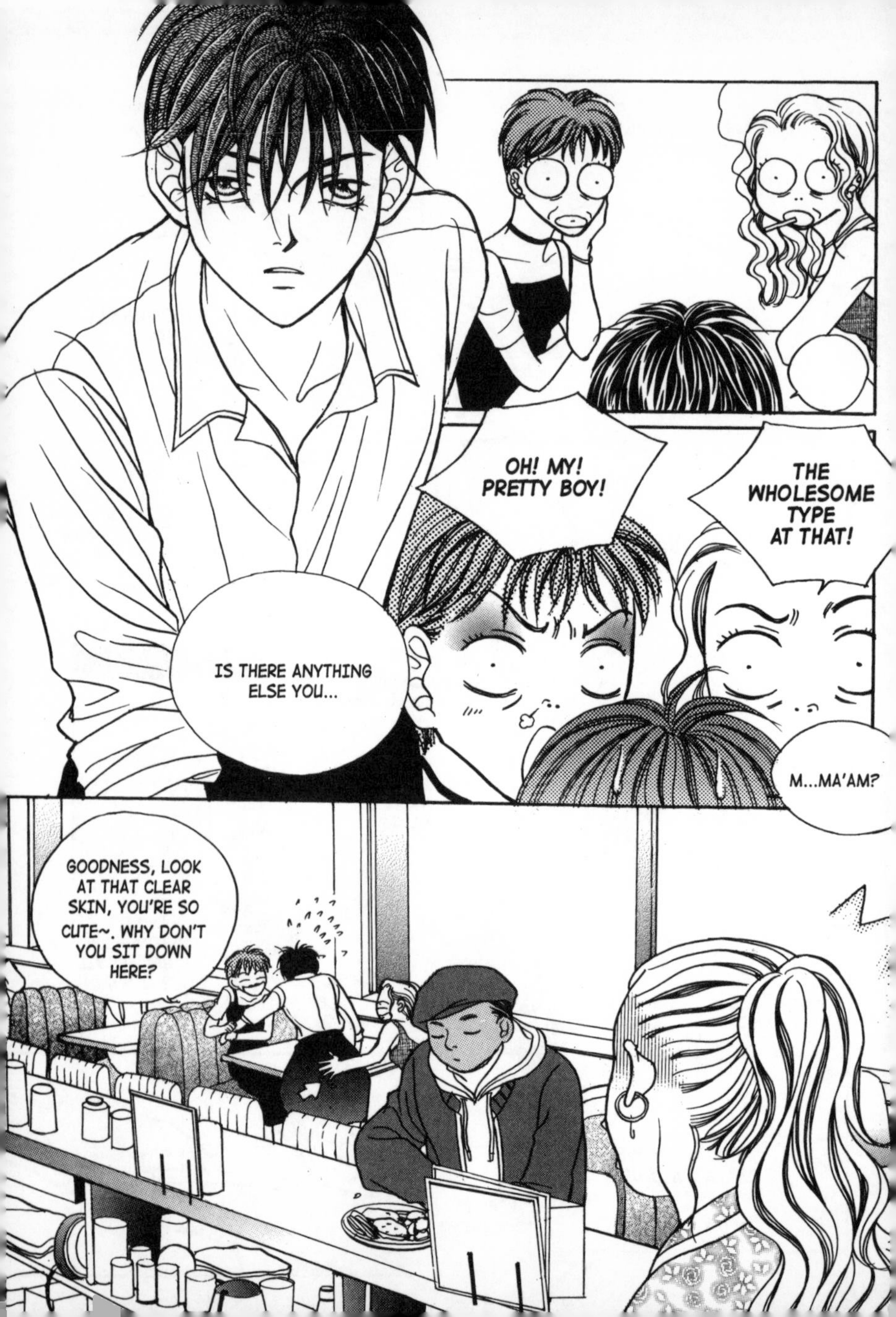
OH! MY! PRETTY BOY!
THE WHOLESOME TYPE AT THAT!
IS THERE ANYTHING ELSE YOU...
M...MA'AM?
GOODNESS, LOOK AT THAT CLEAR SKIN, YOU'RE SO CUTE~. WHY DON'T YOU SIT DOWN HERE?

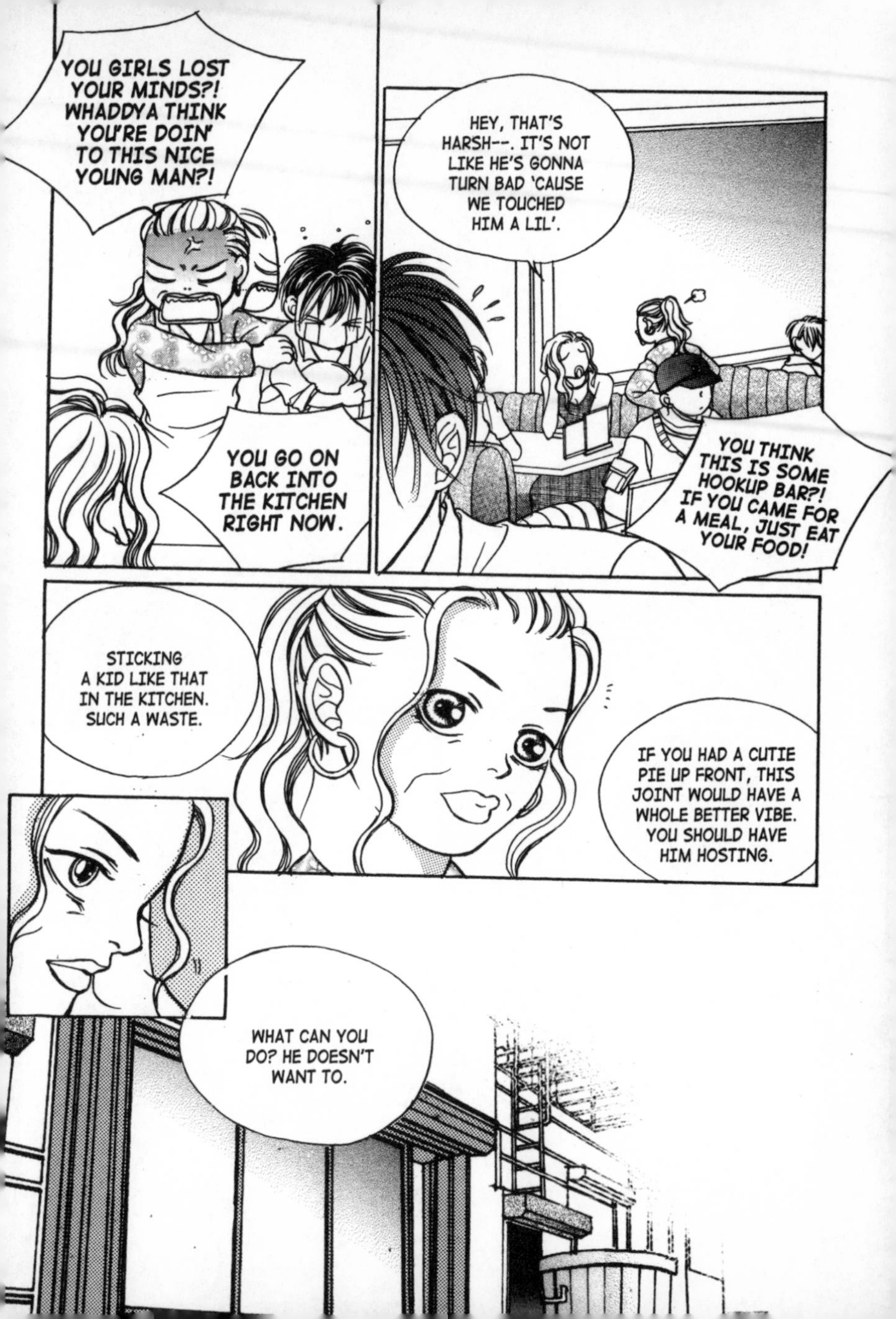
YOU GIRLS LOST YOUR MINDS?! WHADDYA THINK YOU'RE DOIN' TO THIS NICE YOUNG MAN?!
YOU GO ON BACK INTO THE KITCHEN RIGHT NOW.
HEY, THAT'S HARSH--. IT'S NOT LIKE HE'S GONNA TURN BAD 'CAUSE WE TOUCHED HIM A LIL'.
YOU THINK THIS IS SOME HOOKUP BAR?! IF YOU CAME FOR A MEAL, JUST EAT YOUR FOOD!
STICKING A KID LIKE THAT IN THE KITCHEN. SUCH A WASTE.
IF YOU HAD A CUTIE PIE UP FRONT, THIS JOINT WOULD HAVE A WHOLE BETTER VIBE. YOU SHOULD HAVE HIM HOSTING.
WHAT CAN YOU DO? HE DOESN'T WANT TO.

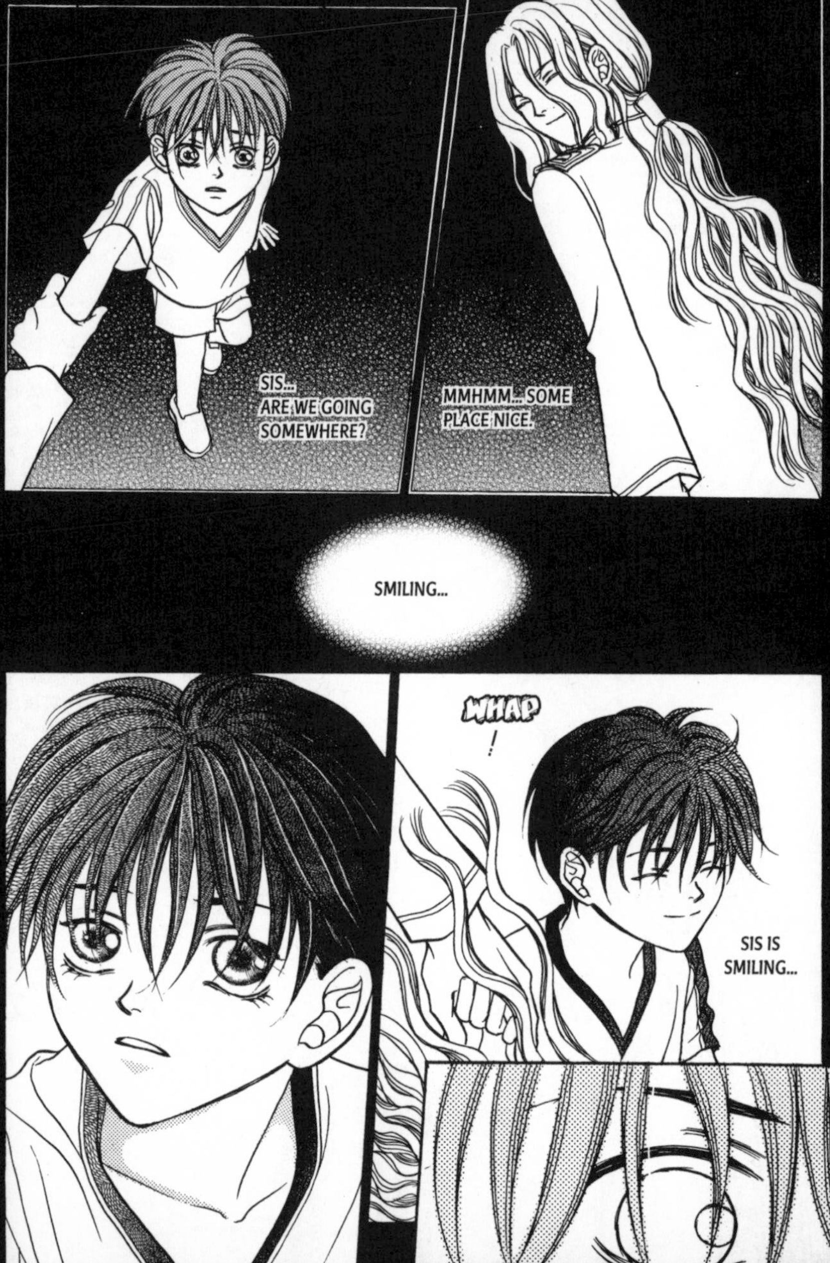
SIS...
ARE WE GOING
SOMEWHERE?
MMHMM... SOME
PLACE NICE.
SMILING...
WHAP
!
SIS IS
SMILING...

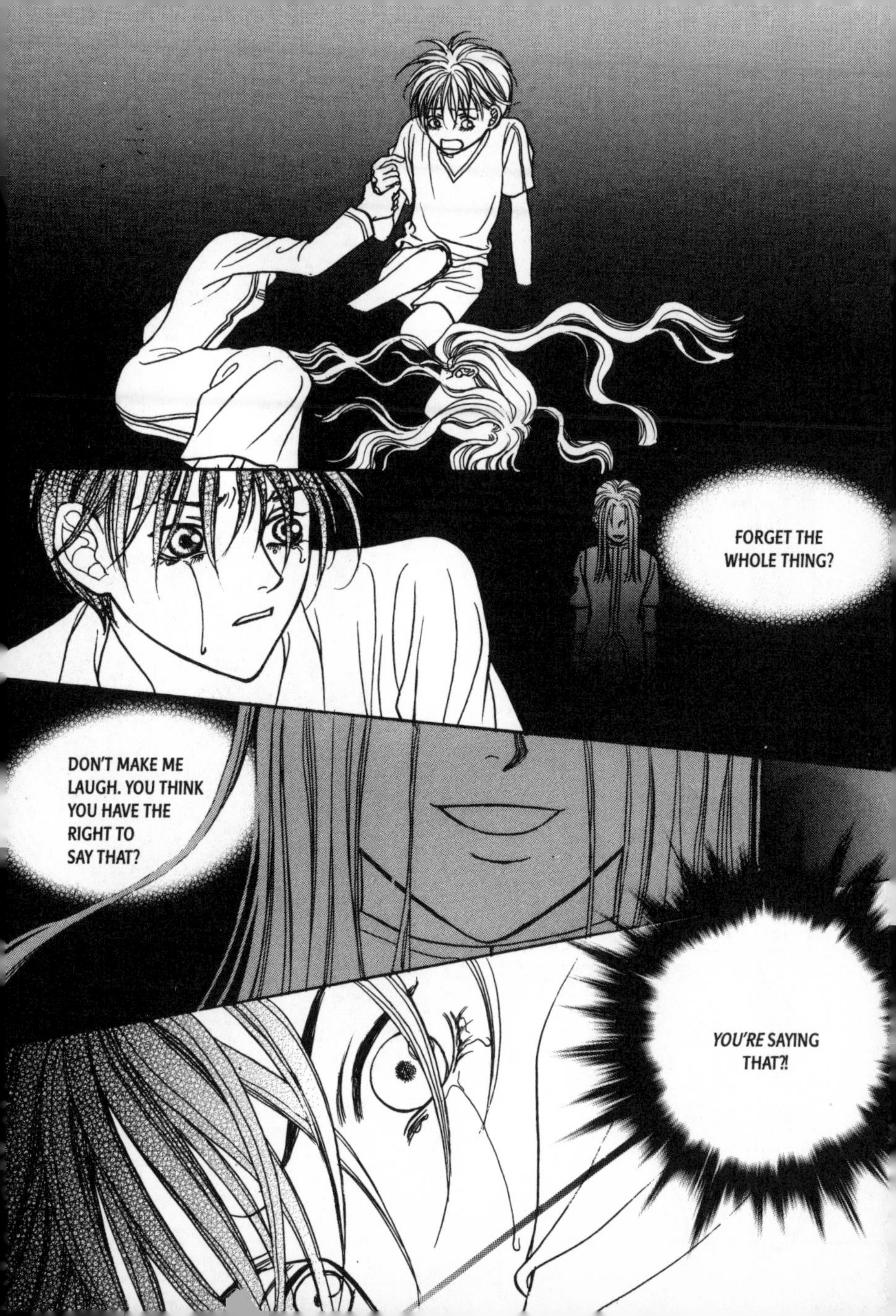
FORGET THE WHOLE THING?
DON'T MAKE ME LAUGH. YOU THINK YOU HAVE THE RIGHT TO SAY THAT?
YOU'RE SAYING THAT?!

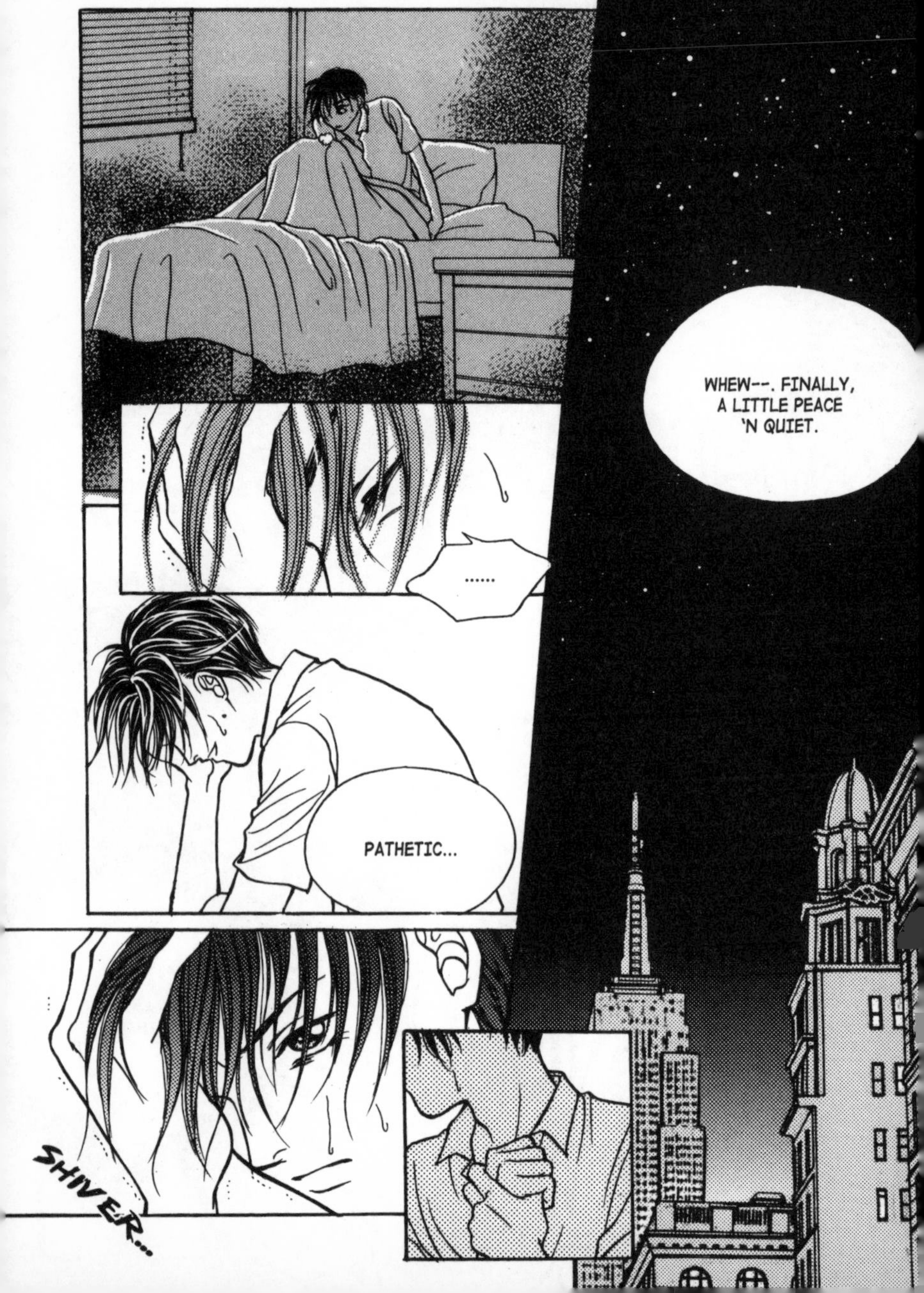
......
PATHETIC...
SHIVER...
WHEW--. FINALLY, A LITTLE PEACE 'N QUIET.

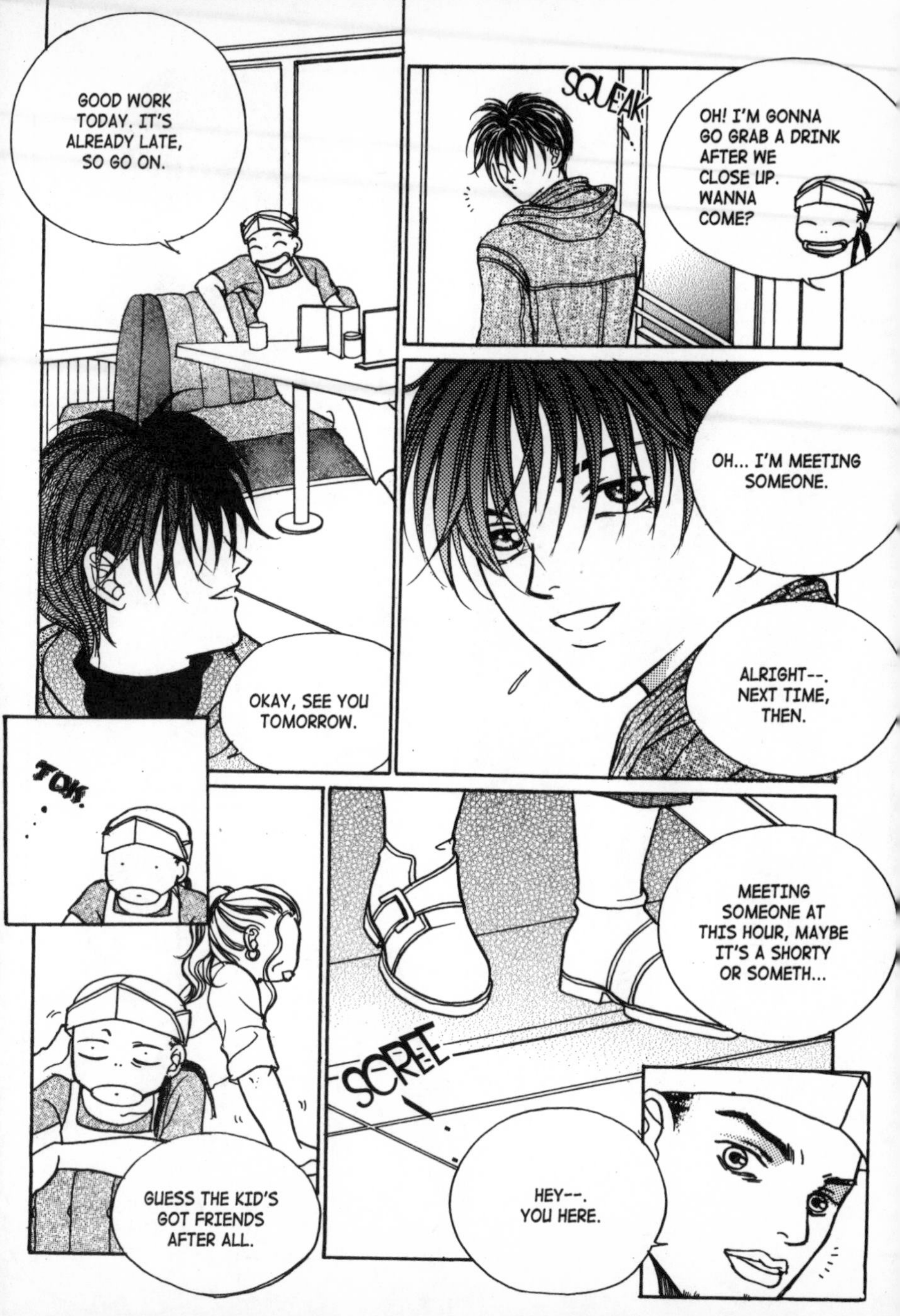
GOOD WORK TODAY. IT'S ALREADY LATE, SO GO ON.
OKAY, SEE YOU TOMORROW.
SQUEAK
OH! I'M GONNA GO GRAB A DRINK AFTER WE CLOSE UP. WANNA COME?
OH... I'M MEETING SOMEONE.
ALRIGHT--. NEXT TIME, THEN.
TOK.
GUESS THE KID'S GOT FRIENDS AFTER ALL.
MEETING SOMEONE AT THIS HOUR, MAYBE IT'S A SHORTY OR SOMETH...
SCREE
HEY--. YOU HERE.

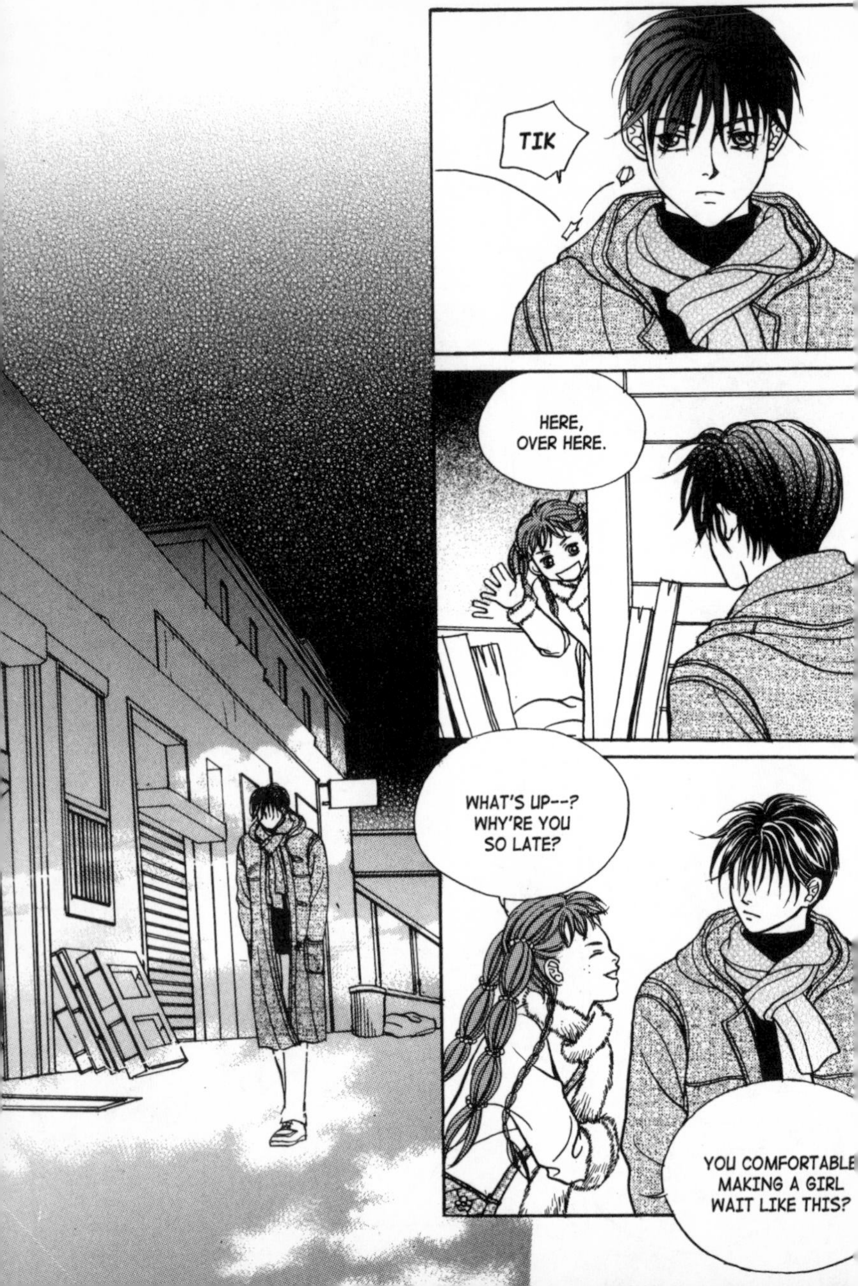
TIK
HERE, OVER HERE.
WHAT'S UP--? WHY'RE YOU SO LATE?
YOU COMFORTABLE MAKING A GIRL WAIT LIKE THIS?

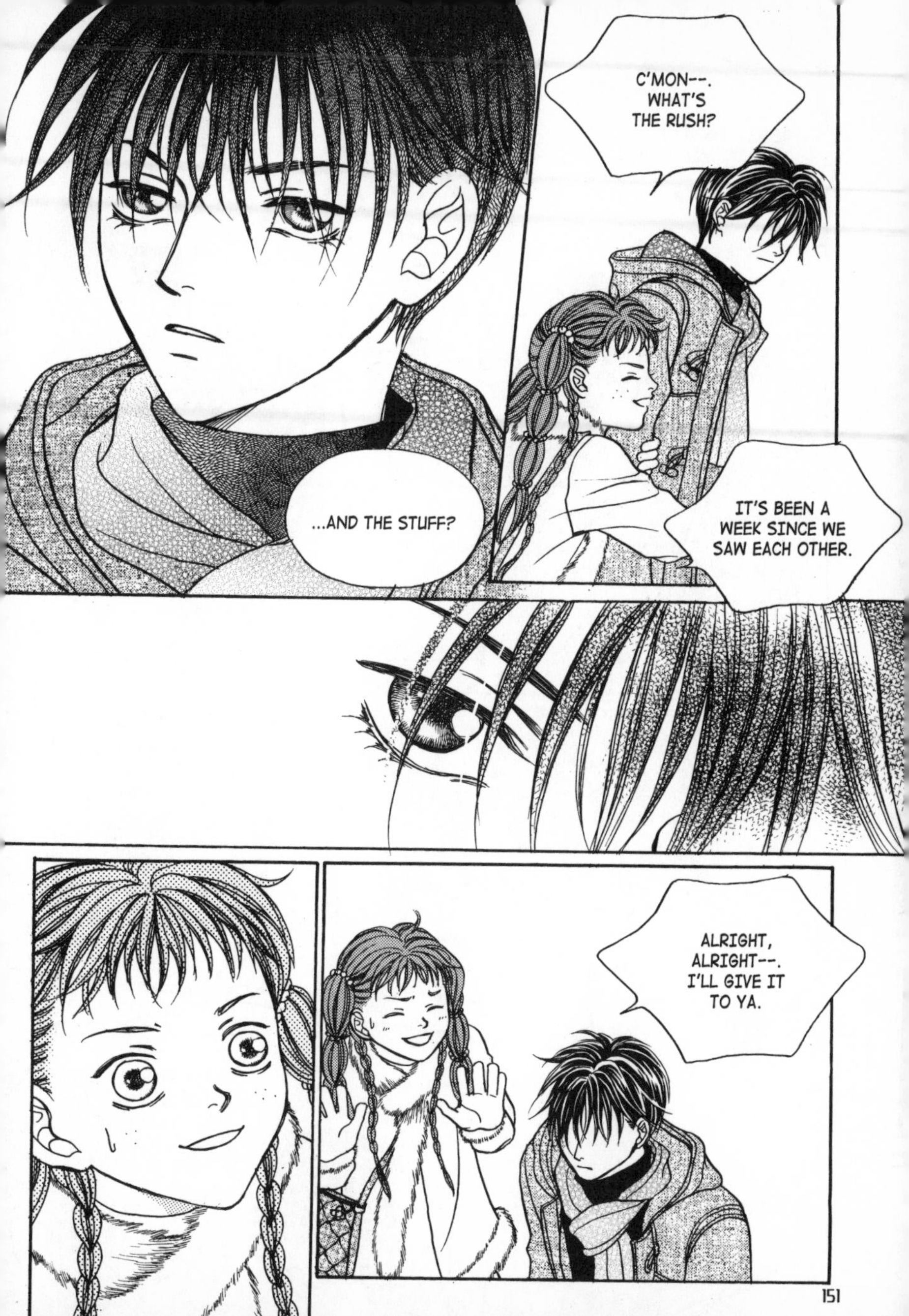
...AND THE STUFF?
C'MON--. WHAT'S THE RUSH?
IT'S BEEN A WEEK SINCE WE SAW EACH OTHER.
ALRIGHT, ALRIGHT--. I'LL GIVE IT TO YA.

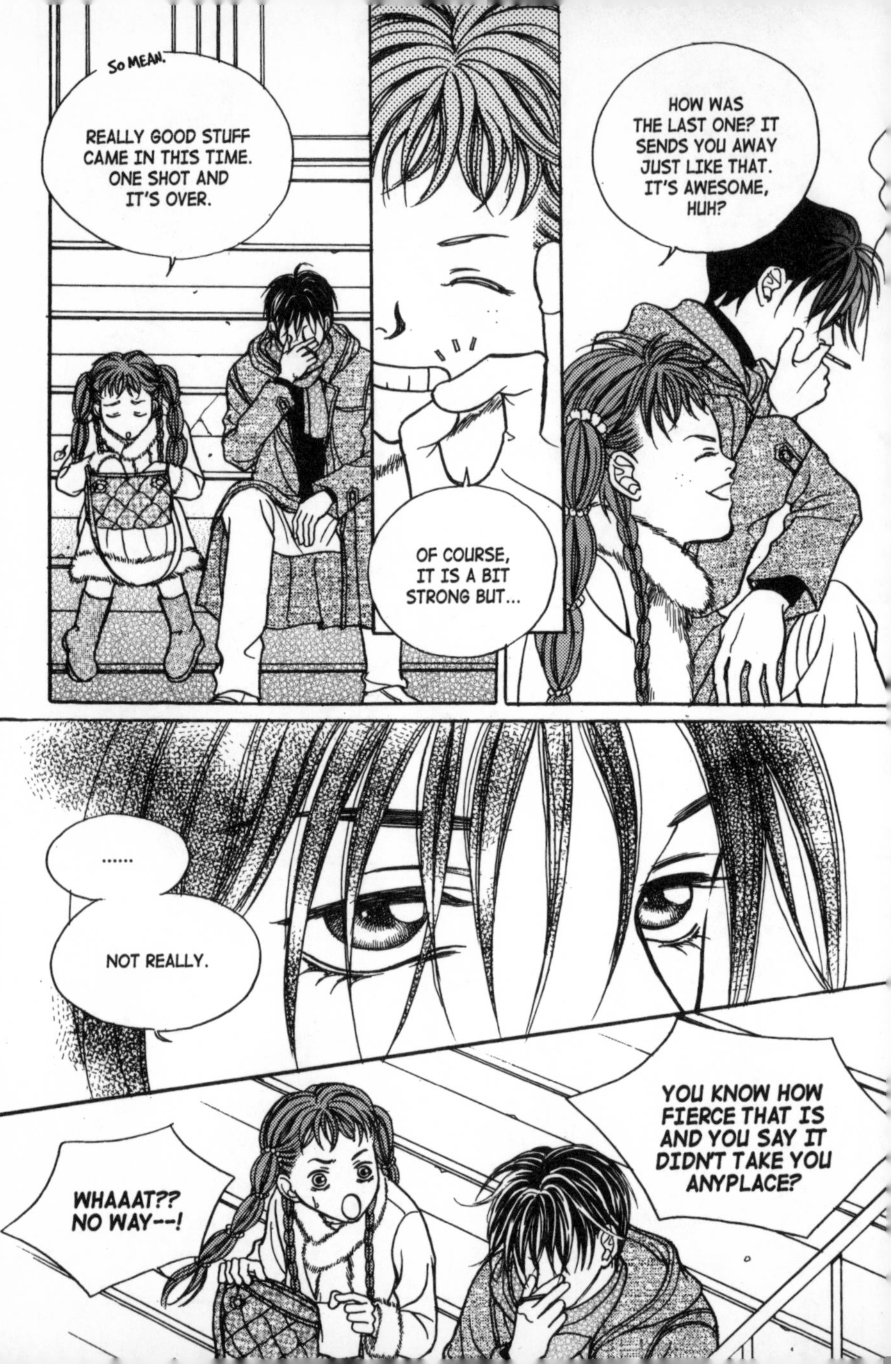
SO MEAN.
REALLY GOOD STUFF CAME IN THIS TIME. ONE SHOT AND IT'S OVER.
OF COURSE, IT IS A BIT STRONG BUT...
HOW WAS THE LAST ONE? IT SENDS YOU AWAY JUST LIKE THAT. IT'S AWESOME, HUH?
......
NOT REALLY.
WHAAAT?? NO WAY--!
YOU KNOW HOW FIERCE THAT IS AND YOU SAY IT DIDN'T TAKE YOU ANYPLACE?

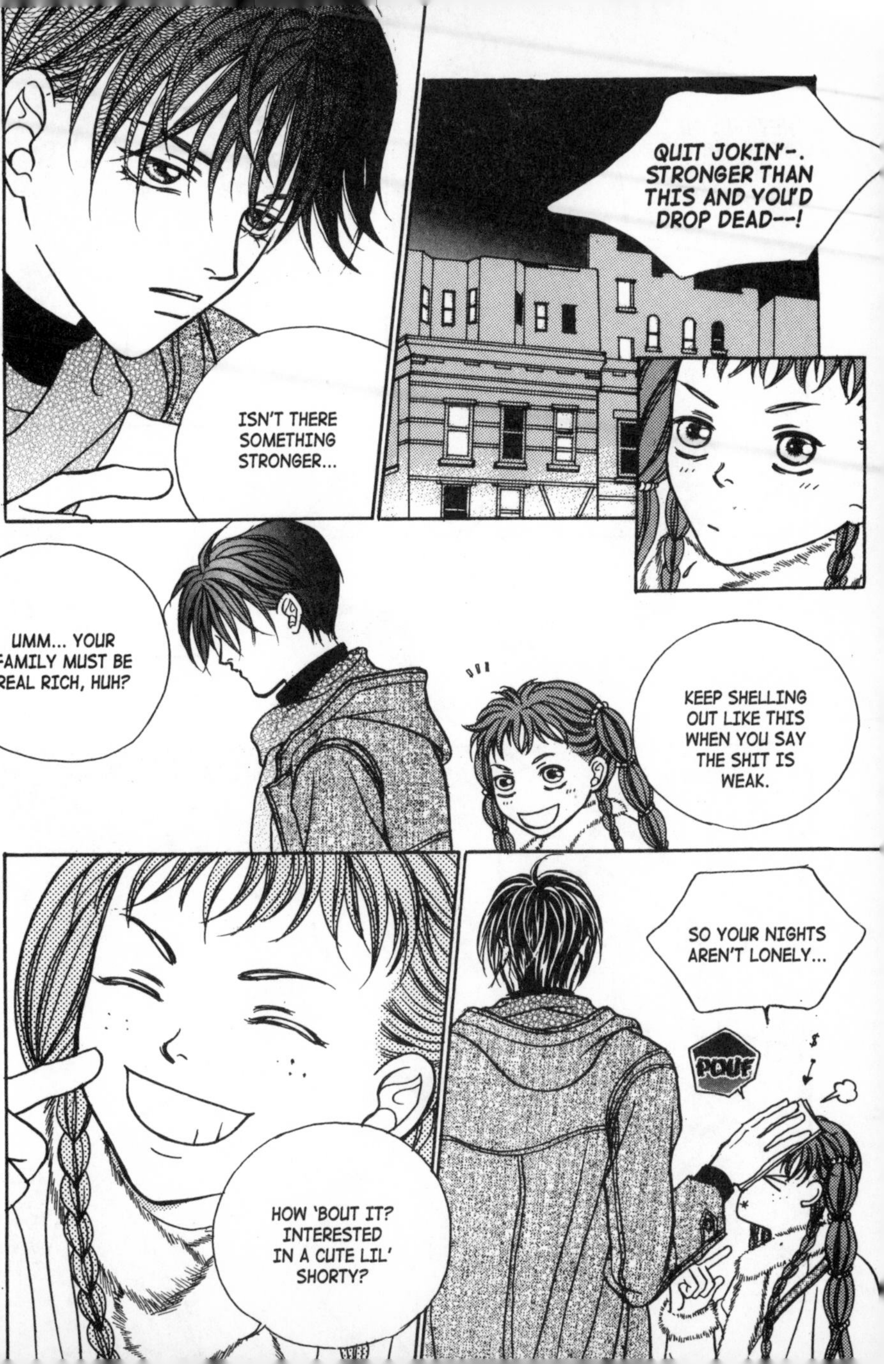
ISN'T THERE SOMETHING STRONGER...
QUIT JOKIN'-. STRONGER THAN THIS AND YOU'D DROP DEAD--!
UMM... YOUR FAMILY MUST BE REAL RICH, HUH?
KEEP SHELLING OUT LIKE THIS WHEN YOU SAY THE SHIT IS WEAK.
HOW 'BOUT IT? INTERESTED IN A CUTE LIL' SHORTY?
SO YOUR NIGHTS AREN'T LONELY...
POUF

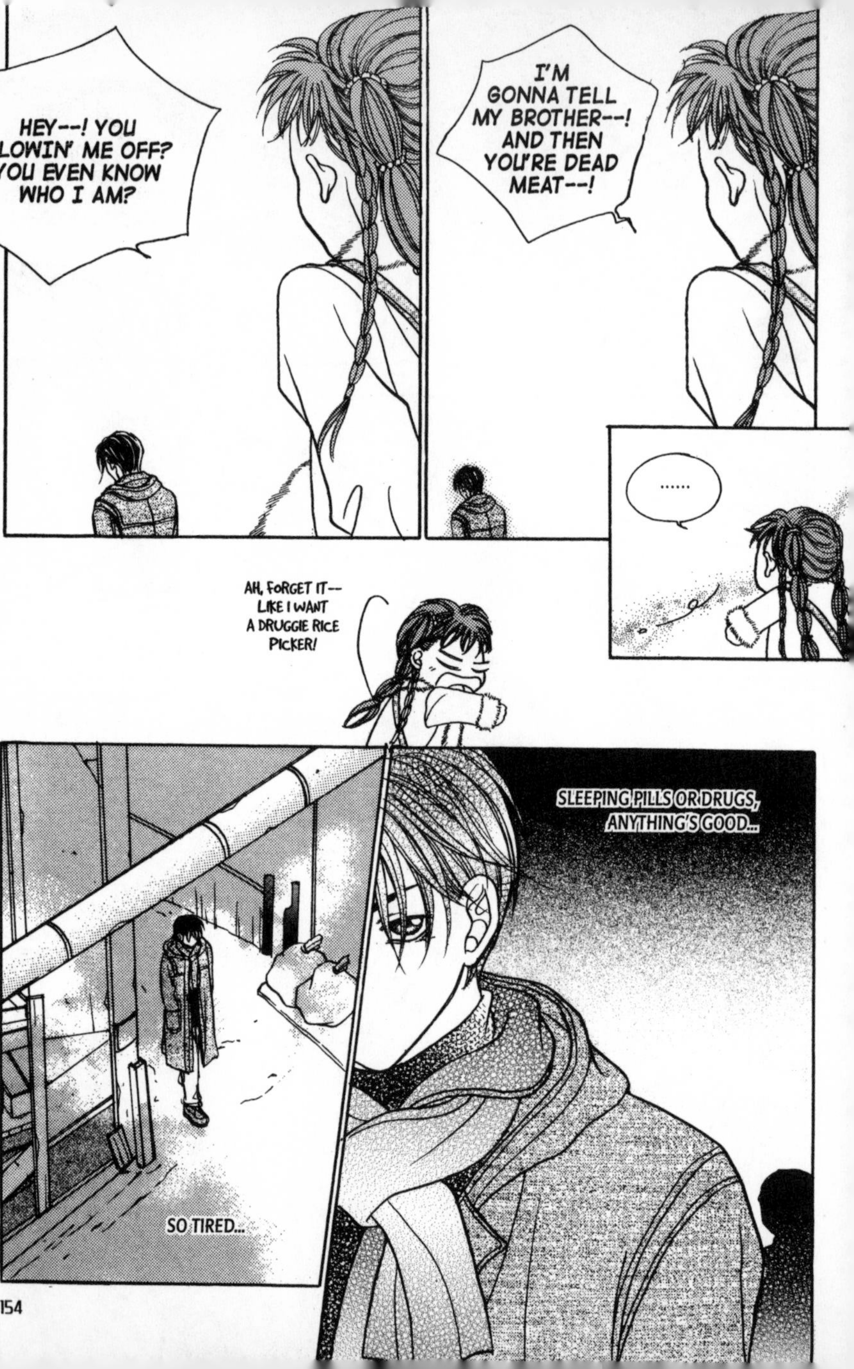
HEY--! YOU BLOWIN' ME OFF? YOU EVEN KNOW WHO I AM?
I'M GONNA TELL MY BROTHER--! AND THEN YOU'RE DEAD MEAT--!
......
AH, FORGET IT-- LIKE I WANT A DRUGGIE RICE PICKER!
SO TIRED...
SLEEPING PILLS OR DRUGS, ANYTHING'S GOOD...

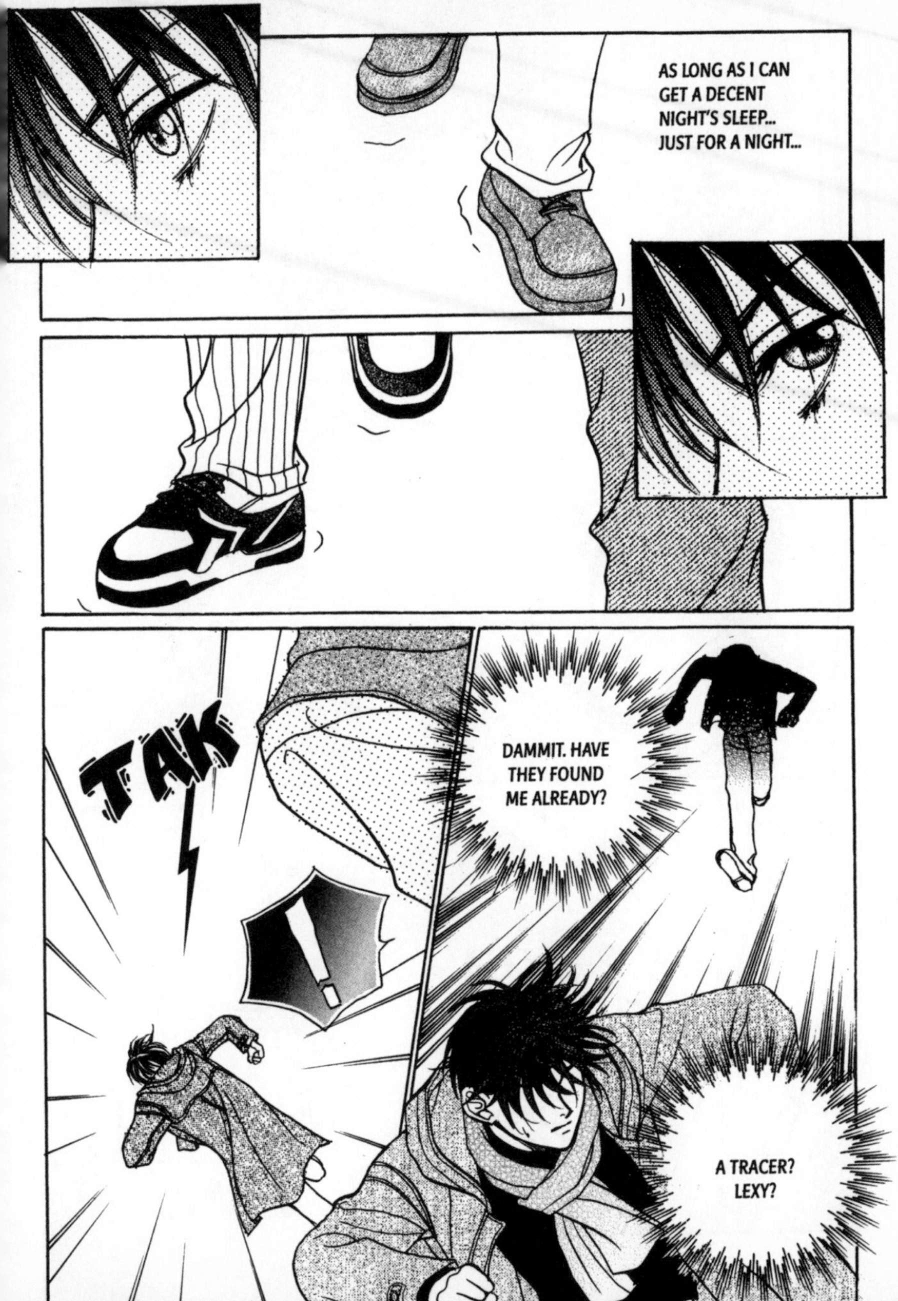
AS LONG AS I CAN GET A DECENT NIGHT'S SLEEP... JUST FOR A NIGHT...
TAK
!
DAMMIT. HAVE THEY FOUND ME ALREADY?
A TRACER? LEXY?

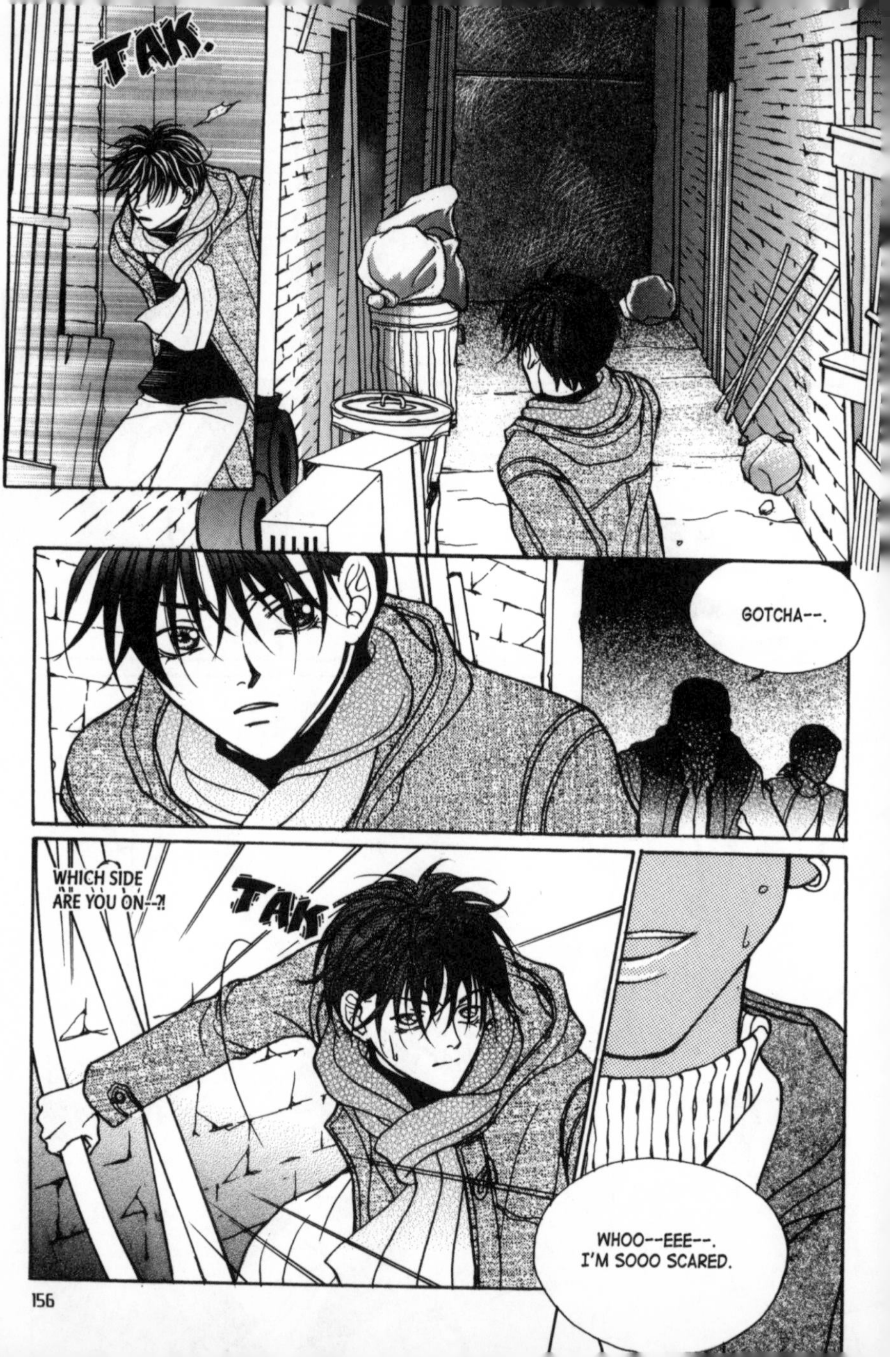
TAK.
GOTCHA--.
WHICH SIDE ARE YOU ON--?!
TAK
WHOO--EEE--. I'M SOOO SCARED.

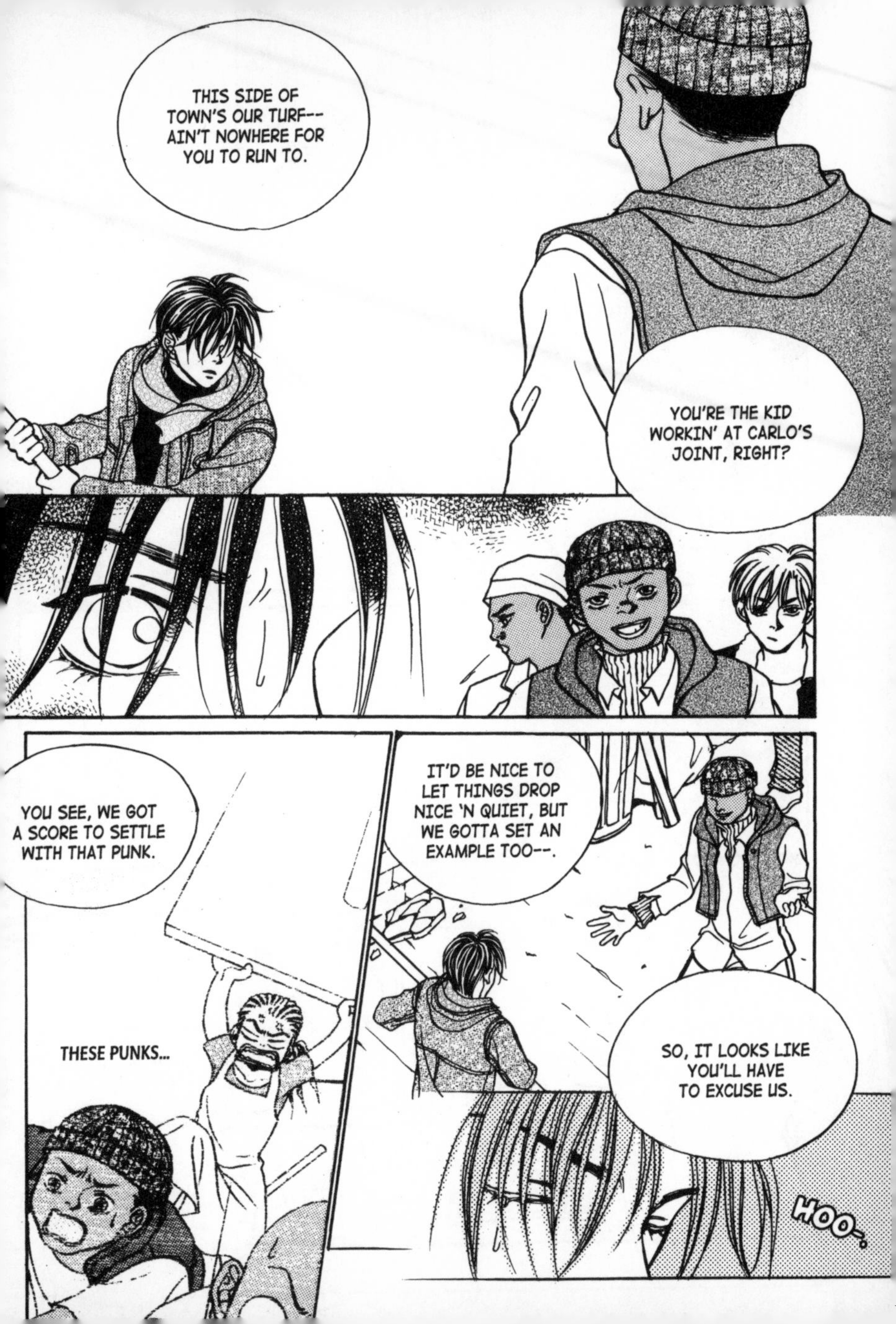
THIS SIDE OF TOWN'S OUR TURF-- AIN'T NOWHERE FOR YOU TO RUN TO.
YOU'RE THE KID WORKIN' AT CARLO'S JOINT, RIGHT?
YOU SEE, WE GOT A SCORE TO SETTLE WITH THAT PUNK.
THESE PUNKS...
IT'D BE NICE TO LET THINGS DROP NICE 'N QUIET, BUT WE GOTTA SET AN EXAMPLE TOO--.
SO, IT LOOKS LIKE YOU'LL HAVE TO EXCUSE US.
HOO-.

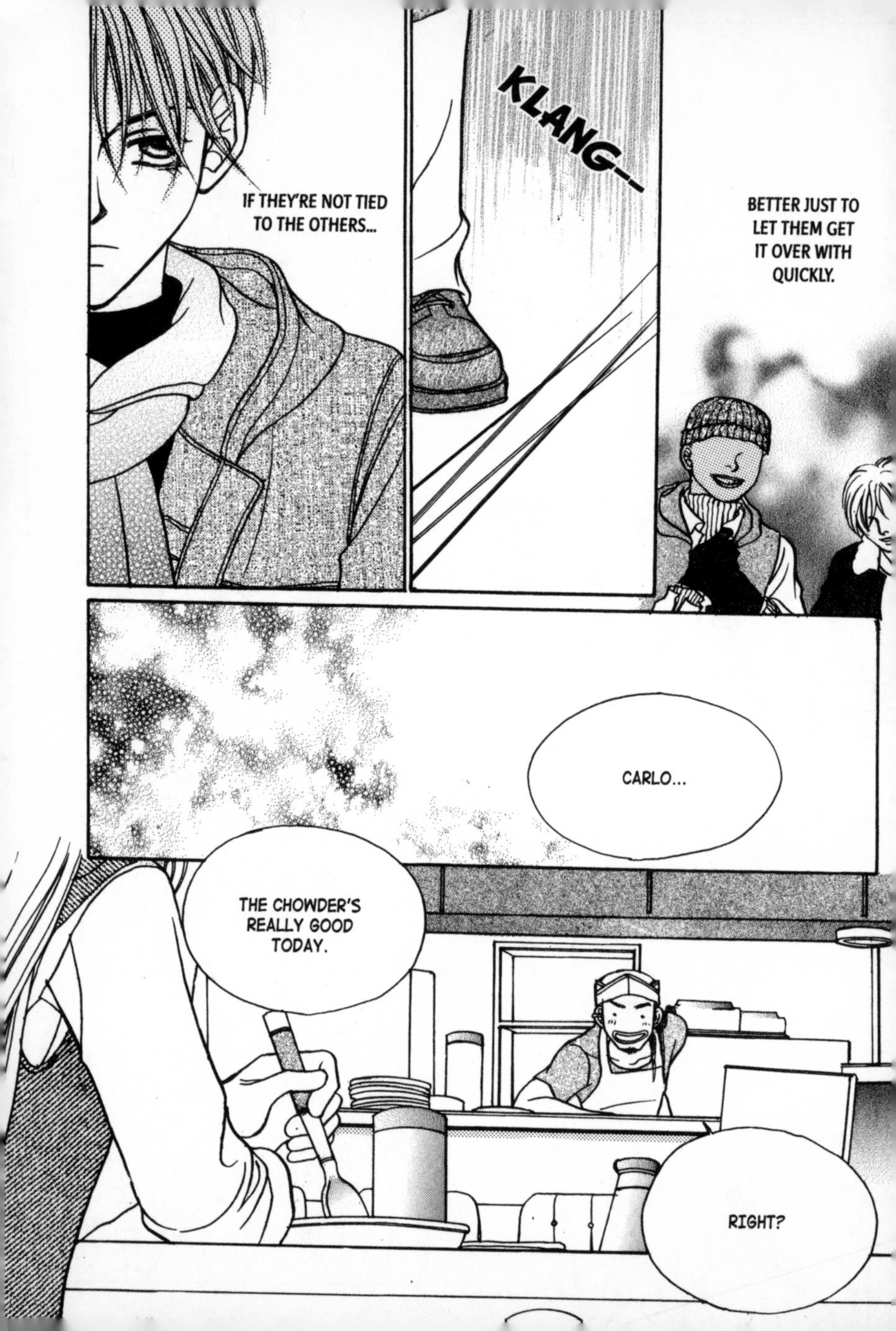
IF THEY'RE NOT TIED TO THE OTHERS...
KLANG--
BETTER JUST TO LET THEM GET IT OVER WITH QUICKLY.
CARLO...
THE CHOWDER'S REALLY GOOD TODAY.
RIGHT?

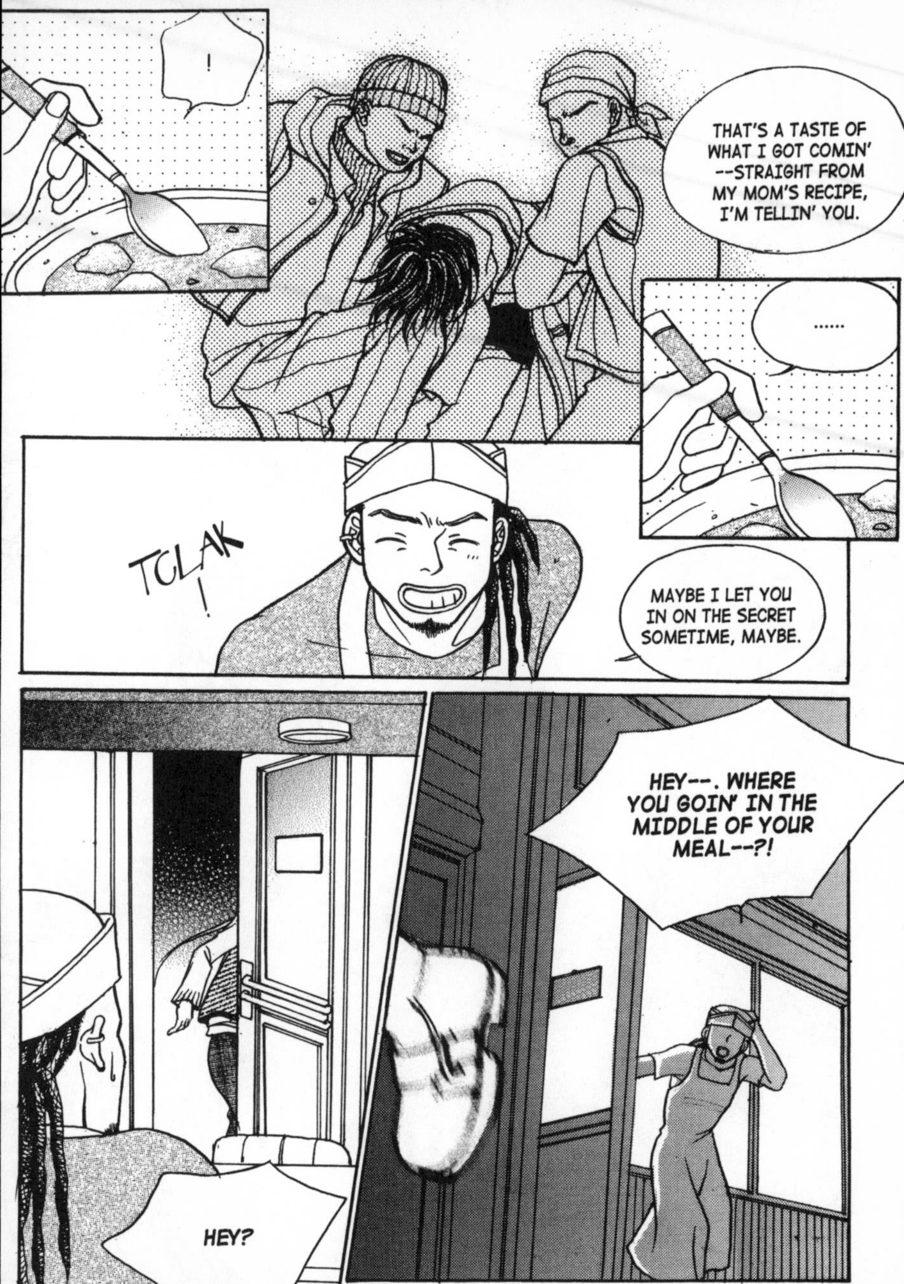
!
THAT'S A TASTE OF WHAT I GOT COMIN' --STRAIGHT FROM MY MOM'S RECIPE, I'M TELLIN' YOU.
......
TCLAK !
MAYBE I LET YOU IN ON THE SECRET SOMETIME, MAYBE.
HEY?
HEY--. WHERE YOU GOIN' IN THE MIDDLE OF YOUR MEAL--?!

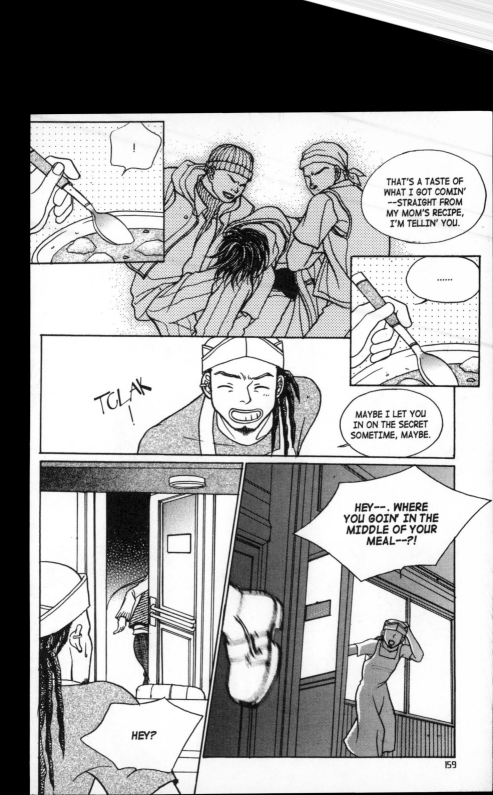

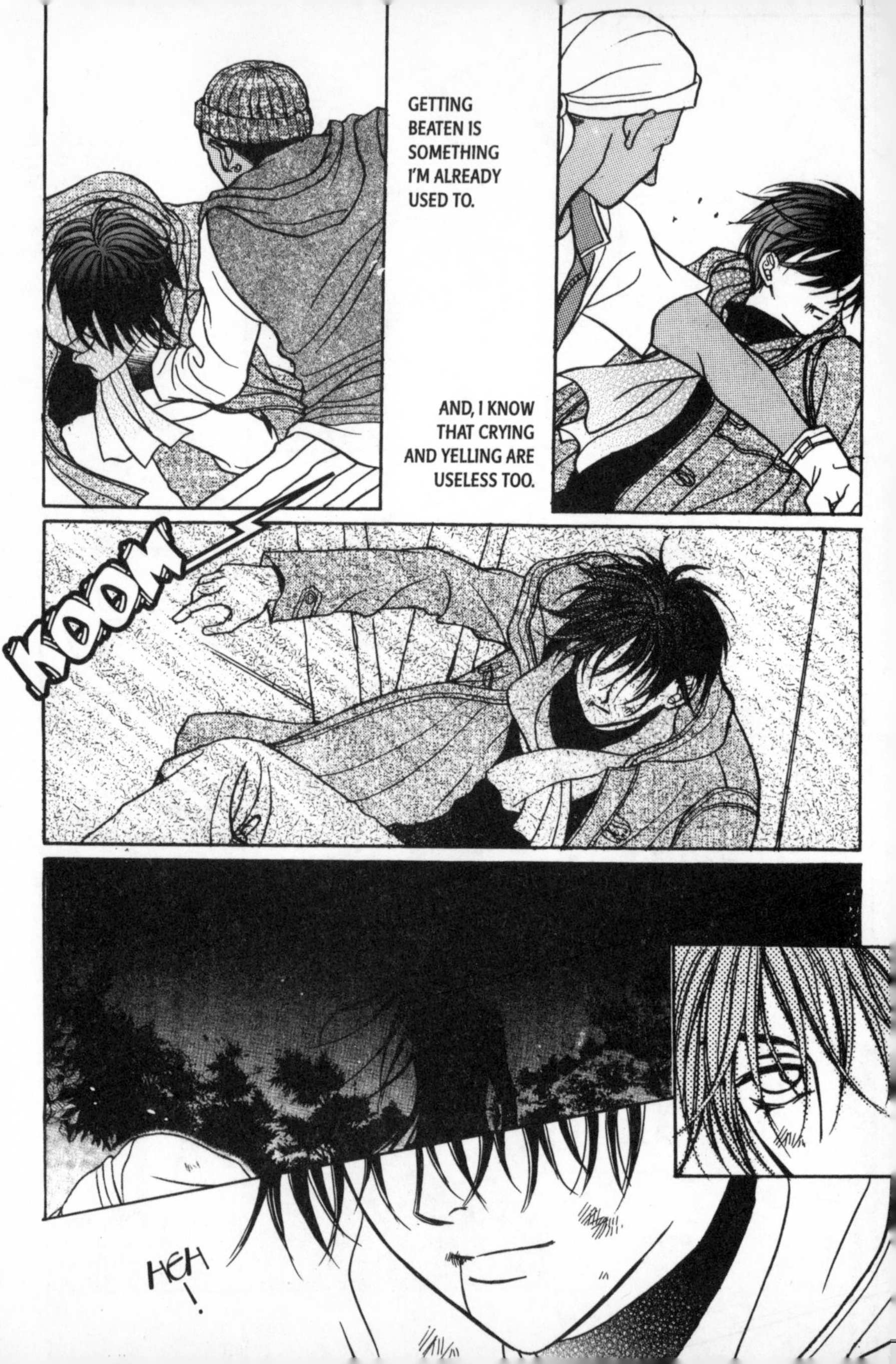
GETTING BEATEN IS SOMETHING I'M ALREADY USED TO.
AND, I KNOW THAT CRYING AND YELLING ARE USELESS TOO.
KOOM
HEH

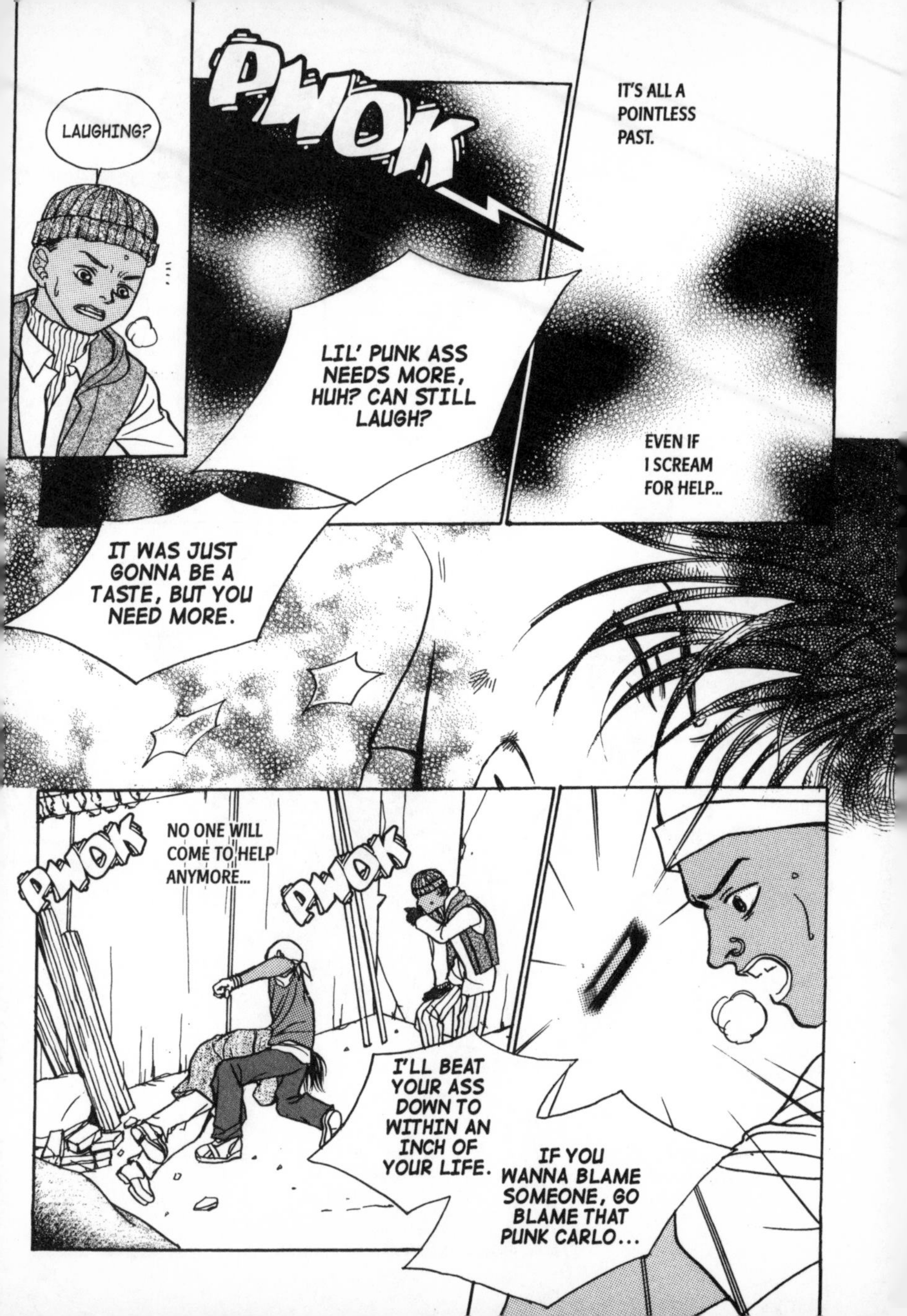
LAUGHING?
PWOK
LIL' PUNK ASS NEEDS MORE, HUH? CAN STILL LAUGH?
IT'S ALL A POINTLESS PAST.
EVEN IF I SCREAM FOR HELP...
IT WAS JUST GONNA BE A TASTE, BUT YOU NEED MORE.
PWOK
NO ONE WILL COME TO HELP ANYMORE...
PWOK
I'LL BEAT YOUR ASS DOWN TO WITHIN AN INCH OF YOUR LIFE.
IF YOU WANNA BLAME SOMEONE, GO BLAME THAT PUNK CARLO...

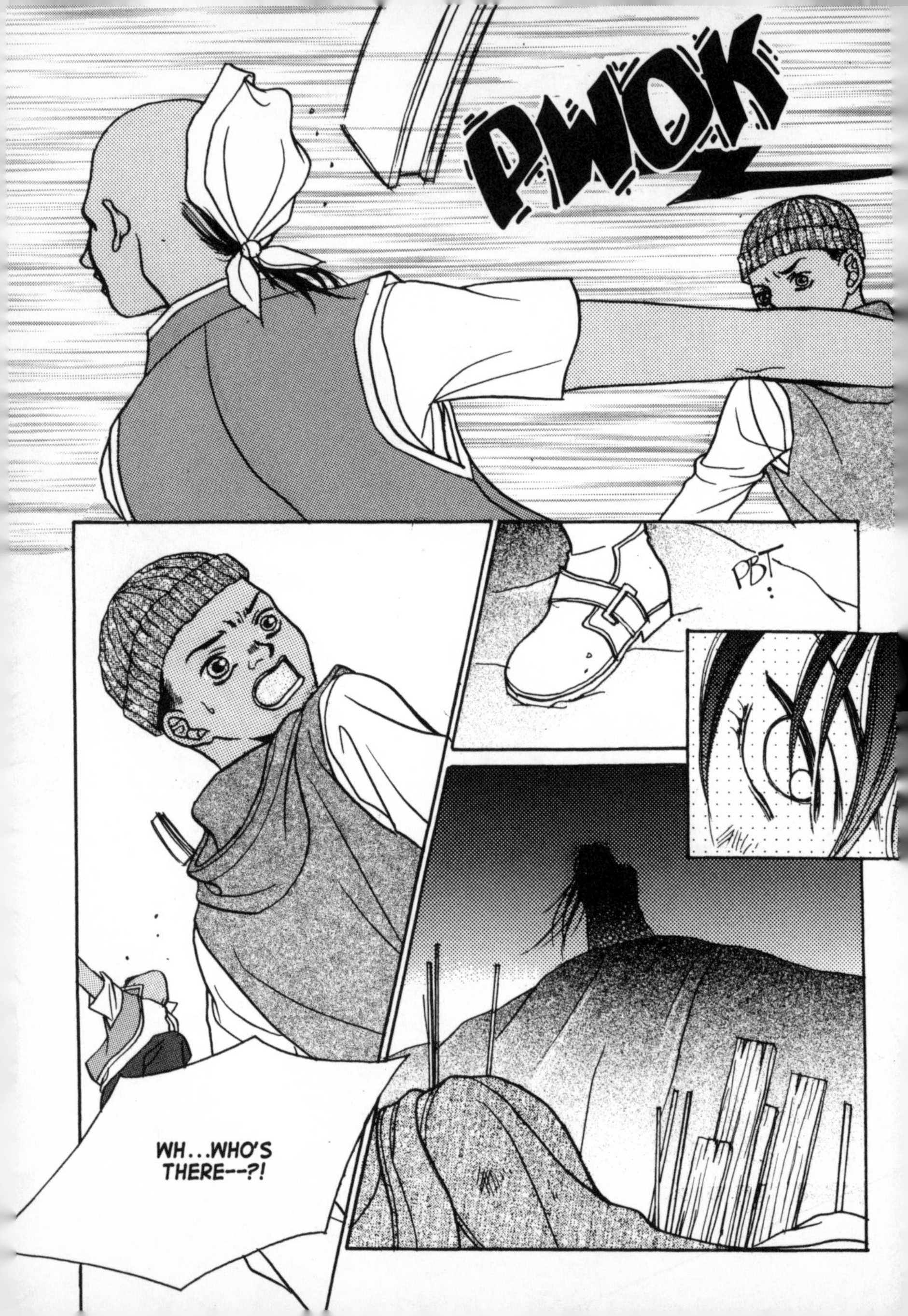
PWOK
WH...WHO'S THERE--?!
PBT

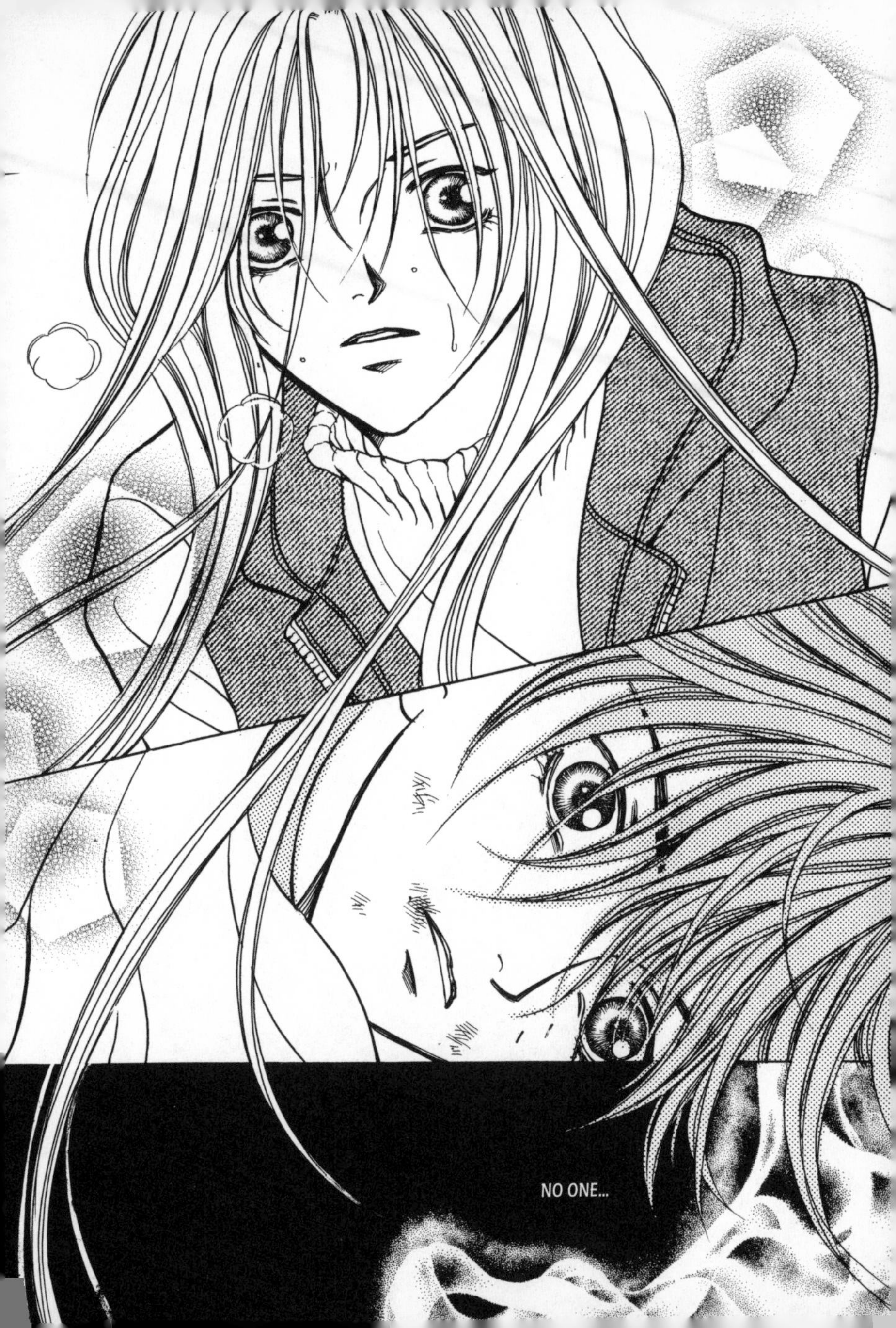
NO ONE...

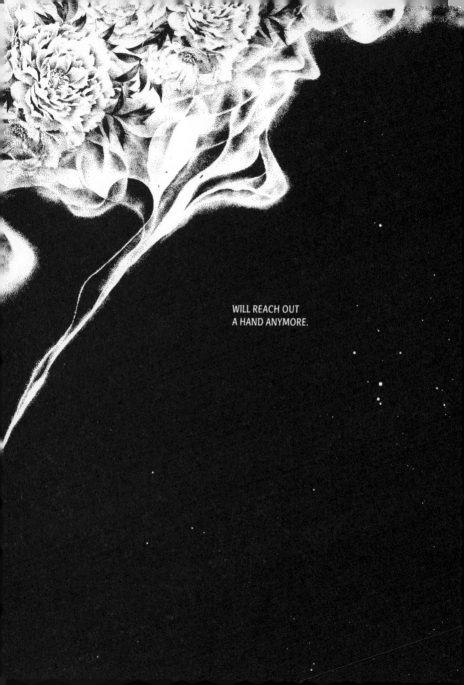

WILL REACH OUT
A HAND ANYMORE.

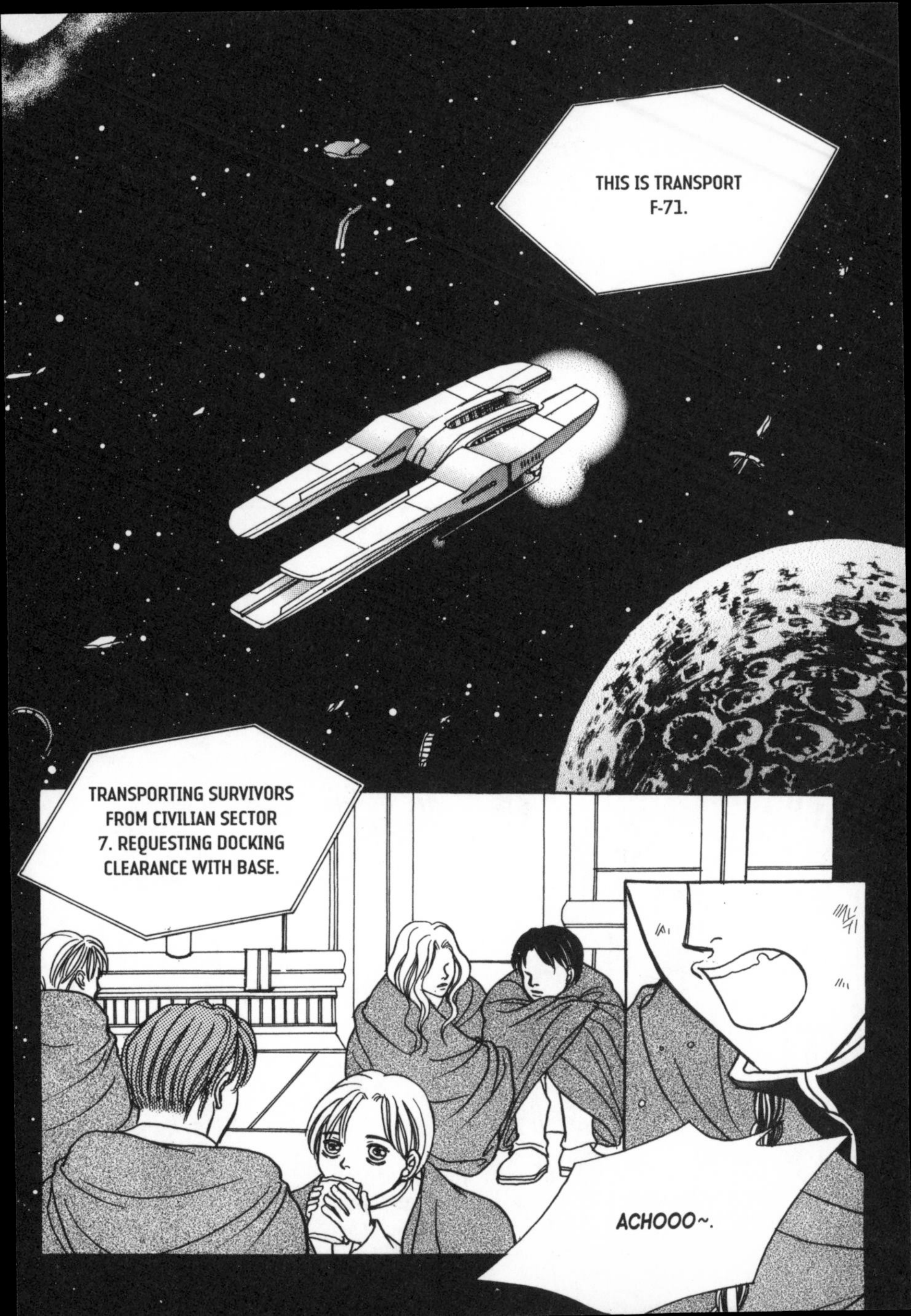
THIS IS TRANSPORT F-71.
TRANSPORTING SURVIVORS FROM CIVILIAN SECTOR 7. REQUESTING DOCKING CLEARANCE WITH BASE.
ACHOOO~.

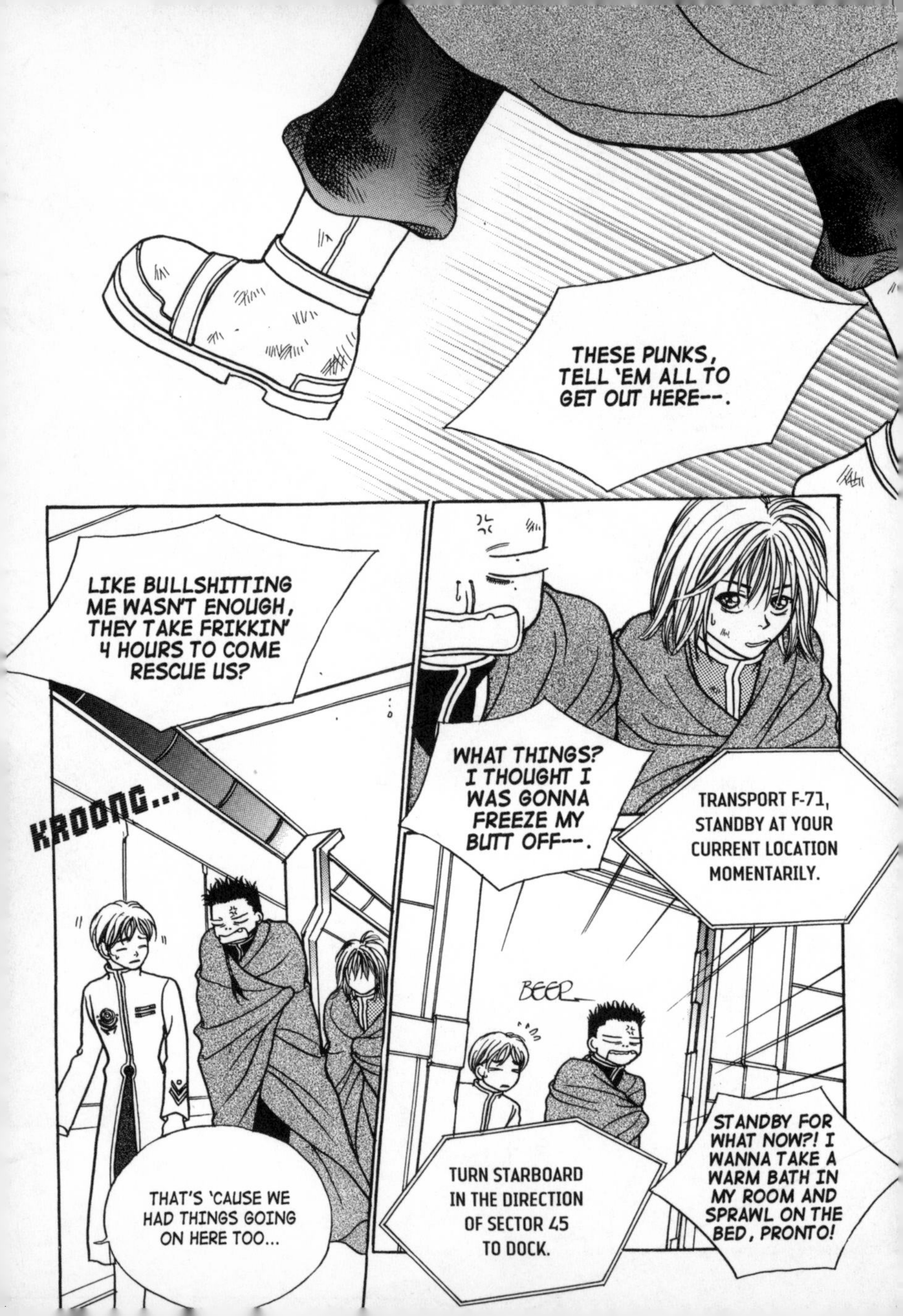
THESE PUNKS, TELL 'EM ALL TO GET OUT HERE--.
LIKE BULLSHITTING ME WASN'T ENOUGH, THEY TAKE FRIKKIN' 4 HOURS TO COME RESCUE US?
KROONG...
THAT'S 'CAUSE WE HAD THINGS GOING ON HERE TOO...
WHAT THINGS? I THOUGHT I WAS GONNA FREEZE MY BUTT OFF--.
TRANSPORT F-71, STANDBY AT YOUR CURRENT LOCATION MOMENTARILY.
BEEP
TURN STARBOARD IN THE DIRECTION OF SECTOR 45 TO DOCK.
STANDBY FOR WHAT NOW?! I WANNA TAKE A WARM BATH IN MY ROOM AND SPRAWL ON THE BED, PRONTO!

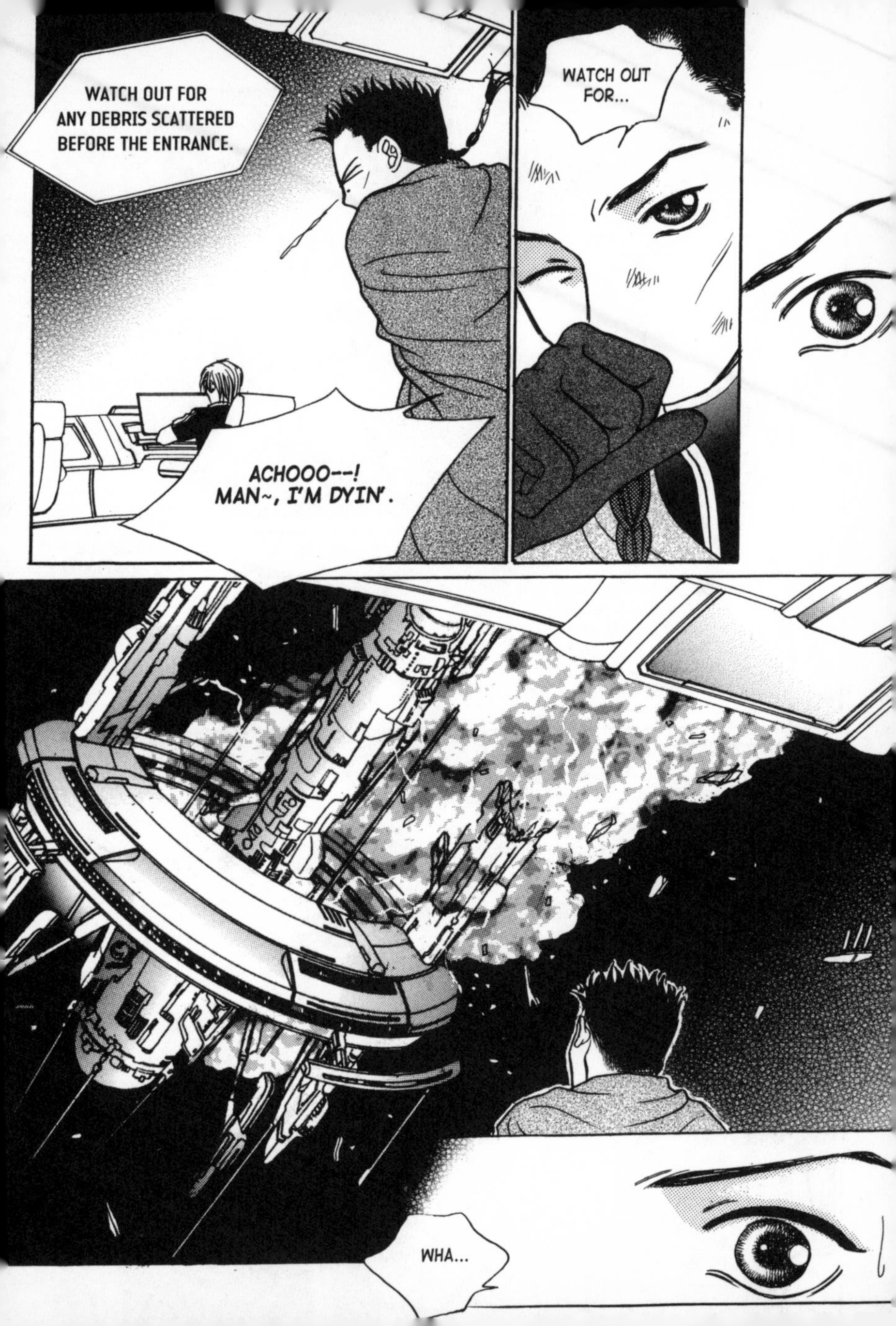
WATCH OUT FOR ANY DEBRIS SCATTERED BEFORE THE ENTRANCE.
ACHOOO--! MAN~, I'M DYIN'.
WATCH OUT FOR...
WHA...

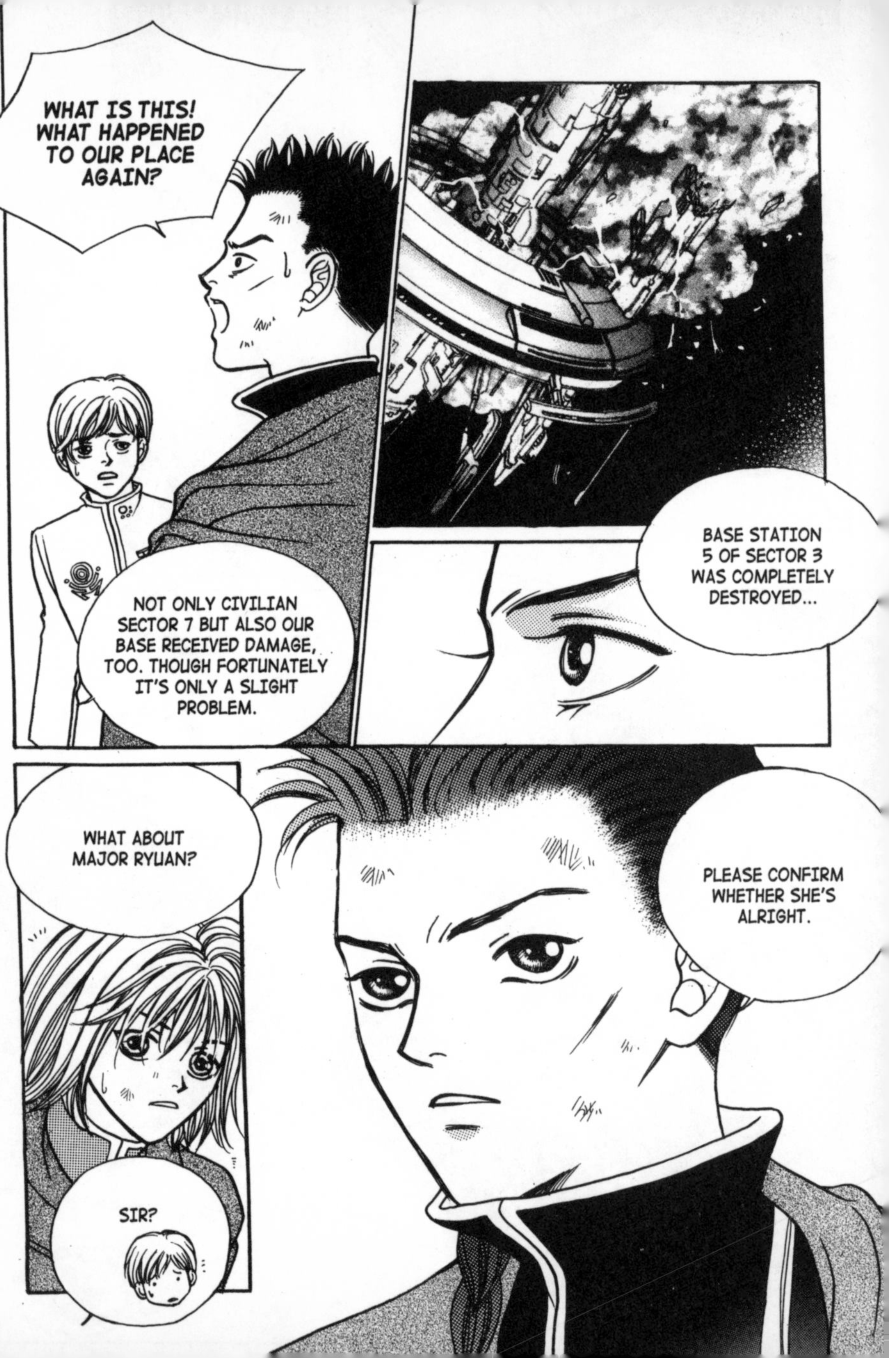
WHAT IS THIS! WHAT HAPPENED TO OUR PLACE AGAIN?
NOT ONLY CIVILIAN SECTOR 7 BUT ALSO OUR BASE RECEIVED DAMAGE, TOO. THOUGH FORTUNATELY IT'S ONLY A SLIGHT PROBLEM.
BASE STATION 5 OF SECTOR 3 WAS COMPLETELY DESTROYED...
WHAT ABOUT MAJOR RYUAN?
SIR?
PLEASE CONFIRM WHETHER SHE'S ALRIGHT.

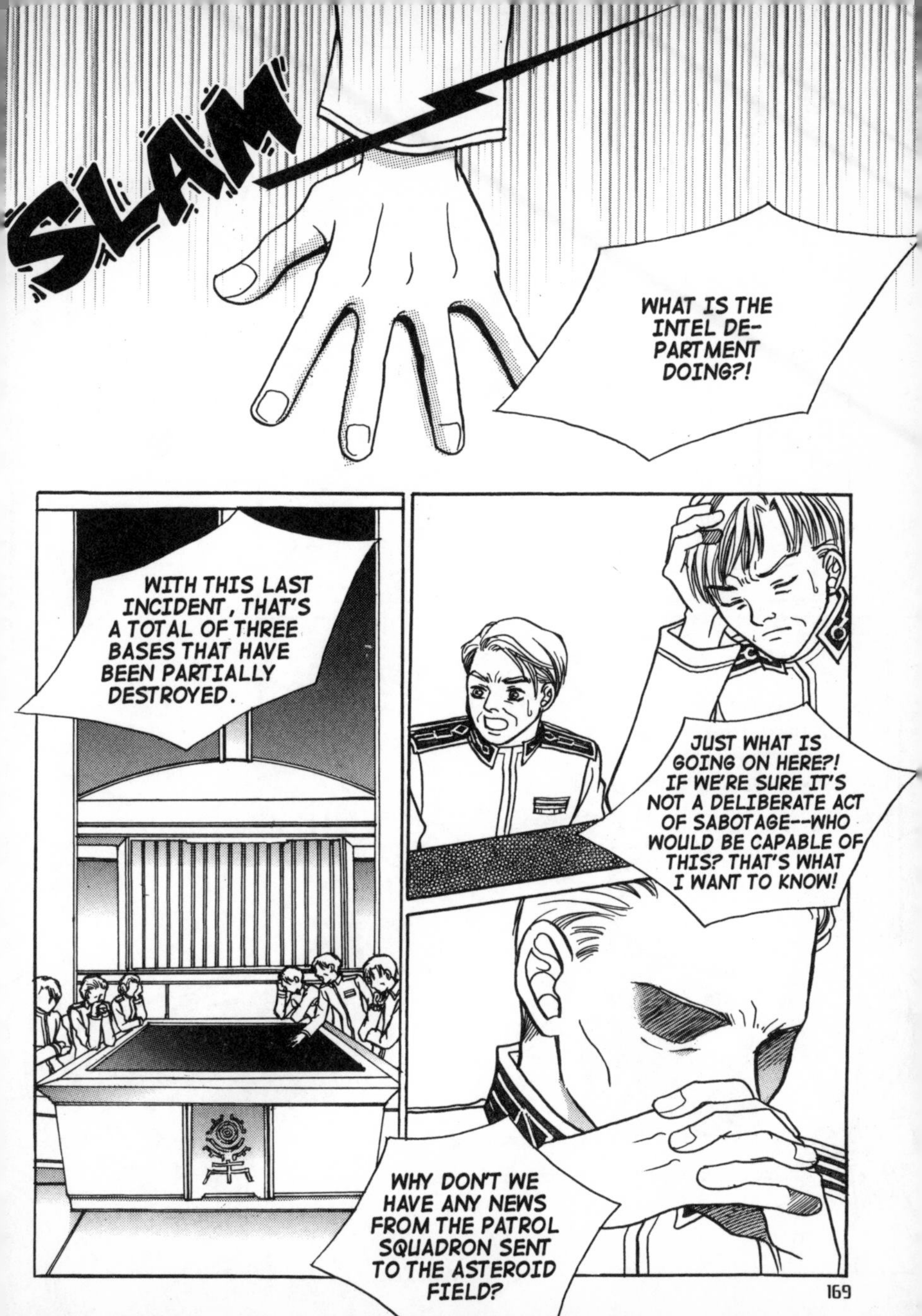
SLAM
WHAT IS THE INTEL DE-PARTMENT DOING?!
WITH THIS LAST INCIDENT, THAT'S A TOTAL OF THREE BASES THAT HAVE BEEN PARTIALLY DESTROYED.
JUST WHAT IS GOING ON HERE?! IF WE'RE SURE IT'S NOT A DELIBERATE ACT OF SABOTAGE--WHO WOULD BE CAPABLE OF THIS? THAT'S WHAT I WANT TO KNOW!
WHY DON'T WE HAVE ANY NEWS FROM THE PATROL SQUADRON SENT TO THE ASTEROID FIELD?

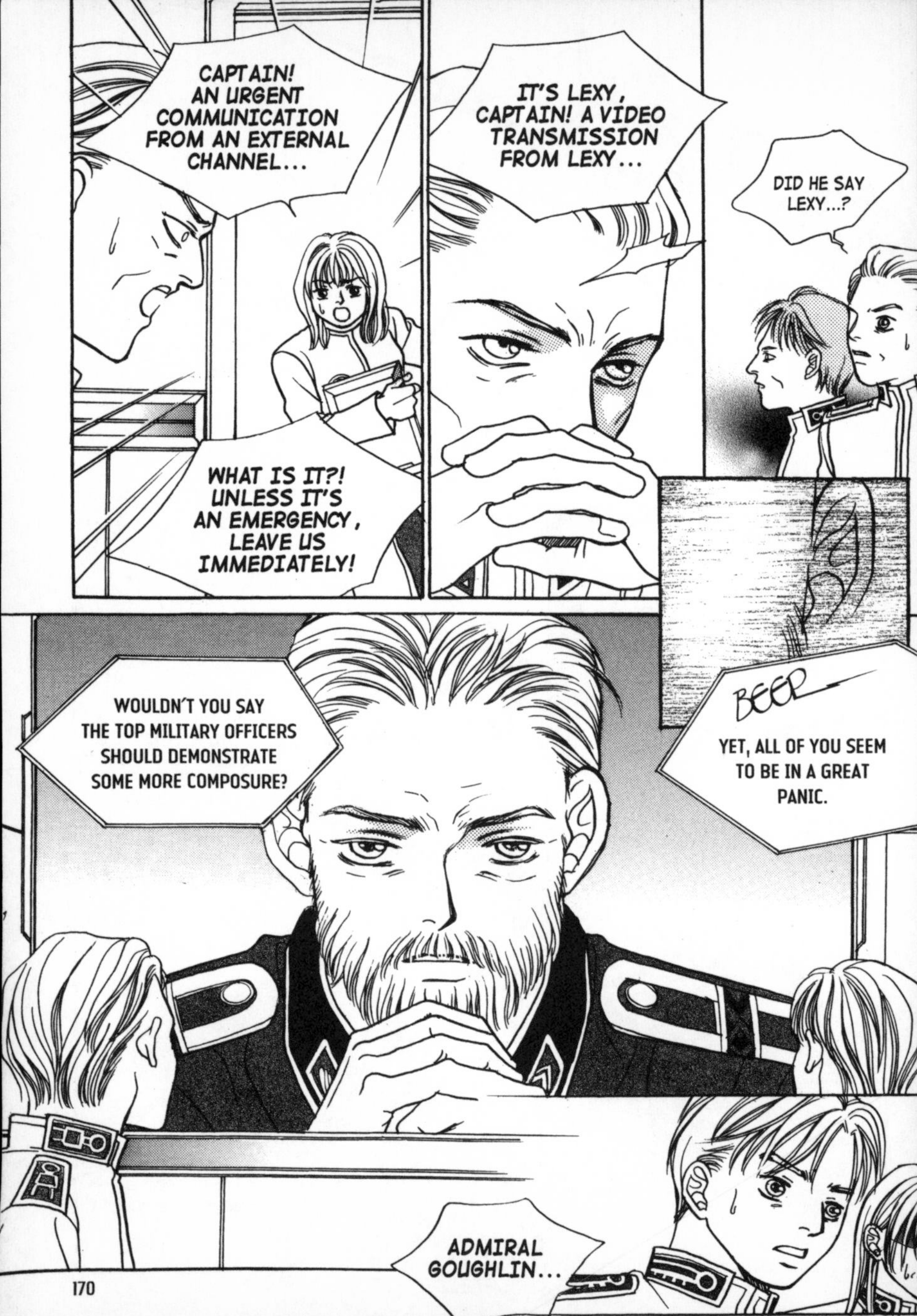
CAPTAIN! AN URGENT COMMUNICATION FROM AN EXTERNAL CHANNEL...
WHAT IS IT?! UNLESS IT'S AN EMERGENCY, LEAVE US IMMEDIATELY!
IT'S LEXY, CAPTAIN! A VIDEO TRANSMISSION FROM LEXY...
DID HE SAY LEXY...?
BEEP
WOULDN'T YOU SAY THE TOP MILITARY OFFICERS SHOULD DEMONSTRATE SOME MORE COMPOSURE?
YET, ALL OF YOU SEEM TO BE IN A GREAT PANIC.
ADMIRAL GOUGHLIN...

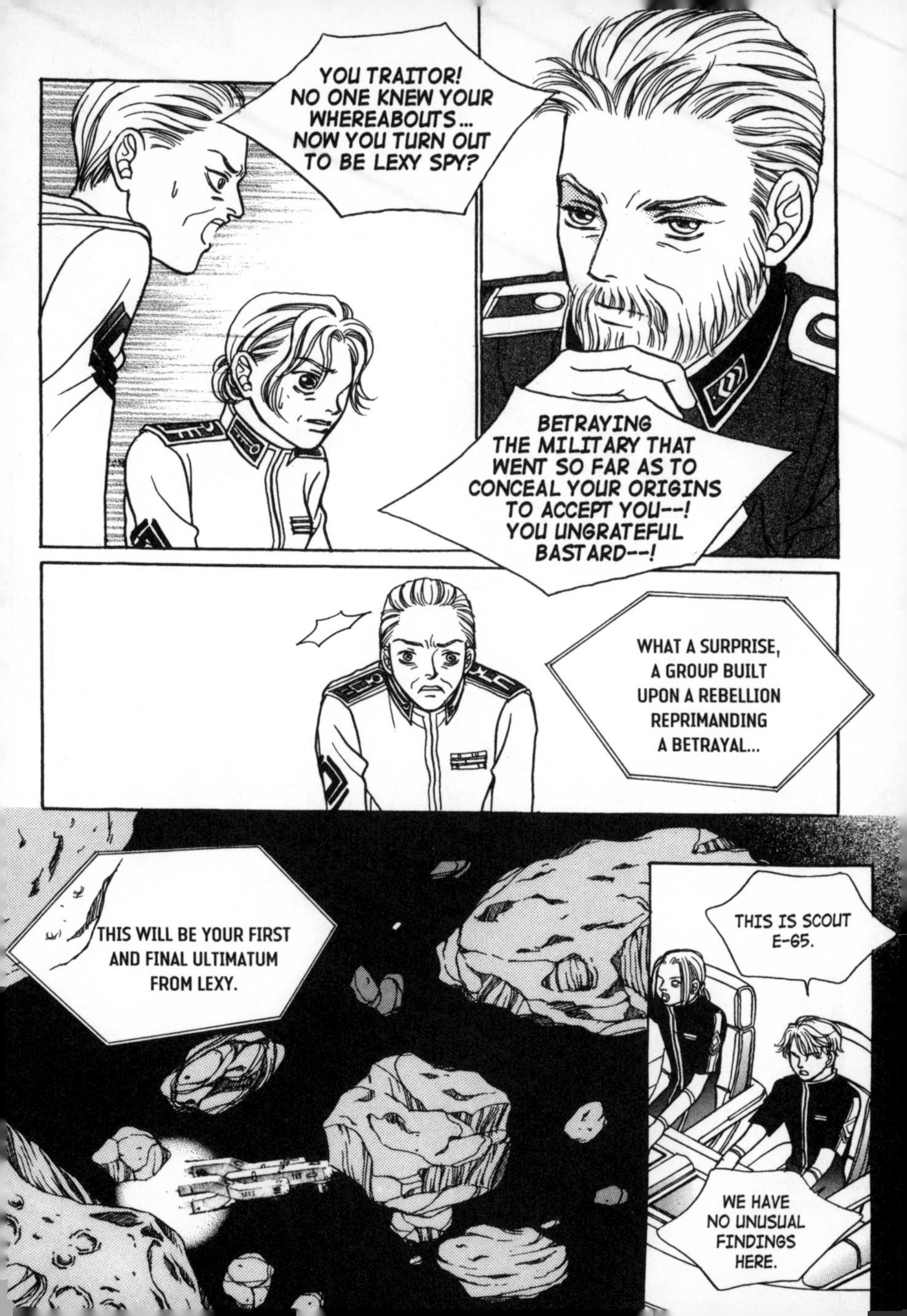
YOU TRAITOR! NO ONE KNEW YOUR WHEREABOUTS... NOW YOU TURN OUT TO BE LEXY SPY?
BETRAYING THE MILITARY THAT WENT SO FAR AS TO CONCEAL YOUR ORIGINS TO ACCEPT YOU--! YOU UNGRATEFUL BASTARD--!
WHAT A SURPRISE, A GROUP BUILT UPON A REBELLION REPRIMANDING A BETRAYAL...
THIS WILL BE YOUR FIRST AND FINAL ULTIMATUM FROM LEXY.
THIS IS SCOUT E-65.
WE HAVE NO UNUSUAL FINDINGS HERE.

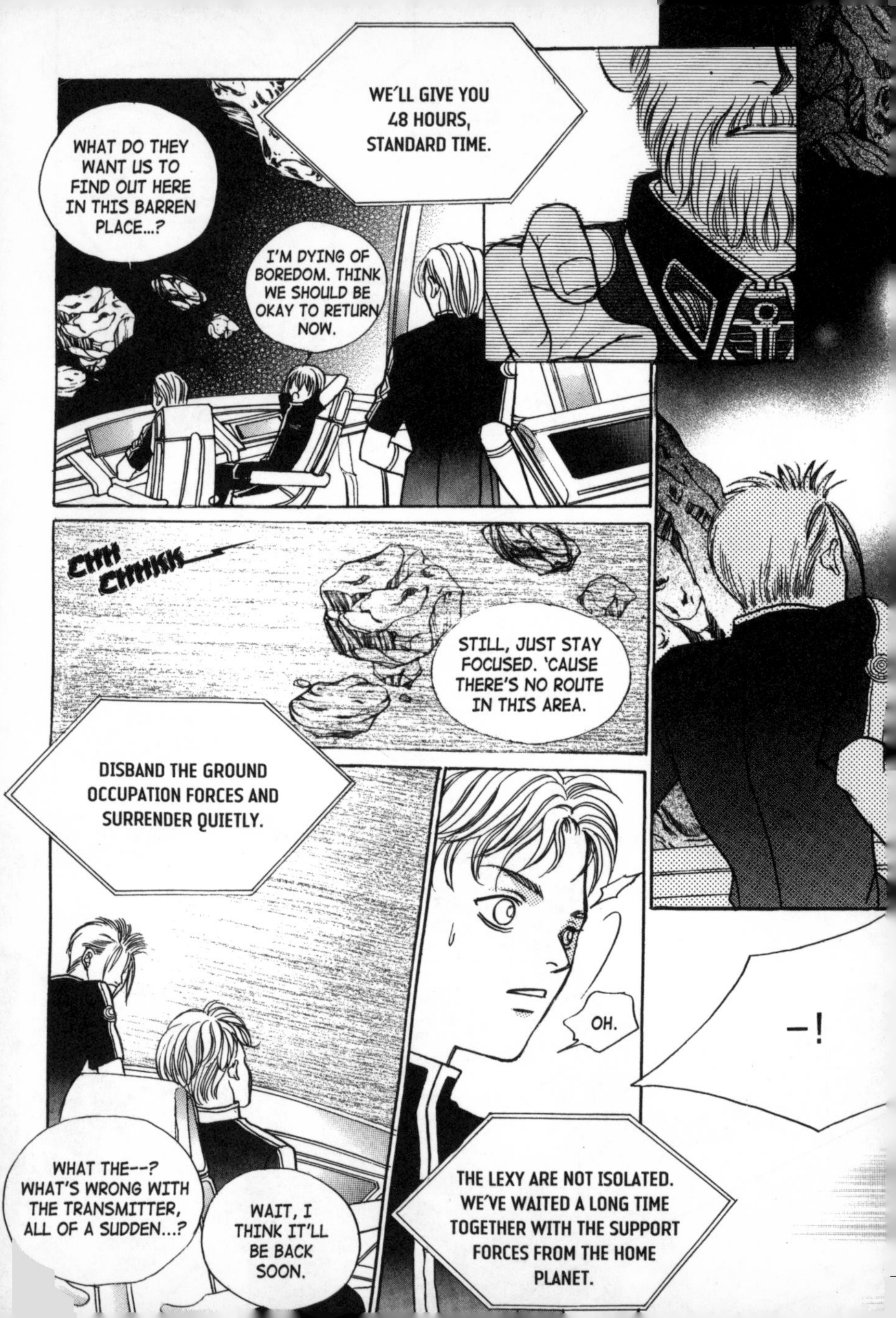
WHAT DO THEY WANT US TO FIND OUT HERE IN THIS BARREN PLACE...?
I'M DYING OF BOREDOM. THINK WE SHOULD BE OKAY TO RETURN NOW.
WE'LL GIVE YOU 48 HOURS, STANDARD TIME.
CHH CHHKK
STILL, JUST STAY FOCUSED. 'CAUSE THERE'S NO ROUTE IN THIS AREA.
DISBAND THE GROUND OCCUPATION FORCES AND SURRENDER QUIETLY.
WHAT THE--? WHAT'S WRONG WITH THE TRANSMITTER, ALL OF A SUDDEN...?
WAIT, I THINK IT'LL BE BACK SOON.
OH.
THE LEXY ARE NOT ISOLATED. WE'VE WAITED A LONG TIME TOGETHER WITH THE SUPPORT FORCES FROM THE HOME PLANET.
—!

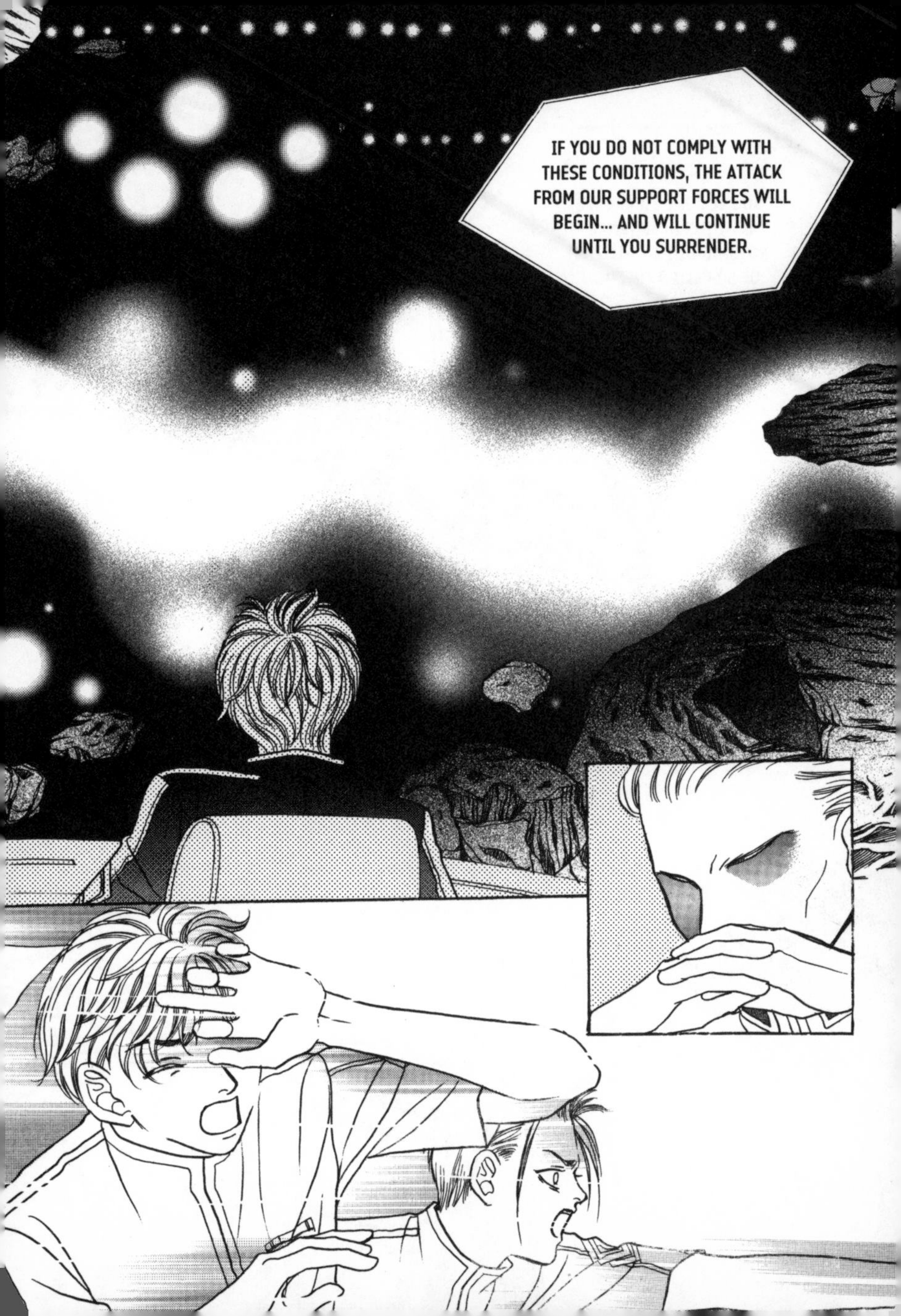
IF YOU DO NOT COMPLY WITH THESE CONDITIONS, THE ATTACK FROM OUR SUPPORT FORCES WILL BEGIN... AND WILL CONTINUE UNTIL YOU SURRENDER.

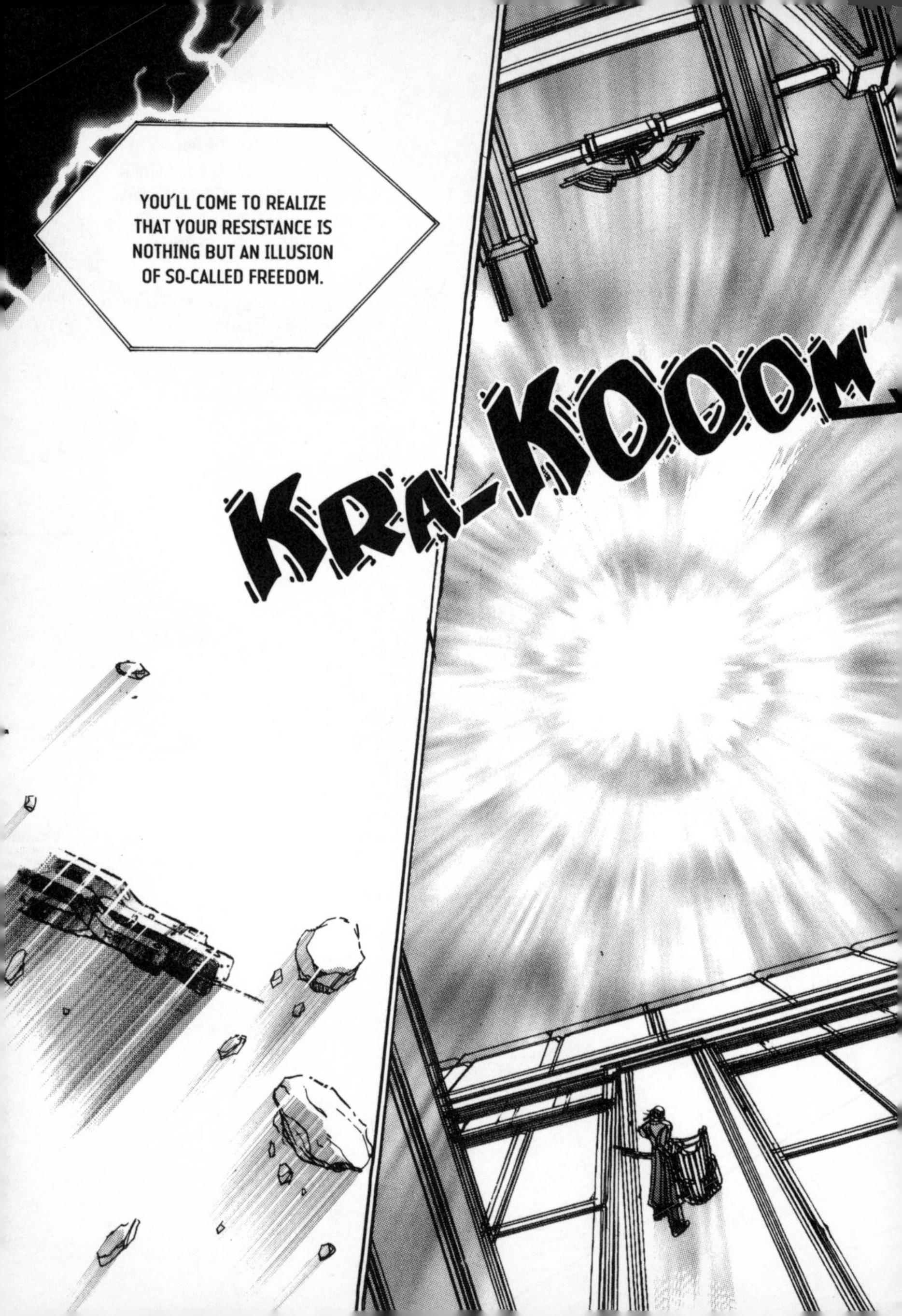
YOU'LL COME TO REALIZE THAT YOUR RESISTANCE IS NOTHING BUT AN ILLUSION OF SO-CALLED FREEDOM.
KRA-KOOOM

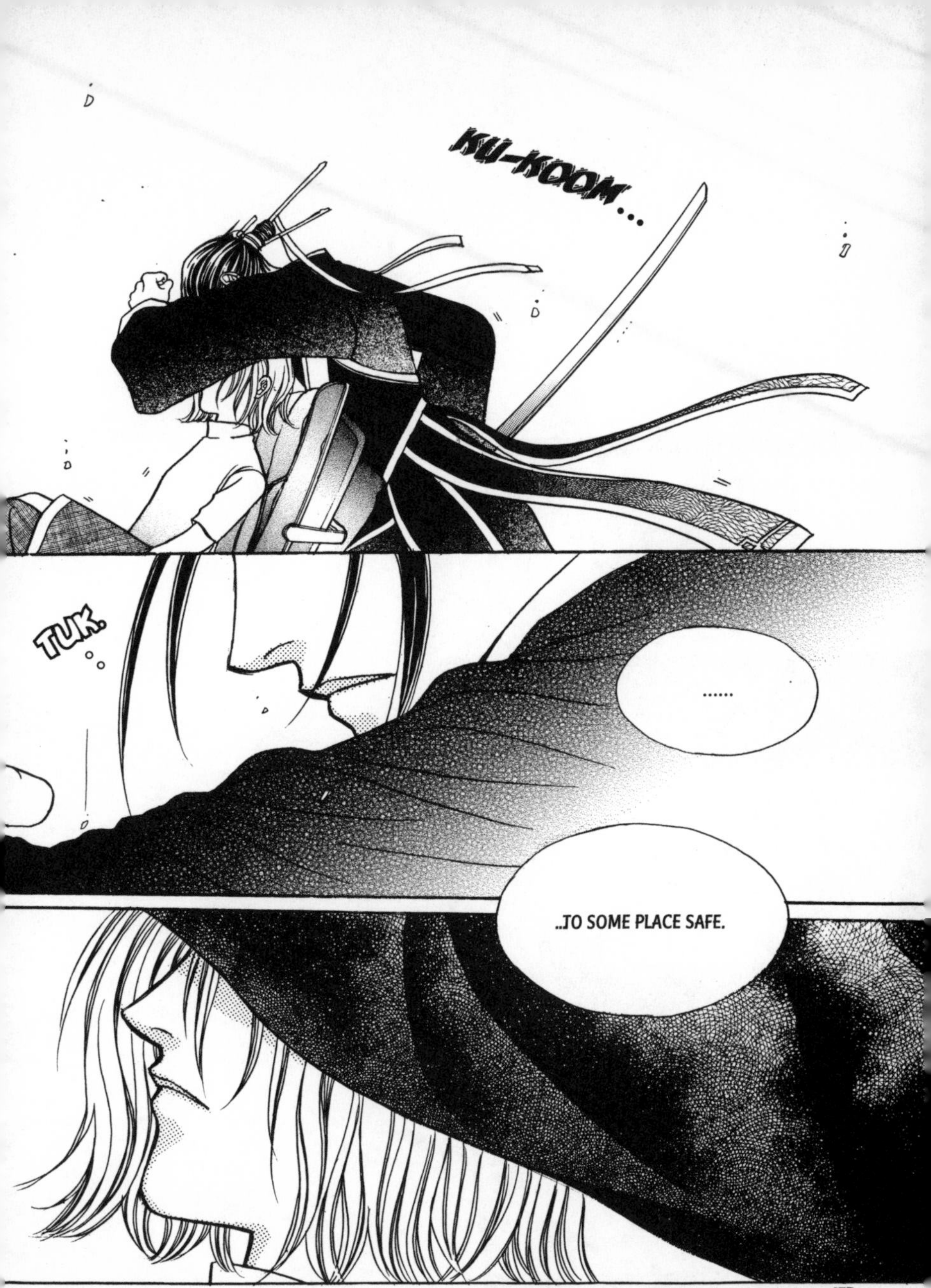
KU-KOOM...
TUK.
......
..TO SOME PLACE SAFE.

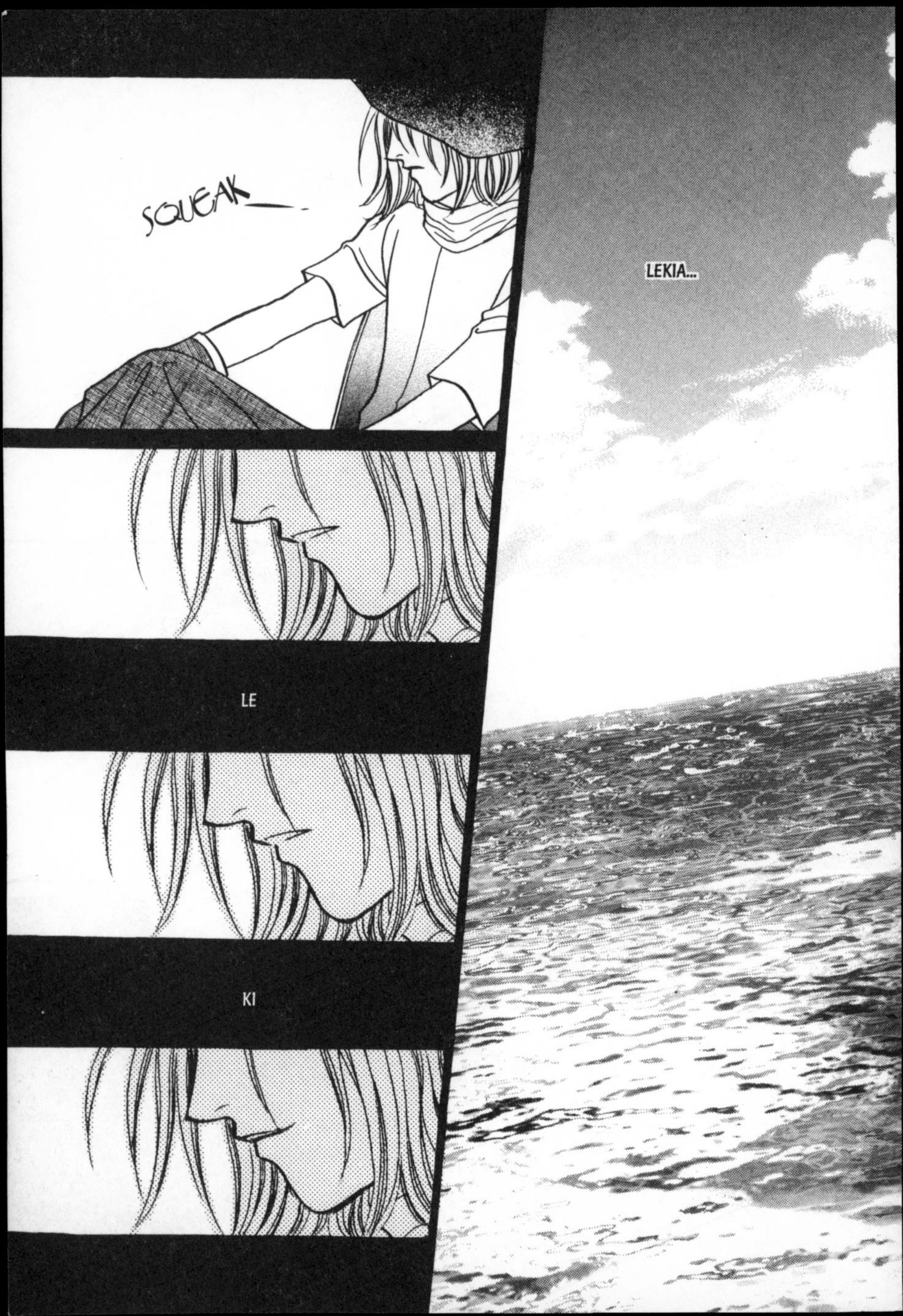
SQUEAK
LE
KI
LEKIA...

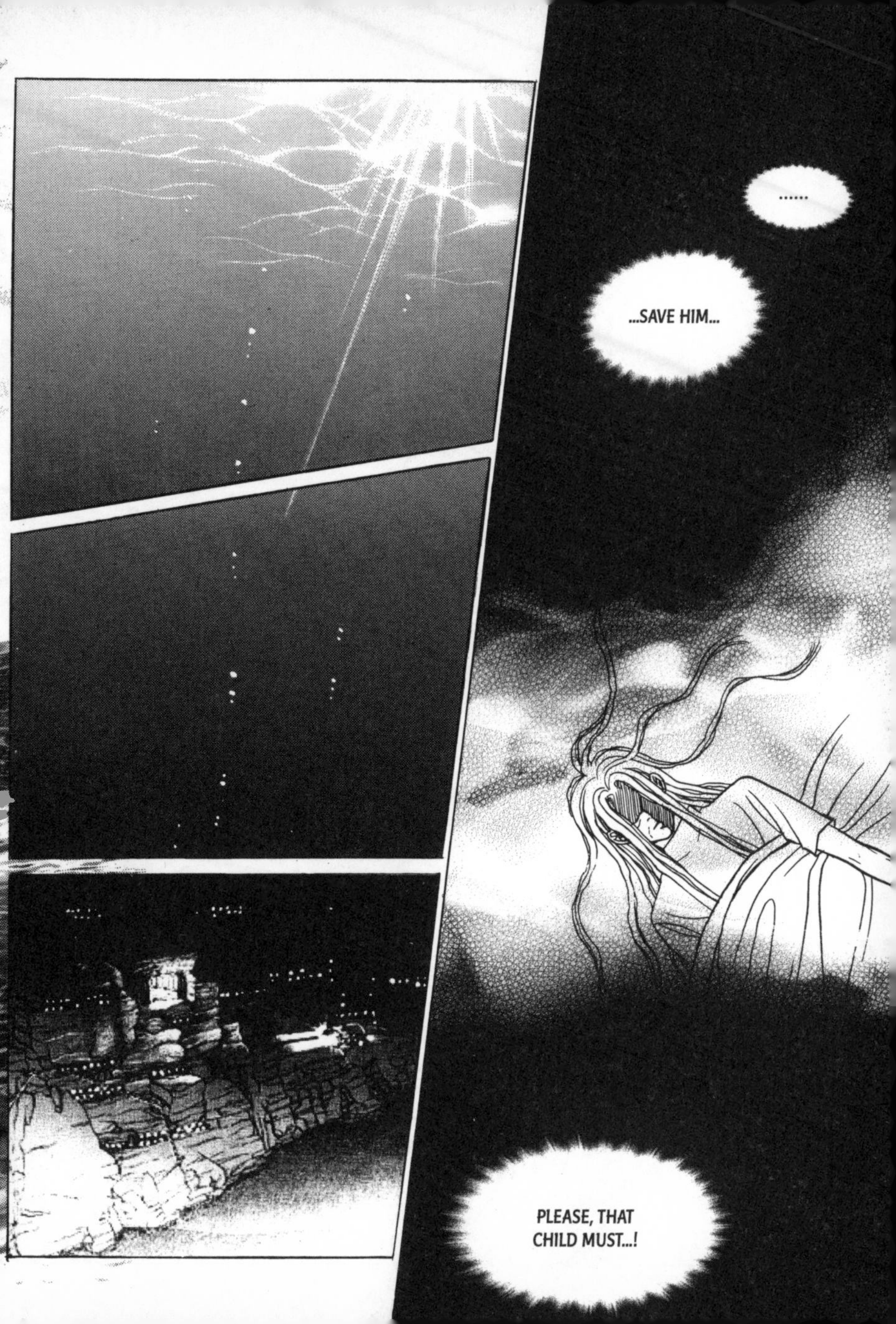
......
...SAVE HIM...
PLEASE, THAT CHILD MUST...!

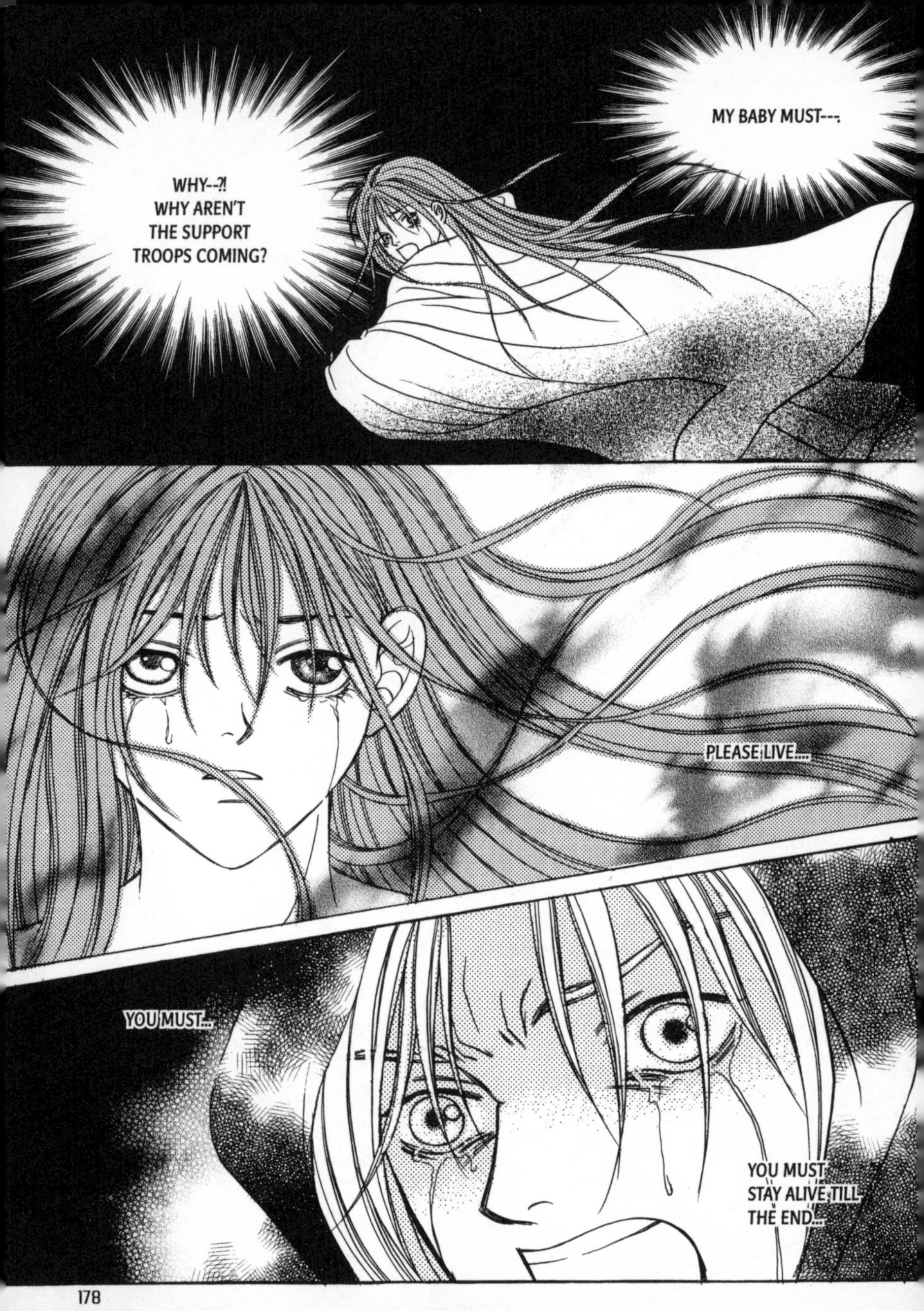
WHY--?! WHY AREN'T THE SUPPORT TROOPS COMING?
MY BABY MUST---.
PLEASE LIVE...
YOU MUST...
YOU MUST STAY ALIVE TILL THE END...

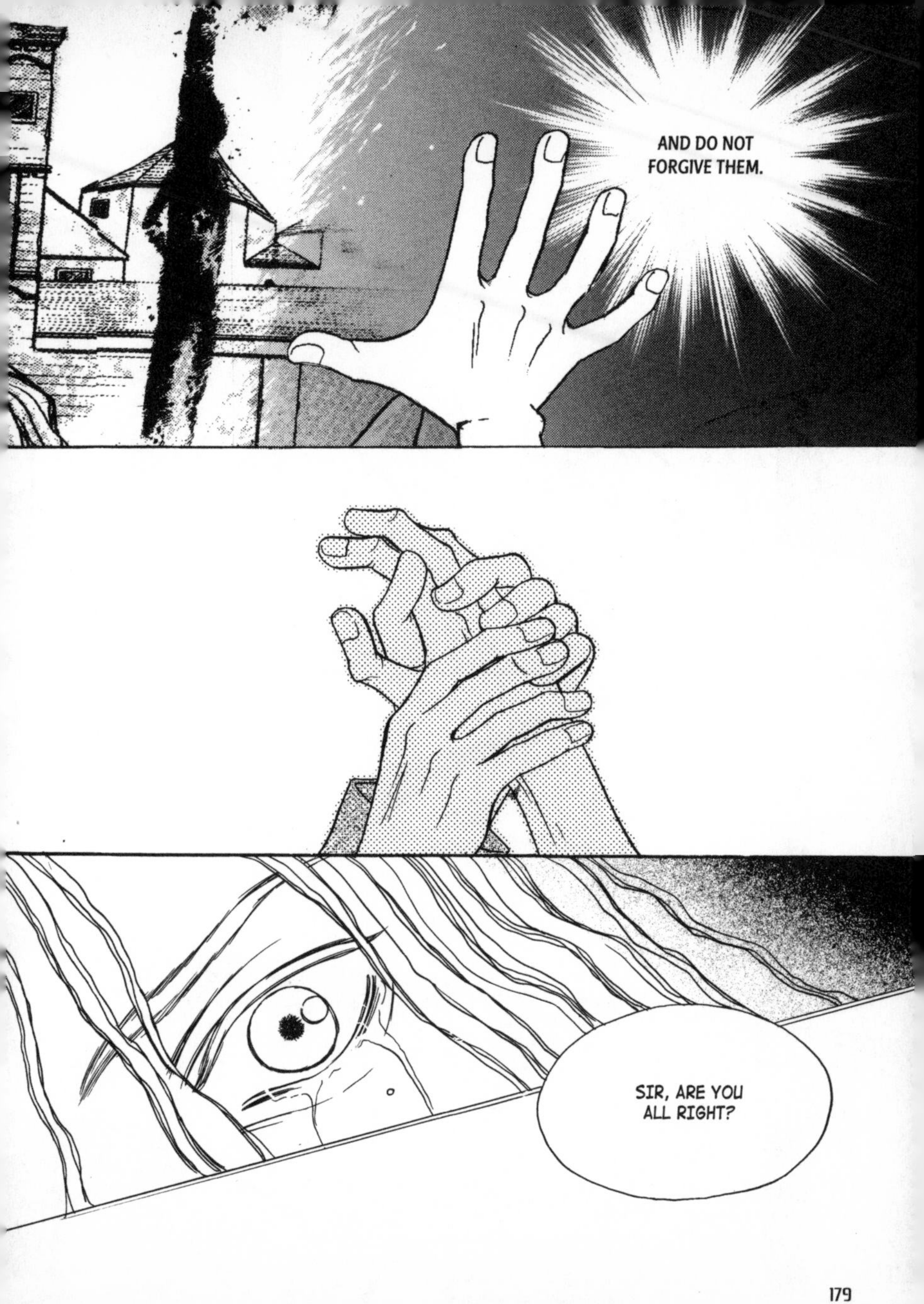
AND DO NOT FORGIVE THEM.
SIR, ARE YOU ALL RIGHT?

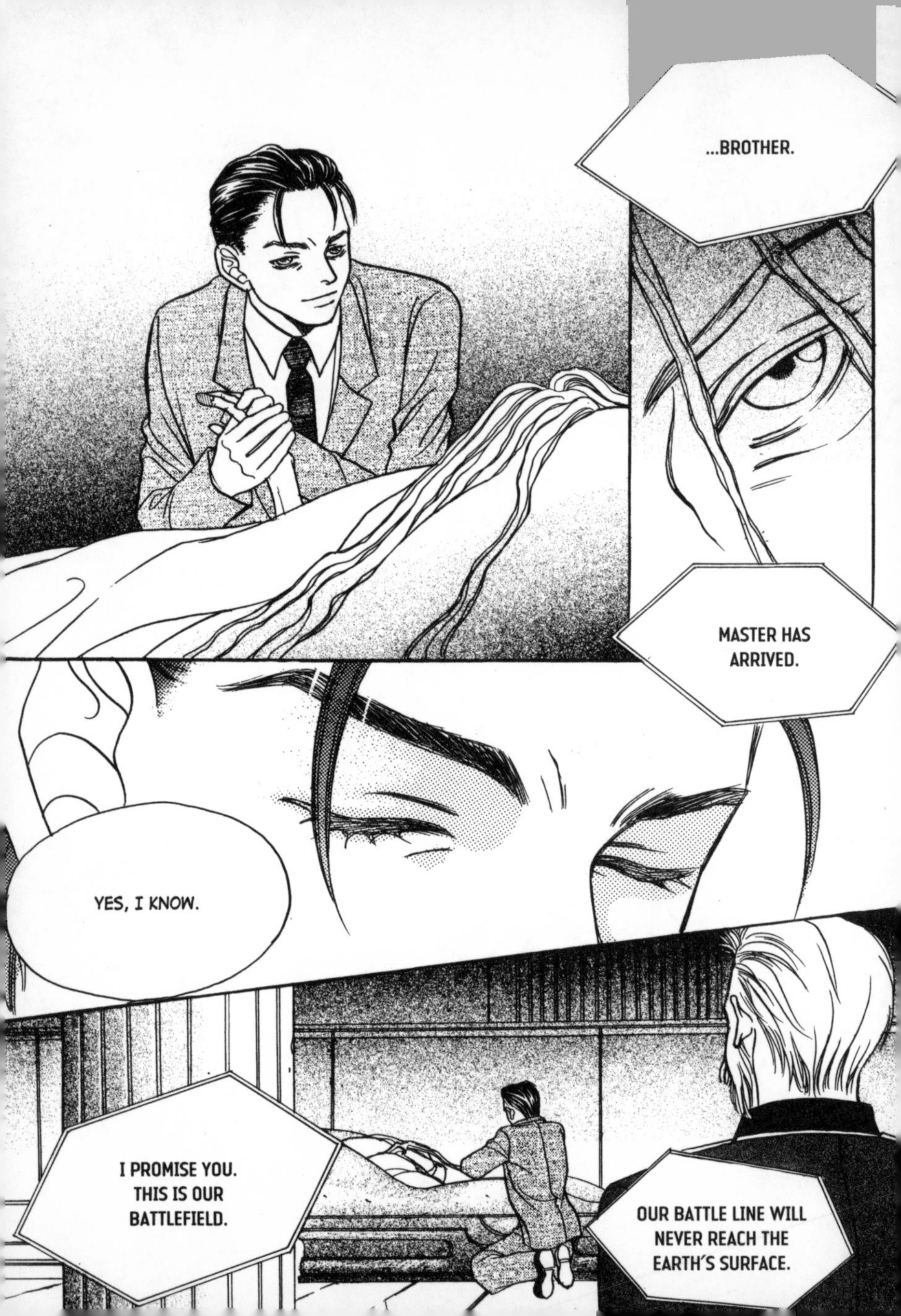
...BROTHER.
MASTER HAS ARRIVED.
YES, I KNOW.
I PROMISE YOU. THIS IS OUR BATTLEFIELD.
OUR BATTLE LINE WILL NEVER REACH THE EARTH'S SURFACE.

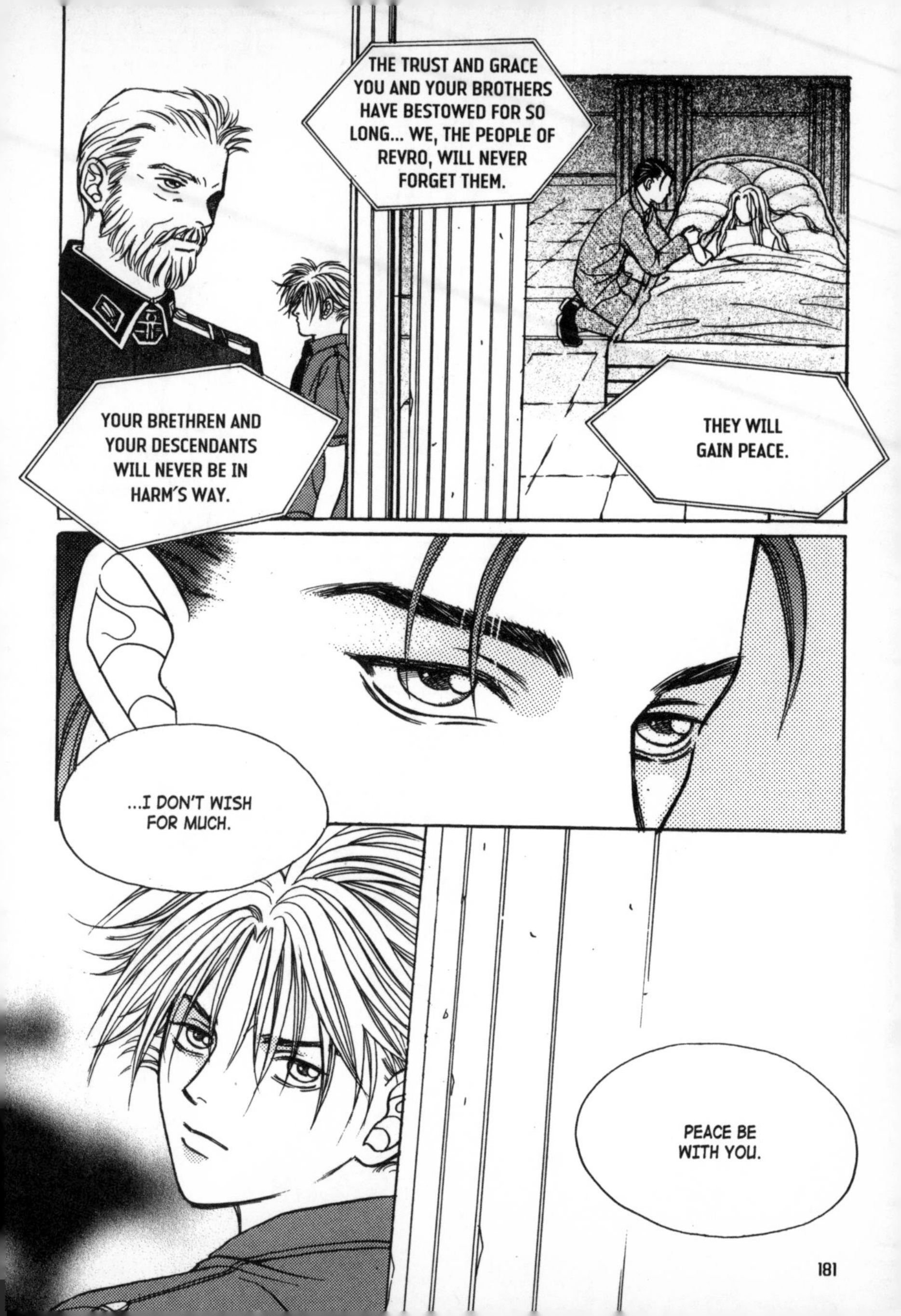
THE TRUST AND GRACE YOU AND YOUR BROTHERS HAVE BESTOWED FOR SO LONG... WE, THE PEOPLE OF REVRO, WILL NEVER FORGET THEM.
YOUR BRETHREN AND YOUR DESCENDANTS WILL NEVER BE IN HARM'S WAY.
THEY WILL GAIN PEACE.
...I DON'T WISH FOR MUCH.
PEACE BE WITH YOU.

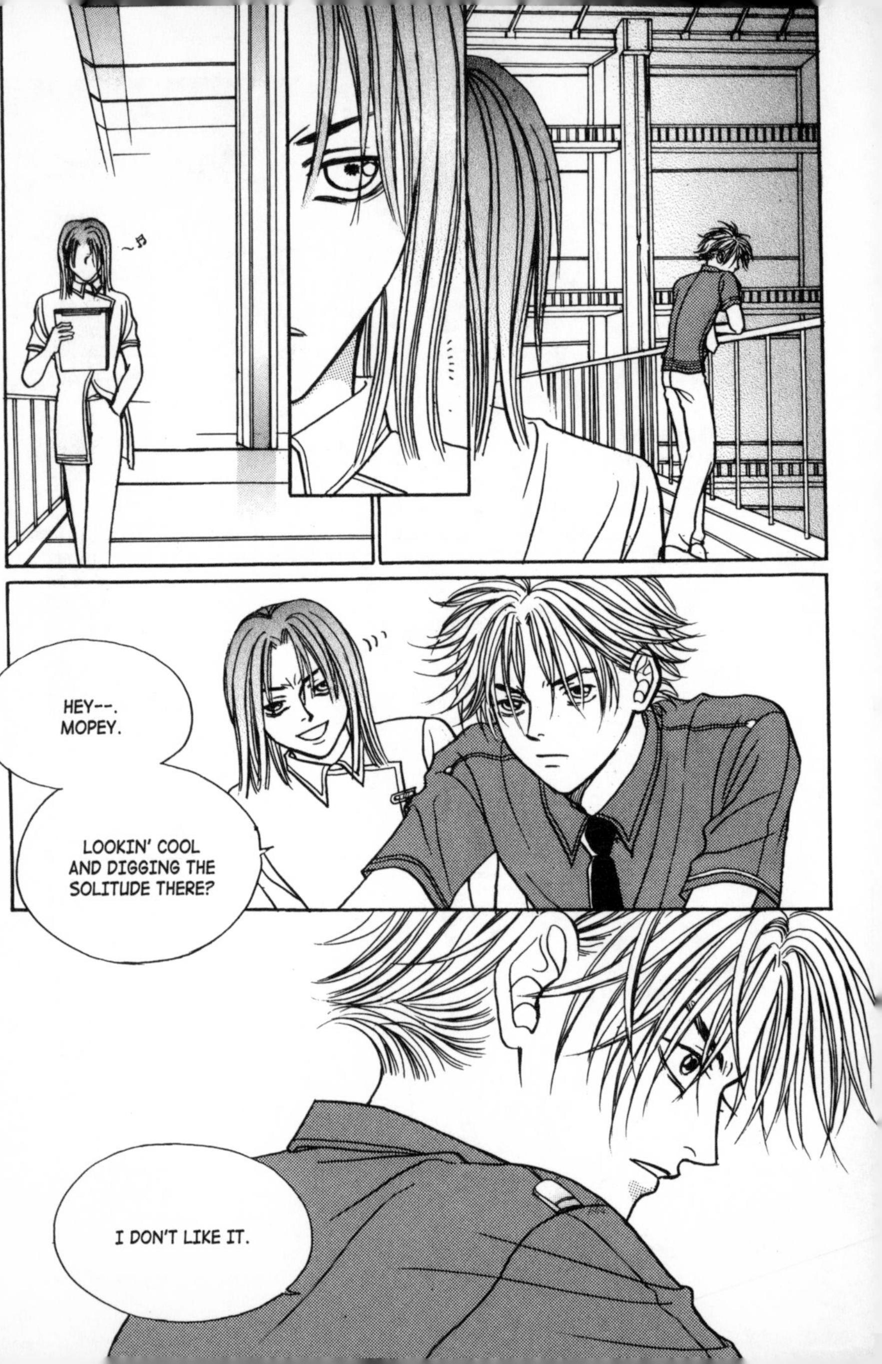
HEY--.
MOPEY.
LOOKIN' COOL AND DIGGING THE SOLITUDE THERE?
I DON'T LIKE IT.

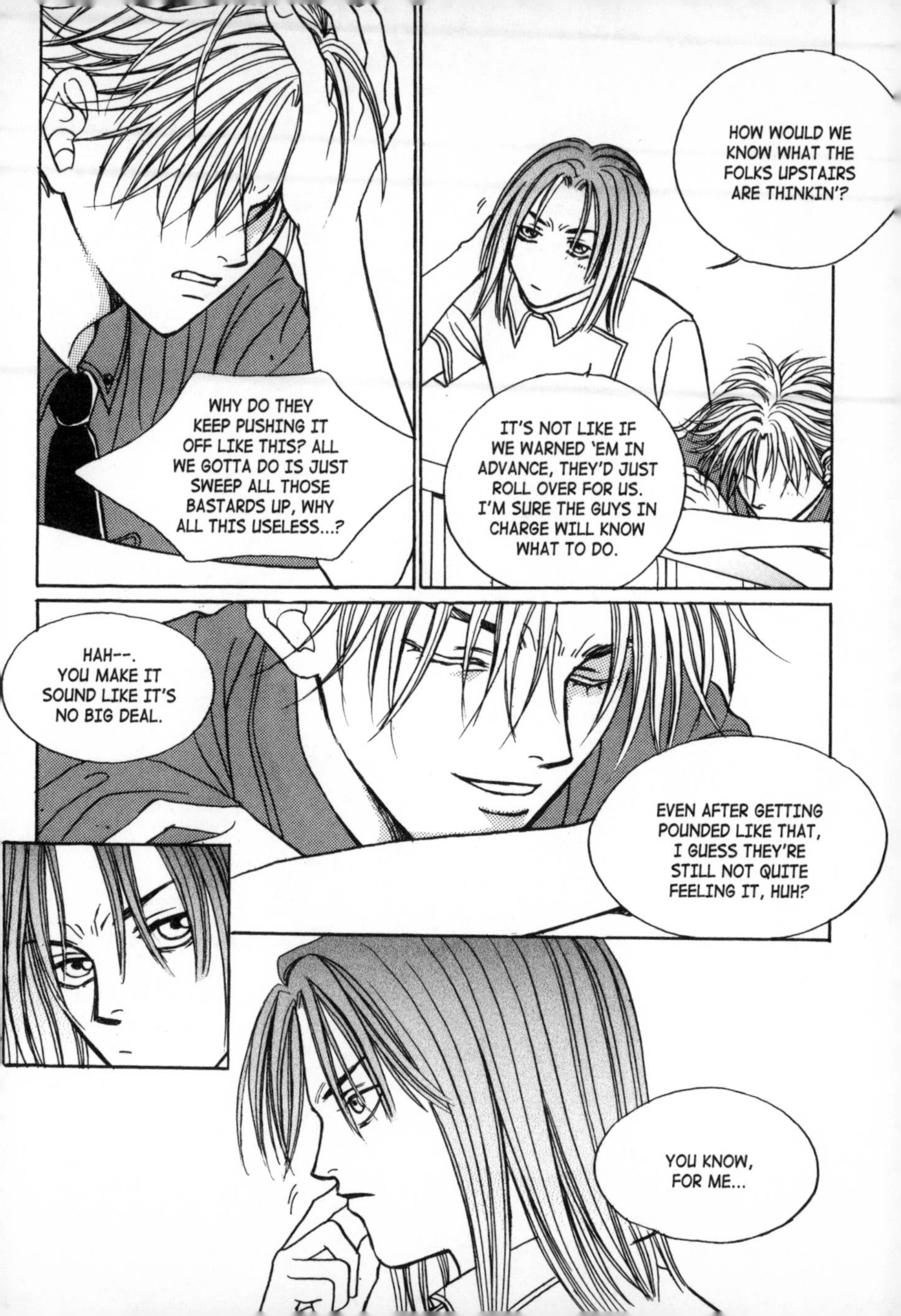
WHY DO THEY KEEP PUSHING IT OFF LIKE THIS? ALL WE GOTTA DO IS JUST SWEEP ALL THOSE BASTARDS UP, WHY ALL THIS USELESS...?
HOW WOULD WE KNOW WHAT THE FOLKS UPSTAIRS ARE THINKIN'?
IT'S NOT LIKE IF WE WARNED 'EM IN ADVANCE, THEY'D JUST ROLL OVER FOR US. I'M SURE THE GUYS IN CHARGE WILL KNOW WHAT TO DO.
HAH--. YOU MAKE IT SOUND LIKE IT'S NO BIG DEAL.
EVEN AFTER GETTING POUNDED LIKE THAT, I GUESS THEY'RE STILL NOT QUITE FEELING IT, HUH?
YOU KNOW, FOR ME...

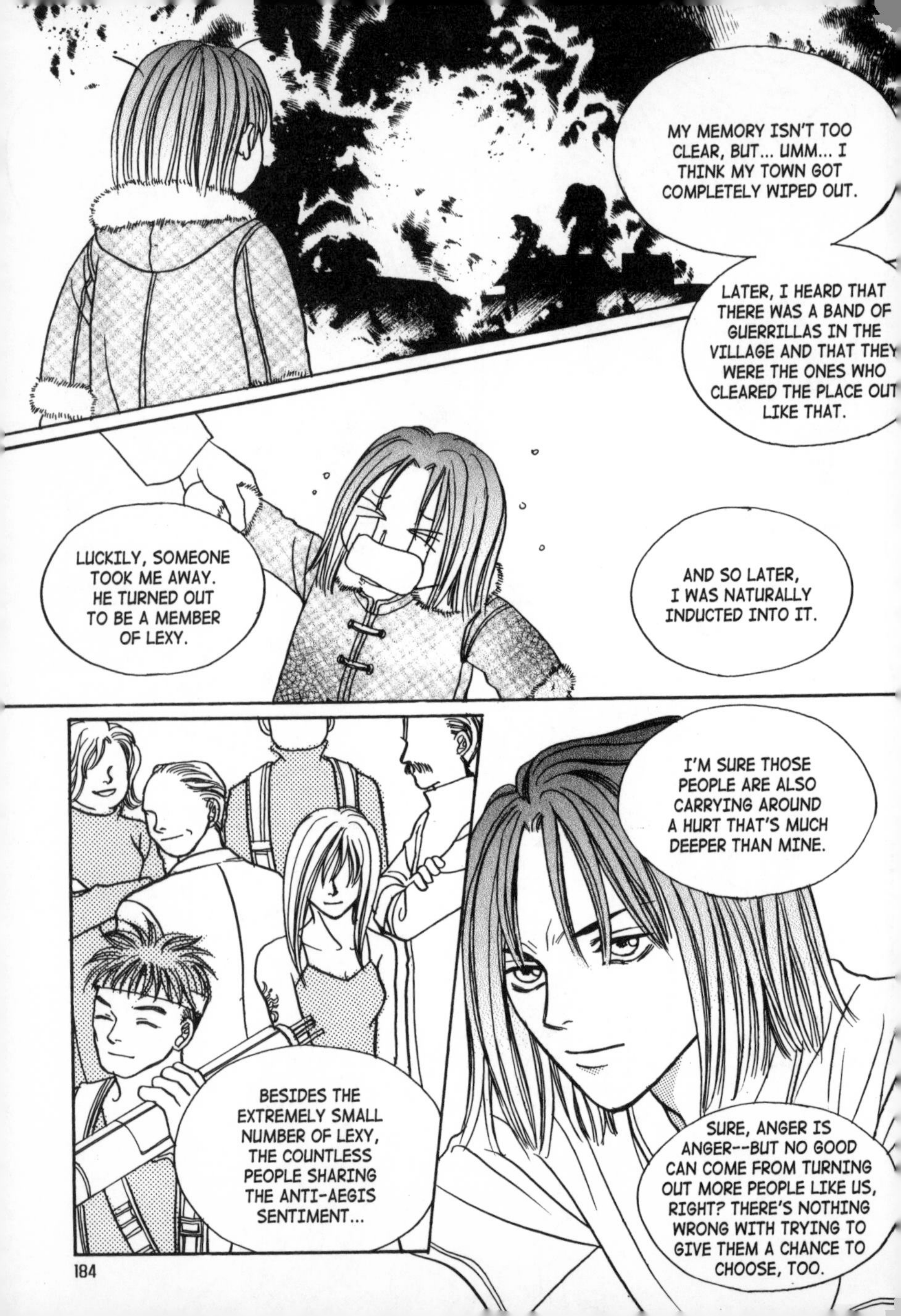
MY MEMORY ISN'T TOO CLEAR, BUT... UMM... I THINK MY TOWN GOT COMPLETELY WIPED OUT.
LATER, I HEARD THAT THERE WAS A BAND OF GUERRILLAS IN THE VILLAGE AND THAT THEY WERE THE ONES WHO CLEARED THE PLACE OUT LIKE THAT.
LUCKILY, SOMEONE TOOK ME AWAY. HE TURNED OUT TO BE A MEMBER OF LEXY.
AND SO LATER, I WAS NATURALLY INDUCTED INTO IT.
BESIDES THE EXTREMELY SMALL NUMBER OF LEXY, THE COUNTLESS PEOPLE SHARING THE ANTI-AEGIS SENTIMENT...
I'M SURE THOSE PEOPLE ARE ALSO CARRYING AROUND A HURT THAT'S MUCH DEEPER THAN MINE.
SURE, ANGER IS ANGER--BUT NO GOOD CAN COME FROM TURNING OUT MORE PEOPLE LIKE US, RIGHT? THERE'S NOTHING WRONG WITH TRYING TO GIVE THEM A CHANCE TO CHOOSE, TOO.

PLUS, WOULDN'T YOU SAY THAT ADMIRAL GOUGHLIN IS AN AMAZING LEADER, TOO?

I CAN NEVER BE AS UNDERSTANDING AS YOU OR THE ADMIRAL.

I'M AFRAID...

THE GUY LAID OUT LIKE A LIVING CORPSE, I WONDER WHETHER HE THINKS THAT WAY TOO.

SIGHHH...

A CHANCE TO CHOOSE?

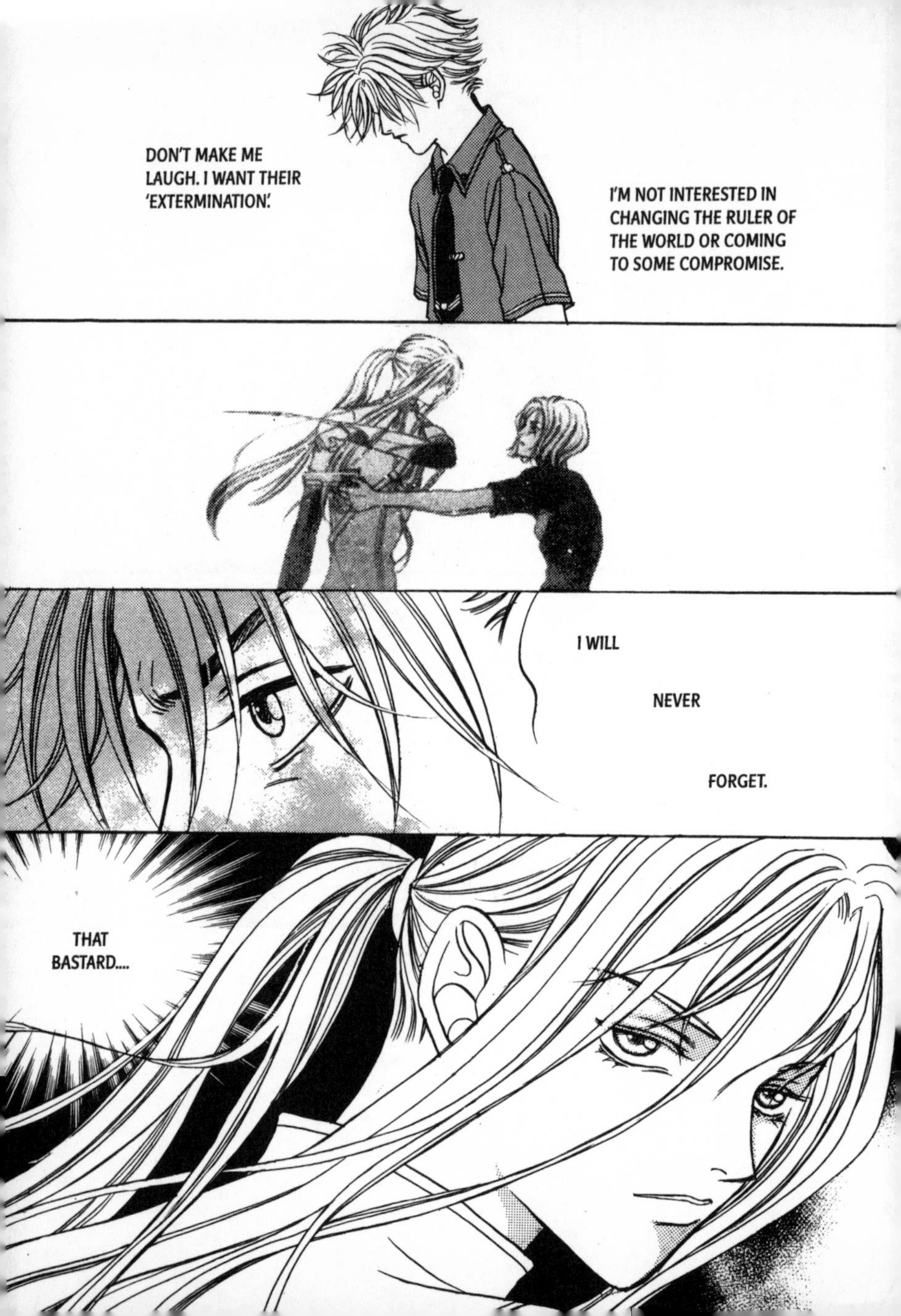
DON'T MAKE ME LAUGH. I WANT THEIR 'EXTERMINATION.'
I'M NOT INTERESTED IN CHANGING THE RULER OF THE WORLD OR COMING TO SOME COMPROMISE.
I WILL
NEVER
FORGET.
THAT BASTARD....

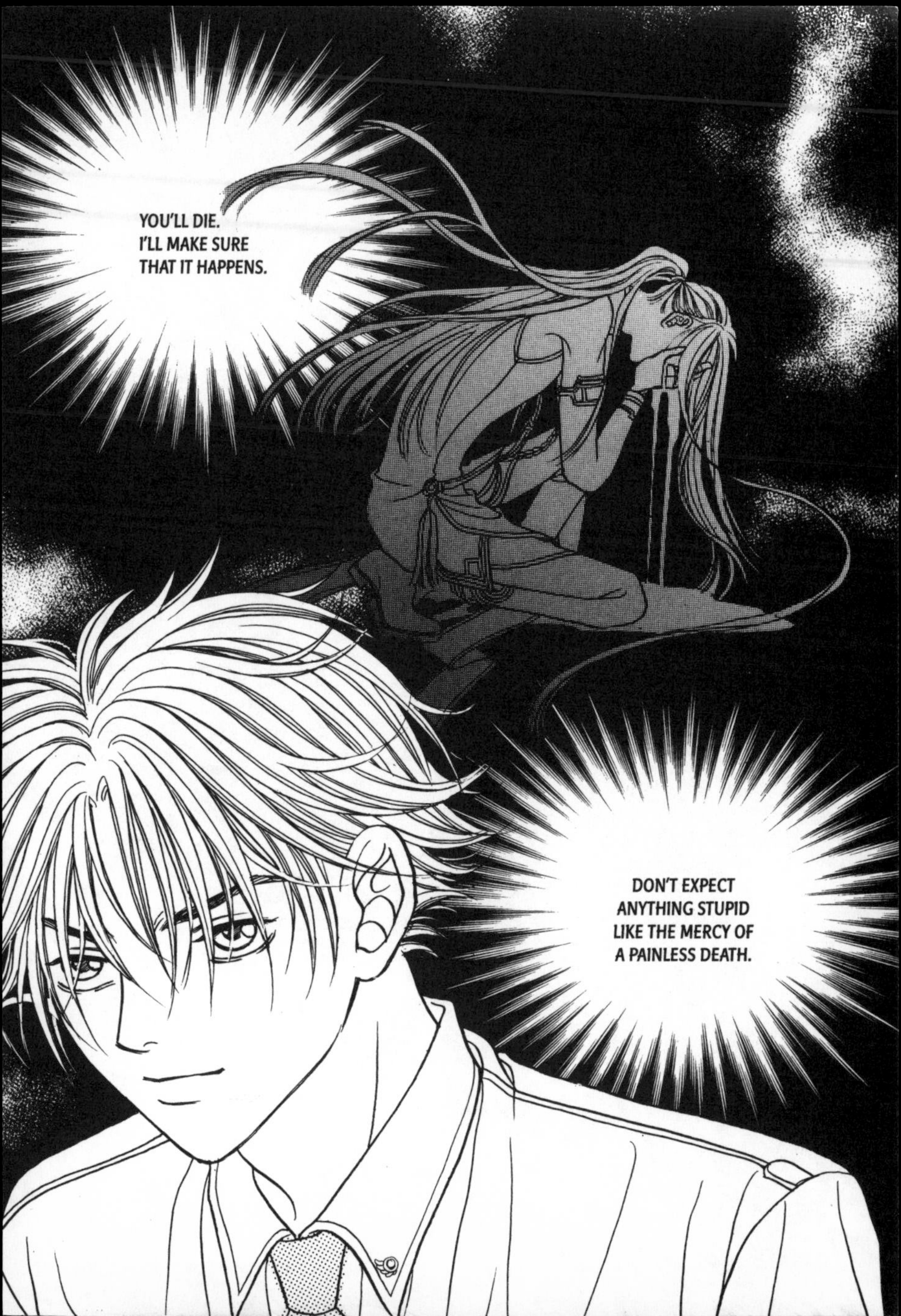
YOU'LL DIE.
I'LL MAKE SURE
THAT IT HAPPENS.
DON'T EXPECT
ANYTHING STUPID
LIKE THE MERCY OF
A PAINLESS DEATH.

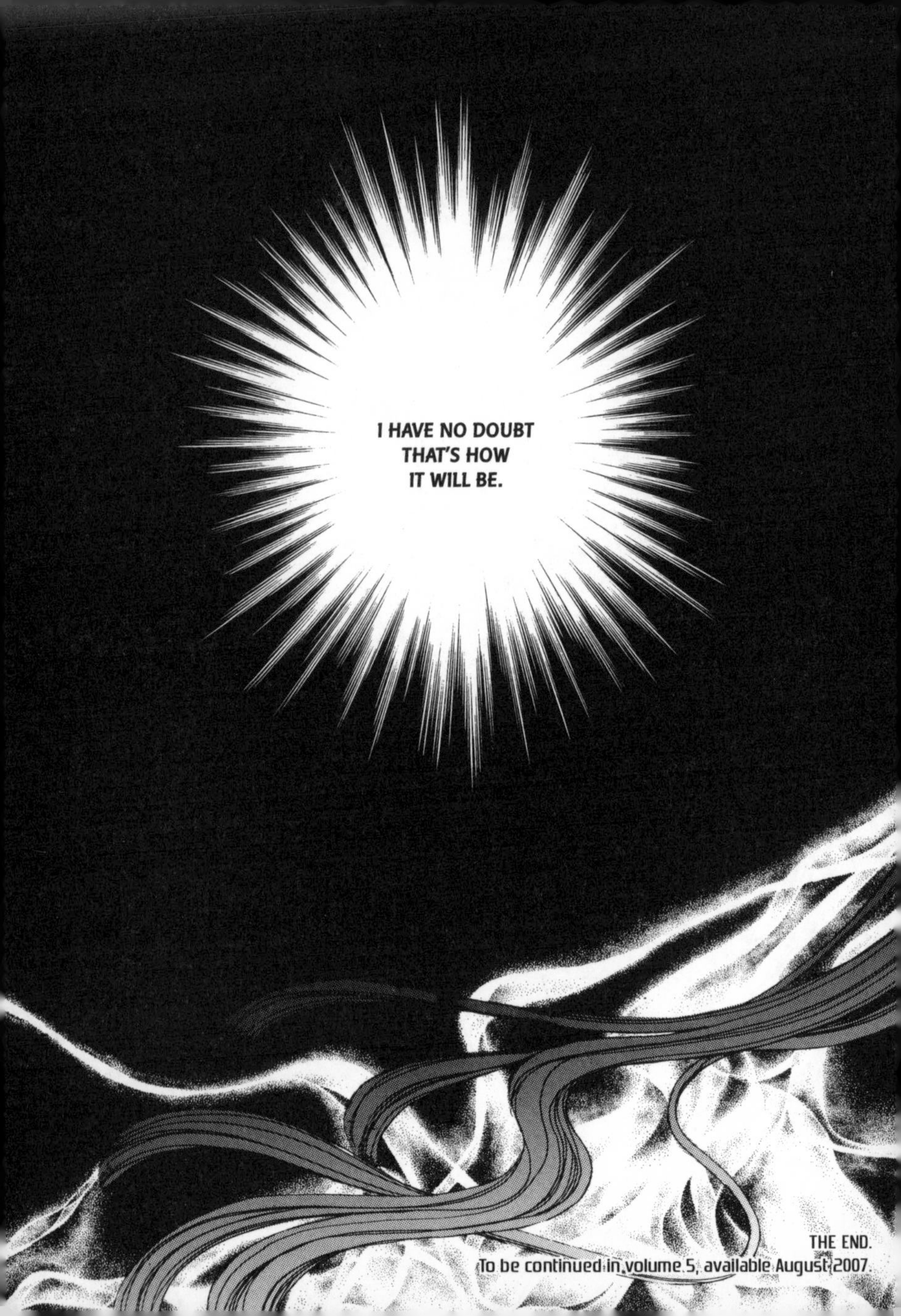
I HAVE NO DOUBT THAT'S HOW IT WILL BE.
THE END.
To be continued in volume 5, available August 2007.

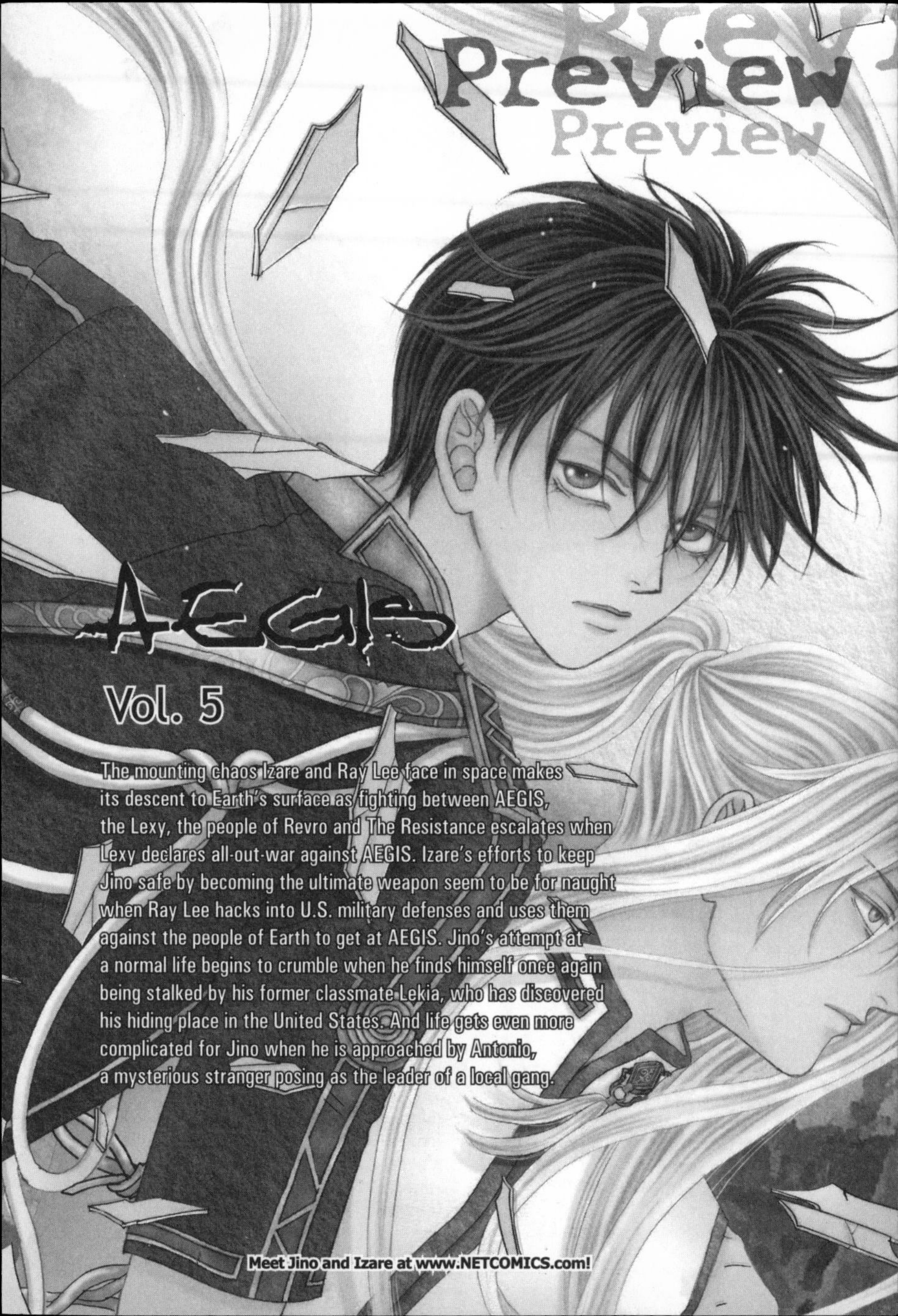
Preview
Preview
AEGIS
Vol. 5
The mounting chaos Izare and Ray Lee face in space makes its descent to Earth's surface as fighting between AEGIS, the Lexy, the people of Revro and The Resistance escalates when Lexy declares all-out-war against AEGIS. Izare's efforts to keep Jino safe by becoming the ultimate weapon seem to be for naught when Ray Lee hacks into U.S. military defenses and uses them against the people of Earth to get at AEGIS. Jino's attempt at a normal life begins to crumble when he finds himself once again being stalked by his former classmate Lekia, who has discovered his hiding place in the United States. And life gets even more complicated for Jino when he is approached by Antonio, a mysterious stranger posing as the leader of a local gang.
Meet Jino and Izare at www.NETCOMICS.com!

in the STARLIGHT

by Kyungok Kang

Ever since Shinhye was young, when she used to sit on a hill watching the night sky with her father, she has always admired the stars and dreamed of what is out there in the universe. But she never expected that her dreams—and nightmares—would come true. As a beautiful and intelligent 17-year-old, she attracts the attention of Donghoon, whose uncle works with the Department of Science. As it happens, Donghoon's uncle is in charge of finding a home for a visiting foreigner...who has ESP! Guess who the foreigner shacks up with?

TWO Will Come

by Kyungok Kang

Ordinary high school girl Jina discovers that she is heir to a terrible legacy handed down from her family's sinister history. Long ago, her ancestors killed a magical serpent known as an Imugi, believing that it would bring them good luck. Unfortunately, the creature cursed them as it died, decreeing that one family member of each generation from that day forth will be killed by two people closely acquainted with that person. In this day and age, no one wants to believe in such outmoded superstitions, but one of Jina's relatives has been murdered without fail in every generation. Now, Jina has been informed that she will be next to die...